Alcohol, Drugs and Employment

Mike McCann MB Bch MA MD (Dublin)
DIH (London) MFOM (UK)

Nadine Harker Burnhams BA (Hons)
(Health and Welfare Management) MA (UPE)

Christopher Albertyn BA (Hons) (Wits) B Proc
(Unisa) LLB (KZN)

Urmila Bhoola BA (Hons) LLB (Wits) LLM (Toronto)

JUTA

First Published 2011

© JUTA & CO LTD
First Floor
Sunclare Building
21 Dreyer Street
Claremont 7708
lawproduction@juta.co.za

ISBN 978 0 7021 94061

Production co-ordinator: Karen Froneman
Editor: Mark McClellan
Indexer: Adami Geldenhuys
Cover design and diagrams: Drag and Drop
Typeset in 10/12.5 ITC Stone Sans Std by Trace Digital Services
Printed and bound by Print Communications

About the Authors

MIKE MCCANN

Dr Mike McCann has worked as a specialist Occupational Physician for the past 26 years. His work in South Africa involved research into alcohol abuse in the workplace, which culminated in a doctoral thesis. He worked as Chief Medical Officer for SAPPI SAICCOR and since then has worked for GlaxoSmithKline, the London Metropolitan Police, Kent County Police and as the Occupational Physician Adviser for organisations as varied as banks, communications organisations, the civil service, media and retail sectors.

He is a non-executive director of Castlecraig Hospital Ltd, a private hospital treating patients with drug and alcohol problems in Scotland, and he is on the executive committee of the Medical Council on Alcohol, London. He is a member of the Society of Occupational Medicine and the Association of Local Authority Medical Advisers UK.

He was joint author with Christopher Albertyn of the first edition of Alcohol, Employment and Fair Labour Practice published in 1993. He has written two previous booklets, Taking Care of Alcohol Abuse at Work and Alcohol Problems for Occupational Physicians through the Medical Council on Alcohol, London.

NADINE HARKER BURNHAMS

Nadine is researcher with the Alcohol and Drug Abuse Research Unit of the South African Medical Research Council. She holds an MA in Health and Welfare Management from the University of Port Elizabeth and is currently pursuing a PhD in Public Health through the University of Cape Town. She has specific interests in improving the quality of substance abuse prevention services, monitoring and evaluating the performance and outcomes of such services, and designing and implementing substance abuse prevention services for the work sector. She has advised local and provincial government on issues related to alcohol and drug abuse prevention and has acted as a technical advisor and consultant to the United Nations Office on Drugs and Crime (UNODC) on the drafting of guidelines for substance abuse prevention initiatives in the workplace. She served as a member of the expert prevention panel for the International Federation of the Blue Cross. She is the principal investigator on a study assessing the effectiveness of a substance abuse and substance-related HIV workplace prevention programme.

CHRISTOPHER ALBERTYN

Christopher Albertyn is an arbitrator and mediator, principally in Ontario, Canada. He was appointed a Vice-Chair of the Ontario Labour Relations Board in October 1994 and has held the position since then. In 1997, he was appointed Chair of the Ontario Education Relations Commission and the Colleges Relations Commission. He was appointed a member of the federal Public Service Labour Relations Board in 2007 and he is an arbitrator on the list of arbitrators of the Canadian Federal Mediation and Conciliation Service. He was appointed a Vice-Chair of the Ontario Public Service

Grievance Settlement Board in 2008. He is a member of the National Academy of Arbitrators of the US and Canada.

Prior to residence in Canada, he was a mediator and arbitrator in South Africa, and before that practised as a labour lawyer in Durban with the firm Chennells Albertyn & Brunton.

URMILA BHOOLA

Urmila Bhoola is a Judge of the Labour Court of South Africa. She was formerly a consultant to the International Labour Organization in Fiji and Nepal, as well as founder and director of the Resolve Group, a labour law and human resource consultancy based in Johannesburg. She has practised law as an attorney and partner at Cheadle Thompson & Haysom and Rosen Wright Rosengarten Attorneys. She served as a part-time member of the Competition Tribunal for eight years from 2001 to 2009.

Table of Contents

Health (☤)   Human Resources (👫)   Legal (🏛)

TABLE OF CASES

Acknowledgements

With this latest edition and the addition of the difficult area of drugs we have been helped immensely by the South African Medical Research Council through Nadine Harker Burnhams.

We are very grateful to Imelda Neate of Drug Testing SA who provided written material on testing for us to work from and also provided advice for these chapters. A thank you to Mr Grant Wilkinson from Global Business Solutions who provided material used in the legal chapters but also gave useful advice on the health chapters from a legal perspective.

We would like to thank the addiction psychiatrist Dr Brian Hore of the Medical Council on Alcohol (London) and book editor of the journal Alcohol and Alcoholism for his useful input and critique of one of the earlier drafts. The Medical Council on Alcohol gave us permission to use information from their publications, for which we are grateful.

Dr Margaret Ann McCann the Medical Director of CastleCraig Hospital for Addictions in Scotland provided valuable input.

We would also like to thank the following people who kindly assisted us:
- Colleagues in Occupational Medicine, namely Dr Andrea Junker and Dr John Challenor, who read draft chapters through the eyes of occupational physicians;
- Professor Leslie London of the School of Public Health and Family Medicine, University of Cape Town, provided sound advice and critique on one of the later drafts.
- Ms Rehana Kader from the Alcohol and Drug Abuse Research Unit of the South African Medical Research Council for her inputs on theories of addiction.

Finally we would like to thank Professor Charles Parry of the South African Medical Research Council for his invaluable support and encouragement for the duration of this project.

Mike McCann
Nadine Harker Burnhams
November 2011

Foreword: Health

In 1996 I purchased a copy of *Alcohol, Employment and Fair Labour Practice* (1993) and over the past 15 years have frequently referred to the book, as it contains a wealth of information on how to identify and address alcohol problems in the workplace. It is a very practical book that, among other things, contains procedures for breath alcohol and urine testing and a draft policy for the management of alcohol in the workplace. However, it is 18 years since the book was first published and it has now gone out of print. South Africa is also a very different country from what it was at the time the book was published. Not only has labour legislation changed dramatically, but so too has the scene with regard to substances being used and abused.

Since 1993 we have seen increased availability of natural, synthetic and semi-synthetic drugs of abuse, including khat, methamphetamine, methcathinone, heroin and drugs with interesting local names such as 'nyaope', 'pinch', 'sugars', and 'whoonga'. Poly-substance use is increasingly common. There have also been dramatic shifts in the demographic profile of drug users and in drug availability in smaller towns and cities, and also in rural areas. Alcohol has continued to be the dominant substance of abuse and has now been determined to be the third largest contributor to death and disability in the country. Increased globalisation and the AIDS epidemic, among other things, place increased stress on employees, which no doubt contributes to increased substance abuse in this and other sectors of society. There is now a greater onus on employers to address substance abuse among their employees in a sensitive way.

As a result of these factors there has been an urgent need to update and expand the material in the 1993 book. To achieve this, the original authors, Mike McCann and Christopher Albertyn, have drawn in local co-authors to assist them. Nadine Burnhams is a scientist at the Medical Research Council's Alcohol & Drug Abuse Research Unit who gained her extensive hands-on experience in working with companies to address substance abuse in the workplace, during the years she worked at the South African National Council on Alcoholism & Drug Dependence (SANCA). Urmila Bhoola is a Labour Court judge based in Johannesburg who practised law for many years with Cheadle Thompson & Haysom Attorneys before co-founding a business and law consultancy, the Resolve Group. The second edition of the book, now titled *Alcohol, Drugs & Employment*, has 20 chapters (increased from the original 17). Drug abuse is no longer confined to one chapter and has also been integrated into several other chapters. New chapters on alcohol/drug testing and preventing substance abuse in the workplace have also been added.

The workplace is increasingly being recognised as an important frontier for addressing substance abuse. Increasing involvement by employers will not only help them to meet the requirements of labour laws, but also makes good business sense as they seek to reduce the costs associated with substance-related health problems (including injuries, infectious diseases, liver cirrhosis, and mental health concerns), absenteeism and loss of productivity. This book will aid companies in rising to the challenge!

In the foreword to the first edition, Justice Richard Goldstone referred to the understanding and compassion displayed by the authors. This has continued in the second edition which likewise provides sensible policy guidelines to meeting the challenge posed by substance abuse in the workplace. *Alcohol, Drugs & Employment* (2011) should be compulsory reading for labour lawyers, human resources managers, occupational health practitioners, persons involved in running employee assistance programmes, trade union leaders, academics working in the substance abuse and labour fields, and policy makers.

Professor Charles Parry
Director: Alcohol & Drug Abuse Research Unit
South African Medical Research Council (Cape Town), November 2011

Foreword: Legal

The first edition of *Alcohol, Employment and Fair Labour Practice* (1993) has for many years been an invaluable resource guide to identifying and managing issues of alcohol problems in the workplace. However, it is 18 years since the book was first published and apart from being out of print, an update is necessary to reflect new labour laws in South Africa post-1994, as well as the increasing variety of drugs prevalent in the market and the shifts in the demographic profile of drug users internationally. Alcohol continues to be the dominant substance of abuse. In addition, with the workplace increasingly being recognised as an important frontier for addressing substance abuse given the increasing stresses that employees have to contend with, a greater onus has now been placed on employers to sensitively address substance abuse among their employees.

The 2nd edition of the book, now titled *Alcohol, Drugs and Employment*, has 20 chapters (increased from the original 17). This book will no doubt prove to be an important tool for human resource managers, labour lawyers, trade unions, occupational health service providers and academics. It provides valuable assistance in the form of both scientific facts and practical tools for addressing the issues of substance abuse in the workplace in a compassionate, legal and fair manner through balancing employee and employer interests.

Dunstan Mlambo
Judge President of the Labour Court and Labour Appeal Court of South Africa
November 2011

Preface

This book follows the first edition which was written in 1993. This new edition was prompted by significant changes in the fields of alcohol and drugs in the past 18 years, particularly around the issue of testing. Conversely In some areas of the field, in some respects, there has been little change.

We have introduced to this edition the challenging field of drugs, which has increased our undertaking considerably. The field of substance abuse is one which produces many different theories and treatments, as well arguments, as to the best way of dealing with a complex problem. We have tried to steer a middle path providing as much information as possible and often allowing readers to judge for themselves which route to take.

The impact of alcohol and drugs on health has taken a major toll in South Africa and companies can play their part in helping to reduce these problems by providing good alcohol and drug policies and procedures designed for their specific businesses, as well as providing education and support to their employees.

We have designed this edition of the book to be more of a reference book, so that different readers can benefit from the varied chapters pertaining to their specific needs. The book is designed to provide information to occupational lawyers, occupational health professionals, human resource specialists, managing directors, line managers and employee assistance professionals, on how best to address this complex and varied problem. It includes chapters on organisational factors that companies should address in order to rid themselves of the risks which can emanate from these problems. The chapters also touch on treatment and prevention options which are a useful guide for occupational health professionals and employee assistance professionals. The chapter on risk assessment for an organisation should provide a search tool for management to identify significant risks in their own organisation. There are also 11 Appendices to help the reader put into practice what they are planning to implement as well as a quick reference source.

Mike McCann
Nadine Harker Burnhams
November 2011

Chapter 1

A Framework for Analysing Alcohol Problems in the Workplace

Mike McCann & Nadine Harker Burnhams

This book starts by looking at the alcohol problems affecting work, and goes on to describe the drug problems. We have decided to separate these two aspects of substance abuse because they are dealt with differently, particularly in treatment and testing. However, they may be considered together in management procedures or policies.

This chapter explores the different theories of alcohol abuse and dependence, starting with a historical perspective. We aim to show the relation between consumption, intoxication and dependence and the impact of tolerance, an important concept because it describes how some individuals appear less intoxicated than others on similar consumption. An understanding of the measurements of alcohol, such as percentage concentration and its relation to the volume of alcohol, is also necessary.

It is important to consider the different categories of drinkers: whether someone is a social, moderate, heavy or problem drinker. These categories help us analyse, understand and ultimately assist those who are problem drinkers. It also helps us to see the correlations between level of alcohol consumption and associated risk to the individual, the public, other workers and the organisation.

The social benefits of moderate alcohol consumption are well known, and the distinctive effects of alcohol dependency (or alcoholism) have been proclaimed for many years. Although alcohol can induce dependence, the major alcohol problem in the workplace is abuse, not dependence. Alcohol abuse[1] impacts on industry and exacts an enormous toll in terms of manpower, production and finance. This problem is more often than not, hidden, and difficult to identify—until you purposefully start looking for it.

International experience leads to the conclusion that in many countries more serious problems of national magnitude arise from other types of drinkers than from those who are termed 'alcoholic' in America. The latter do, of course, exist in every country where alcoholic beverages are consumed, but they may form a small group or, even if they are numerous, the problems arising from them may be overshadowed by the problems which other types of drinking present.[2]

---

1   In the United Kingdom the terminology 'inappropriate drinking' instead of 'alcohol abuse' has been used by some practitioners. The advantage of the category 'inappropriate drinking' is that it broadens consideration of problem drinking beyond heavy drinking.

2   Jellinek *The Disease Concept of Alcoholism* (1960) 15.

Problem drinkers display a wide range of behaviours—from the heavy social drinker to the excessive and troubled drinker, the weekend binge drinker and, finally, to the dependent drinker. What then, do we mean by a 'problem drinker in the workplace'? An employee may be a problem drinker who causes loss and harm to a company without being dependent on alcohol. This drinker may be at risk of becoming alcohol dependent, yet he or she do not necessarily meet the criteria.

The definition of alcohol dependency is important because there are various interpretations of it, many of which are subjective or misleading but which can nevertheless influence an employer or employee's thinking on the subject.

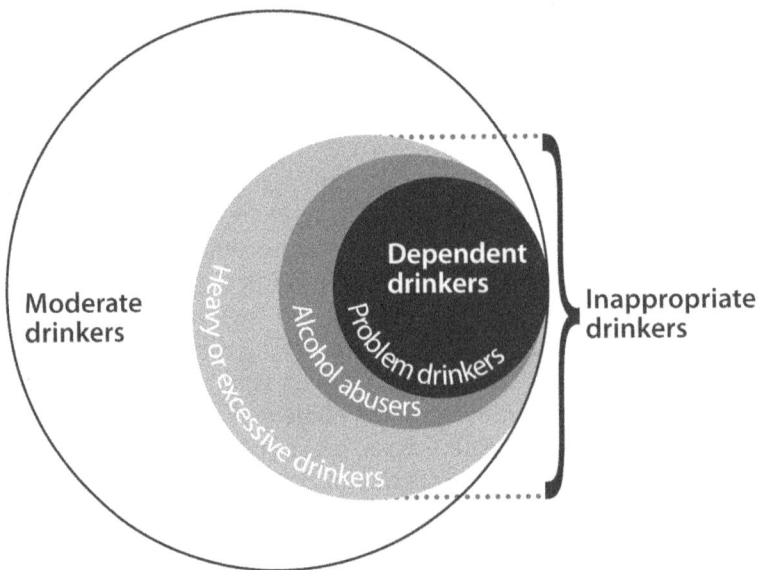

Figure 1.1 It is estimated that up to 85% of employees drink alcohol, of whom 30% will be heavy, excessive and/or problem drinkers while 6–10% will be dependent drinkers, according to figures derived from the South African National Council on Alcohol and Drug Dependence (SANCA).

However, whereas a relatively high proportion of South Africans abstain from alcohol, 45% of males and 18% of females do drink and amongst these drinkers the rate of consuming alcohol is one of the highest in the world.[3]

---

3   Parry CDH et al 'Alcohol use trends in South Africa: Findings from the first demographic and health survey' (2005) 66 *Journal of Studies on Alcohol* 91-97.

Table 1.1

Common terms for alcohol use	Characteristics of use	Term may include
Social drinker, alcohol user	Use of alcohol • Open use of alcohol within, for example, the family setting (at celebration meals or in keeping with cultural customs) or a glass with the evening meal. • Responsible use of alcohol—no more than 2 standard drinks at one sitting, and within the legal driving limits. • Frequency of use varies—however, there is no significant increase in frequency of use. • Use for medical reasons (with a doctor's prescription).	No excessive drinking
Heavy or excessive drinker, inappropriate drinker	Misuse of alcohol • Has control over quantity and frequency of use and can still choose whether or not to use. • Begins to develop a pattern for use. • Starts devising reasons for using without others' knowledge. • Starts making self-imposed rules to govern use. For example, 'I'll only drink at parties and on the weekend.'	Periodic binge drinker (including weekend binge drinker), symptomatic drinker, inappropriate drinker, alcohol-related disability
Alcohol abuser	Abuse of alcohol • Less control over whether to use. • Rituals for using are established—for example, using after work. • Starts anticipating and planning times and occasions for use. • Becomes more clever about hiding use from others and at work. • Solitary use begins. • Self-imposed rules are modified and more exceptions are allowed. For instance, I will drink only after work, but not at work. • Repeated promises about intentions to cut down or quit use.	Problem drinker, troubled drinker, binge drinker, symptomatic drinker, excessive or heavy drinker, alcohol-related or alcohol-induced disability
Dependent drinker	Dependency • No control over alcohol use. • Binge use: may remain intoxicated throughout the day for two or more days. • Exhibits grandiose and aggressive behaviour. • Generally more defiant. • Increased risk-taking and battles to hide use. • Obsessed with alcohol and needs to keep a constant supply on hand. • Spends a lot of time getting and using alcohol. • Solitary use increases in amount and frequency. • Abandons self-imposed rules; because of the obsession and the compulsion to use, life becomes alcohol.	Binge drinker, alcohol-induced disability

An employee falling within any but the first of the above categories of drinkers may arrive at work intoxicated or suffering from the effects of alcohol. If chronic, one alcohol problem could lead to another. Employers and managers should understand the different categories of drinkers so that they can take appropriate action if the need arises. This may involve either disciplinary processes or referral to an Occupational Health Professional (See later chapters 15, 16 and 17).

1. THEORIES OF ALCOHOL DEPENDENCE

No single theory adequately defines alcoholism or problem drinking. It is not a disease state with a clear diagnosis such as diabetes. According to Hore,[4] 'Alcoholism is best regarded as more than an undimensional illness involving more than a single factor.' The American Institute of Medicine[5] states, 'There is no likelihood that a single cause will be identified for all instances of alcohol problems.'

Researchers have looked at various criteria which can indicate the onset of alcohol problems, including the following:
- the quantity of alcohol consumed;
- the frequency of consumption and the drinking pattern;
- the social, psychological and physical damage; and
- dependence in its psychological and physical forms.

There are many theories which attempt to explain alcohol dependence and related problems. The most prominent theories focus on the following: sociocultural factors, psychological characteristics, behavioural indicators, physiological criteria, and genetic and innate personality factors. In addition, ethnic and cultural factors must be considered: What are regarded as alcohol abusers and problem drinking in one ethnic or cultural group might not be considered as such in another. Historically the most prevalent theories relating to alcohol dependence have been the following:
- the moral theory;
- the medical theory;
- the behavioural theory;
- the genetic theory; and
- the alcohol-dependence syndrome theory.

We shall briefly look at each of these in turn.

1.1 The moral theory

Historically, the moral theory had been the most dominant. In 18th-century Britain an Act was passed to repress 'the odious and loathsome sin of drunkenness'.

---

4   Hore *The Disease Concept of Alcoholism—a re-appraisal* Paper presented at 8th International Conference on Alcoholism, Liverpool (April 1990).

5   Institute of Medicine (US) *Broadening the Base of Treatment for Alcohol Problems: Report of a Study by a Committee of the Institute of Medicine, Division of Mental Health and Behavioral Medicine* (1990) 35.

Gin, cursed Fiend, with Fury fraught,
Makes human Race a Prey.
It enters by a deadly Draught
And steals our Life away.

Virtue and Truth, driv'n to Despair
Its Rage compells to fly,
But cherishes with hellish Care,
Theft, Murder, Perjury.

Damn'd Cup! that on the Vitals preys
That liquid Fire contains,
Which Madness to the Heart conveys,
And rolls it thro' the Veins.

Published according to the British Act of Parliament Feb 1, 1751.

The moral theory still exerts a powerful influence on contemporary attitudes towards alcohol problems. Even though alcohol abuse is labelled today as an 'illness', many who value self-control, self-restraint and respectability believe, at root, that it stems from a moral failing. The underlying value judgment in present-day attitudes to alcohol problems is evidenced in the frequent use of expressions such as 'she displays a lack of moral fibre' or 'he should pull himself together'.

1.2 The historical medical or disease theory

The medical or disease theory, based on the concept of illness or disease, gradually succeeded the original moral theory. It originated and gained acceptance in the United States of America, owing its origin largely to the development of the Alcoholics Anonymous (AA) movement and later the research of Jellinek.[6] Here the perception is that the individual suffering from alcohol dependence has an incurable disease and that his only salvation is to abstain from alcohol. The classic AA approach states that he or she is and always will be an alcoholic and must seek spiritual empowerment. The classic disease theory was defined in terms of tolerance to alcohol (see below in this chapter), withdrawal symptoms, craving, loss of control and an inability to abstain. Few modern adherents of the disease theory believe in the classic model but rather in revised and attenuated forms which consider the various states of alcohol dependence as a continuum, or that the individual is dependent or not dependent on alcohol.[7]

Jellinek is historically perhaps the most quoted scientist who has researched alcohol problems and it is due to his work that both the medical profession in the United States and the World Health Organisation (WHO) came to accept alcoholism as a disease. Too often Jellinek's work has been oversimplified in interpretation. He tried to give an unbiased and factual description of a subject which usually had been treated subjectively.

---

6   Jellinek *The Disease Concept of Alcoholism* (1960) 35–41.
7   Glatt 'Alcoholism'—disease, learned disorder or just heavy drinking? A review of Professor Herbert Fingarette's book, *Heavy Drinking—the Myth of Alcoholism as a Disease'* (1991) 26(5–6) *Alcohol and Alcoholism* 499–503.

He was able to dissociate himself from an American cultural bias and to look at the problem from the viewpoint of other cultures and ethnic groups in the world. He did not intend to produce a rigid, narrow model or theory.[8]

In the field of alcohol studies, which involves much controversy and antagonistic feelings, it was predictable that the various schools of thought would interpret Jellinek's work with a leaning towards their own view and that he would be quoted with various and often differing interpretations.

The term 'alcoholic' is outdated and imprecise, yet is still likely to be used by the general public for some time. When Jellinek used the term, however, it was to describe five different types of 'alcoholics': alpha, beta, gamma, delta and epsilon. The gamma and delta are the only two truly dependent types.

The alpha alcoholic is a psychological or symptomatic type of drinker and does not necessarily progress to more severe drinking dependence. The symptomatic drinker can be considered to be in a predependent state.[9] He or she has not totally lost control over alcohol, but finds it increasingly difficult not to rely on alcohol to cope with the stresses of working life. Other researchers have suggested that symptomatic drinking occurs when heavier drinking is resorted to in order to change the mood of individuals to make them feel more powerful and self-confident. Increased drinking usually results in feelings of assertiveness and a sense of being aggressive, dominant and competitive, with the ability to take risks being a further characteristic. These feelings are often accompanied by frequent intoxication.

The beta alcoholic is a problem drinker with deteriorating health due to alcohol abuse. Typically, they may suffer from cirrhosis of the liver, hypertension, cardiac arrhythmias or tuberculosis. Again, this type of drinker may or may not progress to full dependence.

The epsilon alcoholic is the bout or binge drinker; his drinking habits can constitute a distorted version of one of the other four types.[10]

It is important to distinguish between a problem drinker and a dependent drinker

---

As far as the only two truly dependent types are concerned, the gamma type is unable to stop drinking once he or she has started (loss of control) and the delta type is unable to abstain. The delta type, who is likely to drink every day without necessarily losing control, is associated with a high level of physical illness. Jellinek identified only these two types as real illnesses; he regarded the others as pre-morbid or pre-alcoholic states.

Later researchers felt that the notion of loss of control was too rigid and in reality is variable with 'impaired control or relative lack of control rather than of absolute loss of control, and many would hold with the concept of degrees of dependence rather than the old all or nothing theory of alcoholism popular with AA'.[11]

---

8   Pattison, Sobell & Sobell *Emerging Concepts of Alcohol Dependence* (1977).

9   Gallanter *Recent Developments in Alcoholism* vol 6 (1988) 120.

10   Jellinek *The Disease Concept of Alcoholism* (1960); Edwards *The Treatment of Drinking Problems* (1982). In the preface to *The Disease Concept*, Jellinek qualifies his book, stating that it was a viewpoint, a conception (a concept in the making) rather than a concept and that his brief to write on alcoholism rather than alcohol problems 'represents not more than a small section of the problems of alcohol—a very small section indeed'.

11   Glatt (n 7) at 499–503.

Inadequate information has led to a degree of misinterpretation of these categories, one of the main reasons being that use of the term 'alcoholic' has led some to believe that only a person in the dependent state (the alcoholic) has a problem and that all other drinkers are free of problems. This is not the case. Modern thinking on the subject subscribes to the view that it is imperative to distinguish between an alcohol abuser or a problem drinker and a dependent drinker (or alcoholic). It could be argued that there is no clear-cut demarcation between an alcohol abuser or a problem drinker and a dependent drinker, only a gradual continuum in which the one merges into the other at some point. The process of dependence is a further continuum leading to variations of degree and type.[12]

A heavy or excessive drinker (or inappropriate drinker) need not be a dependent drinker, but could still be affected by the impact of alcohol abuse as regards alcohol-related diseases, social problems, poor productivity and accidents.

The distinction between an alcohol abuser or problem drinker and a dependent drinker is important when handling the individual in the occupational setting, though management tends to be primarily concerned with alcohol abuse. Dependence and its sequelae, though secondary factors in respect of the workplace, are nevertheless important and need to be attended to when considering treatment.

1.3 The behavioural theory

The behavioural theory offers an alternative view to the alcohol-dependence symptom theory in that it stresses that substance abuse is a learned behaviour and that problematic or inappropriate behaviour coupled with external influences is the prime consideration in developing an abnormal drinking or drug-abuse state. According to the theory, the individual can be cured if the behaviour problem can be solved or if empowerment can be developed. Changing the environment and the behaviour of the problem drinker or drug user is regarded as significant in altering their substance-abuse pattern. The following are some of the tenets of the behavioural perspective of substance abuse.

Alcohol and drugs can provide a temporary sense of relief from tension or stress and provide a feeling of wellbeing for individuals who are unable to cope with life's stressors. This temporary relief of symptoms can have a reinforcing effect on the individual which could increase the likelihood that the individual would seek out drinking or drug use again. This behaviour pattern is termed *operant conditioning*—when certain behaviours such as alcohol and drug use are seen as a positive reinforcement and not as harmful to one's health. Reinforcement theorists believe that individuals take alcohol or drugs to medicate themselves and escape the unpleasantness of their lives when they experience high levels of anxiety, depression or anger.[13] The use of alcohol or drugs to reduce tension and promote a feeling of relaxation is known as the *tension-reduction hypothesis*.[14] This hypothesis possibly explains the association of substance abuse with individuals working in jobs considered to have a higher risk of injury, jobs with a high work demand and jobs with a high stress factor.

According to the *classic conditioning theory*, environmental stimuli associated with using a particular substance of abuse becomes linked with the effect that the substance

---

12 Ibid. See also Edwards *The Treatment of Drinking Problems* (1982).
13 Comer *Abnormal Psychology* 3 ed (1997).
14 Kendall & Hammen *Abnormal Psychology* (1995).

has on the body. For example, the smell, sound, lighting and other familiar objects in the environment can elicit the craving for or urge an individual to continue seeking the substance irrespective of its negative effects.[15]

According to the *modelling and vicarious reinforcement perspective* an individual's substance-abuse habits and behaviour are shaped by observing others (such as parents, peers, social groups and partners) in their environment. So an individual learns a drinking or drug-use habit from people around them.[16] Therefore, if individuals perceive their drinking behaviour as good or acceptable and justified instead of it being harmful and undesirable, then they will be more likely to continue engaging in this behaviour. The major reinforcement for continuation of substance abuse according to modelling or vicarious reinforcement theorists, is the continued interaction or engagement with people (work colleagues, peers, family, partners, spouses and groups) who engage in such behaviours. For instance, many companies as part of the business culture would perhaps close an important deal over a meal with drinks and thereby endorse that behaviour.

The *social-learning model* proposes that individuals and groups provide a conducive social environment in which exposure to alcohol or other substances takes place. Individuals are then exposed to people whose behaviour they imitate (model on) and who are social reinforcers for use of the substance: the act of drinking is seen as socially desirable by the group that the individual associates with.[17]

1.4 The genetic theory

The genetic theory contends that certain individuals are either born with a susceptibility to alcohol dependence or, due to a possible lack of certain as yet unknown metabolic factors, are inevitably alcohol dependent. There has been much research on the implication of genetic susceptibility in the past two decades. There is now plentiful data from both human and animal studies supporting the importance of genetic influences in substance abuse and dependence. The evidence to support genetic influences and their association with environmental factors needs to be considered.[18]

1.5 The alcohol-dependence syndrome theory

The alcohol-dependence syndrome put forward by Edwards and Gross[19] describes a syndrome and therefore a disease or state of illness. However, Edwards[20] argues against the pigeonholing of drinking problems. He feels that to do so is to oversimplify a complex and varied problem. The task is to identify each individual's drinking pattern as it exists and only then try to identify the influences which shape this pattern.

---

15   Wilson, Nathan, O'Leary & Clark *Abnormal Psychology: Integrating Perspectives* (1996).

16   Ibid.

17   Akers, Krohn, Lanza-Kaduce & Radosevich 'Social learning and deviant behaviour: A specific test of a general theory' (1979) 44 *American Sociological Review* 636–655.

18   Mayfield, Harris & Schuckit 'Genetic factors influencing alcohol dependence' (2008) 154(2) *British Journal of Pharmacology* 275–87.

19   Edwards & Gross 'Alcohol dependence: Provisional description of a clinical syndrome' (1976) 1 *British Medical Journal* 1058–61.

20   Edwards *The Treatment of Drinking Problems* (1982).

> Alcohol dependency should be destigmatised and alcohol abuse should be stigmatised

The WHO and the Diagnostic and Statistical Manual for Mental Disorders (DSM-IV) distinguish between problem drinking and dependency, and thereby associate with the definition of alcohol-dependence syndrome described by Edwards and Gross.[21] The WHO has updated its definition of alcohol dependency in the International Classification of Diseases (ICD).[22] It no longer uses the term 'alcoholic', instead preferring the term 'alcohol dependant' or person suffering from the alcohol-dependence syndrome.

Alcohol-dependence syndrome is defined by seven criteria, later expanded to nine:

1. A narrowing of the dependant's repertoire in type of drink, timing and frequency of drinking. There is a tendency to drink at set times of the week or weekends, irrespective of a change in social restraints.
2. Drinking alcohol becomes of prime importance to the individual, who begins to neglect other interests.
3. Tolerance to alcohol increases, so that sufferers can consume excessive amounts of alcohol without showing signs of intoxication; later, when liver failure ensues, this tolerance is lost.
4. Repeated withdrawal symptoms occur, causing tremor, nausea, sweating and disturbances of mood.
5. Withdrawals are avoided or relieved by continued drinking or 'topping up', not necessarily only in the morning before work but throughout the day.
6. The sufferer knows that he or she is unable to stop drinking once started. This loss of control is variable and not necessarily consistent.
7. Dependent drinking is easily reinstated after periods of abstinence which suggests a long-lasting change in the dependant's body.

If one of the criteria is well developed, then it is likely that all will be present, though in varying degrees.[23] Masking of symptoms will occur particularly if the history is inconsistent and if there is co-existent drug abuse.

The WHO has added the following two criteria to the above list in its ICD-10:

8. Persistence with alcohol abuse even though overt signs of harm have been identified.
9. A strong desire or compulsion to drink and a craving for alcohol, particularly in familiar situations.[24]

The DSM-IV also refers to substance-related disorders. Substance-related disorders range from the taking of a drug of abuse (including alcohol) to the side effects of medication and toxin exposure. The DSM-IV groups substances into eleven classes: alcohol, amphetamines, caffeine, cannabis, cocaine, hallucinogens, inhalants, nicotine, opioids, phencyclidine, sedatives, hypnotics and anxiolytics. 'Substance' is defined as

---

21 Edwards & Gross (n 19) at 1058–61.
22 'Mental, behavioural and development disorders' (1987) *ICD-10* ch 5; Lader, Edwards & Drummond *The Nature of Alcohol and Drug Related Problems* (1992) 86–9.
23 Edwards *The Treatment of Drinking Problems* (1982).
24 WHO 'Mental, behavioural and development disorders' (1987) *ICD-10* ch 5; American Psychiatric Association *DSM-IV Diagnostic and Statistical Manual of Mental Disorders* (1994).

any drug of abuse, medication or toxin. Similar to the ICD-10, the DSM-IV distinguishes between substance dependency and substance abuse (problem use).

Substance dependency is defined by the following criteria:
1. Tolerance: the need for increased amounts of the substance to achieve a desired effect (or the effect diminishes with continued use of the same amount of the substance).
2. Withdrawal: the same substance is taken to relieve or avoid withdrawals.
3. The substance is often taken in larger amounts or over a longer period than was intended.
4. Unsuccessful efforts to cut down or control the substance.
5. A great deal of time is spent on activities to obtain the substance.
6. Participation in important social, occupational or recreational activities is given up because of substance use.
7. Continued use despite knowledge of persistent or recurrent physical or psychological problems that could have been caused or worsened by the substance.

The criteria for substance abuse include:
1. Recurrent substance use resulting in a failure to fulfil major role obligations at work or home.
2. Recurrent substance use in situations in which it is physically dangerous, eg driving or operating machinery while intoxicated.
3. Recurrent substance-related legal problems, eg arrests for drug offenses.
4. Continued use despite the presence of recurrent social or interpersonal problems.

It is important to note that diagnostic criteria and categories used in the DSM-IV and ICD-10 are meant to be employed by individuals with appropriate clinical training and experience.

2. CONSIDERATION OF THE MOST PREVALENT THEORIES

Jellinek[25] has criticised the medical theory of alcohol problems as propounded by the American AA. He contends that this point of view deals only with extreme cases of alcohol problems and is 'too cut and dried', with the result that substantial areas of the phenomenon are overlooked. A result of such a narrow definition is that persons with alcohol problems are stigmatised, since historically only extreme cases of 'down-and-out' alcoholics have been regarded as meriting concern.

Proponents of the behavioural theory of alcohol problems argue that the medical theory is too narrow and tends to characterise the alcohol-dependent person as an extreme 'alcoholic', thus encouraging stigmatisation and the consequent need of the sufferer to deny alcohol abuse. The AA approach has, ironically, influenced public opinion in such a way that nowadays the alcohol-dependent person is stigmatised and often treated with embarrassment and little sympathy. However, the AA approach has been successful when the individual recognises the problem in him- or herself, is willing to accept that he or she should abstain from alcohol and admits that the need for support and comfort provided by a group whose approach he or she accepts.

The image of the 'alcoholic' is still powerful in the mind of the general population. It permeates the historically influential moral theory which judges and blames the

---

25 Jellinek *The Disease Concept of Alcoholism* (1960).

'alcoholic', regarding him or her as a person with no moral fibre. No matter how many authorities declare it to be a disease, people are still embarrassed to discuss or confront the problem and the individual is almost invariably socially stigmatised. This social stigma, whatever its cause, appears to be one of the main reasons for the widespread denial of the problem, and denial is the main initial problem to combat. By way of contrast, smokers have little difficulty admitting their nicotine dependence. Lay beliefs about biological versus nonbiological causes of mental versus substance-abuse disorders are also related to the beliefs regarding what should be the appropriate treatment.[26]

The moralistic, judgmental stance which society often adopts towards the alcohol-dependent person differs markedly from other, more patently physical ailments, which are often met with sympathy and concern. Thus, when a doctor diagnoses a particular physical disease, there is usually acceptance by the patient and possibly relief that at least he or she knows what is wrong. This is not so in the case of a diagnosis of alcohol dependency: both doctors and patients tend to avoid the diagnosis.

While the behavioural perspective is an interesting one, it must be remembered that it is not only alcohol problems that are stigmatised by society. Many psychological problems are socially stigmatised—despite theoretical recognition that the sufferer is usually blameless.

Our view is that there is value in considering both the alcohol-dependence syndrome theory and the behavioural theory. The former deals with the end result of alcohol dependence, while the latter looks at the condition as it progresses. Whichever theory is used will naturally affect the treatment. Some patients respond well to the alcohol-dependence syndrome approach, others to the behavioural approach; their response often depends upon the stage of their condition.

We believe in the eclectic approach that treatment should be designed for each individual patient, depending on his own circumstances. No single treatment approach has been objectively demonstrated to be better than all others. The treatment of alcohol problems remains a complex, arduous task for both treaters and treated.[27]

3. A THEORY FOR ALCOHOL PROBLEMS IN THE WORKPLACE[28]

The theoretical model which we feel is most useful for considering alcohol problems in the workplace is illustrated in Figure 1.2 below.

---

26 Kuppin & Carpiano 'Public conceptions of serious mental illness and substance abuse, their causes and treatments: Findings from the 1996 General Social Survey (2008) 98 (9 Suppl) *American Journal of Public Health* S120–S125.

27 Institute of Medicine (US) *Broadening the Base of Treatment for Alcohol Problems: Report of a Study by a Committee of the Institute of Medicine, Division of Mental Health and Behavioral Medicine* (1990) 35.

28 Gorman, 1989 criticised the use of the term 'model' without describing it as a discrete entity. The terminology 'theory', 'hypothesis', 'concept' and 'model' have been used inconsistently and interchangeably by the majority of researchers. Instead of using 'model', which suggests conforming to specific criteria, we will use the term 'theoretical model'. A 'theory' describes an established but not proven principle or a concept to be proved, and a 'model' concerns a plan or design (*Chambers English Dictionary* (1988) 919 and 1524). When quoting, we shall maintain the author's own terminology.

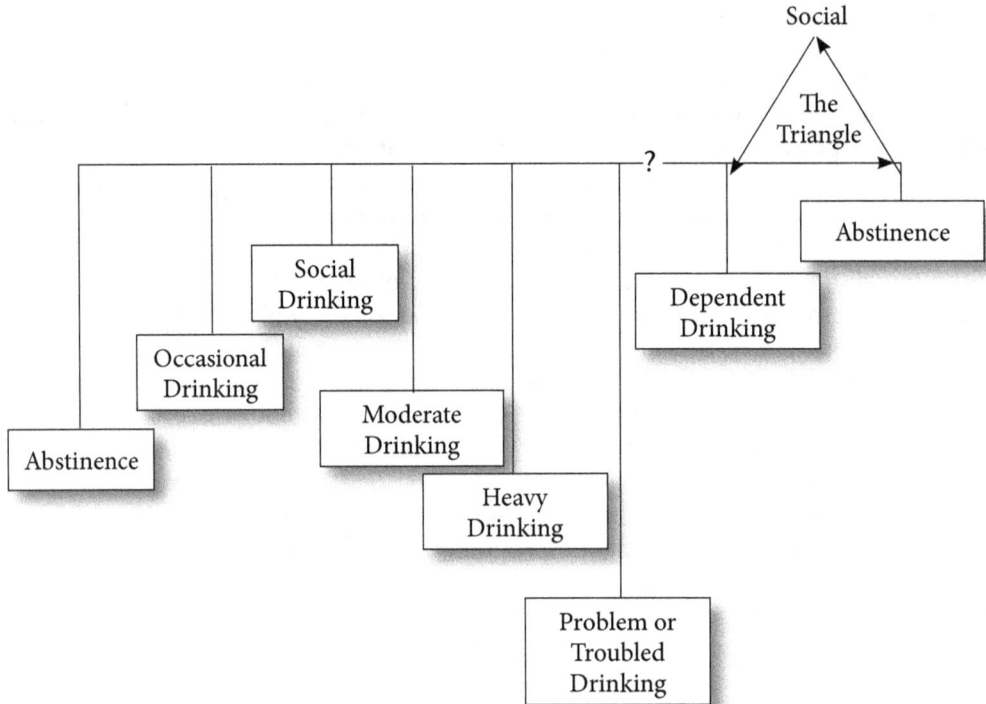

Figure 1.2 A theoretical model for alcohol problems in the workplace.

Definitions of each type of drinker identified by the theoretical model, are given below.

Everybody is situated somewhere along the model's continuum. Individuals are abstinent or occasional drinkers, social or moderate drinkers, heavy drinkers, problem or troubled drinkers, or dependent drinkers. The last-mentioned condition culminates in conditions characterised in the triangle (see next paragraph). A question mark is placed on the line between problem drinkers and dependent drinkers as the differentiation between the two is, at this stage, ill-defined but is now considered to be a continuation of the continuum.[29]

3.1 The triangle of alcohol dependence

The triangle is derived from a long-term follow-up study of 68 male alcoholics conducted over a period of 10 years.[30] Originally, 99 male alcoholics were included in the study but only those who survived the entire 10 years were ultimately used in the study. The researchers were able to produce a barycentric (pertaining to the centre of gravity) plot of the total time each behaviour category spent in the triangle over the 10 years. Thus, each individual in the study was plotted somewhere on the triangle. It was established that the subjects generally fluctuated to and fro between the dependent and the abstinent states. Some attempted social drinking, but virtually all of them soon reverted to the dependent state. They moved around the triangle with a brief period

---

29 Glatt (n 7) at 499–503.
30 Taylor, Brown, Edwards et al 'Patterns of outcome: drinking histories over ten years among a group of alcoholics' (1985) 80 *British Journal of Addiction* 45–50.

of social drinking between abstinence and dependent drinking. Some individuals were consistently in either one of the bottom corners, ie abstinent or dependent, but the majority fluctuated along the line between the two. Only one individual was able to maintain a social drinking status during the entire 10-year period and could therefore be classified as a 'controlled drinker'. Three other individuals partially succeeded, but had occasional relapses into the dependent drinking state, intermingled with periods of abstinence. Thus, out of a total of 68 recorded histories, only one subject could be considered to have escaped from the triangle.

It must be remembered that we are considering only those in this study who have reached the triangle, ie the dependent state. The study does not include heavy and troubled drinkers. Those two categories are to be distinguished from dependent drinkers: it is our belief that heavy and troubled drinkers are able—through education, therapy and counselling—to work their way back down the line which is portrayed in Figure 1.2 without falling into the more intractable dependency triangle. Treatment of a heavy or a problem drinker before he or she becomes alcohol dependent is far more successful than treatment once he or she has become dependent.[31]

In our opinion the workplace is the most appropriate and potentially most successful setting for dealing with alcohol problems.[32] In the workplace there are far more moderately heavy and troubled problem drinkers than there are dependent drinkers and they can be readily assisted to restore reasonable drinking patterns before they become dependent. Here we are dealing with a captive population who are already participating in a structured working environment and where constructive persuasion can control the development of the problem.

Turning our attention again to the theoretical model for the workplace, we observe that the line to the left of the triangle is not static. Individuals move up and down the line due to the impact of various stresses on their lives. The carefree and uninhibited excesses of youth may yield to an attitude of responsibility towards work and family, and as the body ages, it is often unable to maintain the earlier excesses; on the other hand, continued carefree drinking from youth may lead to problem and dependent drinking.

3.2 Defining the terms

In South Africa, standard serving sizes of beer (340 ml), wine (120 ml per glass) and spirits (25 ml per tot) are all officially defined as containing the equivalent of 12 grams of ethanol.[33] While these official definitions of standard drinks may exist, the sizes of drinks poured in serving establishments in South Africa often do not conform to them. A significant amount of beverage alcohol consumption occurs in homes and other private settings (such as shebeens and taverns) where drinks are rarely measured.[34]

---

31 Rosalki (ed) *Clinical Biochemistry of Alcoholism* (1984) 15; Chick 'Do alcoholics recover?' (1982) 285 *British Medical Journal* 3–4.

32 This opinion is supported by Von Weig and 'Alcoholism in Industry' (1972) 67 *British Journal of Addiction* 181–7.

33 Parry, CDH & Bennetts, AL *Alcohol Policy and Public Health in South Africa* (Oxford University Press 1998).

34 Grant, M (ed) *Alcohol and Emerging Markets: Patterns, Problems, and Responses.* International Centre for Alcohol Policies.

The categories listed in Figure 1.2 above are based on average consumption levels.[35] Consumption is measured in units of alcohol. A unit of alcohol, irrespective of its quantity or form, is classified as 8 g. Thus, one unit of whisky is approximately equivalent to one half-pint of 3,5% alcohol per volume of beer. The quantities are different, but the alcohol content is the same. A unit (or 8 g) of alcohol is an important guideline for assessing the extent of drinking. It is also an invaluable tool for helping to educate moderate, heavy and problem drinkers to become conscious of their drinking patterns and control their drinking. A tot measure can be a metric measure (25 ml); or one-sixth of a gill (23,66 ml) as in England and Wales; or one-fifth of a gill (28,4 ml) as in Scotland; or one-quarter of a gill (35,5 ml) as in Ireland. It varies from country to country and from area to area. In South Africa, the standard measure is the metric tot = 25 ml = 8,5 g alcohol, slightly more than one unit of alcohol.

Beer in South Africa is generally stronger than its British counterpart, but the spirits are standardised to 43% v/v alcohol. The outdated proof system, used to measure a concentration of alcohol in spirits, dates back to the time when the Department of Customs and Excise in Britain used to ignite gunpowder soaked in spirits to identify the strength—thus 'proof' of its concentration. Proof spirit was the weakest alcohol which would ignite the gunpowder: 100% proof was equivalent to 57,1% v/v alcohol. Spirits and beer generally have on their label the quantity of alcohol measured as a percentage of volume. Up until a few years ago wines in South Africa only rarely had their concentration of alcohol stipulated on the label, but today all wine bottles have on their label the quantity of alcohol. Table 1.2 gives examples of certain types of alcohol available in South Africa with their relevant concentration and units. The grams of alcohol in a particular drink can be calculated by the formula:

Alcohol in grams = Volume in millilitres x% alcohol per volume/100 x 0,789

---

35   For lay people to understand the concept of alcohol abuse it is easier to address the problem in the context of 'quantity consumed', although this is not strictly true when describing dependent drinkers. In this case the approach should be the effect of drinking rather than quantity consumed. A dependent drinker might drink less than a heavy drinker, but the effect when they drink and the necessity to drink can still be the focus (or obsession) of the dependent drinker's life. As regards the workplace, the main concern is alcohol abuse and not alcohol dependence.

Table 1.2 Types of alcohol and their range of percentage volume alcohol (approximated)

	% volume alcohol	1 bottle (750 ml)	Tots: 1/4 gill (35,5 ml)	1/5 gill (28,4 ml)	metric tot (25 ml)	1/6 gill (23,6 ml)
SPIRITS Whisky Cane Vodka Gin Brandy	43%	254,5 g alcohol or 32 units	12,4 g	9,6 g	8,5 g	7,8 g
WINE					340 ml	
Red	13–14%	77–83 g alcohol or 9,6–10,4 units			35 g or 4,4 units	
White	11–13,5%	65–80 g alcohol or 8–10 units			30–36 g or 4,5 units	
Light	8%	47 g alcohol or 6 units			21,5 g or 2,7 units	
FORTIFIED WINE	± 18%					
BEERS	2–6%					

The following table indicates some specific brands of beer and cider found in Southern Africa and their alcohol concentrations.

Table 1.3 Some brands of beer, cider and spirit coolers (flavoured alcoholic drinks) available in South Africa

	% alcohol/volume*	Grams per 100 ml
BEERS		
Urbock	7,0	5,52
Castle Milk Stout	6,0	4,73
Black Label	5,5	4,34
Hansa Marzen Gold	5,2	4,10
Amstel Lager	5,0	3,94
Becks	5,0	3,94
Castle Lager	5,0	3,94
Heineken	5,0	3,94
Windhoek Special	5,0	3,94
Millers	4,7	3,7
Hansa Pilsener	4,5	3,55
Windhoek Export	4,5	3,55

	% alcohol/volume*	Grams per 100 ml
Castle Lite	4,0	3,15
Guinness	4,0	3,15
Tafel Lager	4,0	3.15
Windhoek Lager	4,0	3,15
Sorghum beer	3,5	2,76
Windhoek Light	2,4	1,89
CIDERS AND SPIRIT	COOLERS	ALCOHOLIC(FLAVOURED DRINKS)
Smirnoff Storm	7,0	5,52
Burchell	6,3	4,97
Blakes & Doyle	5,5	4,34
Foundry	5,5	4,34
Sarita	5,5	4,34
Savanna Dry	5,5	4,34
Vawter	5,5	4,34
Archers Aqua	5,0	4,34
Redds Dry	5,0	4,34
Smirnoff Spin/Ice	5,0	4,34
Bacardi	4,5	3,55
Brutal Fruit	4,5	3,55
Hunters Gold	4,5	3,55
Redds Original	4,5	3,55
Savanna Light	3,0	2,36

* These percentages are as they appear on the websites of manufacturers or as identified on labels. They are averages and there is some variation in the figures.

3.3 Defining categories of consumption

We are now in a position to define the terms of our model represented in Figure 1.2 above and Table 1.4 below (where a range is indicated, the lower level is the recommended level for females and the higher level for males).

The social drinker is defined as someone who drinks usually not more than two to three units of alcohol a day. He or she does not become intoxicated, nor is the drinking likely to affect his or her health or cause problems in his or her social life or at work.

The moderate drinker consumes between three and four units of alcohol a day and will, on certain special occasions, possibly become intoxicated—perhaps twice a year.

The heavy drinker consumes more than six units of alcohol a day—eg three double whiskies or three and a half dumpies (340 ml each) of beer. This is approximately 41–44 units of alcohol a week. Some heavy drinkers will be periodically intoxicated.

A *problem or troubled drinker* will drink seven to nine units of alcohol a day—eg three and a half to four and a half double tots of spirits or 4–5 dumpies (340 ml each). This is approximately 50–60 units of alcohol a week. He or she is known to become intoxicated periodically and his or her social environment, family or work may have suffered either occasionally or more often due to drinking. As already mentioned, Edwards[36] points out that binge or bout drinking (Jellinek's epsilon alcoholic) occurs due to a degree of variation of the alcohol-dependence syndrome often caused by external factors or pressures changing the shape of the drinking pattern and not due to a unique type of dependence.

The dependent drinker consumes 80 g or 10 units of alcohol daily (eg five double whiskies or six dumpies (340 ml each) of lager. This is approximately 70 units of alcohol a week. He or she has a marked tolerance of alcohol and can sustain a blood-alcohol level greater than 150 mg per 100 ml of blood without necessarily looking intoxicated. He or she will start developing withdrawal symptoms as the alcohol level drops and has probably had bouts of 'delirium tremens' (DTs). To avoid the withdrawal symptoms and the DTs, he or she starts topping up, even in the morning. He or she could be described initially as 'never drunk, but never sober'. At a much later stage, when the liver is dramatically affected, there can be a sudden loss of tolerance and imbibing only a few units can produce severe intoxication. Dependent drinkers will continue to drink in spite of the psychological, the social and the physical problems which ensue.[37] Another description of dependent drinking is the repeated 'intermittent or continual' ingestion of alcohol which leads to dependency, physical disease or other harm.[38] This description would include excessive 'binge' drinkers.

Table 1.4 Consumption categories[39]

Category	Units or grams per day	Units or grams per week
Social drinker	2–3 units or 16–24 g	14–21 units or 112–168 g
Moderate drinker*	3–4 units or 24–36 g	21–28 units or 168–224 g
Heavy drinker	6 units and more	42 units or 336 g
Problem or troubled drinker	7–9 units or 56–72 g	49–63 units or 392–504 g
Dependent drinker	10 units or 80 g	70 units or 560 g

* Harper (1989) defines a moderate drinker as one who consumes 30–80 g of alcohol daily. But he includes heavy or problem drinkers in his category of moderate drinkers. This could be related to cultural differences, as Harper's work was done in Sydney, Australia.[40]

---

36 Edwards *The Treatment of Drinking Problems* (1982).
37 Royal College Physicians *A Great and Growing Evil: The Medical Effects of Alcohol* (1987) 7.
38 Davies 'Implications for medical practice of an acceptable concept of alcoholism' in Rosalki (ed) *Clinical Biochemistry of Alcoholism* (1984).
39 Royal College Physicians *A Great and Growing Evil: The Medical Effects of Alcohol* (1987).
40 Harper C, Kril J 'Neuropathology of alcoholism'(1990) 25 (2–3) *Alcohol and Alcoholism* 207-216.

4. DEFINITION OF ALCOHOL PROBLEMS IN THE WORKPLACE

A worker with an alcohol problem is someone whose drinking or dependency interferes with his work, his performance or ability to do his work, or with his relationships at work. Problem drinking in the workplace can be divided into two categories: drinking which results in incapacity and that which results in misconduct.

Incapacity as a result of problem drinking is defined as a physical incapacity (physical damage or absence through sickness) or such serious deterioration of behaviour at work as to render the employee unable to fulfil his work duties. Misconduct brought about by problem drinking is a form of behavioural, rather than physical incapacity: the worker's drinking interferes with his capacity to perform his work diligently and productively. Examples of this are abusive, disobedient or violent behaviour, and sleeping while on shift.

5. CONSUMPTION AND INTOXICATION

What is the relationship between alcohol consumed and level of intoxication, and how does alcohol have its inebriating effect? The influence of alcohol consumed depends on many factors, the most important of which are body mass, gender and level of alcohol in the blood. The body mass and the gender of the individual are related to the total body water. The greater the total body water, the greater the dilution factor. One's body mass consists of muscle and fat; muscle mass helps to dilute the alcohol concentration in the body and so will lower the alcohol level; fat, on the other hand, does not absorb alcohol to the same extent and does little to dilute the alcohol consumed. Females have a higher percentage of body fat and a lower muscle mass compared with males and therefore a given amount of alcohol consumed is more concentrated in a woman's blood than in a man's.[41] Thus, in a man of large build the alcohol will be diluted in his body more than would be in the case of a small male or a woman.

By way of example, a 70 kg man will require 25 g of alcohol for his blood alcohol to reach 50 mg per 100 ml of blood—the legal driving limit in South Africa for a holder of standard driver's licence.[42] A person's blood alcohol is an important measure because it is in direct contact with the central nervous system, where alcohol has its influence, which includes the lowering of inhibitions. There is less suppression of excitability and impulses. This leads to an initial feeling of wellbeing as inhibitions are relaxed and the effects of stresses are reduced, which occurs when the blood-alcohol level is at

- 50 mg per 100 ml of blood
- or 0,05 g per cent (g%)
- or 0,05 g per 100 ml of blood (the legal calculation)
- or 50 mg per cent (mg%) (mg/dl)
- or 10,09 millimolars (see Appendix 5 for conversion tables).

All of these units of volume are the same

---

41 This can be calculated from the Widmark formula (as amended by Schwar in Cooper, Schwar & Smith *Alcohol, Drugs and Road Traffic* (1979)): A = p x c x r x 10 x 0,947. A = amount of alcohol absorbed in grams; p = body mass in kilograms; c = blood-alcohol concentration in grams per 100 ml of blood; r = diffusion rate, which varies with percentage of body fat. For example: obese r = 0,5; muscular r = 0,75; average male r = 0,7; average female r = 0,6.

42 Section 65 of the National Road Traffic Act 93 of 1996. A different standard applies to people registered as professional drivers: 20 mg per 100 ml of blood.

At 100 mg per 100 ml of blood, or 0,1 g%, there is a progressive loss of sensory perception, a staggering gait, emotional instability and reduced judgment, which get worse as the blood-alcohol level rises. Between 100 and 250 mg (0,1 to 0,25 on the legal scale) of alcohol per 100 ml of blood, there is loss of self-control, argumentativeness, slurred speech and amnesia. At 250–350 mg of alcohol per 100 ml of blood (0,25 to 0,35 on the legal scale) drowsiness and overt emotional instability, including laughter, depression, crying and anger, can be displayed within a few minutes of each other. At 400 mg per 100 ml (0,4 on the legal scale) unconsciousness inevitably prevails, and death occurs between 500 and 600 mg per 100 ml (0,5 to 0,6 on the legal scale).

These figures are based upon a moderate drinker and are therefore relative, depending on the drinker's degree of tolerance which is built up over many years of drinking. A hardened drinker could quite comfortably tolerate blood-alcohol levels of 250 mg per 100 ml (0,25 on the legal scale) of blood without showing overt signs of intoxication, yet a 15-year-old schoolgirl upon her first introduction to alcohol would be violently ill, possibly comatose (which could lead to death) with the same level of alcohol in her blood.

At 9 am a contract painter in a large factory fell from a height of three floors and fractured both his femurs, his left radius, his skull and jawbone. A blood-alcohol test was taken soon after the accident and the result was 280 mg/100 ml or 0,28 g% of blood. This man had walked into the factory, collected his equipment and been instructed by his supervisor and yet no one, from the security guards at the gate to the line supervisor, had observed that he was intoxicated. He was obviously a dependent drinker with a high degree of tolerance.[43]

6. TOLERANCE

Tolerance is the acquired resistance of the body to the same blood-alcohol concentration. It means that the drinker must consume more alcohol to achieve the same effect and it can be due to persistent excessive drinking or genetic susceptibility.[44] Tolerance has been shown to have a possible genetic influence by the ability of researchers selectively to breed out certain differences in the capability of rats to develop tolerance.[45]

Tolerance is a very important factor. It is the reason for the insidious way in which alcohol problems creep up on the unaware individual. It gradually leads to a progressive increase in alcohol intake. This is why many heavy or troubled drinkers do not manifest any overt physical signs of alcohol dependence until it is too late—the true extent of the problem is masked. The dependence has been gradual but progressive, through tolerance.

Tolerance can be divided into metabolic and functional forms. Metabolic tolerance is the adaptation of or increase in the chemical breakdown of alcohol in the body due to the induction of specific metabolic enzymes;[46] functional tolerance is the development of resistance to the effects of alcohol on the cells of the central nervous system and

---

43   McCann unpublished case (1989).

44   Metabolic tolerance will have only a minimal impact on the acquired resistance to and progressive dependence on alcohol, but it will affect the metabolism of other drugs which use the same metabolic enzyme system due to cross-tolerance.

45   Kiianmaa 'Neuronal mechanisms of ethanol sensitivity' (1990) 25(2–3) *Alcohol and Alcoholism* 252–62.

46   Hoffman & Tabakoff 'Mechanisms of alcohol tolerance' (1989) 24(3) *Alcohol and Alcoholism* 251–2.

is an adaptive response of the central nervous system to alcohol.[47] This adaptation changes the response of the brain in relation to behaviour and physiology.[48] Functional tolerance has been thought to be due to adaptation of the lipid content of the brain cell membrane (see chapter 7).

Once the changes in metabolism causing tolerance have been made, they are long-lasting and, irrespective of periods of abstinence, easily reactivated. This theory reinforces the thinking that with chronic alcohol abuse biochemical changes occur which can eventually lead to dependence. For instance, a heavy drinker with a high level of tolerance and a blood alcohol of 0,08 g% may feel no intoxication, but at that level they may necessarily and objectively lack 'that clearance of intellect and control which they would otherwise possess'.[49]

A temporary tolerance called the Mellanby effect also occurs.[50] This is caused by the adaptation of the central nervous system to the effects of the alcohol in the elimination phase so that the rising blood alcohol at the absorption phase will cause more marked intoxication than either the equivalent blood alcohol at the elimination phase or the declining blood alcohol. Thus the employee is more able to mask behaviour during the elimination phase of intoxication.

Tolerance is affected by the speed of drinking. Rapid drinking will produce discernible intoxication at levels as low as 20–30 mg/100 ml.

SUMMARY

The particular alcohol-dependence theory you believe in will influence your thinking towards the type of solution that you feel will solve the problem. It must be emphasised that you are dealing with the alcohol abuser and problem drinker and not simply the dependent drinker. The alcohol abuser and problem drinker are made up of the moderately heavy, the heavy, the troubled, the binge and the dependent drinker. These are listed in order of increasing severity and there are far more of the former than the latter (viz the dependent group). Alcohol problems in the workplace are best shown by the model of a linear continuum from abstinent through to dependent. It is important to remember that the individual moves up and down the line in response to influences and pressures in his life. This can lead to symptomatic drinking or, eventually, to dependent drinking.

It is important to be aware of the alcohol concentration of different drinks as this aids our understanding of the effects of alcohol. Understanding the effects of tolerance to alcohol is important for employers and employees wishing to develop an alcohol programme for their organisation. The effects of tolerance mask the true extent of the problem for the individual, and therefore for the organisation in which he or she works.

---

47 Hore *The Disease Concept of Alcoholism—a reappraisal* Paper presented at 8th International Conference on Alcoholism, Liverpool (April 1990).

48 Gradwohl *Legal Medicine* (1954), cited in Cooper, Schwar & Smith *Alcohol, Drugs and Road Traffic* (1979) 154.

49 Walls & Brownlie *Drinks, Drugs & Driving* (1985) 48–9.

50 Ibid.

Chapter 2

The Extent of the Problem: Alcohol

Mike McCann & Nadine Harker Burnhams

Too often employers (and trade unions) are unaware of alcohol problems among the workforce until they start looking for them; and, even if they are aware of alcohol abuse, there is often an unwillingness to admit that a problem exists. Employers frequently avoid confronting the issue. There are many reasons for this, including:

1 fear of a situation about which they know little, and uncertainty about how to deal with it;
2 a respect for individuals' privacy and a fear of involving the organisation in a programme in which the lifestyles of individuals may be exposed or jeopardised;
3 peer group pressures;
4 fear of committing management to a policy which they perceive would be unpopular not only among the employees but also with members of management and perhaps even with sections of the community at large;
5 fear of confrontation with the trade unions; and
6 an unwillingness to address their own drinking behaviour, particularly if this takes place in the company of those being supervised.

In considering why employers frequently avoid confronting alcohol abuse, attention must be given to the managers at lower levels since it is they who are often pivotal to the efficient running of the workplace. The managers are often afraid of confronting alcohol problems; especially lower-level managers, who are only one level above the employee they manage and who often come from the same socioeconomic background. This proximity has its advantages; for example, employees are more likely to trust in and cooperate with someone they consider to be 'one of them'. This sense of shared identity is particularly noticeable in rural areas, where it is likely that managers and employees, and their respective families, participate in shared social activities. Thus at this level of management one may find a manager who wants to be accepted and liked and for whom confronting an abusive and potentially aggressive intoxicated employee is difficult. The greater the distance between employee and supervisor/manager in the organisational hierarchy, however, the easier it becomes to address issues such as alcohol abuse: a senior manager will find it much easier to confront an intoxicated employee than will this employee's immediate superior.

Co-workers, often including superiors, may cover up for fellow employees who have a drinking problem. This misplaced loyalty not only leads to potential safety risks and disruption of the work group, but it also increases the co-workers' frustrations because they must perform additional work for the sake of their alcohol-abusing colleagues.

An American study of 1 300 railroad workers indicated that there was a collective awareness of alcohol problems amongst the employees. In the past year, 36% of employees had seen a co-worker drunk on duty; 15% had experienced co-workers too drunk or with too severe a hangover to work; and 60% said they had worked harder to cover-up for an inebriated co-worker. Only 14% said they would report an alcohol-abusing employee if they caused serious damage and 7% would not report at all, even if the culprit killed someone.[1]

The detrimental effects of alcohol have a daily impact on the local community in many countries throughout the world. In Britain it has been estimated that one in five men admitted to hospital have an alcohol-related problem.[2]

The British Home Office estimated that 45% of violent crimes are committed by people who have consumed alcohol immediately prior to the crime.[3] In South Africa 42,4% of arrestees or prisoners reported drinking at risky levels just before or at the time of their most recent offence.[4] A 2004 study by Parry et al revealed that 15% of arrestees were intoxicated at the time of the alleged offence, although it must be noted that in this case intoxication was due to drugs rather than alcohol. For violent offences the range was 10% to 49%.[5]

In the past five years, in South Africa, elevated blood alcohol concentrations accounted for 50% of homicides and transport accidents and 30–40% of suicides (Peltzer and Ramlagan 2009: see footnote).

In the United States it has been estimated that 8% of the nation's workforce are problem drinkers and that three-quarters of this group must have a continuous level of alcohol in the bloodstream in order to undertake their daily work.[6] Eighty per cent of `alcoholics' go undetected at their place of work despite their performance being consistently below their capacity.[7] Although these studies are early studies the trends have not changed significantly.

What is interesting is that in South Africa the lifetime current use of alcohol and binge drinking has remained similar over the past 12 years for adults as well as between the various race groups but the burden of alcohol use is higher.[8] Also based on production figures there does not seem to have been any significant increase in overall consumption

---

1   Seaman, FJ `Problem drinking among American rail-road workers' in Hore, BD & Plant, MA (eds) *Alcohol Problems in Employment* (1981).

2   Jarman, CM & Kellett, JM `Alcoholism in the general hospital' 1979 *BMJ* 469–471.

3   Robertson, C `Alcohol a public health problem. Is there a role for the GP?' 1990 (83) *J Royal Soc Medicine* 232–236.

4   Rocha-Silva, L & Stahmer, I *Nature, Extent and Development of Alcohol/Drug Related Crime* (Human Sciences Research Council 1996).

5   Parry, CDH, Plüddemann, A, Louw, A & Leggett, T 'The 3-Metros Study of Drugs and Crime in South Africa: Findings and policy implications' (2004) 30 *American Journal of Drug and Alcohol Abuse* 167–185.

6   *American Drug Abuse and Mental Health Administration* (ADAMHA Data Book, Fiscal Year 1978 (1979)).

7   Murray, R `Alcoholism and employment' 1975 *J on Alcohol* 23–26.

8   Peltzer, K & Ramlagan, S 'Alcohol Trends' (2009) 18 (1) *South Africa J Soc Sci* 1–12.

between 1994 and 2004.[9] In South Africa, the level of adult per capita consumption of absolute alcohol in 2000 was estimated to be 10,3 litres per year (12,4 litres if estimates of unrecorded consumption are included), which is substantially lower than many countries.[10] However, when the large population of non-drinkers in South Africa was taken into account the amount consumed per drinker was closer to 20 litres per adult, which is among the highest in the world.[11] A recent review of harmful drinking patterns and levels of consumption in 20 African countries showed that, in terms of the proportion of heavy drinkers as a percentage of current drinkers, South Africa ranked fourth highest.[12]

In the Health Statistics II—Diseases in the South African population[13] it is estimated that between 25–30% of admissions to general hospitals appears to be alcohol-related, either directly or indirectly, and there is no reason to believe that there is likely to be any less an association between alcohol and non-political violent crime in South Africa.

Further, South African data shows that more than 50% of all fatal traumatic injuries are alcohol-related. According to the Third Annual Report of the National Injury Mortality Surveillance System, 51,9% of patients who died in a transport-related accident had an elevated blood-alcohol level. In the majority of these cases (91%) the level was above 0,05 g/100 ml. Pedestrians and drivers had the highest proportions with positive blood-alcohol levels. Ten per cent of chronic psychiatric hospital bed occupancy is alcohol-related. Over 60% of acute psychiatric hospital admissions of black patients are alcohol-related.[14]

These figures are in keeping with the data produced by a 1988 SANCA study, which revealed that in many hospitals 30% of beds were occupied by patients with alcohol-related diseases.[15] Nothing has changed. There has been no improvement. In fact the burden of alcohol has intensified and so too the economic costs. The general rule is that alcohol beverage consumption rises with improving economic circumstances, and that this necessarily creates a concomitant rise in alcohol-related problems.[16]

The implications of this data for a country's economy are significant. In the United States, economist Leonard Schifrin estimated that in 1979 the cost to industry and to the country of alcohol misuse was US $113 billion (R927 bill.), of which lost production was US $77,5 billion (R635 bill.) or 67,4% of the total.[17] A study by the US Research Triangle Institute found that alcohol accounted for $89,5 billion (R734 bill.) in lost productivity

---

9   Parry, CDH, Plüddemann, A, Steyn, K, Bradshaw, D, Norman, R and Laubscher, R 'Alcohol use in South Africa: Findings from the first demographic and health survey (1998)'(2005) 66 *Journal of Studies on Alcohol* 91–97.

10 Parry (n 9).

11 Parry (n 9) .

12 Clausen, T, Rossow, I, Naidoo, N & Kowal, P 'Diverse alcohol drinking patterns in 20 African countries' (2009) 104 *Addiction* 1147–1154.

13 http://www.myfundi.co.za.

14 Van As, AB, Parry, CDH & Blecher, M 'The alcohol injury fund' (2003) 93 (11) *South African Medical Journal* 828–829.

15 De Miranda, S 'Alcoholism: the incidence, treatment and rehabilitation–South African perspective' (1988) 32(3) *Rehabilitation in South Africa* 83–87.

16 Obot, IS 'Alcohol use and related problems in Sub-Saharan Africa' (2006) 5 (1) *African Journal of Drug and Alcohol Studies* 17–28.

17 Schifrin, LG 'Social costs of alcohol abuse in the United States: an updating' in Royal College of Physicians *A Great and Growing Evil: the medical consequences of alcohol abuse* (1987) 8–9.

and that combined illicit drugs accounted for $46,9 billion (R384 bill.). Lost productivity was measured as lost worker earning power.[18] What is notable in this study is that the impact of alcohol abuse was found to be twice that of illicit drug abuse. This would fit in with the results of other studies that show alcohol to be the greater problem.[19]

Many papers still relate to the US Research Triangle figures, which were then updated in 1992 to $148 billion and extrapolated by Harwood in 2000 to $184,6 billion.[20] Estimates in 2002, which allow for increases in inflation, health care and protection services costs, place this economic burden at $665 billion (R5,453 bill.).[21]

In the United Kingdom, the economic cost of alcohol misuse to the NHS (the public health care system) in 2007 was put at approximately £3 billion per annum (R25 bill.).[22] Alcohol misuse significantly contributes to mortality and morbidity. One-third of all premature deaths are alcohol related and alcohol contributes substantially to 40,000 deaths per year.[23] Alcohol-related deaths for men and women have doubled between 1990 and 2000. Deaths caused by cirrhosis of the liver have doubled in this period and drug-related deaths are one-fiftieth of this.

In South Africa a conservative estimate of the health and other social costs associated with alcohol abuse is R9 billion per year or 1% of the country's gross domestic product (GDP). Excise duties on alcoholic beverages amounted to approximately R4,2 billion in 2003/4.[24]

During the 1960s, researchers in Cambridge, England, carried out a study on productivity levels in one of England's counties. They discovered that 52% of male 'alcoholics' experienced alcohol problems at work, yet only 4,2% had been dismissed or retired as a result of these problems.[25]

The sickness absence of employees experiencing a problem with alcohol has been researched, particularly in the United States,[26] where researchers discovered that the majority of productivity problems of a particular company were caused by a small number of workers with alcohol problems (these workers represented 20% of the sample size: n = 764). Most of these workers were identified as being in the late stages of alcohol dependence and were therefore classified as dependent drinkers.[27]

Although no comprehensive alcohol- or drug-related absenteeism data exists for South Africa, Steinman et al interviewed a sample of male alcoholics of which 67%

---

18 Harwood, H 'Economic costs to society of alcohol and drug abuse and illness' in Zeese, KB *Drug Testing Legal Manual* (1980) 6. Although the statistics do not marry Schifrin's, both reveal a considerable problem which is difficult to quantify.

19 Zeese, KB *Drug Testing Legal Manual* (1990) 6.

20 Harwood, H 'Economic costs to society of alcohol and drug abuse and illness' in Zeese *Drug Testing Legal Manual* (1980) 6.

21 Baumberg, B 'The global economic burden of alcohol: a review and some suggestions' (2006) 25 (6) *Drug Alcohol Review* 537–551.

22 Balakrishnan,R, Allender, S, Scarborough, P, Webster, P & Raynor, M 'The burden of alcohol-related ill health in the United Kingdom' (2009) 31(3) *Journal of Public Health* (Oxford) 366–73.

23 Joint report of the Royal College of Physicians and General Practitioners *Alcohol and the Heart in Perspective Sensible Limits Reaffirmed* (RCP 1995).

24 Van As, AB, Parry, CDH & Blecher, M 'The Alcohol Injury Fund' (2003) 93 (11) *South African Medical Journal* 828–829.

25 Moss, MC & Davies, EB *A Survey of Alcoholics in an English County: A Study of the Prevalence, Distribution and Effects of Alcoholism in Cambridgeshire* (1967) Table 48.

26 Pell, S & d'Alonzo, CA 'Sickness absenteeism of alcoholics' (1970) 12 *J Occup Medicine* (USA) 198–210.

27 Ibid.

were in employment.[28] He found that each alcoholic lost 86 working days a year due to absence. Further, 66% of the sample was often late for work, 61% reported Monday-morning absenteeism, and 62% sometimes drank alcohol at work, with 12% doing so regularly.[29]

If we look at early identification of the problem in South Africa in respect of heavy, troubled, and dependent drinkers, the employee prevalence figure is likely to reach 20%. If moderately heavy drinkers, who periodically cause personnel performance problems, were also included, this figure could rise to more than 30%, depending on the culture of the organisation and the community.[30] Data collected by the South African Medical Research Council on cases related to drug or alcohol abuse presenting at specialist treatment centres shows that employee referrals for substance abuse treatment are mostly for alcohol-related problems.[31]

Table 2.1 contains information regarding the issue of substance abuse among employees in South Africa. Specifically, the table shows the proportion of employees referred by their employers for specialist treatment for substance abuse, together with a breakdown in percentage terms of the primary substance of abuse used by employees. This information is mainly presented province-by-province, though there are two instances of grouping (Free State-North West-Northern Cape; Limpopo-Mpumalanga).

These figures correlate well with a survey of 1,338 employees in a South African chemical factory in which all employees underwent a periodic medical examination. Part of the examination comprised blood tests (eg cholesterol, uric acid, full blood count, gamma GT and blood alcohol). At some of these periodic examinations it was ascertained that 31,9% of the employees could be classified as falling into the early identification phase of alcohol abuse (moderately heavy, heavy, troubled and dependent drinkers). If the females were removed from the survey (since no females were identified as problem drinkers), then the percentage rose to 33,7%.[32]

More recently, in a study of mineworkers it was found that 15,3% were classified as alcohol dependent on the CAGE screening test for alcohol abuse.[33] Similarly the lifetime consumption of alcohol findings from a 1993 study amongst farm workers in the deciduous fruit industry in the Western Cape reported average usual weekend (Friday–Sunday night) consumption in grams of pure alcohol to be equivalent to the consumption of six 750-ml bottles of wine or a 750-ml bottle of spirits.[34]

---

28 Steinman, S & Senekal, 'A Solving psychosocial problems in the workplace' (2003) Department of Sociology, RAU.

29 Ibid.

30 These figures correlate well with the statistics provided by SANCA.

31 Plüddemann, A, Dada, S, Williams, Y, et al South African Community Epidemiology Network on Drug Use *Monitoring Alcohol and Drug Abuse Treatment in South Africa* (2008) Phase 24 Medical Research Council.

32 McCann Unpublished survey (1989).

33 Peltzer, K and Ramlagan, S 'Alcohol trends in South Africa' (2009) 18 (1) *Journal of Social Science* 1–12.

34 London, L 'Alcohol consumption amongst South African farm workers: a challenge for post-apartheid health sector transformation' (2000) 59 *Drug and Alcohol Dependence* 199–206.

Table 2.1 Employer referrals for specialist substance abuse treatment services by substance of abuse and province

	Western Cape	Free State, North West and Northern Cape	Eastern Cape	Gauteng	KwaZulu-Natal	Limpopo and Mpumalanga
Percentage of referrals by employers	7	16,8	12,2	9,1	13,9	12,2
Primary substance of abuse	%	%	%	%	%	%
Alcohol	12	24	23	15	25	23
Methamphetamine	6	–	–		22	–
Heroin	4	17	–	4	2	–
Cocaine	7	6	7	4	6	7
OTC/prescription medications	6	17	–	4	–	–
Ecstacy	–	–	–	20	–	–
Cannabis	2	1	3	3	3	3
Whitepipe (Cannabis + Mandrax combination)	2	–	5	4	17	5

An American study[35] that analysed the cost of hospitalising alcohol-problem employees noted that 24%, who were dependent drinkers, accounted for 78% of the total employee disability income and 89% of the total medical benefits paid out. It also showed that the majority were over the age of 40 and that, in 86% of these, alcohol problems were the cause of the main presenting symptom.

However, as mentioned earlier, these problems are not identified unless employers and trade unions start to look for them. Furthermore, identification of the extent of the problem can come as quite a shock. One Scottish company discovered that 14% of its managers were `alcoholic'. Of further interest was the fact that none had been disciplined as a result of manifest alcohol problems.[36]

In another survey, 279 London companies were asked for the number of employees they believed had an alcohol problem at work. This information was compared to

35 Burton, WN, Eggin, PR & Keller, PJ 'High-cost employees in occupational alcoholism programmes' 1981 23 (4) *J Occup Medicine* 259-262.
36 Gray, J 'The Scottish experiment' (1969) 4 *J of Alcoholism* 461.

the World Health Organisation's statistics for Britain and the results suggested that companies were missing nine out of ten cases.[37]

In one Scottish study,[38] 702 patients admitted to the casualty department of a general hospital due to a non-work-related accident were asked to take a confidential breathalyser test for research purposes. Only two of these patients refused to be tested. By contrast, all the patients attending the casualty department who had had an accident at work, refused to be subjected to a breathalyser test for research purposes, under the same conditions. It is reasonable to conclude that for at least some, and possibly the majority of these employees, the refusal to take the test was because they had consumed alcohol prior to the accident and wished to avoid detection.

Sometimes it takes a number of serious accidents to alert an organisation to the fact that an alcohol problem exists. For example, in one company a series of falls from heights in excess of 10 m culminated in drastic action. One accident involved a contract painter surviving a fall from a height of three floors; a test revealed his blood-alcohol level to be 280 mg/100 ml (0,28 g%)—at 9 o'clock in the morning. Another less fortunate accident occurred in the same company only 10 weeks later. On this occasion, the man landed on his head and was killed instantly. The accident occurred at 9.20 am and his blood-alcohol level was found to be 310 mg/100 ml (0,31 g%).[39] It is tragic that these types of incidents have to occur before the reality of the problem sinks in.

As a result of these accidents, the company decided to introduce immediate random breathalyser testing of employees as they entered the factory. On the first day, 50 employees were tested and 1 in 7 were found to be intoxicated, ie to have more than the limit of 0,05 g% alcohol in their blood. Statistically, representing a random sample of the workforce, this figure indicated that 7,14% of the total workforce were arriving at work intoxicated. These figures agree with the general trends revealed by other researchers. In this particular study, the results of random testing gradually evened out to 5,25% in the first week and gradually dropped to 0,75% by the fourth week. Interestingly enough, the figure climbed to 3,75% by the sixth week but dropped further as the weeks went by. [40]

The extent of the problem can also be determined by consulting records of accidents on duty, where statistics reveal the high prevalence of accidents related to alcohol abuse. In May and June 1985, all accident patients attending the clinic of a company in South Africa were tested for alcohol abuse. The tests consisted of gamma GTs (gamma glutamyl transferase or GGT), MCV (mean corpuscular volume), and blood alcohol.[41] In these two months 100 accidents on duty were identified as falling within the study, of which 38 were identified as relating to alcohol-abuse employees. Of this number, 18% tested positive for blood alcohol.[42]

---

37   Hawker A, Edwards, G, & Hensman , C 'Clients of alcoholism information centres' (1967) 4 *BMJ* 346.

38   Little, K 'Common factors in accident prevention—-alcohol and drugs' Conference on Health and Education for Safety (Peebles, 1983).

39   McCann, MG *The effect and impact of breath analysis in a workplace* paper presented at Medichem Conference London (October 1992).

40   Ibid.

41   McCann, MG Unpublished research, 1985. See chapter 7 at 84–91 for explanation of tests.

42   McCann, MG (n 39).

SANCA makes the point that in South African society we are dealing with a Third World unsaturated drinking population compared to the First World's almost saturated drinking population. This important point is explained in the next paragraph and is the reason why the South African population is vulnerable to progressively increasing problems. Table 2.2 on page 30 shows patterns of alcohol consumption among men and women and across various South African population groups.

Levels of current drinking differ substantially by population group and gender, with the highest level of drinking reported by the white male population, followed by those within the coloured and Indian populations. The lowest levels were reported by African females. For both men and women, higher rates of current (past seven days) drinking were recorded in urban as compared to non-urban areas. For men, the highest levels of current alcohol use were recorded in the 35–44 age group, and the lowest levels in the 15–24 age group. For women, the highest levels of current alcohol use reported were in the 35–44 and 55–64 age groups, while the 25–34 age group recorded the lowest levels. 'These findings suggest that alcohol use is more prevalent in the age groups where individuals are more likely to be employed.

Although the findings are fairly consistent it should be noted that in comparison to the previous demographic and health survey conducted in 1998, and other more localised surveys, and given what is known about alcohol consumption in South Africa from estimates of consumption, the figures for both men and women in the 2003 SADHS are likely to grossly underestimate the true prevalence of alcohol use in South Africa. Other factors may also mask the true picture. For example, certain cultural groups maintain that women should not drink alcohol and censure or ostracise those that do. In such circumstances it is unlikely that these women would make public their drinking habits, which implies that there may be widespread under-reporting in certain subpopulations, eg African women.

Jellinek[43] has shown that 27–30% of those who drink periodically abuse alcohol in an irresponsible manner, and may develop an alcohol problem once or twice during their lifetime. He goes on to say that these individuals often belong to the 'unsaturated drinking population'. By 'unsaturated', Jellinek means that the percentage of persons drinking in the population group is continuing to increase.

The unsaturated groups usually consist of the young, the women and the recently urbanised or westernised. He also calls them the 'unlearned' or inexperienced drinkers. They are particularly susceptible to greater saturation. The saturated portions of the unsaturated drinking population groups are on the increase and potential drinking problems among these groups are therefore also increasing.

Hawker et al[44] interviewed a sample of male 'alcoholics' attending alcoholism information centres, of which 67% were in employment at the time of interview. He found that they had on average each lost 86 working days due to absence in the previous year; 66% of the sample were often late for work and 61% reported Monday-morning absenteeism; 49% had been in their present employment for more than two years; the longest period in one job (more than five years) had been held by 65% of the sample; for 76%, drinking had interfered with promotion and 90% said they had not been promoted during the previous five years; 47% were in a lower-paid position

43   Jellinek, EM 'Phases of alcohol addiction' (1952) 13 *Quart J Studies on Alcohol* 673–684.
44   Hawker (n 37).

than in their immediate previous job and 75% had been dismissed at least once through drinking; 12% had been dismissed more than five times through drinking; 62% had at some time carried a bottle of alcohol to work to drink there and 12% consistently carried a bottle to work; 88% of the sample drank at times before arriving for work and 91% drank occasionally throughout the working day; 52% of the sample said that the organisation they worked for had no consistent policy on drunkenness and 14% said that their organisation ignored drinking problems completely.

SUMMARY

Economic arguments for acting on health issues are increasingly important for policymakers. The problem of alcohol abuse in the workplace is generally agreed to be a particularly important issue and one that exerts a considerable economic burden worldwide. Alcohol misuse can undermine productivity, cause accidents and jeopardise the health of the workforce, all of which will threaten the financial stability of an organisation. The supervisor who deals with the workers on a daily basis can find confronting the issue both challenging and time consuming. Senior management may avoid the problem to avoid upsetting employees and their trade union representatives, or because they feel ill-equipped to deal with such a sensitive, intensely personal issue.

In South Africa, the research shows that the problem of alcohol in the workplace is an ongoing problem. In addition, there is a population group who remain unsaturated in their drinking habits and this group would be vulnerable to developing more significant problems.

Further research and debate is needed to determine the precise extent of the economic burden created by alcohol abuse, and this is something to be done on a worldwide basis given the universal nature of 'the alcohol problem'. In the meantime, employers, and more specifically their senior managers, need to commit time, energy and resources to confronting the problem of alcohol abuse in the workplace. As this chapter has shown, alcohol abuse and dependency remain the main reasons why organisations continue to experience diminished productivity, which implies that the media's preoccupation with the dangers posed by drug abuse is to some extent misleading.

Table 2.2 Patterns of drinking, risky drinking and symptoms of alcohol problems among men and women as percentages: Findings from the 2003–2004 South African Demographic and Health Survey.[45]

Background characteristics	Ever drank alcohol		Drink past 12 months		Abstainers in past 12 months	
	M	F	M	F	M	F
Age						
15–24	38.5	18.5	32.7	14.7	67.4	85.3
25–34	52.8	20.8	43.3	14.7	56.7	85.3
35–44	55.3	25.0	45	19.6	55.0	80.4
45–54	55.8	21.0	42.6	13.4	57.4	86.6
55–64	54.6	27.1	41.3	17.0	58.7	83.0
65+	44.7	19.8	32.9	12.2	67.1	87.8
Residence						
Urban	53.4	26.7	43.5	19.5	56.5	80.5
Non-urban	38.6	12.5	30.2	8.3	69.8	91.7
Population Groups						
African	44.2	16.4	35.2	11.4	64.8	88.6
African urban	48.0	20.3	38.7	14.2	61.3	85.8
African non-urban	38.0	11.1	29.5	7.5	70.5	92.6
Coloureds	68.0	40.2	52.3	27.7	47.7	72.3
White	74.5	58.6	69.9	50.9	30.1	49.1
Indian	66.3	37.7	50.3	24.4	49.7	75.6

45   SADHS Department of Health (2008).

Responsible <4 drinks males; females <2 drinks		Hazardous 4<6 drinks for males; 2-<4 drinks for females		Harmful 6+ drinks for males; 4+ drinks for females		Drink past 7 days		Number	
M	F	M	F	M	F	M	F	M	F
25.7	11.5	1.8	0.5	1.4	0.9	21.5	8.2	1 121	1 256
33.6	12.4	3.1	0.7	3.2	0.8	34.4	7.9	735	979
35.5	15.6	2.5	0.9	4.2	2.1	36.8	13.3	593	883
33.9	9.9	3.1	1.9	2.1	0.7	33.8	9.3	438	714
33.1	14.0	2.9	0.8	1.9	1.0	29.7	13.6	297	483
28.6	8.6	0.6	2.0	1.9	0.7	27.7	8.0	240	378
35.2	16.0	3.0	1.2	2.7	1.1	34.1	12.0	2289	2995
22.5	5.7	1.2	0.5	2.0	1.1	20.7	5.9	1133	1697
26.9	8.9	2.3	0.9	2.5	0.8	27.1	7.1	2 838	3 857
30.2	11.7	2.9	1.1	2.8	0.6	31.2	8.5	1 747	2 250
21.6	5.1	1.2	0.5	2.0	0.9	20.4	5.3	1091	1607
43.5	20.2	3.5	1.0	3.0	3.8	36.4	19.7	268	456
64.8	43.9	1.9	2.9	1.9	1.1	53.1	31.3	220	257
40.6	21.2	5.0	0.2	1.3	0.3	36.2	12.8	83	112

Chapter 3

Drugs and Drug Abuse:
An Introduction

Mike McCann & Nadine Harker Burnhams

Although alcohol remains the predominant abuse and addiction problem in the workplace, there is a significant rise in the number of employees using illicit or licit drugs. Employers should take cognisance of the fact that alcohol is classified as a drug, albeit a socially and legally accepted one. Furthermore, a large proportion of drug abusers also abuse alcohol and the interaction of the two has a profound effect on the individual's level of intoxication.

In Western industrialised countries more emphasis is being placed on the impact of illegal drugs in the workplace, particularly with increasingly widespread use since the 1980s. In South Africa the use of cannabis, crystal methamphetamine (more centralised in the Western Cape), heroin and cocaine has become quite widespread over the last few years with many companies now recognising that the overall approach to substance-related issues should be general and related to all drugs of abuse. The introduction of such general programmes, however, should not dilute the impact of a programme directed towards alcohol abuse because illegal drug abuse is sometimes erroneously looked upon as a more serious problem.

Alcohol-related problems, contrary to drug-related problems, often go undetected until much later in the disease process. As a result the extent of the prevalence of alcohol abuse is more often greater and the long-term effects for the company are more profound. Attention should be paid to the similarities and differences between alcohol and drug abuse. The two should remain key focal points for prevention and treatment instead of one occupying a greater role than the other. Though drug abuse is looked upon as a major problem in American and increasingly in South African companies, it is still less prevalent than alcohol abuse. Research confirms this: every study on the effects of drugs in the workplace shows that alcohol is the greater abuse and addiction problem. For example, Harwood et al had[1] estimated that the economic costs of alcohol abuse was US $166.5 billion in the United States in 1995 whereas drug abuse accounted for US $109.8 billion. Anecdotal feedback from companies in South Africa also highlights this contrast.

It is practical to consider introducing drug abuse under a similar programme as substance abuse, as long as the need to emphasise both alcohol and drugs is borne in mind. The main consideration in the workplace is abuse, whether abuse of alcohol, legal drugs or illegal drugs. The legality or illegality of the latter is not really an issue for

---

1   Harwood H and Lewin Group Updated estimates for 1995 in the Report of the economic costs of Alcohol and Drug Abuse in the United States, 1992. NIDA. US Dept of Health & Human Services.

the workplace; rather, it is their effect on safety, health and productivity that should be considered.

The question of the illegality of the drug is the concern of the state and therefore relates to the workplace only indirectly. Care must therefore be taken to ensure that the substance-abuse policy in the workplace does not differentiate between legal and illegal abuse of drugs as this could undermine the programme. The important point to note is that the abuse of any drugs whatsoever should not be condoned by management and, in particular, the selling of drugs in the workplace should always be treated with the severest discipline and referral to the police.

In this chapter we consider abuse of drugs under the headings of legal drugs and illegal drugs (and their interactions with alcohol). As regards the progressive use of urine drug testing, emphasis is given to the implications of testing for drug metabolites rather than the active substance and to the complications associated with the chain of custody procedures.

1. LEGAL DRUGS

The main legal drugs which are abused are the barbiturates and the benzodiazepines. These are often obtained legally via prescriptions from unsuspecting doctors. It is possible to move from one doctor to another collecting prescriptions (often repeated for up to six months) and then to use different pharmacies to maintain a consistent supply. Patients can also put subtle pressure on a doctor, particularly in a fee-for-service consultation, to supply them with prescriptions. Both barbiturates and benzodiazepines are classified as minor tranquilliser or anxiety-reducing (anxiolytic) drugs, and their main effect is as a depressant on the nervous system, in a way similar to alcohol. This can cause drowsiness, a lack of co-ordination, slurred speech and poor productivity, with an increased likelihood of accidents.

In combination with alcohol the effects are additive and, as some benzodiazepines have a long half-life, the effects could be prolonged over a considerable period of time. Valium, for example, will have such an effect for at least eight hours. The phenobarbiturates and some of the benzodiazepines are metabolised in exactly the same way as alcohol by the smooth endoplasmic reticulum found in the liver. Chronic alcohol abusers will have an increased ability to metabolise these drugs as long as there is no liver damage, because the alcohol excess will have induced an increase in enzyme production for metabolism. An increased tolerance of these drugs will develop and they will have less effect on the chronic alcohol abuser as long as he or she is sober. However, if combined with alcohol ingestion, the drug competes for the same metabolic enzymes as the alcohol, which is always metabolised first. This sequence produces a build-up of the drug and therefore increases its effect. (This process is one reason why anaesthetists giving general anaesthetics have great difficulty sedating the sober abuser, because his tolerance is so high.) If cirrhosis of the liver has developed, then the ability to metabolise the drug is reduced and an overdose could build up in the abuser. Antabuse (disulfiram) inhibits the hepatic metabolism of Valium or Pax (diazepam) and can therefore increase the effect of the drug.

The legal drugs which are generally abused fall under the heading of central nervous system depressants, and they fall into three groups:
- Sedatives and hypnotics
- Barbiturates
- Narcotic analgesics

1.1 Sedatives and hypnotics

This group consists of the benzodiazepines, meprobamate and antihistamines. The benzodiazepines are by far the largest group of legal drugs abused and are the most easily available. They are prescribed for anxiety states, sedation, sleeplessness, acute withdrawal from alcohol, muscular spasmodic pain and as anticonvulsants. They are grouped roughly by the length of time the drug acts on the body (though the activity levels or half-lives given here are only a guideline). Some of the ultra-short-acting types have a very short effect (less than six hours). The short-acting, intermediate-acting and long-acting benzodiazepines progressively increase the duration of their effect, up to 24 hours and sometimes longer.

Benzodiazepines used to be liberally prescribed, but it has been well proven that they induce physical dependence, particularly at high doses or if taken for a prolonged time or by patients with other dependency problems. There is a definite withdrawal state when the drug is stopped after a prolonged period of time. It was estimated that up to 40% of patients taking benzodiazepines for at least a year will become physically dependent on the drug.[2] Short-acting and intermediate-acting benzodiazepines are more likely to cause dependence and their withdrawal symptoms are likely to occur more rapidly and more severely than with the long-acting drugs. The ultra-short-acting benzodiazepines can induce rebound withdrawal effects owing to the rapid elimination of the drug. This causes anxiety and early morning awakening if taken as a sleeping tablet.[3]

Meprobamate is used very little now as the benzodiazepines are more effective, but it does cause sedation and is sometimes abused, leading to dependence. It also lowers the body's tolerance to alcohol, so that the combined effect of the two is considerably greater than either taken alone.

Examples of benzodiazepines are:[4]

Table 3.1 Examples of benzodiazepines

Pharmaceutical name	Principal constituent (generic name)	Period of action
Valium	diazepam	long half-life
Tranqipan, Ativan	lorazepam	intermediate half-life
Serepax	oxazepam	short half-life
Lexotan	bromazepam	intermediate half-life
Librium/Karmoplex	chlordiazepoxide	long half-life
Urbanol	clobazam	long half-life
Tranxene	chlorazepate	long half-life
Rohypnol	flunitrazepam	long half-life
Mogadon	nitrazepam	long half-life

---

2   Conradie, EA & Straughan, JL *South African Medicines Formulary* (1988) 36.

3   Van Rooyen, JM & Offermeier, J 'Pharmacokinetics of the benzodiazepines' (1985) *South African Medical Journal* Suppl 10–13.

4   For a more complete list refer to Conradie & Straughan (n 2) at 38–40, from which this list has been adopted.

Pharmaceutical name	Principal constituent (generic name)	Period of action
Halcion	triazolam	ultra-short half-life
Dormonoct	loprazolam	short half-life
Dormicum	midazolam	ultra-short half-life
Normison	temazepam	short half-life
Demetrin	prazepam	long half-life
Dalmadorm	flurazepam	long half-life

Identification signs of acute intoxication are drowsiness, lethargy, unsteady gait, and possibly slurred speech with poor co-ordination. High doses can produce euphoria, irritability and confusion.[5]

1.2 Barbiturates

Barbiturates (colloquially named 'downers' or 'barbs') are minor tranquillisers and have anticonvulsant properties. They cause sedation but can lead to dependence in some people. Withdrawal effects occur if they are suddenly stopped. Barbiturates have a potentiating or resonant effect with alcohol rather than being merely additive.[6] The shorter-acting barbiturates are the ones which are generally abused.

Table 3.2 Examples of barbiturates

Pharmaceutical name	Principal constituent (generic name)	Period of action
Gardenal	phenobarbitone	long half-life
Balladenal, Bellergal	phenobarbitone	long half-life
Vernased	phenobarbitone	long half-life
Amytal	amylobarbital	short half-life
Seconal	secobarbital	short half-life
Pentothal	thiopentone	ultra-short half-life

Identification signs of acute intoxication are drowsiness, lethargy, poor co-ordination, slurred speech, unsteady gait and, as with the benzodiazepines in high doses, euphoria, irritability and confusion.

1.3 Narcotic analgesics

These are members of the opiate family and cause depression of the central nervous system in addition to alleviating pain. They can produce feelings of euphoria, which

---

5   Cooper, WE, Schwar, TG & Smith, LS *Alcohol, Drugs and Road Traffic* (1979) 358.
6   Sandberg, F 'A quantitative study on the alcohol-barbiturate synergism' (1951) 22 *Acta Physiologica Scandinavica* 311–325.

is the main reason they are abused. They are highly predisposed to causing physical dependence:[7]

Table 3.3 Main narcotic analgesics and route of administration

Pharmaceutical name	Principal constituent (generic name)	Administration
Morphine	morphine sulphate	injectable
Pethidine	pethidine hydrochloride	injectable
Cyclomorph	morphine tartrate with cyclizine	injectable
DF-118	dihydrocodeine tartrate	tablets (oral) and injectable
Sosegon	pentazocine	injectable and tablets (oral)
Omnopon	papaveretum	injectable
Valoron	tilidine hychochloride	capsules or drops (oral) or injectable
Wellconal	dipipanone hychochloride and cyclizine	tablets (oral)
Physeptone	methadone	injectable
Codeine	codeine	oral

It must be remembered that the severe restrictions on the availability of these drugs make them difficult to abuse legally; inevitably, therefore, they are acquired and abused illegally.

Identification signs of acute intoxication are similar to those of the illegal opiate narcotics.

2. ILLEGAL DRUGS

The illegal drugs can be divided into three groups:
- Narcotics
- Stimulants
- Hallucinogens

2.1 Narcotics

The narcotic drugs have a depressant effect on the central nervous system, causing drowsiness, slowed reflexes and a feeling of euphoria. Tolerance is rapid and they are highly addictive. Physical and psychological dependence are severe.

---

7 Methadone is a longer-lasting opiate which is given to addicts as a substitute for heroin in drug rehabilitation programmes. In the United States and in the UK it is provided as an oral treatment lasting up to 12 hours. Thus the addict can work rather than spend time on illegal activities to support the addiction. Methadone can cause significant sedation and can be dangerous.

2.1.1 Heroin

The opiate heroin ('H', 'smack', 'junk') is the main illegal narcotic drug which is abused. This drug is sniffed, smoked or heated on a piece of aluminium foil and inhaled ('chasing the dragon'). Otherwise it is powdered and diluted with a mild acid such as lemon juice to dissolve the powder, and then injected. The other opiates, especially the legal narcotic drugs which are used illegally, are often crushed to a powder and injected in the same way. The sudden high which the injection provides cannot be simulated if the drugs are taken orally. This difference explains the popular use of injections in the consumption of heroin.

Identification signs of acute intoxication: pinpoint pupils, drowsiness with euphoria, nausea, vomiting, constipation, itching, flushing, depressed breathing, loss of appetite, lethargy, and depressed reflexes and responses to stimuli.[8]

2.2.2 Mandrax

Mandrax (methaqualone) is a narcotic that produces an initial euphoric state followed by a period of profound sedation. The therapeutic effect of this drug occurs close to the toxic dose and because of this it can be dangerous. Locally, the drug is often powdered, mixed with cannabis and smoked from a broken bottleneck (known as 'white pipe').

Identification signs of acute intoxication: poor co-ordination, slurred speech, sluggish pupils, unsteady gait, clumsy movements, and drowsiness leading to sleep. When smoked in combination with cannabis: red, bloodshot eyes, mood changes, loss of appetite, faulty judgment and a persistent cough.[9]

2.2 Stimulants

The symptoms of intoxication mirror those of a psychotic episode. The stimulant (or psychomimetic) drugs are listed and described below.

2.2.1 Amphetamines

Amphetamines ('speed', 'uppers', 'whizz', 'blues', 'sulph') are sniffed in powder form, injected or swallowed as capsules or tablets. They increase the heartbeat and give a feeling of confidence, excitement and alertness. There is an accompanying loss of appetite and they also distort hearing and vision and can cause paranoia, aggression and panic. The after-effects can often lead to feelings of depression and exhaustion. They are highly likely to cause marked psychological dependence after long-term use and withdrawal symptoms do occur—the withdrawal can be extremely severe in patients with high levels of addiction.

Identification signs of acute intoxication: increased blood pressure, agitation, dilated pupils, increase in temperature at high doses, loss of weight, and high levels of energy and activity. Amphetamines can be identified in urine and blood. Urine amphetamines can be identified up to 48 hours after absorption.

---

8   Sciberras, M *Reaching the Drug Abuser* (1992) 32.

9   Baumann, S *Primary Health Care Psychiatry: A Practical Guide for Southern Africa* (2007) 308.

2.2.2 Crystal methamphetamine

The use of crystal methamphetamine ('tik') has risen dramatically in certain parts of South Africa. Methamphetamine is a powerfully addictive stimulant that affects many areas of the central nervous system. It is a white, odourless, bitter-tasting crystalline powder that readily dissolves in water or alcohol. The drug can easily be made in clandestine laboratories from relatively inexpensive over-the-counter ingredients and can be purchased at a relatively low cost (about R15–R30 per 'straw'). Methamphetamine triggers release of epinephrine, norepinephrine and dopamine in the sympathetic nervous system. Common effects of intoxication are euphoria, increased energy and self-confidence, insomnia, restlessness, irritability, heightened sense of sexuality, and tremors. Respiratory effects include increased respirations, pulmonary edema, pulmonary hypertension and decreased lung capacity. Cardiovascular effects include increased heart rate and blood pressure, tachycardia (abnormally rapid heartbeat) and/or arrhythmias. Users run the risk of overdose characterised by dehydration, hyperthermia, convulsions, renal failure, stroke and myocardial infarction.[10]

A major concern for public health practitioners is the association of methamphetamine use with risky sexual behaviour—a precursor for various sexually transmitted infections including HIV and AIDS. The use of methamphetamine enhances sexual desire in the user, resulting in more risky sexual risk behaviour, such as having multiple sex partners and having unprotected sex.[11] In Cape Town, for example, recent studies found that two adult community populations studied were more likely to engage in risky sex if they were methamphetamine users.[12]

Identification signs of acute intoxication: severe weight loss, severe dermatological problems, uncontrollable rage, violent behaviour, impaired concentration and memory, hallucinations, insomnia, depressive reactions, psychotic reactions, paranoid reactions, and panic disorders.

2.2.3 Cocaine

Cocaine ('coke', 'snow', 'crack') is sniffed, injected or smoked. It produces feelings of euphoria and elation with overt excitement and a sense that nothing is impossible. But the effect is short-lived, lasting less than half an hour. Cocaine can cause psychological dependence and produces feelings of paranoia with delusions if taken in excess for a prolonged period.

Identification signs of acute intoxication: irritability, increased heart rate, high blood pressure and fast pulse, dilated pupils, increase in temperature and high levels of energy and activity. Cocaine can be identified in the urine as a metabolite.

---

10 Plüddemann, A, Flisher, AJ, Mathews, C, Carney, T & Lombard, C 'Adolescent methamphetamine use and sexual risk behaviour in secondary school students in Cape Town, South Africa' (2008) 27 *Drug and Alcohol Review* 687–692.

11 Ibid.

12 Carney, T & Parry, CH *Harm Reduction in Southern Africa: Strategies used to address drug-related HIV (and Hepatitis C)* report by Alcohol and Drug Abuse Research Unit, Medical Research Council (July 2008).

2.3 Hallucinogens

These drugs alter a person's mood and modify visual stimuli (giving heightened and often distorted sensory perceptions) rather than giving rise to the perception of non-existing stimuli. The use of these drugs changes in response to the dictates of fashion, their availability and cost; new drugs are entering the market continually. The main hallucinogens are:

2.3.1 LSD

LSD (lysergic acid diethylamide or 'acid') is taken orally as small squares of paper or tablets. It heightens sensory experiences and causes perceptual distortion. Feelings experienced during a 'trip' may recur years after a dose has been taken. These flashbacks are thought sometimes to be precipitated by alcohol. The symptoms of LSD may last for up to 10 hours following a single dose and only very small quantities are required to have a dramatic effect. Work is virtually impossible and the use of moving machinery or driving is positively dangerous. Because of the rapid breakdown of the drug and the small amount required, identification by analysis is problematic, and analysis is almost impossible after four hours.[13]

Identification signs of acute intoxication: dilated pupils, tremors, increase in temperature, disturbed emotions, acute anxiety and hallucinations.

2.3.2 Mescaline

Mescaline is a hallucinogen obtained from a small spineless cactus, peyote (lophophora williamsi). Mescaline is also found in certain members of the *fabaceae* (bean family). From earliest recorded time, peyote has been used by natives in northern Mexico and the southwestern United States as part of traditional religious rites. Although mescaline has a similar effect to LSD, it is not as long lasting. Mescaline results in visual hallucinations and drastically alters the individual's state of consciousness. Users report pleasurable and illuminating experiences and may also experience anxiety or feelings of revulsion. Other effects include: open and closed eye visualisations, euphoria, dream-like states, laughter and psychedelic experiences.[14]

2.3.3 Psilocybin

Psilocybin ('magic mushroom') is derived from the psilocybe mushroom and is taken either by eating fresh or dried mushrooms or it can be brewed like tea. The effect is similar to LSD, but there is a high risk of poisoning. The drug's effect is also of shorter duration.

2.3.4 Designer drugs

Examples of designer drugs are phencyclidine ('PCP', 'angel dust') and MDMA ('Ecstasy', 'E', 'Adam', 'Eve'). These drugs are synthetically produced. They enhance visual, auditory and tactile perception and induce mild intoxication. Some designer drugs may damage the central nervous system. Chronic users develop antisocial behaviour, aggressiveness, and a high risk of accidents when driving.

---

13   Cooper, WE, Schwar, TG & Smith, LS *Alcohol, Drugs and Road Traffic* (1979) 353.
14   Drug Information Online at http://www.drugs.com/mescaline/html acessed 26 July 2011.

2.3.5 Ketamine

Ketamine ('Special K') is an anaesthetic used in emergency medical situations. It acts quickly, stimulates the cardiovascular system and can produce hallucinations similar to LSD. The danger lies in the high percentage of bad trips which an abuser can experience with it.

2.3.6 Cannabis

In cannabis ('dagga', 'marijuana', 'pot', 'grass', 'reef', 'Mary Jane', 'Durban Poison') the active ingredient is delta-9 tetrahydrocannabinol (THC). The drug is taken either in its compressed form as a resin or as loose dried plant, when it is usually smoked together with tobacco and is called a 'reefer' or 'joint'. It is also smoked in small pipes, and occasionally eaten or boiled to form a tea. When cannabis is smoked, the effects occur within minutes and can last for up to five hours. When it is absorbed orally, the effect takes longer to occur (up to an hour). Cannabis is also mixed with Mandrax ('white pipe').

Cannabis is classified as a hallucinogen but it can also be classified as a central nervous system depressant. The drug releases inhibitions and accentuates the mood which was prevalent at the time of taking it. It increases tactile, auditory and visual sensations which can, in larger doses, lead to a form of hallucination. Paranoid feelings are quite common. Cannabis is capable of producing psychotic reactions and there are references to violent behaviour during these episodes. Such cannabis-related violence has been described in reports from traditional cannabis-using cultures.[15] Whether psychosis can be induced by cannabis or whether it is due to an underlying predisposition is still the subject of debate. Generally, if the drug is withdrawn, the psychotic reaction falls away within a few weeks.

It can adversely affect performance and safety at work, developing what is called the amotivational syndrome. This syndrome occurs when frequent use of the drug leads to lethargy, lack of interest, reduced drive and loss of the desire to succeed.

Cannabis is dangerous when associated with driving or moving machinery. It affects motor co-ordination, reduces reaction time, and hinders tracking ability and perception of time, hearing and distance. In heavy doses it can cause disorientation. Potentiation can occur with simultaneous alcohol intake, and this can lead to further paranoia, agitation and even chest pain.

The breath of the smoker has a characteristic smell shortly after cannabis use The whites of the eyes are invariably red due to a general vacillation, but the pupils are normal. With cannabis it has been difficult to demonstrate tolerance and withdrawal phenomena, but it is considered to induce only psychological dependence.

Identification signs of recent consumption: apathy, low energy levels, red eyes, slow speech, tachycardia, sweating, poor reaction time, poor motor co-ordination, labile emotions, anxiety, a dry feeling in the mouth and throat, and increased appetite. Urine levels of THC associated with recent absorption can vary from 100 ng/dl to 1000 ng/dl (ng/dl = nanogram per decilitre).[16]

---

15   WHO *Assessment of Public Health and Social Problems Associated with the Use of Psychotropic Drugs* Technical Report Series 656 (1981) 35.

16   Solomons, K & Neppe, VM 'Cannabis—its clinical effects' (1989) 76(3) *South African Medical Journal* 102–104.

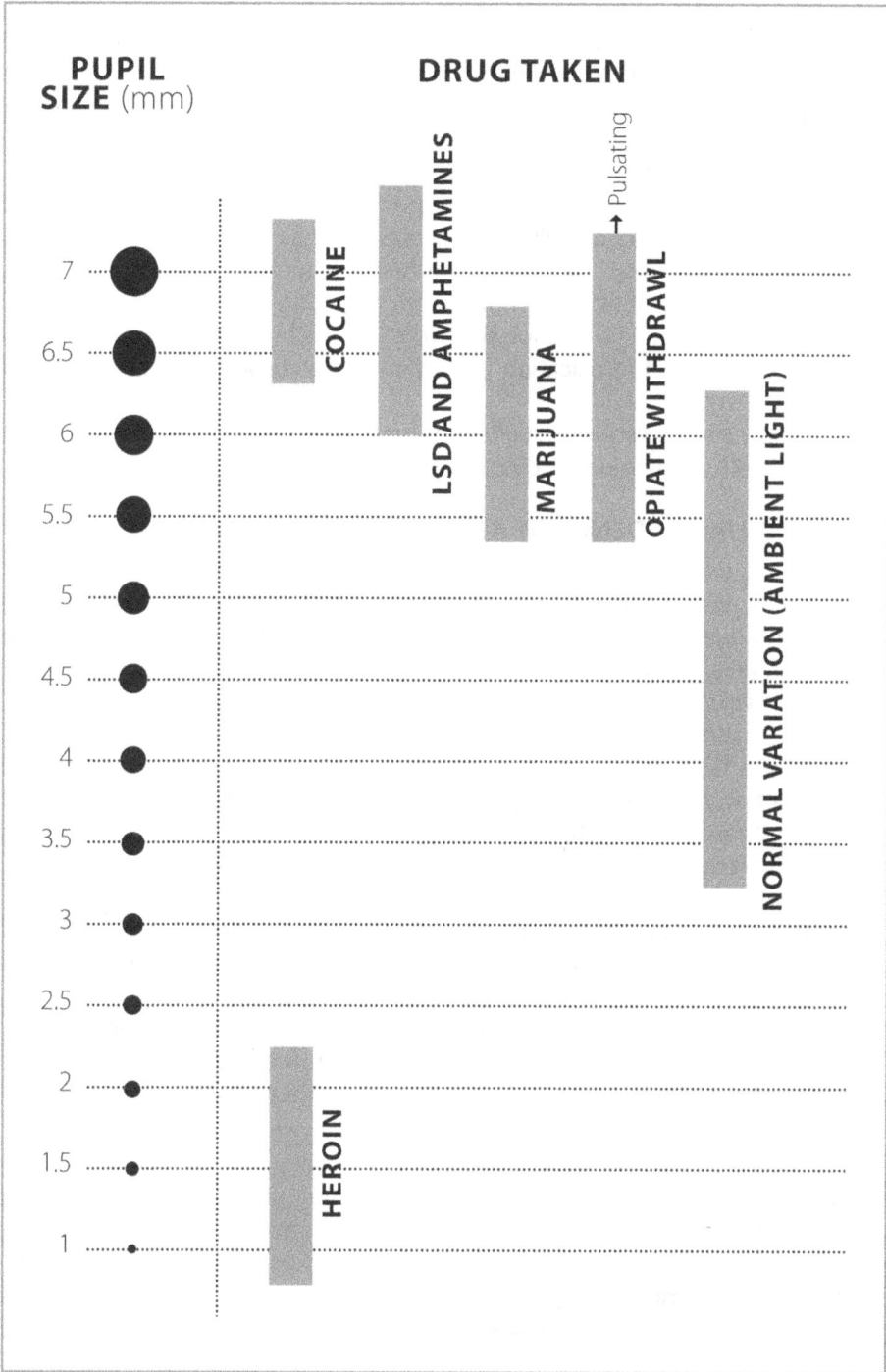

Figure 3.1 Pupil size

3. SOLVENTS

All solvents have narcotic properties and many are related to some general anaesthetic agents. The ability to produce narcosis or drowsiness associated with euphoria depends on the particular solvent used, but the main solvent of abuse is toluene, which is found in glues and paint. Taken in high concentrations, toluene can cause hallucinations. At this level of intoxication there is also a dangerous cardiac effect which can produce ventricular arrhythmias that lead to heart failure.

The solvents or glues are invariably inhaled or sniffed and in cases of extreme abuse (found increasingly among schoolchildren) the abuser inhales the vapour with a plastic bag over the head to heighten its effect. The milder effects of solvents can produce symptoms similar to those of alcohol intoxication.[17] This is yet another reason why it is important to have an objective test for alcohol abuse such as the breathalyser, which would identify whether the intoxication was alcohol-related or not. Access to solvents at work should be regulated.

Identification signs of acute intoxication: confusion, disorientation, dizziness, blurred vision, slurred speech, and an unsteady gait leading to drowsiness.

4. CIRCUMSTANTIAL EVIDENCE OF ABUSE

Drug abuse during work hours may occur at the workplace itself. There is evidence to suggest that employees are more likely to use drugs after hours, but some will go to work under the influence. It is important to be able to identify the telltale signs and methods used to take the drugs.

Broken bottlenecks found with silver paper or aluminium foil that is scorched or charred indicate cannabis and/or Mandrax use. Short lengths of brown kraft paper or newspaper with both ends twisted closed are used for the packaging of cannabis. Syringes, needles and/or needle caps indicate intravenous drug use. Spoons bearing scorch marks indicate the dissolving of a drug for use intravenously, as in the case of heroin. Small pieces of glass or mirror with razor blades used for pulverising and separating powder into fine lines; and straws or tightly folded squares of paper for holding powder indicate possible cocaine use. The straws are used to inhale the lines of cocaine powder via the nostrils ('snorting'). Large plastic bags smelling of solvent could be a possible indicator of solvent abuse.

Although previous studies have reported cannabis as the main substance of abuse in the workplace besides alcohol, companies are now faced with an influx of various substances of abuse and sophisticated methods of substance abuse.

SUMMARY

Drug abuse, although not as predominant as alcohol abuse in the workplace, is now being recognised as a growing problem and companies must prepare themselves for it. This factor needs to be borne in mind when developing a substance-abuse policy, but simultaneously we must ensure that the impact of alcohol abuse is not paid less attention in the process. A substance-abuse policy needs to address safety, health and productivity issues.

---

17 Waldron, HA 'Industrial toxicology 2: organic solvents' in *Lecture Notes on Occupational Medicine* (1990) 44.

In South Africa by far the most prevalent drug of abuse after alcohol is cannabis, followed by cocaine, heroin and methamphetamine. There is a significant problem with methamphetamine abuse in the Western Cape, with concern for the link between methamphetamines and risky sexual behaviour. However, it should be noted that other drugs including alcohol have also been associated with multiple risks for HIV transmission.

Management should be alert to the telltale signs of drug abuse. This highlights the value of using a breathalyser. It gives a direct objective test to differentiate between alcohol intoxication and drug intoxication. The majority of drugs, like alcohol, cause both physical and psychological dependence, the exception being cannabis, which is often considered to induce only psychological dependence because it has been difficult to demonstrate tolerance or withdrawal phenomena.

Chapter 4

Extent of the Problem: Drugs

Mike McCann & Nadine Harker Burnhams

1. INTRODUCTION

Since South Africa's first democratic elections in 1994, the country saw an increase in economic opportunities and a massive growth in employment patterns. Since then the economically active population increased steadily and is currently estimated to stand at 17 million persons.[1] Gauteng has 27% of the working population, followed by KwaZulu-Natal (19%), the Western Cape (13%), and Eastern Cape (12%).[2] Unfortunately this growth in employment patterns has been paralleled over the same period by an increase in drug trafficking.[3] South Africa has seen a surge in illicit substances such as heroin, cocaine and crystal methamphetamine in the country with more and more individuals seeking treatment for drugs and alcohol.[4] In addition, South Africa has become a convenient trans-shipment point for illicit drugs, due to its geographical location. Drugs are shipped from drug-producing countries to drug markets and an unfortunate side effect of this has been that the problem of drug abuse has become more pronounced in South Africa.[5]

Due to the increase in drug abuse, awareness and concern over drug use and its impact on the general health and productivity of the population increased. In 1999, the National Drug Master Plan (NDMP) was drafted, in accordance with the stipulations of the Prevention and Treatment of Drug Dependency Act 20 of 1992, as a direct response to the rise in alcohol and drug abuse. The NDMP reflects the country's responses to the alcohol and drug-abuse problem as set out by UN Conventions and other international bodies with the aim of reducing the supply and demand for drugs. The NDMP recognises that specific occupational groups seem to be more at risk of developing a substance-abuse problem and makes reference to those involved in the entertainment business, emergency personnel, farm workers, transport industry workers (such as long-distance truck drivers) and other industry workers. Interestingly, research conducted in Australia

---

1   Adams, S, Morar, R, Kolbe-Alexander, T & Jeebhay, MF 'Health and Health Care in the Workplace' in Harrison, S, Bhana, R & Ntuli, A (eds) *South African Health Review 2007* http://www.hst.org.za/uploads/files/chap7_07.pdf (accessed March 2011).

2   Statistics South Africa *Labour Force Survey September 2006* (2006) http://www.statssa.gov.za/publications/P0210/P0210September2006.pdf (accessed March 2011).

3   Parry, CDH & Pithey, AL 'Risk behaviour and HIV among drug using populations in South Africa' (2006) 5(2) *African Journal of Drug and Alcohol Studies* 140–157.

4   Ibid.

5   Harker,N, Myers, B, Kader, R, Fakier, N, Flisher, A, Peltzer, K, Ramligan, S & Davids, A *Substance Abuse Trends in the Western Cape: A Review of Studies Conducted Since 2000* Technical report. Medical Research Council, South Africa (2008) http://www.sahealthinfo.org/admodule/substance.pdf (accessed March 2011).

verifies this assumption and concluded that the use of illicit drugs varied significantly across different industries but workers in the hospitality, retail and construction industries were leading in use of all drug types.[6]

2. DRUG PREVALENCE

Accurate national statistics on the prevalence of the use of illicit drugs and on the inappropriate use of over-the-counter or prescription medicines (lifetime use, use in last 12 months, and use in last 30 days) are not routinely collected in South Africa.[7] Although the first South African Stress and Health Survey (SASH) conducted in 2004 and the South African Democratic Health Survey (SADHS) provide quality estimates on alcohol and drug prevalence in South Africa, the former was only conducted once in 2004 and the latter collects prevalence estimates for alcohol but not drugs. As a result much of the available information on drug prevalence has come from ad hoc cross-sectional and intervention research studies very often conducted in specific locations.[8]

In the same vein, although we know that South Africa has a lifetime prevalence estimate of 13.3% for substance abuse and dependence,[9] a national estimate on substance abuse in the workplace is not currently available. Various literature and anecdotal data sources, however, do allude to a growth in substance use amongst employed persons. For instance, a study conducted in mines found that alcohol and cannabis were the most common substances abused and were mainly associated with coping, socialising and relaxation.[10] This study estimated that approximately 6% to 16% of the average labour force is likely to experience an alcohol-dependence problem and that 20% is likely to be afflicted with drug problems. The latter figure, however, may be an overestimation and should be viewed with caution considering the lack of national household surveys to verify these estimates. National treatment data collected through the South African Community Epidemiology Network on Drug Use (SACENDU) provide an indication of the percentage of persons referred for substance-abuse treatment by their employers which ranges on average from 5% to 20% of referrals. In addition, anecdotal data collected from two companies in the food and retail sector in Cape Town highlight an increase in drug abuse amongst their employees. One of the companies has had several drug-related dismissals over the last four years.[11]

---

6   Bywood, P, Pidd, K & Roche, A *Information and Data Sheet 5: Illicit Drugs in the Australian Workforce: Prevalence and Patterns of Use* National Centre for Education and Training on Addiction Flinders University (2006) http://www.nceta.flinders.edu.au/workplace/documents/NCETA_info_sheet_5. pdf (accessed March 2011).

7   Parry, C 'Alcohol and other drug use' in Ntuli, A, Crisp,N, Clarke, E & Barron, P (eds) *2000 South African Health Review* (2001) 441–454.

8   Myers *Access to Substance Abuse Treatment for Historically Underserved Communities in the Cape Town Metropole* Medical Research Council (2007) http://www.sahealthinfo.org/admodule/accessreport. pdf (accessed March 2011).

9   Stein, DJ, Seedat, S, Herman, AA, Heeringa, SG, Moomal, H, Suliman, S, Koza, L, William, D & Myer, L *Findings from the First South African Stress and Health Study* MRC Policy Brief (2007).

10   Pick, W, Naidoo, S, Ajani, F, Onwukwe, V, Hansia, R & Bielu, O 'Prevalence of Alcohol and Cannabis Use and Reported Knowledge, Attitudes and Practice regarding its Relationship with Health' *Safety in Mines Research Advisory Committee Project HEALTH* (2003) 1 Vol 1 (2003). 712.

11   The two companies provided access to their records, but requested that they remain anonymous.

3. RANGE OF SUBSTANCES USED

Alcohol remains the most commonly abused substance in South Africa, followed by dagga (cannabis). The diagram below depicts treatment-demand data highlighting the primary and secondary substances of abuse by all patients accessing treatment services in South Africa. The last five years, however, have seen a dramatic increase in methamphetamine (locally known as tik) use. Although all provinces have documented increases in tik use, the extent of use is greatest in Cape Town.[12] As a result, it has become the most commonly used drug in Cape Town. Treatment admissions for cocaine-related problems have also seen slight increases but appear to have stabilised.[13] Although prevalence rates for heroin consumption are generally low in Africa, there have been reports of a steady increase especially in countries located along primary drug trafficking routes such as South Africa.[14]

Local and international data on the prevalence of licit medicine abuse is minimal.[15] Although the SACENDU project also collects information on treatment demand related to OTC and prescription medication abuse, the last seven years have shown very little change in the proportion of persons admitted to treatment centres with OTC/prescription medication abuse. This is not saying that OTC/prescription medication abuse is not a problem; on the contrary, it highlights the lack of research in the area. However, it should be understood that OTC/prescription medication is associated with multiple harms, such as damage to physical health, dependency on medications and increasing risk of potential overdose.[16]

The array of substances used by the broader population provides an idea of the types of drugs that may be commonly used by those that are employed.

---

12 Parry, CDH, Myers, B & Plüddemann, A 'Drug policy for methamphetamine use urgently needed' (2004) 94(12) *South African Medical Journal* 964–965.

13 *South African Community Epidemiology Network on Drug Use (SACENDU) Research Brief* Medical Research Council meeting May 2009.

14 Parry, CDH, Plüddemann, A & Myers, B 'Heroin treatment demand in South Africa: trends from two large metropolitan sites (January 1997–December 2003)' (2005) 24(5) *Drug and Alcohol Review* 419–423.

15 Harker, N, Myers, B, Kader, R, Fakier, N, Flisher, AJ, Peltzer, K, Ramligan, S & Davids, A *Substance Abuse Trends in the Western Cape: A Review of Studies Conducted Since 2000* Technical report. Medical Research Council, South Africa (2008) http://www.sahealthinfo.org/admodule/substance. pdf (accessed March 2011).

16 Ibid.

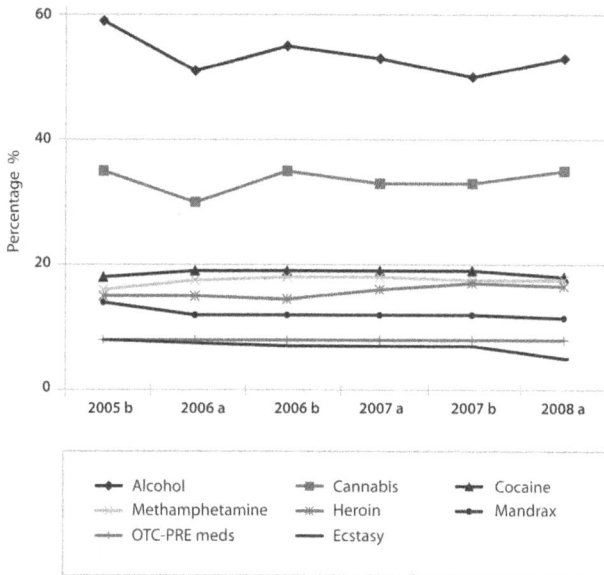

Figure 4.1
* Data for 2005b–2006a reflect data of 5 provinces; data for 2006b–2007b reflect 8 provinces; and data for 2008a reflect 9 provinces. (Source: SACENDU Update MRC May 2008.)

4. CHARACTERISTICS OF SUBSTANCE ABUSERS

In respect of alcohol and drug use, differences have been noted in respect of gender, socio-economic status and geographic location.[17] Several studies have reported on higher alcohol and drug prevalence rates amongst males than females.[18] This, however, does not necessarily reflect dramatically lower levels of use among women but may allude to women experiencing more barriers in accessing treatment services and it is highly likely that data on substance abuse in certain populations are skewed in favour of men.[19]

Differences in socio-economic backgrounds are also thought to influence drugs of choice.[20] For instance, the inhalation of glue or petrol is more common amongst street

---

17 Parry, CDH *Substance Abuse in South Africa: Country Report Focussing on Young Persons* Paper prepared for Regional Consultation—Global Initiative on Primary Prevention of Substance Abuse Among Young People, Harare (February 1998) http://www.sahealthinfo.org/admodule/countryreport.pdf (accessed March 2011).

18 Ibid; Myers, B *Access to Substance Abuse Treatment for Historically Underserved Communities in the Cape Town Metropole* Medical Research Council (2007) http://www.sahealthinfo.org/admodule/accessreport.pdf (accessed March 2011); Shisana, O, Rehle, T, Simbayi, L, Parker, W, Zuma, K, Bhana, A, Connolly, C, Jooste, S & Pillay, V *South African National HIV Prevalence, HIV Incidence, Behaviour and Communication Survey, 2005* (2005) http://www.hsrcpress.ac.za (accessed March 2011).

19 Myers, B, Parry, CHD & Plüddemann, A 'Indicators of substance abuse treatment demand in Cape Town, South Africa (1997–2001)' (2004) 5 *Curationis* 27–31.

20 Parry, CDH *Substance Abuse in South Africa: Country Report Focussing on Young Persons* Paper prepared for the Regional Consultation—Global Initiative on Primary Prevention of Substance Abuse Among Young People, Harare (February 1998) http://www.sahealthinfo.org/admodule/countryreport.pdf (accessed March 2011).

children or those from a lower socio-economic group.[21] Although the use of harder drugs such as cocaine and heroin are synonymous with the more affluent person, recent research data have reported an increase in cocaine and heroin use amongst men and women from historically disadvantaged communities.[22]

Patterns of drug use also vary according to geographic location. This is confirmed by a study of substance use among educators which found higher rates of risky drinking within the West Coast district (8%), followed by 6% in the Eden district (which includes Oudtshoorn, Mossel Bay, George and Knysna) and 5% in the Boland district. The West Coast also had the highest proportion of binge drinking (19%) followed by the Eden (14%) and Boland (13%) districts.[23] Conversely the study found higher lifetime prevalence rates for cocaine use in urban formal settings as opposed to rural formal settings.

5. IMPACT OF DRUG ABUSE

Drug abuse costs South Africa millions of rands a year due to productivity losses as a result of drug-related illnesses and deaths. In addition, alcohol and drug abuse by employees on-or off-site inevitably impacts on the work performance of each employee resulting in decreased productivity, work errors, accidents, wasted materials, tardiness and absenteeism—all translating to massive losses each year.[24]

It is estimated that over 50% of accidents in the workplace are substance related, and theft and other criminal activities at work are trebled as a result of substance abuse. Overall, an undetected drug abuser costs his employer a further 25% of his wages.[25]

At a Cosatu-sponsored safety and health conference it was revealed that every day in South African industry on average 5 people die from injuries received, 430 people are injured and 52 people are permanently disabled.[26]

The National Council on Smoking estimates that about 25 000 smoking-related deaths occur annually in South Africa and that 2,5 million workdays are lost due to absenteeism arising from tobacco-related illnesses. Tobacco smoke affects smokers as well as non-smokers, hence the legislation prohibiting smoking in the workplace and in other public places.

Drug abuse not only has a negative impact on the workplace but also beyond it. The burden alcohol and drugs place on developing countries is reflected in the breakdown of families, trauma, violence (often gender-based), crime, risky sexual practice and

21 Parry, CDH 'Alcohol and other drug use' in Ntuli, A, Crisp, N, Clarke, E & Barron, P (eds) 2000 South African Health Review (2001) 441–454.

22 Myers, B, Louw, J & Fakier, N 'Alcohol and drug abuse: removing structural barriers to treatment for historically disadvantaged communities in Cape Town' (2008) 17(2) International Journal of Social Welfare 156–165.

23 Shisana, O, Peltzer, K, Zungu-Dirwayi, N & Louw, J The Health of our Educators: A focus on HIV/AIDS in South African public schools (2005) http://www.hsrcpress.ac.zar (accessed March 2011).

24 Kew, G 'A descriptive study of alcohol consumption patterns on a South African gold mine' (1994) 21 Urbanisation and Health Newsletter 39–42; Garcia, FE 'The determinants of substance abuse in the workplace' (1996) 33(1) The Social Science Journal 55–68; Roman, PM & Blum, TC The Workplace and Alcohol Problem Prevention (2008) http://pubs.niaaa.nih.gov/publications/arh26-1/49-57.pdf (accessed March 2010).

25 Rose-Inness, O Drugging on the Job (2008) http://www.health24.com/mind/sexualdysfunction (accessed July 2008).

26 Presentation by Raymond Meneses at http://www.kwazulunatal.gov.za (accessed April 2010).

injury-related trauma. Substance abuse also places a large burden on the health, social development, criminal justice and economic sectors.

SUMMARY

Drug abuse in the workplace is a global phenomenon and too often organisations are unaware of the extent of the problem until they start looking into it. South Africa has seen a considerable increase in drug trafficking and the use of drugs. The country is a staging post for drug transportation to the Americas and Europe and this has contributed to the pronounced increase of the problem in South Africa. According to the South African Stress and Health Survey, the country has the second highest prevalence for substance-use disorders, when compared with 14 other countries surveyed.[27] Although national statistics on substance-abuse prevalence in the workplace are limited, it is estimated that approximately 6% to 16% of the average labour force is likely to suffer an alcohol-dependence problem and that 20% is likely to experience drug problems.[28] The impacts of drug abuse can be felt beyond the borders of the workplace, placing an enormous burden on the health, social development and economic sectors of the country.

---

27 Stein, DJ, Seedat, S, Herman, AA, Heeringa, SG, Moomal, H & Myer, L *Findings from the First South African Stress and Health Study* MRC Policy Brief (2007).

28 Pick, W, Naidoo, S, Ajani, F, Onwukwe, V, Hansia, R & Bielu, O *Prevalence of Alcohol and Cannabis Use and Reported Knowledge, Attitudes and Practice regarding its Relationship with Health* Safety in Mines Research Advisory Committee Project HEALTH (2003) 1712.

Chapter 5

Causes of the Problem: Psychosocial, Environmental and Cultural

Mike McCann & Nadine Harker Burnhams

The question is often put, why do we drink too much? Or, why do we use drugs? If we exclude those people who have a genetic susceptibility to dependence, we are left with many and diverse reasons which centre on the individual and his interaction with his environment. Over the last three decades, two views on the possible causes of substance abuse in the workplace have evolved. The first view is that alcohol and drug problems are external to the workplace and are often carried into the workplace. In such instances consideration is given to factors such as genetic susceptibility, environmental, cultural and other psychosocial factors as well as the presence of certain personality attributes. The second view assumes that conditions within the workplace contribute to employees' alcohol or drug use,[1] signifying contributing factors such as organisational culture and climate. This chapter aims to discuss some causes of the problem, from mainly three perspectives: psychosocial, environmental and organisational culture.

1. A PSYCHOSOCIAL PERSPECTIVE

1.1 Negative emotional states as a predictor of alcohol or drug abuse

Alcohol is the fastest acting, most effective and most easily available tranquilliser. Its immediate relaxing effect and social acceptance makes it attractive as a reducer of inhibitions and as a means of providing a feeling of wellbeing, an escape from reality or depression, and it makes us feel powerful and assertive when feelings of inadequacy are present. Similarly, illicit drugs provide an escape from the sometimes painful and stressful realities of life by creating a happy diversion for the users, a chance to escape from challenging life circumstances. These effects make us vulnerable to the risk of excessive drinking and harmful drug use.

In a study of a group of patients suffering from addictive behaviour, three quarters of the group's relapses were attributable to negative emotional states, interpersonal

---

1   Lehman, WEK, Farabee, DJ, Holcom, MC & Simpson, DD 'Prediction of substance use in the workplace: Unique contributions of personal background and work environment variables' (1995) 25(2) *Journal of Drug Issues* 253–274.

conflicts, and social pressures.[2] Negative emotional states caused 35 per cent of all the relapses. Although various negative emotional states such as frustration, anger, anxiety, depression and boredom were documented, the largest number of relapses, by far, occurred in situations involving frustration and anger.

There is a strong association between anger and alcohol or drug abuse. Heavy drinkers consume more alcohol when they are feeling frustrated and angry and this increases the probability of the heavy drinker developing aggressive behaviour.[3] Stress at work, whether real or perceived, can produce a negative emotional state in an individual employee, rendering them vulnerable to alcohol or drug abuse. The same job done by two employees may produce different levels of stress depending on the individual's innate ability to handle the stress. Often the stress is not recognised by the individual.

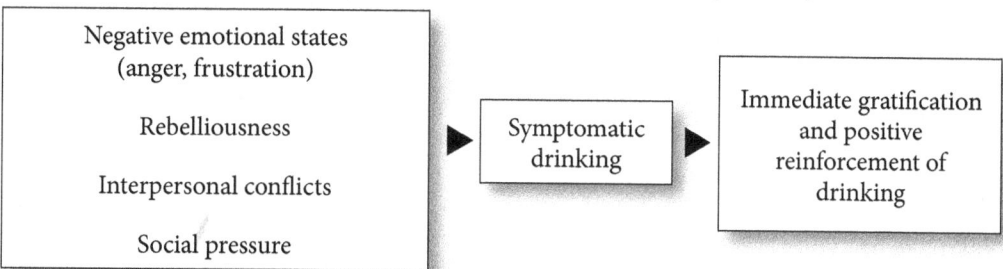

Figure 5.1 Negative emotional states as a cause of drinking

1.2 Negative emotional states as a cause of alcohol or drug abuse

> Rapid drinking will lead to greater intoxication than slower drinking of the same quantity of beverage

The transition period between the end of the working day, after the pressures of work, and the relaxation period which follows is often difficult to control. For too many employees, a quick and effective way of climbing down from that state of high arousal after work is to have an alcoholic drink or take some form of drug. The high arousal state can encourage rapid drinking as everything in the process is being done fast, and often unconsciously, by the individual. Blood-alcohol levels will therefore peak high and fast, particularly if no food has been taken. This is an example of symptomatic drinking, where one action is responded to by another, namely drinking. Galanter refers to those whom Jellinek calls symptomatic drinkers ('those who consume large amounts of alcohol to relieve bodily or emotional stress'), and suggests that the psychological or symptomatic drinker is in a pre-alcoholic stage of addiction. Control has not yet been lost, but alcohol is necessary to cope with the stresses relating to work.[4]

There are other situations which can encourage drinking or drug use in order to increase arousal. These include circumstances where arousal is too low: when work is

---

2   Marlatt, GA & Gordon, JR *Relapse Prevention: Maintenance Strategies in the Treatment of Addictive Behaviors* (1985) 71–92.

3   Ibid.

4   Jellinek, EM *The Disease Concept of Alcoholism* (1960); Galanter, M *Recent Developments in Alcoholism* vol 6 (Plenum 1988) 120.

routine, boring, non-taxing or repetitive, and where employees are working well below their experience or capabilities.

High-risk situations at work

The stresses of work impact on all job levels. Galanter identifies job competition, time pressures, unusual work hours or excessive working hours, and dirtiness or heaviness of work as significant factors.[5] Freedom from supervision, where the job has too little structure or where there is too little visibility of job performance, is also a high-risk situation for alcohol problems. Other factors such as role conflict within the workplace or between the work and an outside source as well as jobs with a high work demand but characterised by non-participation in outcomes and decision-making have also been found to contribute significantly to the experience of occupational stress.[6]

The less balance in one's daily lifestyle the more the desire for immediate gratification. Supervisory or middle-management jobs can be stressful if they are not properly structured or if the persons concerned have not adapted to the status required of them. Jobs which have accountability without authority can be very stressful. Jobs which entail high stress but provide poor recognition induce feelings of low self-esteem, frustration and anger. Middle management is at a particularly high risk, caught between the employees and senior management. Members of middle management have much responsibility but are provided with little authority. Features of such jobs are excessive demands from the employees and, likewise, excessive demands from senior management. People in such positions often work extra hours without extra pay or recognition, they can be overlooked for promotion or are too old to change their jobs. They are also often free from supervision and can be encouraged to participate in lunches where excessive drinking occurs. This situation of low potential for both intrinsic and extrinsic reward has been associated with the experience of stress[7] and is particularly high risk for developing alcohol and drug problems.

Shift workers are an at-risk group due to the stresses of their work, namely irregular hours and poor sleeping patterns. A study conducted on the occupational stressors experienced by shift workers in the South African motor industry found that shift workers often use alcohol or other prescription medications to help induce sleep after working a night shift.[8] Poor supervision has also been cited as increasing the risk of substance abuse amongst shift workers. In one company a man would continually turn up to his shift intoxicated only to be locked up in the toilets out of harm's way by his co-workers. Where supervision is poor, the subculture of substance use can develop inside the workplace. Alcohol is smuggled inside and is distributed to the group, usually disguised as a soft drink. Here the cover-up is developed as a form of camaraderie.

The degree of balance in one's daily lifestyle has an impact on the desire for indulgence or immediate gratification. An equilibrium has to be reached between what we want to do, such as achieving self-fulfilment, and what we have to do. Tedious, difficult, repetitive tasks cause us stress that we unburden by pleasure. A lifestyle weighed down

---

5   Galanter, M *Recent Developments in Alcoholism* vol 6 (Plenum 1988) 120–127.

6   Harker Burnhams, N & Pretorius, B '*Occupational stress and coping among shift workers at a motor manufacturing plant*' (2009) 21 *The Social Work Practioner-Researcher* (1).

7   Ibid.

8   Ibid.

by perceived difficulties and obligations gives an increased feeling that we are deprived and produces a reciprocal desire for indulgence and immediate gratification.[9]

Learned behaviour contributes to our subconscious desire for alcohol or drugs. Immediate gratification produces a strong positive reinforcement which, due to the immediate nature of the gratification, is difficult to combat. The reality of the situation soon returns and the short-term gain is lost, but the negative reinforcement is distanced from the drinking or drug use and therefore is less effective than its positive reinforcement. The negative reinforcement can consist of the hangover effects of nausea, vomiting, weakness, tremors, and headache. It also includes the inability to work effectively, being chastised by family or superiors, and feeling depressed and agitated. Inevitably, though, the drinking or drug-use is repeated sooner or later as a positive reinforcement. Only when the negative reinforcement becomes effectively more powerful can it influence the individual's behaviour to consider change.[10] The work environment can also have a positive impact on decreasing drinking or drug use. Specifically, group cohesion or teamwork has been shown to buffer the negative impact of drinking climates.[11]

1.3 Interpersonal conflicts as a predictor of alcohol or drug abuse

In the study by Marlatt and Gordon,[12] interpersonal conflicts accounted for 16 per cent of the relapses and in this category the majority of relapses were related to anger and frustration stemming from confrontations or arguments with marriage partners, employers or co-workers. The anticipation of negative criticism was also a significant factor and even the potential threat of a conflict was a likely cause of starting to drink.

1.4 Family influences

Family role models play an important part in whether an individual will develop a substance dependence or not, with parents' drinking and even smoking habits being modelled by offspring. In particular, the stability of family life at the age of onset of drinking is an important family or social risk factor. Even though workplace culture is fairly distinct from the culture of the wider community, the values an individual gains within the family unit interact with workplace norms, perceptions and values concerning the use of alcohol or drugs.[13] If an employee's existing family values, norms, behaviours and perceptions encourage responsible use of alcohol and zero tolerance towards illicit drugs, it is more likely that he or she may have a negative view of lax organisational norms or a culture of substance abuse in the workplace—and therefore may not succumb as easily to internal work pressures to abuse alcohol or drugs.

---

9   Marlatt & Gordon (n 2).

10 Lied, ER & Marlatt, GA 'Modeling as a determinant of alcohol consumption: Effect of subject sex and prior drinking history' (1979) 4 *Addictive Behaviors* 47–54.

11 Bennett, JB & Lehman, GA 'Workplace drinking climate, stress, and problem indicators: Assessing the influence of teamwork (group cohesion)' (1998) 59 *Journal of Studies on Alcohol* 608–618.

12 Marlatt & Gordon (n 2) at 71–92.

13 Pidd, K *Work-related Alcohol and Drug Use: Key Issues and Interventions* Paper presented at Work-Related Alcohol and & Drug Use: A National Forum Conference, Flinders University, Adelaide (June 2006).

2. AN ENVIRONMENTAL PERSPECTIVE

2.1 Work conditions

Work conditions can be conducive to alcohol or drug abuse, but it must be remembered that those abusing alcohol or drugs can also choose a job which favours a subculture of drinking or drug use (see below), and stress can be a consequence rather than a precursor of excessive drinking and drug use.

Plant[14] discusses three main occupational factors that increase the likelihood of alcohol abuse:

(a) When alcohol is readily available for consumption during working hours.

(b) When there are strong social pressures to drink (as in a culture of drinking).

(c) When workers are separated from 'normal' sexual or social relationships.

Social pressure to drink occurs frequently in the workplace. Business lunches are a prime example as alcohol is invariably available at the company's expense or at the expense of the company entertaining the employee. A manager under treatment for alcohol problems explained how the pressures at a business lunch are affected by the number of the people with whom one is having lunch. If the business lunch is a situation where there are only two people present, the pressures are minimal and usually any refusal to drink alcohol is accepted without question. But as the numbers at the luncheon increase, there is both direct verbal pressure and indirect social pressure to drink, particularly if there is an underlying culture of drinking.

Separation from conventional sexual or social relationships, an occupational factor of alcohol abuse, can be found in those whose work takes them away from their normal home environment eg deep-sea fishermen, members of the armed forces, travelling salespersons, pilots and employees such as migrant mine workers, imported for their labour and living in hostels. Workers in physically hazardous or safety-sensitive jobs report more alcohol or drug use and more acceptance of drinking at work than workers in less risky jobs. The influence of culture on alcohol use can be especially problematic in high-risk occupations and for younger workers who may be socialised into an occupation that supports drinking. When safety risks are high, drug or alcohol abuse by employees make them and their co-workers particularly vulnerable.[15]

Does the job attract heavy substance abusers or do they become heavy substance abusers at the job? Some occupations are especially tolerant of heavy drinking and among such groups drink-related problems are greater than elsewhere. More heavy drinkers are recruited into the drinks trade than to other companies and this preference is the result partly of self-selection because heavy drinkers are attracted to this type of work.[16] The hospitality industry in Australia had the largest percentage of workers reporting long and short term drinking behaviours. Factors such as the availability of

14   Plant, MA 'Alcoholism and occupation: A review' (1977) 72 *British Journal of Addiction* 309–316.

15   Bennett, JB, Patterson, CR, Reynolds, GS Wiitala, WL & Lehman, WL 'Team awareness, problem drinking, and drinking climate: Workplace social health promotion in a policy context' (2004) 19(2) *American Journal of Health Promotion* 103–113.

16   Plant, MA 'Occupation and alcoholism: cause or effect? A controlled study of recruits to the drinks trade' (1978) 13(4) *The International Journal of Addictions* 605–626.

alcohol and a culture of alcohol promotion accounts for this.[17] Any employment in which there is little checking of references, which has little direct supervision and which offers environmental features that allow employees to camouflage their drinking or drug-use behaviours, will naturally attract those suffering from alcohol or drug addiction.[18]

2.2 Alcohol legacies

The legacy of the 'dop system' is considered a contributing factor to alcohol abuse in South Africa. The term 'dop system' refers to the provision of alcohol to farm workers as partial payment for their labour.[19] Historically it formed form part of their conditions of service. Although the system is now illegal in South Africa, alcohol dependence among farm workers continues to play a major role, entangling farm workers in a cycle of poverty and dependence, and is likely to be a contributing factor to alcohol abuse.[20] This is particularly evident on farms in the Western and Northern Cape.

Similarly, the mining industry in South Africa has also encouraged alcohol use amongst its workers. During colonial and apartheid rule alcohol was used as a means of labour mobilisation. It was often used to control migrant workers and as a social outlet for them, as part of their relaxation time.[21] Today unsatisfactory work and living conditions on mines encourage unhealthy drinking. Despite the new political dispensation, the farming and mining industries are still characterised by poor social conditions such as poverty and ill health—aggravated by substance abuse.

The European impact in Africa influenced drinking patterns in many cultures. The Europeans introduced stronger commercialised alcoholic drinks than those to which traditional societies were accustomed. The consumption of bottled beer has become the most visible, most widely and easily attainable symbol of African social drinking.[22] The traditional role of alcohol in Africa for ritualistic celebrations has been progressively eroded as a result of industrialisation and urbanisation and the resultant changed lifestyle, which have undermined traditional cultural supports and restraints.[23] A lack of recreational facilities in disadvantaged communities is viewed as contributing to alcohol and drug abuse, especially among the youth.[24]

---

17 Pidd, K *Work-related Alcohol and Drug Use: Key Issues and Interventions* Paper presented at Work-Related Alcohol and & Drug Use: A National Forum Conference, Flinders University, Adelaide (June 2006).

18 Von Wiegand, RA 'Alcoholism in industry (USA)' (1972) 67(3) *British Journal of Addiction to Alcohol & Other Drugs* 181–187.

19 Parry, CD & Bennetts, AL *Alcohol Policy and Public Health in South Africa* (1998).

20 London, L 'Addressing the legacy of the dop system: Tackling alcohol abuse among South African farm workers' (1999) 2(1) *Urban Health and Development Bulletin* 33–35 http://www.sahealthinfo. org/admodule/dopsystem.htm (accessed March 2011); Parry & Bennetts *Alcohol Policy and Public Health in South Africa* (1998).

21 Parry, CD & Bennetts, AL *Alcohol Policy and Public Health in South Africa* (1998).

22 Molamu, L & Mbere, N 'Alcohol use & abuse in Botswana—A community study in *Alcohol & Developing Countries* (1990) 93.

23 Odejide, AO, Ohaeri, JU, Ikuesan, BA & Adelekan, MF 'The promotion of alcohol research in Nigeria—A need for cross-cultural collaborative research' in Maula et al (eds) *Alcohol in Developing Countries* (1990) 59–69.

24 Molamu, L & Mbere, N 'Alcohol use and abuse in Botswana: A community study' in Maula et al (eds) *Alcohol in Developing Countries* (1990) 93.

Although there are many similarities in causal factors for alcohol and drug abuse in South Africa, there are differences which are worth mentioning. Rocha-Silva et al[25] mentioned habitual behaviour (doing it out of habit) as a common reason for drug use. There is also the need to seek a heightened state of awareness by altering one's mood state. This has often been associated with religious practices (for example, those of Rastafarians).[26]

2.3 Advertising

As regards environmental pressures, advertising plays a role, and its impact can be seen in the way advertisements present alcohol as an easy way to attain an attractive lifestyle. It is not the taste or effect of alcohol that is promoted, but an escape into an unattainable world of pleasure. Furthermore, television soap operas utilise the continual glass in hand as a prop depicting power, affluence, charm and charisma, and this influences our attitude towards the acceptance of alcohol to such an extent that to be without it in certain circumstances is uncomfortable or apparently antisocial. There is a misperception that people who do not drink cannot enjoy themselves.

2.4 Availability

In addition, there is also increased access to and availability of both licit and illicit substances. For example, in South Africa in the late 1990s there were almost 23 000 licensed liquor outlets with an estimated 150 000 to 200 000 unlicensed outlets, yielding approximately one liquor outlet for every 190 persons.[27] The dawn of a new democracy also saw increased trafficking and availability of drugs such as cocaine and heroin in South Africa. The country has become a drug transit point which may be due to factors such as the decrease in local controls following the collapse of apartheid, an increase in tourism as well as increased economic and political migration to South Africa.

3. AN ORGANISATIONAL CULTURE PERSPECTIVE

Throughout this book there is a theme relating to culture whether of the community, the workplace or the organisation. This is because it is one of the most powerful influences to impact on an individual and a work group. It is also the most difficult aspect of an organisation to change. The addicted organisation is analogous to the addicted individual.[28] The process of addiction is sustained by defenses of denial, projection or self-centeredness. This gives rise to strong and pervasive co-dependency between the existence of a serious alcohol or drug problem and its denial. The co-dependence pervades management and employees.

---

25 Rocha-Silva, L *Attitudes towards Drinking and Drunkenness in the RSA* (1987).

26 Parry, CD *Substance Abuse in South Africa: Country Report Focussing on Young Persons* Paper prepared for Regional Consultation—Global Initiative on Primary Prevention of Substance Abuse Among Young People, Harare (February 1998) http://www.sahealthinfo.org/admodule/countryreport.pdf (accessed March 2011).

27 Ibid.

28 Milton,R 'Recovery strategies for addicted organisations' in International Institute on the Prevention & Treatment of Alcoholism *Book of Abstracts* (1990) 153.

3.1 A culture of alcohol and drugs at work

The various cultures of substance use amongst employees at work reflect the cultures in the community at large. Before the corporate causes of the problem can be addressed, employee attitudes towards alcohol and drugs will be discussed. The interpretation of corporate alcohol policies will be influenced by the attitude of the workforce towards alcohol and drug abuse. The impact of the attitudes and cultures of the employees upon the workplace is determined through the drinking patterns of the majority of drinkers and not only of the dependent drinkers. Without doubt, the way in which a community or work group consumes alcohol or uses drugs has a direct influence on the number of people with alcohol or drug problems, irrespective of genetic or personality susceptibility.[29] In turn, the workplace is a major player in the causation and the perpetuation of substance-abuse problems in the community.

The corporate culture can directly or indirectly promote drinking. Some corporate cultures seem to produce more resistance to change in drinking attitudes. The reasons for this are varied and often difficult to define.

The cultural causes of alcohol problems are as diverse as the cultures themselves. There is unlikely to be one single cause of alcohol problems; instead there is a conglomeration of different causes often interwoven, which impact in different ways in different circumstances.

The corporate culture is often made up of subcultures within the company such as ethnic, political or union subcultures. There can also be informal subcultures such as drinking groups. An individual is exposed to cultural pressures in a company due to (a) formal company culture; (b) informal company culture; (c) formal subcultures; and (d) informal subcultures. The culture of drinking can come from one or even all four of the above and the total corporate culture can contribute to the development of a substance-abuse problem regardless of genetic or personality susceptibility.

Corporate cultures can generally affect all employees, whereas subcultures mostly affect groups within a company. Corporate culture can directly or indirectly promote substance use. Moreover, the attitude of management can give misleading messages and be inconsistent. Their preventive measures can be weak or non-existent. There may even be two standards: regular managerial drinking at lunchtime and after hours on the premises, but a substance-abuse policy or disciplinary policy for workers which prohibits all substance use. When employees exhibit substance-use problems, their punishments may be negative and too strong and neither corrective nor fair, thus increasing cover-ups by co-workers and even supervisors at the lower level. Problems are often tolerated because of poor confrontation policies or attitudes—and then finally treated with extremes of discipline once the problem is already out of hand.

An example of the type of formalised corporate culture that can encourage substance use is that in which production parties are held where the reward is alcohol. Not to partake of the reward may sideline an employee from further promotion. Typically, the sales or business conference held in a hotel or conference centre usually starts with a cocktail party. Some breweries supply alcohol to their employees by offering a free pub after work and cases of beer at the end of the month. The armed forces have a significant

---

29 Roberts, R 'Factors influencing alcohol consumption in a workplace setting' (1988) 38(4) *Journal of the Society of Occupational Medicine* 118–122.

culture of drinking around their mess nights where one's chances of promotion may be impacted if not a participator in the drinking games that are played.

Some companies accept less than the best from their employees and, in the worst cases, employees can linger in positions to which they have been sidelined, out of the way, without the underlying problem being addressed. In these circumstances management will avoid rather than address and confront a substance-abuse problem. They often act only when there is overt intoxication at work—the stage when the worker concerned is likely already to have become a dependent substance user.

Another problem is caused by an authoritarian management style which transfers responsibilities to the lower supervisory levels but seldom transfers authority. An authoritarian management often encourages and expects behaviour problems. These companies are likely to experience the more severe substance-abuse problems, in a similar way to companies that enjoy high productivity but which give little or no recognition to achievement, those that have scant or no system in place for dealing with grievances, and those which hardly encourage communication between management and employees. An authoritarian culture will experience difficulty in introducing a caring substance-abuse policy—such a policy will be treated with suspicion, there will be no trust on the part of employees and without change in the management style, the results will fall short of expectations.

An open, participative management style, on the other hand, is more likely to implement a substance-abuse policy successfully as there is less likelihood of denial and cover-up and more chance of co-worker and supervisor referral. As mentioned previously, management's perception of what constitutes a substance-abuse problem is vitally important. The perception is often one of a down-and-out, continually intoxicated, non-functional employee. The reality is far from this. Management is often unable to connect the related problems of unproductivity, sickness, absence, accidents and severe behaviour problems to an underlying substance-abuse problem, which is kept simmering due to a subculture of substance use. An example of formal subcultures exists in South African mining hostels. Here male employees live in barrack-type accommodation. They lack conventional family and sexual relationships. Peer-group pressure to use substances are immense. In the mines the profits from the taverns run by the hostels are used to subsidise sport and other recreational facilities; thus, the greater the profits, the better the facilities. This arrangement can condone and reinforce excessive substance use.

Social pressures to drink occur frequently in the workplace

3.2 Social pressures in a culture of drinking

In the study by Marlatt and Gordon,[30] social pressures caused 20% of all the relapses. The main thrust of the social pressures was from a peer group, either directly by means of verbal persuasion or indirectly in the presence of others displaying the same target-group behaviour. In this category, the majority of relapses were due to direct verbal persuasion. Group behaviour is a powerful influence, particularly in the workplace. Cultural and social pressures to drink are often found in the workplace and need not be associated with verbal persuasion—the presence of a favourable social or cultural environment which endorses drinking or even drug use, is often all that is needed.

---

30 Marlatt & Gordon *Relapse Prevention: Maintenance Strategies in the Treatment of Addictive Behaviors* (1985) 71–92.

An important aspect of the influence of culture is research that shows males are especially influenced by modelling associated with drinking, as there is a perceived 'macho' association.[31] Particularly vulnerable are new employees seeking recognition, apprentices modelling their behaviour on the artisans they wish to emulate and the rehabilitated employees who are thrust back into the environment which encouraged them to drink in the first place. In some occupations there is a culture where employees drink or use drugs together or in unison as a means to unwind from stress and to encourage social bonding, even though this form of bonding could be considered harmful. Such cultural behaviour fortifies individual inclinations toward uncontrolled drinking and drug use, further stigmatising any possibilities for seeking help for alcohol or drug problems. Alternatively and of course positively, responsible social norms can lead co-workers to encourage those who abuse alcohol or drugs to seek some form of help.[32]

> Peer-group pressure is the most often quoted cause of an individual substance-abuse problem

It should be emphasised that informal subcultures play a major role in continuing corporate substance-abuse problems. Such subcultures are (often unknowingly) condoned by lower management. They are difficult to root out because of co-worker cover-up and peer-group pressure.

The majority of substance-related problems start with friends and peer-group pressure. Such pressure is orientated around the 'macho' image and denial is heavily associated with this image: to admit one has a substance-abuse problem is exposing oneself to be thought of as weak. The subcultures of a company can particularly impact on new employees and apprentices, as mentioned earlier, either initiating the habit or encouraging established habits as they seek acceptance and recognition. Young employees such as apprentices are particularly susceptible to observational learning and modelling, while a rehabilitated employee will be up against tremendous pressure when returning to a subculture of substance use at work.

Lunchtime drinking is a subculture which is often condoned by companies, whether recognised or not, and this is particularly noticeable after the weekly wages have been paid. In a survey conducted by the writers in Durban in 1990, 27 per cent of companies surveyed were concerned about their workers' off-the-premises lunchtime drinking. Extended business lunches lead to poor afternoon productivity and, as they are indulged in mainly by senior management, this sets a poor example to other employees.

4. CHALLENGES IN IMPLEMENTING AN ALCOHOL AND DRUG POLICY

A company can implement a substance-abuse policy but individuals can sabotage its impact unless they feel they are participants in the policy and stand to benefit from it. Individuals in an organisation tend to choose information which accords with their own views and ignore that which opposes them. They will tend to resist changes which

---

31   Lied, ER & Marlatt, GA 'Modeling as a determinant of alcohol consumption: Effect of subject sex and prior drinking history' (1979) 4 *Addictive Behaviors* 47, cited in Marlatt, GA& Gordon, JR *Relapse Prevention: Maintenance Strategies in the Treatment of Addictive Behaviors* (1985).

32   Bennett et al 'Team awareness, problem drinking, and drinking climate: Workplace social health promotion in a policy context' (2004) 19(2) *American Journal of Health Promotion* 103–113.

they believe will impact adversely upon their own behaviour. They develop attitudes to protect themselves from threatening realities. Such attitudes in the workplace are formed and influenced by a number of factors, such as the corporate image, the social style of the employees, their comradeship and their conformity and loyalty to one another. These develop into subcultures which are difficult to change due to resistance. To produce behavioural change the two cornerstones, attitude and culture, need to be addressed.[33]

4.1 Attitudes and culture—the cornerstone of a substance-abuse programme

There are significant hurdles in changing the culture of drinking in an organisation. To change the culture is a large undertaking, in which education on its own is not sufficient. It requires a combination of serious commitment from senior management, thorough consultation with and explanation to the employees and their union, and the addressing of issues around job security.

Resistance to change from individuals, particularly management, and from other sections of the organisation, is based on structural, economic and cultural factors.[34] Such resistance is the inevitable result of trying to change behaviour which has been particularly ingrained and previously condoned. Management or union resistance can be due to a fear of exposure of their own problems, admission of the failure of supervision, poor understanding of the difference between normal and problem drinking and because of real or imagined fears of prejudice arising from the change.

Roberts,[35] in a survey done at a large international corporation, found that employees were reluctant to change their drinking behaviour and stressed that they would find it difficult to change anyway. Employees were also reluctant to assist another employee who had a drinking problem. To provide employees with education concerning alcohol was insufficient on its own. Although difficult, they had to change their behaviour towards alcohol.

Organisational resistance due to structural factors may be a consequence of increases in workload, a change in decision-making processes, or of alterations to procedures for dealing with problematic behaviour. Organisational resistance for economic reasons, on the other hand, can be ascribed to an exclusive focus upon production and concern at the cost of investing in any substance-abuse program. Organisational resistance for cultural reasons can be due to the high level of acceptance of alcohol or drug use in the community and to wariness on the part of management introducing the change as to the reaction which such change may produce in the community.

Resistance to change will usually occur in an organisation, but it must be identified and overcome. The most difficult resistance to overcome is individual and cultural resistance.[36] Without changes in attitudes and culture any programme will fail.

---

33 Pidd, K *Work-related Alcohol and Drug Use: Key Issues and Interventions* Paper presented at Work-Related Alcohol and & Drug Use: A National Forum Conference, Flinders University, Adelaide (June 2006).

34 Bijl, R 'Resistance as a potential positive factor in implementing an alcohol policy' in International Institute on the Prevention & Treatment of Alcoholism *Book of Procedures* (1990) 15.

35 Roberts 'Factors influencing alcohol consumption in a workplace setting' (1988) 38(4) *Journal of the Society of Occupational Medicine* 118–122.

36 Bijl 'Resistance as a potential positive factor in implementing an alcohol policy' in International Institute on the Prevention & Treatment of Alcoholism *Book of Procedures* (1990) 15.

The drinking population seems to move in unison up and down the consumption continuum when changes in the culture occur. Individual substance-use habits are closely related to substance-use habits among friends in the social network.[37] For instance, individual drinking habits and heavy drinking in particular are products of a company's culture. This was seen in a study evaluating the effectiveness of an alcohol and drug programme. Findings indicated a significant change in drinking and drug-use patterns amongst employees whose organisation reflected an intolerance of alcohol and drug use.[38] In some cases of addiction the necessary change in culture can be brought about only by changes in regulations or legislation. For example, the general attitude towards smoking has changed only since legislation began to dictate that smoking in public places is not permissible or that cigarette packs and alcoholic beverages must contain health warnings. Education alone was not enough to alter perceptions about smoking.

The necessity of corporate cultural change, as opposed to mere education and counselling, was demonstrated by the introduction of random breathalysing of the workforce of a South African company as part of its substance-abuse policy. Within four months there was a dramatic reduction not only in the number of employees found to be in excess of the limit but also among those who were found to have small amounts of alcohol (below the limit) in their blood. This dramatic reduction has been sustained since then and has been seen to have affected the culture of drinking by employees.[39]

Drug testing by itself, however, has been found to be insufficient in reducing substance abuse or changing the prevailing substance-abuse culture. A comprehensive, integrated, multipronged focus should be used to address substance abuse in the workplace.

---

37 Skog, OJ 'Interpreting trends in alcohol consumption and alcohol related damage' (1988) 23(3) *Alcohol and Alcoholism* 193–202.

38 Marlatt, GA & Gordon, JR *Relapse Prevention: Maintenance Strategies in the Treatment of Addictive Behaviors* (1985) 11 and 353; Heather & Robertson *Problem Drinking: The New Approach* (1985) 223–224; Pidd, K *Work-related Alcohol and Drug Use: Key Issues and Interventions* Paper presented at Work-Related Alcohol and & Drug Use: A National Forum Conference, Flinders University, Adelaide (June 2006).

39 McCann, MG The Effect and Impact of Breath Analysis in a Workplace and the Development of Indicators to Identify Employees at Risk of Alcohol Abuse (MD thesis, Trinity College, Dublin, 1998).

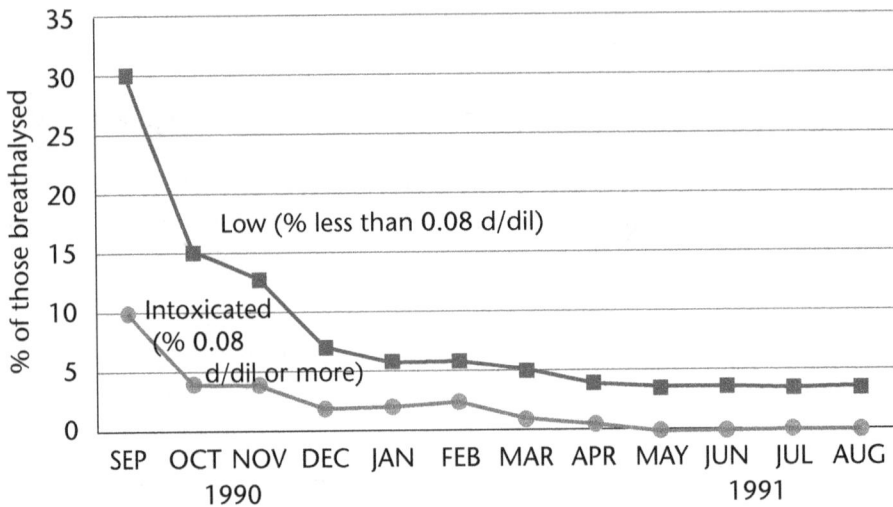

Figure 5.2 Reduction in number of employees identified with low and intoxicated levels of blood alcohol after random breathalysing over a period of one year.[40]

Management must pay more attention to the signals that the cultures of the company are giving, which are both formal and informal, and their influence on any proposed substance-abuse programme. The workplace is the ideal environment to influence and correct the cultures of substance abuse in the community to the benefit of both community and workplace. The workplace can lead and set the example for the development of an overall improved attitude towards substance abuse. On the other hand, a company does not want to become too puritanical. It needs to recognise that although drug abuse may not be tolerated, alcohol is a part of many lifestyles and cultures and that it is only those influences which induce problematic substance use that must be addressed and curtailed in order to create a healthier and more productive employee.

SUMMARY

Negative emotional states, interpersonal conflicts and social pressures are the main triggers of a dependent drinker's relapse. Anger and frustration have been shown to be important factors contributing to relapse. Stress at work and the transition period after the working day can be high-risk situations as regards substance abuse. Immediate gratification can be a powerful reinforcer to the detriment of one's behaviour pattern, and is furthered by cultural and peer-group pressures. Cultural and peer-group or social pressures are one of the main causes of substance-abuse problems in the workplace. The type and style of management in the workplace also plays a role.

Education alone is not enough; a change of culture is required and this can sometimes be brought about only by the introduction of regulation or legislation. Resistance to change is inevitably present, but that resistance must be defined and overcome.

---

40   Ibid.

Corporate cultures will influence employees' attitudes towards the abuse of licit and illicit substances in the workplace. Such cultures can be divided into formal and informal, and one will influence the other. Management often has an incorrect perception of what constitutes a substance-abuse problem. It also might not want to address the problem because of its wariness of the reaction from employees, possibly as management's approach would go against the prevailing culture. An authoritarian type of culture will have great difficulty in instituting a trusting, caring alcohol policy with worker participation.

Chapter 6

The Risk Assessment Approach: Managing Alcohol and Drug Misuse within the Organisation

Mike McCann & Nadine Harker Burnhams

1. INTRODUCTION

The misuse of alcohol and drugs presents several risks; not only to the users themselves but also to their co-workers, to the general public and to the organisation itself. In this chapter we focus on the risks posed to the organisation. We begin by defining *hazard, crisis, risk and risk perception, risk assessment* and *risk management* in the context of alcohol and drug problems. We then consider how the risks associated with alcohol and drug abuse manifest within an organisation and how these risks can be managed through the adoption of a risk assessment approach. The chapter also investigates the reasons why certain types of organisation are more at risk than others to the hazards of alcohol and drug misuse.

To manage alcohol and drug abuse effectively, organisations must understand the serious consequences that could result from failure to do so. Emotional or cultural sensitivities, stigma or ignorance can undermine an organisation's efforts to address problems of substance abuse; a situation made worse by the difficulties associated with identifying and evaluating the extent of an alcohol or drug problem. Despite these challenges it remains vitally important for an organisation to deal with problems of substance misuse. Intoxication, whether through alcohol or drug consumption, is the cause of many catastrophic events in the workplace, and these events can have extremely serious consequences for the well-being of an organisation.

Although the emphasis of this chapter is on alcohol, the approach for drugs is similar. The only real difference is that alcohol is a socially accepted and more frequently utilised substance, which makes it significantly more of a hazard in the context of risk assessment. The examples used are of alcohol related disasters because these have been major incidences that have had significant impact.

2. THE THEORY OF STRATEGIC FAILURE AND CATASTROPHE

Professor Denis Smith[1] in his chapter 'The dark side of excellence: managing strategic failures' used the sinking of the *Titanic* as an example of a failing organisation. He

---

1   Smith, D *The Dark Side of Excellence: Managing Strategic Failures. The Strategic Management Handbook* (1995) 161-191.

describes how the accumulation and interaction of small factors resulted in the calamity. He used 'the 7 Cs' to show how this took place:

Culture—officer of the watch failed to wake the captain; speeding was common operational practice as competing ships raced one another across the Atlantic;

Control—inability to take corrective action when the iceberg was sighted;

Communication—failure on the *Titanic* to heed warnings sent by other ships and failure on other ships to realise why the *Titanic* was sending up distress flares;

Configuration—intense rivalry between shipping companies seeking competitive edge at all costs;

Coupling and complexity—iceberg buckled the hull steel plates below the waterline;

Cost—single-hulled and inferior steel used in construction of the *Titanic* to save cost;

Contingency planning—too few lifeboats for passengers; six of the watertight compartments flooded despite the *Titanic* being considered unsinkable.[2]

> There are many factors which can lead to the demise of an organisation, and one of them could be an unrecognised or unacknowledged culture of alcohol or drug abuse

Denis Smith describes the failing organisation to be one with a crisis that is incubating but that will eventually erupt in a catastrophic event. He describes how failure due to human causes has risen from 20% in the 1960s to 80% in the 1990s—if we extrapolate this to the recent economic downturn in the world economies, we can begin to appreciate the scale of damage attributable to human action or inaction. Smith comments that the implementation of today's sophisticated technology is still subject to the limitations of human thought and behaviour and the flaws that form an intrinsic part of our nature.

It therefore remains the responsibility of management to ensure that alcohol- and drug-related problems are treated seriously; if they are not, the consequences in terms of lost or damaged resources (time, money, people), can be severe, even catastrophic. Neglect of such problems results in a serious risk to an organisation.

3. THE RISK ASSESSMENT APPROACH

The employer, the employee and the public may have different perceptions of risk. If firm policies and procedures are to be developed and implemented to deal with the hazards associated with an organisation's business operations, it is essential for both employer and employee to be aware of the magnitude of the risk resulting from a failure to do so. Smith and Toft describe how 'it is only in the wake of tragedy that organizations seem to accept the nature of the hazard ... Unless we have an event to anchor our concerns, it is often difficult to accept that the worst could happen and that the probability of one in a million does not mean that the event will not occur tomorrow!'[3] It is likewise our opinion that the hazard of alcohol abuse will only be considered in an organisation when a risk evaluation has been made or when some serious or catastrophic event which is attributable to alcohol is identified. For this reason it is important to consider the influence alcohol-related problems can have on the development of risk in an organisation.

---

2   Smith (n 1) at 161–191.
3   Smith, D and Toft, B 'Risk and Crisis Management in the Public Sector' in Public Money & Management October 1998 pp 7-10.

3.1 Hazard and risk

The terms *hazard* and *risk* are defined and interpreted according to the context in which they operate. An environmental hazard is very different to an economic hazard, for example; and both of these are distinguishable from a safety hazard. But while these three hazard types may seem unrelated, at least in some respects, it is clear that alcohol abuse can impact in all three areas. Smith and Calman[4] stated that one of the problems found in the field of risk and crisis management is that there are no general, publicly agreed upon definitions for much of the terminology used. This is particularly so with the definition of hazard, which can refer to some perceptible physical danger, such as a tripping hazard on a factory floor, or to something more abstract, such as the financial risk companies face when venturing into new markets.

3.2 Risk perception

Risk perception can be considered from the viewpoint of the employer and the employees and from the viewpoint of the public. If the employer and the employees do not recognise that a risk exists then it is unlikely that any significant policy or procedures relating to risk management exist. The risk may be substantial but the perception of risk by employers and employees may be different. The public generally becomes aware of risk in the aftermath of an environmental catastrophe or some other devastating event. In the next section we use the Exxon Valdez oil spill of 1989 and the New York subway crash of 1991 to illustrate several points regarding the issue of risk perception.

The Health and Safety Executive (UK)[5] considers *hazard* to be something with the potential to cause harm, while *risk* is the likelihood that the harm from a particular hazard will come about. *Risk* reflects both the likelihood that harm will occur and its severity. A *risk assessment* refers to the identification of the hazards present in any undertaking (whether arising from work activities or from other factors, such as the layout of the premises) and then assessing the risks involved, taking into account whatever precautions are already in place.

3.3 Risk estimation and risk evaluation

Risk assessment (see Figure 6.1) is subdivided into *risk estimation* and *risk evaluation*. *Risk estimation* includes the identification of things that may go wrong, an estimation of how likely it is that they will, and the magnitude of the consequences if they do. *Risk evaluation* looks at the economic and social impact as well as the public perception of negative events, which can be very damaging to the organisation.

The Exxon Valdez oil spillage of 24 March 1989 perfectly illustrates the dangers of failing to undertake risk estimation and risk evaluation. Put another way, the *Valdez* incident is a prime example of what we wish to portray as an incubating crisis about to become a catastrophe. The vessel spilled approximately 41 million cubic metres of crude oil into the sea off the coast of Alaska, which eventually covered 3,400 square

---

4   Calman, K and Smith, D 'Works in theory but not in practice? Some notes on the precautionary principle' (1998) 4 (1) *Industrial Crisis Quarterly* 1-26.

5   Health and Safety Commission, Management of health and safety at work, HMSO. 1992.

kilometres of ocean (Trustee Council, 2009).[6] The *Valdez* incident was one of the most devastating environmental disasters ever to occur at sea as a result of human error.

Employer and employee perceptions and education (or more precisely, lack of education) around alcohol issues were critical to the development of the crisis. The Exxon Corporation did have an alcohol and drug policy, but it was not implemented effectively. In the subsequent investigation it emerged that the master of the *Valdez* had a history of alcohol abuse. The National Transportation Safety Board (NTSB), based in Washington DC, wrote to the chairman of the Exxon Corporation to express its concern at the lack of guidance given to Exxon employees on the dangers of alcohol misuse.

> *The master failed to provide an effective navigation watch, possibly due to impairment under the influence of alcohol or the fact he was sleeping it off below. The master was known to have a dependency problem and had been previously hospitalised for the problem. His superior was unaware of the alcohol dependency until after he had been hospitalised but no records were kept or referral to the Exxon Medical Department after this hospitalisation. There was therefore no indication that the treatment was successful. The lack of records suggests that no guidance, advice, or information was provided by Exxon Management to the Exxon Medical Department [or] to the master's supervisor. Furthermore, no one in the Exxon management structure seems to have consulted an expert on alcoholism about the following issues:*
> 1. *The kind of support the master would need when he resumed work.*
> 2. *The kind of supervision and monitoring he would need.*
> 3. *The chances he would resume drinking.*

The NTSB suggested that the Exxon Corporate Management demonstrated inadequate knowledge of and concern about the seriousness of having an alcohol-impaired master. The Board finally concluded that Exxon should have removed the master from the seagoing employment until there was ample proof that he had his alcohol problem under control.[7]

The economic and social impact of such an event is also apparent from the New York subway train crash of August 1991, when the driver was severely intoxicated with alcohol and five people were killed, some 200 seriously injured and the central part of the New York subway closed for a week.[8]

Risk estimation and risk evaluation are both required for an overall assessment. It includes the study of risk perception and the likely trade-off between perceived risks and perceived benefits. The trade-offs will be different depending on whose perspective is being examined. The drinking employee will have the largest trade-off, whereas the manager may have less concern for benefits. This is important for the

---

6   History of the spill Exxon Valdez Oil Spill Trustee Council http://en.wikipedia.org/wiki/Exxon_Valdez_oil_spill (accessed 26 May 2009).

7   USA National Transportation Safety Board. Safety Recommendation dated 18 September 1990 addressed to the Chairman of the Board Exxon Corporation.

8   Service on the Lexington Avenue IRT was disrupted for six days as transit workers toiled around the clock to clean up the wreckage. The motorman, Robert Ray, who was drunk and doing more than 40 mph when the speed limit was 10 mph, was later convicted of manslaughter and sentenced to 15 years in prison. It was the worst subway accident in 63 years.

impact of identifying alcohol problems in an organisation and will be discussed later. Risk management flows from risk estimation and evaluation and is the process of making decisions concerning risks and their implementation.[9]

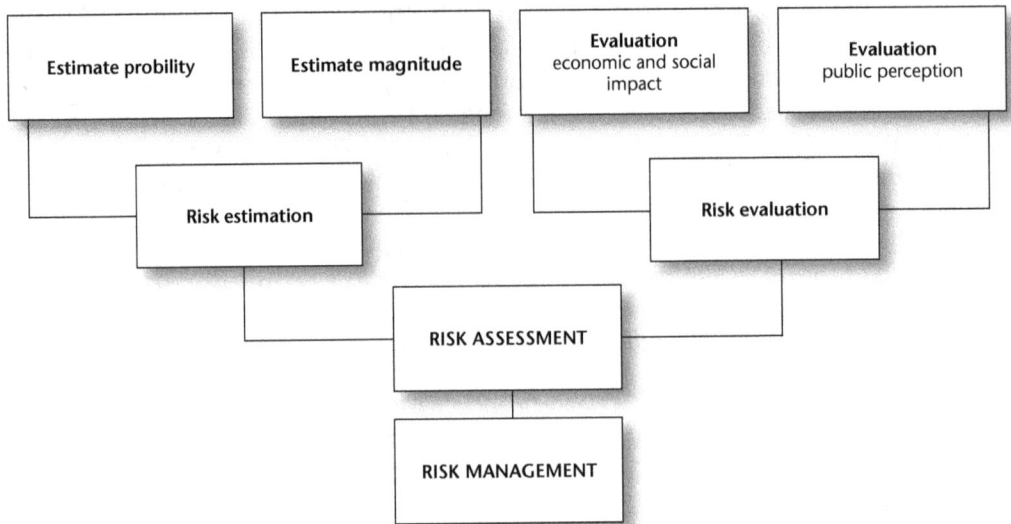

Figure 6.1 Flow chart of risk assessment [adapted from Royal Society (1997) 32].

3.4 The impact of crisis

Crisis is a complex phenomenon and a term that changes meaning according to specific circumstances and contexts. For an organisation, a crisis is something that threatens its integrity and strategic aims. A crisis can lead to a disaster, often with implications extending beyond the organisation itself. It can affect other organisations within its sphere of influence, or have implications for the wider community. The repercussions of the crisis can eventually destroy the organisation.

But despite the very real threat a crisis poses to an organisation's viability, it is often something that is left unconsidered by management. There are reasons why this is so. Firstly, there is the problem of making sense of a crisis. When something happens that is implausible or out of the ordinary, people may hesitate to report it for fear they will not be believed. Secondly, the fact that drinking alcohol (in moderation) is a widespread socially acceptable phenomenon, compromises management's ability to deal with a situation of alcohol abuse among employees. Management may be reluctant to confront employees who have a drinking problem in case this antagonises them, which may in turn lead to a worsening of management–employee relations and a possible downturn in productivity. Thirdly, denial and complacency characterise many organisations' attitude towards alcohol abuse in the workplace, which often leads to a failure to detect the warning signs. (This is an issue we explore more thoroughly in chapter 5.)

Thus, when a crisis occurs, it is associated with managerial failure, and the need to find a scapegoat arises.[10]

---

9   Royal Society, 1992 p 3.
10   Greiner, L 'Evolution and revolution as organisations grow' *Harvard Business Review* (1972).

4. HUMAN FAILURE AND THE INCUBATING CRISIS

As a result of the power of modern technology, many human activities have greater potential for damage today than at any other time in our history. As mentioned earlier in the chapter, the incidence of failure attributable to human error has risen from an estimated 20% in the 1960s to 80% in the 1990s.[11] The reason lies in the increasing complexity of our organisational as well as our technical systems.[12] Combined with the hazard of intoxication, this can have catastrophic consequences, as demonstrated by the Exxon Valdez incident, in which alcohol abuse is alleged to have played a part.[13]

Alcohol problems in an organisation could therefore be considered a symptom of other, more deep-rooted organisational problems that may have been festering prior to the disaster, perhaps for some time. It is often the accumulation of small factors and their interaction that results in the calamity.[14]

5. RISK ASSESSMENT AT THE LEVEL OF THE INDIVIDUAL EMPLOYEE AND OF THE ORGANISATION

In the process of risk assessment, alcohol-related problems can be examined at two levels. The first level is that of the individual employee and the impact that an alcohol problem can have on his or her health and productivity and on the health and safety of others. The second is the organisational level and the possible impact alcohol problems may have on the viability of the strategic management and even the very survival of the organisation.

6. THE PROBABILITY AND MAGNITUDE OF THE PROBLEM

The probability and magnitude of alcohol problems as a hazard in an organisation depends on the type and structure of the organisation and the estimate of the likelihood of there being a risk. Inevitably the alcohol problems will be incubating at the operational level. In some organisations there may be an embedded drinking culture among employees. A drink problem at the operational level can adversely affect the health and productivity of individual employees; it can also jeopardise the health and safety of others since impairment or intoxication increases the risk of workplace accidents.

Although the hazard can be identified as being significant at the individual level it does not necessarily qualify as a risk to the organisation. An employee with a drink problem may not necessarily present an immediate risk to the organisation if he or she has a high tolerance to alcohol. Being less susceptible to alcohol may allow such an employee to function at an acceptable level during his or her working day or shift, and to do so for some time (perhaps for months or even years). But we must stress that this does not mean that a 'problem' employee presents *no threat at all* to the organisation since this is clearly not the case. All instances of alcohol misuse have the potential to endanger organisational performance and cannot be ignored or dismissed as trivial by management. While it may be true that certain types of organisation may be more at

---

11 Hollnagel, E *Human Reliability Analysis: Context and Control* (1993).

12 Smith, D *On a wing and a prayer? Exploring the human components of technological failure* Centre for Risk and Crisis Management (1997) University of Durham.

13 Smith, D 'Exploring the myth: The sinking of the Titanic: A Review essay' (1994) 8 (3) *Industrial and Environmental Crisis Quarterly* 22-26.

14 Smith 'Exploring the myth: The sinking of the Titanic: A Review essay' 161–191.

risk than others (see below), it cannot be said that any organisation is entirely 'risk free' in the context of alcohol abuse among employees.

7. 'AT RISK' ORGANISATIONS

The types of organisations that are especially vulnerable to the damage created by alcohol abuse are listed below. In these organisations, persistent alcohol abuse among employees is likely to incubate a crisis, which could in turn erupt in a catastrophic event that causes severe or sometimes irreparable harm to the organisation itself, as well as to entities within its sphere of influence. 'At risk' organisations include those operating within the following sectors:

- transport of toxic or explosive chemicals by road, rail, sea or air
- public transport by road, rail, sea or air
- manufacture of dangerous substances or by-products or the utilisation of dangerous substances in manufacturing
- construction and engineering industry
- financial institutions
- communication and information technology
- pleasure, sport and tourism
- breweries and distilleries
- offshore oil and refining industry
- security personnel
- nuclear industry
- mining industry.

8. TYPES OF HAZARD

From the heterogeneous list above it is clear that the types of hazards linked to alcohol abuse will be similarly varied. However, it is still possible to separate these hazards into several distinct categories, as shown below.

8.1 Environmental hazards

As we discussed in relation to the Exxon Valdez disaster, when alcohol misuse is wholly or partly responsible for damage to the environment the damage caused is usually extensive (see page 66–67).

8.2 Hazards to the general public

Members of the general public, communities and even entire regions can be affected as a result of alcohol misuse by employees. The New York subway disaster of 1991, discussed above, was the direct result of alcohol abuse on the part of the train driver and the subsequent fatalities and injuries among the general public. As well as these health and safety hazards, the potential for economic loss also arises in these circumstances— the week-long closure of a section of the New York subway system following the 1991 accident was a blow to the local businesses that relied upon the income derived from subway commuters.

8.3 Hazards to the employee

Intoxicated or impaired employees are a danger to themselves and to others. The main concern is that an employee under the influence of alcohol will hurt him- or herself or another person. An impaired or intoxicated employee usually exhibits slower reaction times, poor eye-hand coordination, increased risk-taking behaviour and a reduced decision-making ability. Any one of these factors, or a combination of several, could create the necessary conditions for a workplace accident or incident to arise.

We can also note that certain occupations present more opportunities for alcohol consumption and thus abuse; marketing personnel who travel and entertain extensively would qualify in this respect.[15] Another 'at risk' class of employees would be migrant workers; in this case the misuse of alcohol is often prompted by feelings of anxiety and loneliness at being separated from their families.

8.4 Hazards to the employer

Productivity suffers in organisations where an alcohol problem exists. In a factory setting, this loss can be measured in terms of delays in production, poorer quality control, an increased incidence of machine breakdown, incorrect order processing, and so on. But financial loss can also be the result of poor decision-making at a higher level, where alcohol-impaired managers mistakenly choose a course of action that destabilises the economic security of the organisation. Employers are often held liable for third-party injury, loss or damage caused by the behaviour of intoxicated or impaired employees. Insuring against this possibility is an option but the cost of doing so can still be regarded as a hazard. (Please refer to chapter 2 for further information on the financial losses stemming from alcohol abuse.)

9. THE INFLUENCE OF THE ORGANISATION ON ALCOHOL USE AND ABUSE

9.1 Organisational culture

The causes of the problem of alcohol abuse in an organisation can be encouraged at the organisational level by corporate entertaining, in-house drinking facilities and inadequate recreational facilities when employees are separated from their home environment. Organisational social events very often include alcohol as part of the occasion. End-of-year parties, team-building getaways, corporate functions, and so on, give employees the opportunity to consume alcohol in large amounts. The same observation can be made about companies that have on-site bar facilities.

9.2 Peer group pressure

At the operational level, peer group pressure may strongly influence an individual employee's decision to participate in drinking practices that he or she would otherwise have avoided. This pressure may be exerted explicitly (repeated invitations to attend lunchtime or after-hours drinking sessions, for example) or implicitly (the resisting employee risks losing the friendship and trust of his or her co-workers). Stress-related drinking behaviour is a further 'on-the-job' danger many employees confront.

9.3 Supervision

Poor supervision is often a factor in organisations where alcohol abuse by employees exists. Supervisors are often reluctant to challenge employees they believe to have a

---

15   Albertyn, C and McCann, M *Alcohol, Employment and Fair Labour Practice* (1993).

drink problem in case this alienates or antagonises the workforce. In organisations where a strong drink culture exists, the supervisor's position is compromised even further.

Direct supervision of employees is made more difficult in situations where a significant volume of work is performed off-site, where employees move in and out of the workplace or around the workplace, when there is distant supervision, and at times when reduced or no supervision of employees can be expected (night shifts, for example). An organisation that uses contractors and sub-contractors ostensibly supervises these workers indirectly, though in practice this rarely occurs.

10. THE INFLUENCE OF THE ALCOHOL INDUSTRY

Organisations involved in the production, distribution and sale of alcohol are obviously exposed to the risk of alcohol abuse by their employees. Breweries, public houses, hotels, restaurants, farms and wine estates are sites where such abuse can be anticipated.

The alcohol industry is well known for its sponsorship of various sports—cricket, rugby, football, motor racing, and so on. Organisations linked to these sponsorship activities (for example, corporate hospitality companies, catering firms and advertising agencies) need to be aware of the risks their employees face when working in such proximity to large supplies of alcohol.

11. THE INFLUENCE OF GEOGRAPHIC LOCATION AND CULTURAL GROUPINGS

The use and abuse of alcohol, as well as attitudes towards its consumption can be differentiated by geographical location. In some countries, alcohol is prohibited (Saudi Arabia, Kuwait, and Afghanistan, for example), and even within countries and regions where alcohol is not prohibited, consumption patterns vary. Certain cultural groups— Sikhs, Muslims and Brahmins, to name but three—avoid alcohol and their members can be found across the globe. For organisations with a displaced workforce, the need to take into account the individual local community's attitudes towards alcohol is paramount.

12. THE INFLUENCE OF THE COMMUNITY ON ALCOHOL USE AND ABUSE

The local community's attitudes towards alcohol consumption and abuse have a direct bearing on how alcohol is perceived, used and misused in the workplace. If the community has a thriving drinking culture it is very likely that the businesses within that community will display a high acceptance of alcohol at work.

It is also true however, that community concerns regarding alcohol abuse can influence organisational culture in this respect. Many communities today are troubled by the incidence of alcohol abuse among young female members of the population. This phenomenon can largely be explained by the increasing number of young women who form part of the workforce. Many of these women stay single for longer, pursue careers that generate an above-average disposable income, and spend a significant amount of their leisure time consuming alcohol, often to excess, in a variety of social settings. This state of affairs has led to a progressive increase in the number of young women addicted to or dependent on alcohol as well as an increase in alcohol-related organic damage in this social group.

13. THE INFLUENCE OF LEGISLATION ON ALCOHOL USE AND ABUSE

The impact of prescriptive legislation in changing the culture of drinking in the community must be considered. If this legislation is enforced it can impact on the culture of drinking considerably. This has been seen in the UK with the change of drinking habits due to drinking and driving legislation.[16] Similarly, through an amendment of the 2008 Western Cape Liquor Act, the province now limits on-site and off-site consumption sales of alcohol. Furthermore, trading of alcohol on a Sunday is prohibited, and there is a restriction on the on-site consumption sales of alcohol in outlets operating in residential areas. Legislative changes of this nature help to reduce alcohol consumption and the prevalence of alcohol-related harm.[17]

13.1 Factors associated with high risk drinking

The factors associated with a high risk of excessive drinking are:
1   availability of alcohol
2   social pressures to drink
3   segregation from normal social or sexual relationships
4   freedom from supervision
5   very high or very low income
6   collusion by colleagues
7   strains, stresses and hazards
8   pre-selection of high risk people.[18]

It is clear that in practically all occupations at least some of the factors listed above will be present.

Our focus so far has been on risk assessment, which refers to the need to identify the types of hazards associated with alcohol abuse, how probable it is that these hazards will materialise and the consequences involved. We now turn our attention to risk evaluation, which refers to an appraisal of the costs resulting from alcohol abuse in the workplace.

14. RISK EVALUATION: ASSESSING THE IMPACT OF ALCOHOL ABUSE

It is difficult to express risk evaluation in monetary terms, especially when this relates to the effect alcohol abuse may have on society and what the public's likely reaction will be to an alcohol-related accident or incident. Despite this difficulty, risk evaluation remains a necessary exercise and is often critical to the post-crisis state of the organisation and its long-term viability. To illustrate this point we can look at what happened in the wake of the Bhopal disaster of December 1984, where a gas leak at a chemical plant in Bhopal, India, left more than 3 000 people dead and many thousands more injured. The tragedy caused a public outcry regarding the substandard operating practices of Union Carbide Corporation, the plant's owner. Public pressure eventually forced the company to abandon its plan to build a chemical plant in Scotland. Union Carbide was also

---

16   Albertyn & McCann (n 15).
17   Parry, C 'Curbs on Drinking Limits Harm' in McNiell, A (ed) (2010) 3 *The Globe* at 18.
18   Plant, MA 'Risk Factors in Employment' in Hore, BD & Plant, MA (eds) *Alcohol Problems in Employment* (1981) 32.

subject to a hostile take-over bid, though this did not materialise.[19] Although alcohol was not cited as a cause of the accident, the Bhopal incident is included here to show how the public's reaction to an adverse event can to a greater or lesser extent determine the fate of a transgressing organisation.

An organisation affected by alcohol abuse among employees is likely to incur a number of different costs. We can classify these costs under three headings:

1   costs of alcohol-related incidences
2   costs of alcohol-problem employees
3   relationship costs.

14.1 Costs of alcohol-related incidents

- public liability and third party compensation claims
- damage to organisation's public image and reputation, especially if exposed via press and other media
- asset repair and replacement
- increase in insurance premiums.

14.2 Costs of employees with alcohol problem

- sickness absence downtime
- retirement through ill health
- temporary staff cover
- poor productivity, including drop in quality standards
- injury to employees with alcohol problem, other employees, or members of the public.

14.3 Relationship costs

- unacceptable or inappropriate behaviour that affects other employees, customers, suppliers and members of the public
- damage to employer-employee relationship caused by formal or informal culture of alcohol use
- damage to organisational objectives caused by formal or informal culture of alcohol use
- damage to employer-trade union relations caused by formal or informal culture of alcohol use, most noticeably in situations where the trade union acts on behalf of an employee facing disciplinary action for alleged alcohol abuse.

14.3.1 A worked example using the New York subway crash of 1991

A train driver (motorman) employed on the New York subway system must report to the supervisor (dispatcher) and sign an attendance sheet before taking the train out. The supervisor is required to observe the operator to ensure that he or she is fit for duty—bloodshot eyes, impaired speech, and signs of drug or alcohol use are sufficient grounds for ruling the driver unfit for duty. Improper dress would also disqualify. Mr Ray (the motorman) was wearing tennis shoes when he reported for duty on 28 August 1991; this was unacceptable since he should have been wearing safety shoes. The supervisor must

---

19   Smith, D 'Corporate power and the politics of uncertainty' (1990) 4 *Industrial Crisis Quarterly* 1-26.

report an employee unfit for duty; failure to do will result in disciplinary action. On this occasion the supervisor took no action. Furthermore, a code of silence prevailed among employees regarding the issue of on-the-job drinking. Many drivers acknowledged that they knew of colleagues who drank before or even during working hours; however, they also maintained that reporting on these individuals was regarded as an act of betrayal. In this case it was common knowledge that Mr Ray drank on the job. Alcohol had been smelt on his breath before.

On this particular journey Mr Ray overshot the first station, coming to stop with the first five carriages lodged in the tunnel beyond the end of the platform. The conductor radioed the driver to ask what was going on but received no coherent reply. At the second station Mr Ray overshot the platform again—by one carriage. The conductor again asked the driver if he was alright, to which Mr Ray replied 'I'm okay'. Coming to the next station, Mr Ray drove extremely cautiously and took a considerable time to bring the train alongside the platform. When the conductor admonished him, Mr Ray started speeding up. The conductor warned him that he was now driving too fast. Although the danger was growing rapidly no one took any action—neither the conductor nor one of the 500 passengers pressed the emergency button. In a crisis situation the conductor can also ask the command station to switch off power on the line, but this was not done on this occasion.

Mr Ray then fell asleep at the controls at a point where the train was to switch tracks. It should have been travelling at 10 mph (16 kph) but at this instant it was travelling at four times this speed. Safety devices on the track to slow a speeding train were antiquated and for other braking systems the train was travelling too fast for them to trigger a response. The train derailed killing five passengers and seriously injuring 200 others.

From this brief summary of the events leading up to the crash it is clear that this was an incubating crisis with the potential to erupt into a catastrophic event. We can use Denis Smith's analysis of a failing organisation to describe what went wrong. Smith's contention is that calamities arise out of the accumulation and combination of several smaller problems or factors—the '7 Cs' we looked at earlier in the chapter. Using the 7 Cs typology we can analyse the New York subway crash of August 1991 in terms of the following:

Culture—the code of silence amongst peers about drinking on the job and the stigma attached to reporting intoxication

Control—lack of effective assessment on the part of the supervisor, which, if it had been performed, would have stopped Mr Ray entering and starting the train

Communication—failure of the conductor to radio the command station to stop the train

Configuration—lack of objective processes to identify alcohol intoxication; existing system based on supervisor's subjective assessment of condition of operator, which was strongly influenced by culture and stigma

Coupling and complexity—speed of the train as it jumped tracks and the human frailty of a driver with an alcohol abuse problem and who was responsible for the lives of hundreds of people

Cost—antiquated braking system; other systems unable to cope with trains travelling at high speed

Contingency planning—lack of CCTV monitoring of train drivers' behaviour and actions; no objective means of assessing intoxication among employees; need for annual medical appraisal of drivers and this to include stringent test(s) of their fitness to operate trains.

Despite the several weaknesses this analysis reveals, the probability of the disaster happening would most likely have been low if a risk assessment had been conducted. However, the same risk assessment would also have concluded that *if* an accident were to occur, the consequences would be extremely serious. The New York subway accident also had a significant social and economic impact, which our retrospective risk evaluation has shown. Public perception of the risk was most probably low *before* the accident, but high *after* it.

15. RISK MANAGEMENT

Having considered the two stages of risk assessment (risk estimation and risk evaluation), it is now time to look at the final stage: *risk management.*

An organisation engages in risk management when it attempts to eliminate or reduce the risks associated with a particular hazard or hazards. Risk management of the hazards associated with alcohol misuse in the workplace involves the following:

1   education
2   policy implementation
3   the introduction of procedures and protocols
4   constructive persuasion.

15.1 Education

The education of the workforce regarding the dangers of alcohol abuse consists of two elements. The first element concerns the education of employees at the policy-making level of the organisation, typically senior management and trade union figures; who will lead any forthcoming 'anti-alcohol' initiatives and will need to understand the potentially disastrous impact alcohol abuse can have on the long-term health of the organisation and its workforce. The advantages and complications of the objective and the subjective methods of identifying alcohol misuse also need to form part of the education programme.

The second element refers to the education of the remaining groups or levels of employees, where the focus should be on the risks to personal health that alcohol abuse presents and the counselling, treatment and disciplinary procedures the organisation intends implementing.

The separation of employees into two distinct groups (in simplistic terms, 'executive' and 'non-executive') is understandable if we accept that the information needs of each group are not identical. Senior management and trade union officials require a solid grounding in all aspects of alcohol misuse and abuse if they are to help the organisation achieve its goals and to maintain the health and well-being of the workforce. Because of this their information needs are likely to be greater than the remainder of the workforce, for whom information on how alcohol abuse affects them *personally* is of primary importance.

It is important to note that while the complexity of information delivered to staff may be differentiated according to the level at which they operate, the fundamental facts concerning alcohol abuse and the organisation's policy regarding alcohol abuse in the workplace apply to, and should be communicated to, all members of the workforce. There is very often a huge difference of opinion among employees regarding what constitutes alcohol abuse. Explicit, precise guidelines on the issue will go a long way towards rectifying the confusion and misunderstandings caused by these differing perceptions.

The education process needs to be in a participative format so that employees will be encouraged to share their experiences of and attitudes towards alcohol use and misuse. Employees with an alcohol problem need to know that they can voice their concerns in a sympathetic, supportive environment. The overall aim of the education process is to change any inappropriate or damaging behaviour or attitudes that may exist and to convince all employees of the value of maintaining a balanced approach towards alcohol consumption, and this can only be achieved if the beliefs, values, thoughts and experiences of all employees are solicited. This information will be used during the policy implementation stage of the risk management process, which we consider in the following section.

15.2 Policy implementation

An organisation's policy on alcohol misuse should reflect the views of all its employees, so far as this is possible and provided that these views are not contrary to any statutory requirements. The facilitator of the education process will bring the knowledge that he or she has gained from the sensitisation of both employee groups. Senior management and trade union representatives use this and all other relevant information to construct a policy statement.

15.2.1 Policy statement

The policy statement regarding the consumption, misuse and abuse of alcohol should address the following issues:
- *reason(s) for the introduction of the policy*—compliance with relevant legislation; history of alcohol abuse in the organisation; the potential severity of alcohol-related damage or loss (to employees, to the organisation, to the public and to the environment)
- *role of the organisation*—attitude of organisation towards alcohol abuse in the workplace (caring yet firm, ideally); services offered to alcohol-dependant employees; disciplinary procedures and sanctions
- *definition of 'intoxication'*—the level of alcohol required and why this level has been chosen
- *description of the testing techniques used*—objective and scientific; direct testing and confidential indirect testing.

15.3 Procedures and protocols

The need for sound procedures and protocols in respect of acceptable and unacceptable alcohol use, testing for intoxication, disciplinary processes, and so on, is paramount. For comprehensive coverage of this topic please see end of chapters 5, 6, 12–15, 18, 20, as well as Appendices 1, 2, 4 and 8.

15.4 Constructive persuasion

Denial—the reluctance to admit that a problem exists—is common among alcohol-dependent or addicted employees, which is why a degree of constructive persuasion may be appropriate.

Constructive persuasion is a means of securing employee commitment to organisational objectives (see chapter 15 Treatment of the Organisation for more on this subject). In terms of an organisation's policy on alcohol abuse, the purpose of constructive persuasion is to get employees to 'buy into' the employer's objective of maintaining a safe workplace environment. The employer can achieve this by highlighting the dangers associated with alcohol abuse—injury to self and others, damage to company property, loss of productivity, and so on—but also by making it clear that such abuse will not go unexplored or unpunished. In other words, the employees should be made to understand that job security is dependent on adhering to the company's alcohol (and drug) policy and that this may include submitting to treatment or counselling in the case of alcohol-dependent employees. This should be written into the contract of employment or a separate contract provided to the alcohol dependant employee to commit to treatment and testing.

We can note here that the term 'constructive coercion' can be used to describe the same process. However, the fact that 'coercion' is often associated with intimidatory or threatening behaviour explains why many employers today choose to use the more neutral-sounding 'persuasion'. ('Constructive confrontation' has also fallen out of favour for much the same reason.)

SUMMARY

A risk assessment approach to alcohol and drug misuse is seldom considered by organisations when they do a corporate risk assessment; nor is it included in a corporate hazard strategy. Yet experience tells us that even some large organisations have been involved in a major crisis when ignoring the implications of alcohol and drug abuse. Human failure will always be with us and it is important to consider the consequences of that failure on not only the individual but also other employees, members of the public, the environment and the organisation itself.

This chapter provided an overview of the process an organisation engages in when it seeks to identify, assess and manage the risks associated with the misuse of alcohol and drugs in the workplace.

Chapter 7

The Effects of Alcohol on the Individual

Mike McCann & Nadine Harker Burnhams

This chapter is divided into three sections:
I   Accidents and safety
II Health of the individual
III Effects of alcohol in the working environment.

I ACCIDENTS AND SAFETY

1. INTRODUCTION

Most of the research into alcohol, accidents and safety has been connected to the issue of alcohol and drug abuse when driving. This research is both experimental and epidemiological and often of a good quality. There is no reason why we should not use this research for exploring the issue of the impact of alcohol and drugs in the workplace. While some of the research studies referred to are relatively 'old', their pioneering quality and their explanation of fundamental principles ensures their continued relevance today.

2. THE RELATIONSHIP BETWEEN ALCOHOL CONSUMPTION AND ACCIDENTS

A historical study done in Czechoslovakia in 1960 showed the relationship between the blood-alcohol level of an individual and the probability of him or her having an accident; in this case, a motor vehicle accident (MVA) (see Figure 7.1).[1]

Figure 7.1 shows the relationship between a progressively increasing blood-alcohol level and the risk of having an accident (specifically, a MVA). The figure shows that a blood-alcohol level of 80 mg/100 ml (or 0,08 g%) produces the risk of an accident occurring four times greater than the risk associated with a zero (0) blood-alcohol level. The risk increases as the blood-alcohol level rises; climbing steeply so that by 150 mg/100 ml (0,15 g%), the probability of an accident occurring is 23 times greater than the chance of an accident happening at a zero blood-alcohol level.

A survey performed in 1962 and 1963 in Grand Rapids, USA, produced a similar picture. Here researchers differentiated between those more experienced as drinkers and those less experienced.[2]

As can be seen from Figure 7.2, the two groups (less-experienced drinkers; experienced drinkers) display differing characteristics. Those highly susceptible to alcohol ('Group A'

---

1   Denney, RC *Drinking and Driving* (1979).
2   Borkenstein, RF, Crowther, RF, Shumate, RP, Zeil, WB & Zylman, R 'The role of the drinking driver in traffic accidents: the Grand Rapids study' 1974 (11) *Blutalkoholl* 1-132.

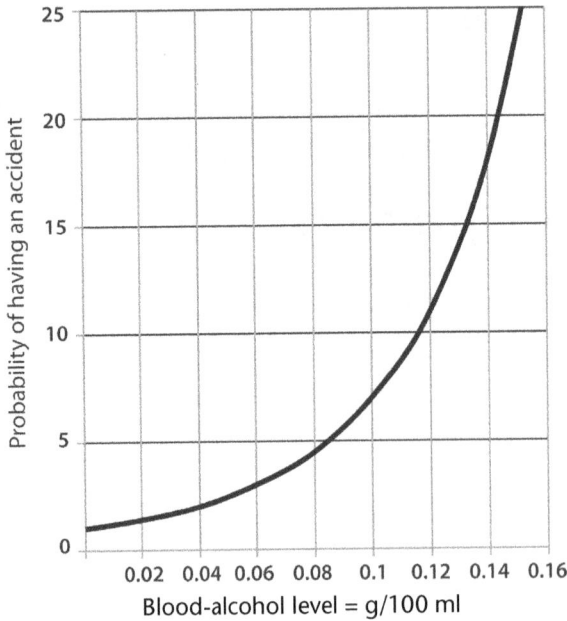

Figure 7.1 Relationship between MVA accident proneness and blood-alcohol levels

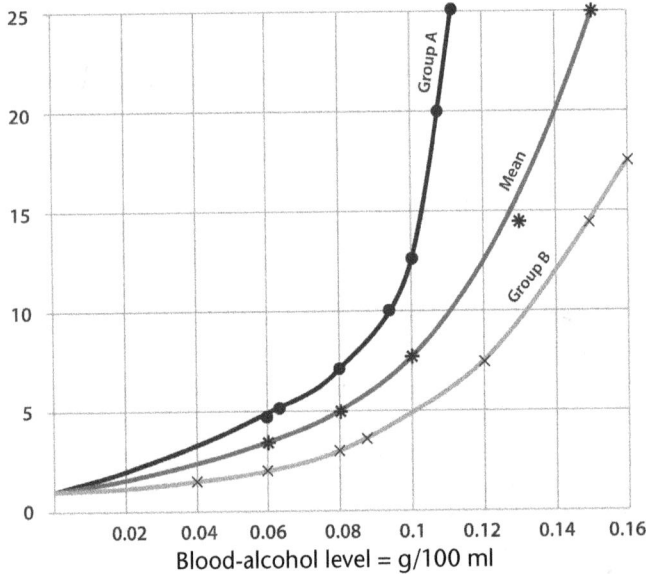

Figure 7.2 Relative probability of causing an accident

on the graph) are six times more likely to have an accident at 80 mg/100 ml (0,08 g%), while those less susceptible to alcohol ('Group B' on the graph) are likely to experience a fivefold increase in accidents at a blood-alcohol level of 100 mg/100 ml (0,10 g%).

Yet care must be taken when interpreting these figures. For example, the regular consumption of alcohol increases alcohol tolerance, which means that the hardened drinker is less likely to display the effects of alcohol, or more likely to mask these effects, despite drinking more than the less-experienced drinker. However, this 'masking' also means that the hardened drinker is more liable to have a much higher blood-alcohol level than the legal limit of 0,08 g%; a fact borne out by the UK Department of Transport's study of road traffic accident deaths, which found that two-thirds of driver fatalities showed blood-alcohol levels in excess of 150 mg/100 ml (0,15 g%).[3]

These studies, although perhaps now rather dated, are still used to highlight the importance of two key factors—the blood-alcohol level and individual susceptibility to the effects of alcohol. The first two studies are referred to as pioneering early studies.[4]

2.1 Blood-alcohol levels and individual susceptibility to the effects of alcohol

Analysing a series of breathalyser tests done at a factory gate, the present author found that, of the readings identified as 'intoxicated' (above 0,079 g %), 73,7 % were 0,1 g % and over, and 28,8 % were 0,15 g% and over.[5]

The Grand Rapids study data was revisited using more sophisticated statistical methods and revealed further information. Hurst, in 1973, identified from the Grand Rapids data, that daily drinkers have the lowest accident rate compared to weekly, monthly, or yearly drinkers. The youngest and oldest drivers, who tend not to drink daily, have higher crash rates than the 25–55 year olds who might be drinking daily. Once the variable of drinking frequency was controlled for, the probability of involvement in collisions increases with any departure from zero blood-alcohol concentration (BAC) and the rate of increase is greatest for the least frequent drinkers. Because of this the J-shaped curve of the Grand Rapid study is changed at the end of the curve.[6] Theoretically, it could be argued that a blood-alcohol level of 0,10 g% (100 mg/100 ml) would be a fairer figure to use in an assessment of intoxication in hardened drinkers. However, for individuals just beginning to drink alcohol and/or those who periodically drink heavily, the 0,10% level would be detrimental, since their susceptibility to the effects of alcohol is likely to be high. As yet there is no objective way of identifying the alcohol tolerance level of an individual.

A 1976 report on drinking and driving, published by the Blennerhausset Committee for the UK, produced similar results to the first study and recommended that the legal limit for driving should remain at 0,08 g% or 80 mg/100 ml.[7]

A blood alcohol concentration (BAC) limit of 80 mg/100 ml (0,08 g%) has for some time been accepted by many countries as the standard measure for determining what constitutes an acceptable blood-alcohol level. However, more recent research suggests that the international community may need to review its approval of the 0,08 g% measure, and that a BAC limit of 50 mg/100 ml (0,05%), if implemented, would be a more effective means of reducing road accidents. A 2004 study in Germany, where the researchers compared a sample of accidents to a sample of 'trips' not leading to an accident, provides the first reliable analysis of alcohol related accident risk. This showed

---

3   Great Britain, Department of Transport *Road Accidents in Great Britain* (1984).

4   Ogden, EJ and Moskowitz, H 'Effects of alcohol and other drugs on Driver Performance' (2004) 5 (3) *Traffic Injury Prevention* 185-198, over 55% of the references were before 1980 highlighting the importance of the earlier research into this subject.

5   McCann, MG 'The effect and impact of breath analysis in a workplace'Conference Paper presented at Medichem Conference London(October 1992).

6   Hurst, PM 'Epidemiological aspects of alcohol in driver crashes and citations' (1973) 5 *Journal of Safety Research* 130-148.

7   *Departmental Committee Report on Drinking and Driving* (1976).

that the attributable risk (AR) was 12% for all accidents attributable to alcohol and that over 96% of these accidents happen with BACs of 0,05% and above.[8]

However it must be stressed that there is no threshold effect below which a driver or worker *does not* become impaired. At least some skills could be impaired with any level of alcohol consumption. The effects of alcohol are dependent on both the quantity consumed and the nature of the performance required. There is no evidence that low BACs improve any human skill.[9]

There are certain categories of jobs for which even a blood-alcohol level of 0,05 % would certainly not be appropriate.[10] For example, this (lower) level would still be excessive for airline pilots, train drivers, bus drivers, oil-rig workers, and those engaged in other hazardous occupations. A four- to fivefold increase in the possibility of an accident occurring on an airplane, train, coach or any other form of public transport would not be acceptable to any responsible public body.

In Salzburg, Austria, a study looked at the influence of alcohol and drugs on driving during the years 2003–2007. The study analysed 1,167 blood samples of drivers suspected of driving while under the influence of alcohol and drugs. Cannabis was identified in 50% of the drivers, opiates in 20%, amphetamines in 18%, cocaine in 15%, and benzodiazepines in 20%.

A new urinary roadside test was used to differentiate between recent and temporal earlier consumption of cannabinoids, and the technology of pupillography (developed by AMTech Pupilknowlogy GmbH, Germany) was applied in cases of drugged driving (see chapter 10 section 5.1 for further information on pupillography). For the first time the authors were able to predict the presence of at least one central nervous active substance in the blood of a drugged driver.[11]

It has been suggested that the different features of alcohol intoxication depend upon the separate effects of alcohol on specific brain functions rather than on an overall non-specific general depressant effect.[12] This is true for frontal executive functions and particularly for the motor programming subset, which is an executive function that is highly involved in driving skills.[13] Similarly, a 2004 study revealed that the consumption

8   Kruger, HP, Vollrath, M 'The alcohol related accident risk in Germany: Procedures, method and results' (2004) 36 (1) *Accident Analysis and Prevention* 125.

9   Moskowitz, H, Burns, M, Williams, AF 'Skills performance at low blood alcohol levels' (1985) 46 (6) *Journal of Studies on Alcohol*482-485. in Ogden, EJD and Moskowitiz, H 'Effects of Alcohol and Other Drugs on Driver Performance' *Traffic Injury Prevention* 185-198.

10   Section 122, Road Traffic Act 29 of 1989. The Road Traffic Amendment Bill 1993 proposed that the alternative of 0,38 mg of alcohol in a litre of breath be included within s 122, being the equivalent of 0,08 g % of blood.

11   Keller, T, Keller, A, Tutsch-Bauer, E and Monticelli, F in 'Driving under the influence of drugs and alcohol in Salzburg and Upper Austria during the years 2003-2007' (2009) 11 (1) *Legal Medicine* Supplement-S98.

12   Kiianamaa,K 'Neuronal mechanisms of ethanol sensitivity' (1990) 25 (2/3) *Alcoholand Alcoholism* 252-262.

13   Domingues, A, Mendonca, B, Laranjena, R & Nakamura, M 'Drinking and driving a decrease in executive frontal functions in young drivers with a high blood alcohol concentration' (2009) 43 (8) *Alcohol* 657.

of even a moderate amount of alcohol can have an adverse effect upon the brain's metabolism and its motor, behavioural and cognitive functions.[14]

3. NEUROPHYSIOLOGICAL AND PHYSIOLOGICAL MECHANISMS AFFECTED BY ALCOHOL CONSUMPTION

Research shows that certain neurophysiological and physiological mechanisms— essential attributes for safety—are affected by blood-alcohol levels as low as 0,05 g% and even 0,03 g%. These figures are based on research that has also analysed the different physiological mechanisms that interact with alcohol to produce an at-risk situation or the potential risk of an accident occurring. It is important to understand these mechanisms.

The neurophysiological and physiological mechanisms just referred to are dealt with below under the following headings:
1   Eye-hand coordination
2   Precision in manipulation
3   Effects on vision
4   Slowing of reaction time
5   Reduced cognitive processing of information:
    a   Reduced concentration
    b   Reduced or poor judgement
    c   Increased risk-taking.

Various research studies have looked at the relationship between alcohol consumption and safety at work. One particular study from the 1970s considered the delayed effects of alcohol consumption on workers before, during and after a measured alcohol intake. Blood-alcohol levels ranged from 0,065% to 0,175%. Delayed effects were noted up to 18 hours after ingestion of the alcohol and included lengthened reaction time, poor motor performance and decreased motor sensory skills. An inability to manipulate and position without tactile or visual facilitation was also noted. Visual scanning and postural configuration were also assessed.[15]

More recently, a number of peer-reviewed studies analysed psychological performance during the 'morning after' hangover following a controlled alcohol intake; disclosing several pathological changes that outlast the acute intoxicant effects.[16]

3.1 Eye-hand coordination

Eye-hand coordination has been shown to consist of three phases and therefore three types of error can occur.

The first phase is the sensory phase. This phase, described as the dwell-time error or delay, concerns the time interval between an individual's observance of a specific stimulus and his or her reaction to it. Dwell-time error (or delay) is increased for high

---

14   Zhu, W, Volkow, ND, Ma, Y, Fowler, J & Wang, GJ 'Relationship between Ethanol-induced changes in brain regional metabolism and its motor, behavioural and cognitive effects' (2004) 39 (1) *Alcohol and Alcoholism* 53-58.

15   Wolkenberg, RC, Gold, C & Tichauer, ER `Delayed effects of acute alcohol intoxication on performance with reference to work safety'(1975) 7(3) *J Safety Research* 104-118.

16   McKinney, A & Coyle, K 'Alcohol hangover effects on measures of affect the morning after a normal night's drinking' (2004) 39 (6) *Alcohol and Alcoholism* 509-513.

levels of alcohol intoxication (up to 0,175 g%) in all subjects, for at least 18 hours after the peak blood-alcohol concentration (BAC) and for at least 10 hours after the BAC has returned to zero. At lower alcohol levels the frequency of dwell-time errors is reduced to normal after much shorter time intervals.[17] This sensory phase affects reaction time. Thus, high blood-alcohol levels—those up to 0,175 g%—produce an extended dwell-time error even after the alcohol has been completely eliminated from the body. For individuals engaged in precise, manipulative work, a high blood-alcohol level therefore represents a particular source of concern.

The second phase of eye-hand coordination relates solely to motor control and reveals errors in motion. In sober individuals there is a smooth acceleration and deceleration of movement but in the intoxicated there are mid-course corrections.

The third phase of eye-hand coordination consists of a combined motor and sensory response and this can produce two types of error: (i) an error where the whole arm moves sideways away from or towards the body; a movement used when placing small objects into position at a short arm's length; and (ii) an error in fine wrist movements; used, for example, in the fine-tuning of a large dial or in manipulating the levers of an overhead crane.

The two movements identified above (movement of the arm sideways; fine wrist movements) are used extensively in the electronics industry and the textiles industry. (It is worth noting that, in respect of the latter, this is particularly true for clothing manufacturers using older types of looms where there is the need to change bobbins.)

Tasks involving the use of conveyors could also cause errors, accidents and injuries as a result of these movements (a conveyor used to grade fruit for quality-control purposes is a good example of where these problems could arise). Another 'high-risk' area can be found in the cellulose industry. Here, pulp processing and paper manufacturing is performed at high speed on machines that are in continuous operation, and operators are required to make quick, accurate decisions. The movements of airline pilots, crop sprayers, and firefighter bombers, which warrant either the flick of a switch or the fine tuning of a dial would be another area where a potentially disastrous error could occur.

3.2 Precision in manipulation

Precise manipulation is required in the electronics industry and this can be affected by difficulty in the perception of depth (see below), which means that past-pointing occurs and fine manipulative movements are affected.

3.3 Effects on vision

The most important effects on vision are a decrease in the lateral field of vision and the impact on depth perception.[18]

The field of vision is defined as the total area that is seen when the eye is looking straight ahead. We often see things 'out of the corner of our eye' without really observing them, but if a sudden movement occurs, our attention is drawn towards the movement and we turn our head in that direction. With a raised BAC, this lateral visual field is dramatically reduced and therefore the perception of any movement that may occur

---

17 Wolkenberg & Tichauer (n15).

18 Mortimer, RG & Jorgeson, CM 'Effects of low and moderate levels of alcohol on steering performance' in Israelstam and Lambert (eds) Alcohol, Drugs and Traffic Safety (1996).

in the periphery is curtailed. This is often the cause of accidents involving intoxicated pedestrians, as they do not see approaching vehicles. Similarly, the lateral field of vision is important for dealing with any moving machinery in an occupational setting.

With depth perception alcohol impairs both fast and slow eye movements, which are needed for different functions. The fast eye movement system allows the eyes to move rapidly to what we need to see; the slow eye movement system allows fixation and the tracking of a moving object.

With alcohol intoxication the slow eye movements become too slow. The brain then adjusts by using the fast eye movement system to compensate (in effect, to 'catch up') and this in turn produces jerky eye movements called horizontal nystagmus. Because of this, an intoxicated person's perception of depth from motion parallax—which relies heavily on the slow eye movement system—is impaired. Several studies have drawn attention to this phenomenon. One particular study suggests that the effect of alcohol on these eye movements produces inaccurate or inadequate information from which to judge the relative depth of obstacles from the subject.[19] In addition, night vision is affected; reducing an individual's ability to see poorly illuminated objects and increasing the difficulty he or she experiences in recovering from the effects of glare.

3.4 Slowing of reaction time

Slowing of reaction time is the most often quoted effect of drinking and driving and is made up of various elements of eye-hand or eye-foot coordination, judgement, and speed of decision-making. Studies employing driving and flight simulators to demonstrate this effect are common in the literature.

3.5 Reduced cognitive processing of information

Cognitive processing of information in order to make decisions comes from the higher centres of the brain. Alcohol interferes with this process and produces the following negative outcomes:
a   Reduced concentration
b   Reduced or poor judgement
c   Increased risk-taking.

3.5.1 Reduced concentration

Reduced concentration in effect means an inability to give proper attention to a particular task or tasks. The implications for safety at work are clear. For example, flight controllers working under the influence of alcohol would experience difficulties in tracking the movements of more than one plane since their ability to focus on a number of tasks (airplanes) would be diminished. Similarly, employees who need to focus intently on a particular task or procedure for a certain period of time (for example, a soldier on sentry duty or an anaesthetist in an operating theatre) the same negative effect would arise.

---

19   Nawrot, M, Nordenstrom, B & Olson, A 'Disruption of eye movements by ethanol intoxication affects perception of depth from motion parallax' (2004) 15 (12) *J Psychological Science* 2004 856-865.

3.5.2 Reduced or poor judgement

Reduced judgement occurs with the consumption of even small amounts of alcohol. This has been shown in a study of bus drivers who were asked to take their buses through a driving course.[20] Some drivers had been given alcohol prior to the test. Certain obstacles were moved to positions where the gap was increasingly narrowed until it was not wide enough for the buses. Those not intoxicated were able to judge the width of the gaps, but a large proportion of those with blood-alcohol levels of 0,06 g% or above were unable to judge that the gaps were too narrow. Errors were noticed with blood-alcohol levels as low as 0,02 g%.

3.5.3 Increased risk-taking

Increased risk-taking is associated with reduced judgement. This phenomenon can be thought of as a dampening of the inhibitory processes related to judgement. In practice, this means that a sober person is capable of making a subjective assessment of the risk(s) associated with taking a particular course of action and to hold back should he or she decide that the potential risk is too great. In the study of the bus drivers above, the intoxicated drivers may have been able to judge that the gap was too narrow but the subjective assessment which would advise caution would have been overridden by the disinhibitory effect which alcohol produces.

Further research has shown the cognitive impairment of alcohol-dependent persons with regard to tasks sensitive to frontal lobe function and that executive frontal lobe function is affected earlier in dependence than previously thought.[21]

When looking at the gender differences in performance of simulated driving motor coordination, speed and capacity of information processing, both genders were significantly affected by a challenge dose of alcohol but women displayed a more significant impairment than men on all behaviour tests and reported higher levels of subjective intoxication compared to men.[22]

SUMMARY

There is a wealth of research which shows that there is a relationship between alcohol consumption and accidents. Furthermore, the higher the blood-alcohol level, the greater the risk tends to be. Tolerance to alcohol, although helping to maintain normal behaviour patterns, does not eliminate the increased potential for accidents to occur. Up to recently a blood-alcohol level of 80 mg/100 ml, (0,08 g%) has been accepted by many countries as the medicolegal level at which intoxication occurs and task performance is adversely affected. As already shown this does not mean that significant effects do not occur at much lower blood-alcohol levels. The need to prevent the effects of alcohol intake upon performance is important at all levels, and not just the 0,08% cut off. As

---

20　Day et al 'An integrated service for patients with a physical disease related to excessive alcohol intake' Paper read at Eighth International Conference on Alcohol-related problems (Liverpool, 1990).

21　Loeber, S, Duka, SD, Welzel, H, Nakovics, H, Heinz, A, Flor, H & Mann, K 'Impairment of Cognitive Abilities and Decision making after Chronic use of Alcohol: the impact of multiple detoxifications' (2009) 44 *Alcohol and Alcoholism* 372-381.

22　Miller, MA, Weafer, J & Fillmore, MT 'Gender differences in alcohol impairment of simulated driving performance and driving skills' (2009) 44 *Alcohol and Alcoholism* 586-593.

we mentioned above, the performance requirements of certain roles in the workplace could be impaired by alcohol consumption lower, sometimes much lower, than the 0,08% norm.

However, in the average person it can be accepted that the neurophysiological mechanisms and neurobehavioural mechanisms affected by alcohol become unacceptably altered at the medicolegal blood-alcohol level of 0,08g%. Some recent research has shown that 50 mg/100 ml (0,05 g%) should be regarded as the medicolegal threshold for accidents. However, the important factor is always the risk assessment that the role indicates. The neurophysiological mechanisms that govern eye-hand coordination and precision in manipulation and vision are impaired via intoxication in terms of a slowing of reaction time, reduced concentration, reduced or poor judgement, and increased risk-taking. Research has also shown that the higher the initial blood alcohol concentration, the more affected and prolonged is the period of disturbances following the return of BAC to normal. In some cases, the impairment of neurophysiological functions caused by a night's drinking has been seen to extend into the afternoon of the following day.

It must be remembered that the majority of workplace accidents resulting from alcohol-induced indiscrete behaviour are caused by employees who are habitual and excessive drinkers and rarely by the occasional or social drinker.

II HEALTH OF THE INDIVIDUAL

1. INTRODUCTION

Alcohol is one of those rare substances that is able to penetrate every part of the body and thus to affect either directly or indirectly every organ. Often a breakdown in health in a person is the first overt indication that he or she has an alcohol problem. The initial signs of a developing problem may have been missed or overlooked due to the reluctance of many employees, relatives and employers to accept that an alcohol problem does indeed exist. The presentation of an alcohol problem can be an incidental finding when the employee-patient complains of particular health problems and all health staff should be aware of this possibility.

Linking alcohol problems to a breakdown in health is beneficial in terms of educating and counselling employee-patients regarding the hazards of alcohol abuse. Researchers in Newcastle upon Tyne, England, compared the acceptance of alcohol problems in two groups of problem drinkers. Those with diagnosed cirrhosis were more amenable to counselling (the therapeutic window) than those in whom a specific health problem had not yet been identified.[23]

2. EFFECTS OF ALCOHOL ON THE HEALTH OF THE INDIVIDUAL

2.1 The nervous system

The nervous system is often the first and predominant system of the body to be damaged by alcohol. Alcohol has a direct neurotoxic effect on the brain and affects both its structure and functioning.

The increasing use of MRI (magnetic resonance imaging) as a diagnostic tool has greatly improved our understanding of the damage alcohol, and its toxic metabolite

---

23 Day et al 'An integrated service for patients with a physical disease related to excessive alcohol intake'. Paper read at 8th Int Conference on Alcohol-related problems (Liverpool, 1990).

acetaldehyde, causes to the brain and nervous system. However, the extent of the damage which develops may be dependent on other factors, such as age, gender, genetics, nutrition, foetal brain damage and other mental health problems, and alcohol liver disease. And because no two people have exactly the same physiology, the damaging effects of excessive alcohol consumption will vary from person to person. A combination of these factors will play a part in the cumulative effect on the severity of brain damage and will impact on the recovery process.[24]

Damage to the nervous system ranges from the development of neuropsychiatric diseases (mental disorders) to the loss of peripheral sensation. Usually the symptoms are put down to other causes until they become more overt, which can take many years. The effects on the nervous system can be acute or chronic, psychiatric or organic.

2.2 Acute alcohol intoxication

The primary effect of alcohol abuse is intoxication itself. Alcohol has the ability to cross the blood-brain barrier with impunity and recent reports discuss its capacity to alter the way that messages are received, distributed and sent back from the brain.

The basic cell of the nervous system is the neuron. Neurons release transmitting substances from their end plates, which transmit the signals or ions to receptor sites or to other neurons. The outer membrane of the neuron is made up of proteins, which provide structural form and fats to help transport messages in the form of charged particles or ions into the cell. It has been suggested that alcohol has the ability to change the fat or lipid of the cell membrane, making it more fluid and therefore causing the protein part of the membrane structure to become haphazard, and to lose its usual structure. This impairs the transmission of messages (or ions) across the membrane, causing distorted signals or messages and creating a feeling of disorientation, cognition difficulties, and changes in behaviour.[25]

Because alcohol readily crosses the blood-brain barrier, the concentration of alcohol in the brain parallels the concentration established in the blood. For sporadic drinkers, obvious intoxication occurs at BACs of 50–150 mg/dL. Symptoms vary directly with the rate of consumption and may include euphoria, uncoordinated behaviour, ataxia, drowsiness, loss of inhibitions, garrulousness, gloominess, and belligerence. With increasing BACs, the direct depressant effects of alcohol predominate and subjects may experience lethargy, bradycardia, hypotension, and respiratory depression, sometimes complicated by vomiting and pulmonary aspiration. As BACs continue to rise, alcohol poisoning manifests with the development of secondary respiratory depression with respiratory acidosis and hypotension, stupor, coma and death. The median lethal BAC is approximately 450 mg/dL.[26]

---

24 Marshall, JE, Guerrini, I & Thomson, AD. 'Introduction to Special issue Alcohol related brain damage' (2009) 44 (2) *Alcohol and Alcoholism* 106-107.

25 Leonard, BE 'Is ethanol a neurotoxin? The effects of ethanol on neuronal structure and function'1986 (21) *Alcohol & Alcoholism* 325-338; Noble 'Alcohol scientists in breakthrough', article by Sandra Blakeslee, *New York Times*, 1989; Goldstein & Chin 'Interaction of ethanol with biological membranes'in Rosalki, SB *Clinical Biochemistry of Alcohol* (1984) 131.

26 Zeigler, D, Wang, C, Yoast , R, Dickenson, B, McCaffree , MA, Robinowitz ,C & Sterling, M 'The neurocognitive effects of alcohol on adolescents and college students' (2005) 40 (1)*Preventive Medicine*23-32.

2.3 Alcohol use in adolescents and young adults

Adolescents typically have smaller bodies (lower body mass) than adults and initially have not developed a physiological or behavioural tolerance to alcohol and its effects. Thus, they often do not need to drink very much to become intoxicated. They are also more prone to drink heavily and rapidly until intoxicated because their social, emotional control, thinking, and decision-making skills are less developed. Moreover, they are more likely to lose control and to take risks than adults.[27]

However, age-related differences in the acute effects of alcohol on performance and behaviour in healthy men, allowing for standardised body mass, showed there was not much difference in men aged between 20 and 59 years of a moderate dose of ethanol on sensory and motor functions.[28]

2.4 Blackouts

An episode of heavy drinking may cause an amnesic episode or 'blackout', where there is a loss of memory of events that occurred during the drinking episode. Blackouts, which appear to be caused by acute dysfunction of the hippocampus, are inevitably associated with a very rapid alcohol intake leading to a blood-alcohol concentration (BAC) in excess of 150 mg/100 ml (0,15 g%) in normal drinkers. Because the occurrence of blackouts is based on the amount of alcohol consumed during a single drinking episode, they are common among binge drinkers, including college students. Typically, an individual wakes up the morning after an episode of heavy drinking and cannot remember what occurred the previous evening, only to later learn that he or she had engaged in risky behaviour. One in four college students who drank reported forgetting where they were or what they did while drinking during the academic year. The incidence doubled (54%) among frequent binge drinkers. Females blacked out after consuming, on average, only five drinks. Males averaged nine drinks per occurrence. Adolescents also seem to have more blackouts and forgetting events than adult drinkers. The memory loss is generally temporary but may persist for some time after the drinking episode that caused it.[29]

Alcoholic fugue is a condition which occurs as a period of amnesia when one has travelled away from a familiar environment and not known how one got there.

2.5 Sleep

Alcohol consumption affects the neurotransmitters serotonin and glutamate, which control the sleep/wake cycle. During the rising limb of the blood alcohol curve, alcohol has a stimulating effect in contrast to a sedative effect which occurs during the descending limb. Alcohol affects the time taken to fall asleep but changes the pattern of sleep throughout the night. It can induce rapid onset of sleep but with a resultant disturbance of the quality of sleep. It increases the time spent in short wave sleep. Alcohol reduces rapid eye movement (REM) sleep during the first half of the night, but increases it during the second half of the night. The complex interaction between

27 Zeigler, D, Wang, C, Yoast , R, Dickenson, B, McCaffree , MA, Robinowitz ,C & Sterling, M 'The neurocognitive effects of alcohol on adolescents and college students' (2005) 40 (1)*Preventive Medicine*23-32.

28 Jones, AW& Neri, A 'Age related differences in the effects of Ethanol on performance and behaviour in healthy men.' (1994) 29 *Alcohol and Alcoholism* 171-179.

29 Jones (n 28).

alcohol and sleep has a direct implication on the effects of alcohol consumption on cognitive performance.[30] Poor sleep efficiency is associated with depression and when combined with alcohol is associated with daytime disturbance of mood.[31]

An experimental study of college students revealed that after four hours drinking late at night the students exhibited the following symptoms: disrupted sleep on the night of the drinking episode and, the next day, increased levels of anxiety, changes in emotions, and fatigue. (The students used themselves as their own controls for comparing when abstinent three weeks later.)[32]

2.6 Alcohol withdrawal syndrome

The most common acute after–effect of intoxication is the alcohol withdrawal syndrome. The degree of the reaction depends on the severity of the blood-alcohol level, the tolerance to alcohol of the individual, and the innate sensitivity of the individual to alcohol. In its mildest form (commonly called a hangover), tiredness, a depressed mood, a headache, tissue dehydration, nausea and hypersensitivity to outside stimuli can occur. Many people will get a hangover on relatively small amounts of alcohol; however, in cases of heavier alcohol consumption where the daily alcohol intake is, on average, 250 g, which represents four-fifths of a bottle of spirits or 15 (340 ml) bottles/cans of beer, the alcohol withdrawal symptoms experienced will, for most individuals, be more extreme. A reaction consists of tremor, nausea, sweating and mood changes. The tremor can involve not only the hand but also the face and even the body; it can be of a fine or a coarse nature, depending upon the degree, and is best described as an increase in the normal physiological tremor; it can be clearly identified by resting a sheet of paper over the extended hands.

Nausea due to alcohol abuse takes two forms: toxic reaction in the central nervous system and gastric irritation.

The withdrawal nausea comes from the toxic reaction of the alcohol on the central nervous system and should be differentiated from the nausea due to gastric irritation. Whereas another alcoholic drink will relieve central nervous system nausea, it will only make gastric nausea worse. Sometimes it can be so severe that even cleaning the teeth in the morning can induce retching. Breakfast is often avoided as it is too traumatic. Sweating can be profuse and is present particularly in the early morning before one gets out of bed. Mood disturbances producing depression, anxiety or agitation can often be severe. In addition, the person often experiences hyperacusis (increased sensitivity to noise), tinnitus (ringing in the ears), muscle cramps, and sleep disturbances or early awakening. However 25–30% of drinkers may be resistant to hangovers.[33] But note that the 'hangover-free' drinker is not as blessed as he or she appears to be; this is because

---

30 Vitiello, MV 'Sleep, alcohol and alcohol abuse' (1997) 2 *Addiction Biology* 151-158.

31 Robert, RE and Shema, SJ 'Sleep complaints and depression in an aging cohort' (2000) 157 *American J of Psychiatry* 81-90. Allgower, A, Wardle, J and Steptoe, A 'Depressive symptoms, social support and personal behaviours in young men' (2001) 20 *Health Psychology* 223-227.

32 McKinney, A & Coyle, K 'Alcohol hangover effects on measures of Affect the morning after a normal night's drinking' (2006) 41 *Alcohol and Alcoholism* 54-60.

33 Howland, J, Rohsenow ,D, Allensworth, D, Greece, J, Almeida, A, Minsky, S, Arnedt, J & Hermos, J 'The incidence and severity of hangovers after moderate alcohol intoxication' (2008) 103 (5) *Addiction* 758-765.

it is the presence of the hangover that can act as an effective negative reinforcement to reduce or stop drinking.

Dependent drinkers may suffer from 'delirium tremens' (DTs), which is a particularly violent reaction that follows withdrawal from alcohol. Halllucinations–both auditory and visual– can occur and these can produce considerable distress. One patient described seeing insects crawling all over his body and another described being attacked by having broken glass hurled at him. *Grand mal,* epileptic seizures can manifest in up to one-third of cases of severe DTs, and the condition becomes very dangerous if not handled carefully. The severity is related to swelling of the brain due to oedema (fluid retention). When using intravenous infusions on head-injury cases who may be intoxicated this is an important point to consider: if there is a high blood-alcohol level, then the intake of intravenous fluids may, due to oedema of brain cells, make the condition worse.[34] Delirium tremens can occur up to three days after drinking has stopped.

Age plays a role in the effects of alcohol abuse, with 50% of cases over 45 years of age beginning to experience cognitive, judgemental, memory and problem-solving difficulties.

3. CHRONIC EFFECTS OF INTOXICATION

With chronic alcohol abuse, fats in the nerve cell membrane tend to harden with increasing cholesterol uptake as they adapt to the persistent consumption of alcohol. Because the fats need to maintain fluidity so that messages (ions) can pass through the membrane and affect the nerve cell, more alcohol (ie liquid) is required. The net result of this increased consumption of alcohol is that the central nervous system becomes less responsive to alcohol, which in turn means that more alcohol is required to achieve the same effect. This condition is known as the state of functional tolerance (refer to chapter 1), which can lead to dependence when the nerve cell membranes become dependent on alcohol in order to function normally.

3.1 Message distortion and nutrition problems

Although the fats in the nerve cells need alcohol to maintain their fluidity and thus their ability to transmit messages through the membrane, too much alcohol will lead to intoxication and, consequently, a distortion of the messages to be transmitted, received and processed. When the intake of alcohol ceases, withdrawal symptoms appear because the fat has difficulty adjusting to normal fluidity and messages are in disarray as the nervous system becomes overly sensitive to some stimuli.[35]

The chronic effects of intoxication on the nervous system are, as mentioned above, due to the toxicity of alcohol and the direct (and harmful) effect this has on the brain and central nervous system. However, heavy or excessive drinking can also create problems in respect of nutrition. In particular, it can result in thiamine deficiency, which deprives the individual of a nutrient that is essential to the healthy functioning of the brain (see the section on encephalopathy and psychosis below). With regular excessive drinking, withdrawal states will occur more frequently unless they are avoided by repeating

---

34 Further reading is essential. The reader is referred to Rosalki ed *Clinical Biochemistry of Alcoholism* chapters 5 and 6, where the dangers of IV therapy in patients undergoing withdrawal is highlighted.

35 Lee, K, Moller, L Hardt, F, Haubek, A & Jensen, E 'Alcohol-induced brain damage and liver damage in young males'1979 (2) *The Lancet* 759-761.

the intake of alcohol (inability to abstain), therefore leading to dependence. In these circumstances, excessive drinking would comprise ten units (80 g) of alcohol daily for four or more days for men, and less for women. In severe excessive drinkers, who drink more than 400 g of alcohol per day (50 units or one-and-a-half bottles of spirits); DTs can occur up to three days after the drinking has stopped.

3.2 Intellectual impairment

Intellectual impairment may be the earliest complication of chronic alcohol abuse. Alcohol abuse is closely associated with depression. Cognitive impairment occurs, producing minor difficulties in judgement, concentration, perseverance, memory, problem-solving and abstract thinking. However, all these faculties can be regained within a few months by abstinence as long as permanent damage has not already taken place. A study by researchers in Copenhagen, Denmark, examined 37 'alcoholic' males under 35 years of age, using three diagnostic criteria: psychometric tests, computerised tomography (CT/CAT Scan) and liver biopsy. They found that 59 % were intellectually impaired, 49 % had cerebral atrophy but only 19 % had severe liver damage, suggesting that intellectual impairment may be the earliest complication of chronic alcohol abuse and could possibly arise early in the subject's career.[36]

3.2.1 Organic disease

Organic disease can occur due to the direct toxic effect of alcohol on brain tissue, causing 'dementia' and can present as a pre-senile condition in individuals in their late fifties. The person will develop a history of periodic personality changes and memory deterioration. Age is a crucial factor, because the older the patient the more susceptible they become. The patient can become morbid and depressed however the link with alcohol can often be missed or incorrectly diagnosed. Alcohol abuse is closely associated with depression, which is often a reflection of a perceived lack of personal power. In excessive drinkers, depression and mood changes can occur both while the individual is intoxicated and during the withdrawal state. Anxiety attacks and phobias also occur and morbid jealousy can be directed at the marital partner. These effects can dissipate dramatically if sustained abstinence is achieved.

3.3 Hallucinosis

A condition of hallucinating without any other symptoms can occur with excessive drinking as well as in the withdrawal state and can persist for weeks or even months.

A high proportion of problem drinkers are suffering from brain damage that has not been identified.

3.4 Encephalopathy and psychosis

Wernicke's encephalopathy and Korsakoff's psychosis are related conditions caused by a deficiency in thiamine (vitamin B). The pathological background of the two conditions is similar. Wernicke's encephalopathy can be considered to be the acute condition and is characterised by confusion, ataxia (loss of equilibrium or staggering gait) and ocular

---

36 Harper, C 'Wernicke's encephalopathy: a more common disease than realised'1979 (42) *J Neurology, Neurosurgery & Psychiatry* 226-231.

palsy (abnormal eye movements). There is also often an associated peripheral neuropathy (tingling and pains or numbness and weakness in the legs). The chronic condition of Korsakoff's psychosis is most likely the final stages of the confusional state of the acute condition. In this case the main finding is a severe loss of short-term memory. Patients often develop confabulation, where stories are invented to cover up for the memory inadequacy.

Considerably more people evince the post-mortem pathological changes of Wernicke's encephalopathy than they reveal evidence of 'alcoholic' symptoms during their lives.[37]

In Harper's study of 51 autopsies revealing pathological changes of Wernicke's encephalopathy, only seven had symptoms that had been diagnosed during their lifetime. The significance of this is that a high proportion of existing excessive or dependent drinkers are suffering from brain damage that has probably not been identified. The three main symptoms of Wernicke's encephalopathy (confusion, ataxia and ocular palsy) can occur separately as the overt symptom without the other two necessarily being identified. Harper has followed up with further studies which have confirmed his initial findings.[38]

3.5 Amblyopia

A further condition which occasionally occurs is a progressive dimness of vision due to the toxic effects of alcohol on the central optic nerve forming a central blind spot (scotoma). This is called amblyopia. There is also an associated loss of colour vision.

3.6 Epileptic fits and hypoglycaemic fits

For people diagnosed with epilepsy, and who therefore have a lower epileptic (seizure) threshold than non-epileptics, alcohol is potentially dangerous. This is because alcohol, like tiredness, stress and lack of sleep, can trigger seizures in an epileptic. Although it may be possible for an epileptic to consume moderate amounts of alcohol without increasing his or her chances of experiencing a seizure, heavy drinking is far more hazardous.

Fits, or seizures, can also occur due to alcohol-induced hypoglycaemia, which is a condition where the body's blood sugar level drops below a certain point. Since alcohol suppresses the liver's production of blood sugar, a person who drinks heavily is more likely to suffer a fit.[38]

3.7 Peripheral neuropathy

Peripheral neuropathy is commonly found in long-term excessive drinkers. The condition is generally thought to be caused by thiamine deficiency and consists of a symmetrical loss of sensory perception and poor reflexes in the lower legs.

3.8 Toxic hepatic encephalopathy

The damaging effects of alcohol on the liver, where cirrhosis distorts the organ's internal architecture, hinders the portal venous blood supply. This venous blood supply then develops an alternative pathway that bypasses the liver. The systemic circulation is then exposed to substances that have not been detoxified by the liver—in particular

---

37 Harper, CG & Kril, JJ 'Neuropathology of alcolism' (1990) 25 (2/3) *Alcohol & Alcoholism* 207-216.
38 Seixas, L (1984) (33) *Alcoholism Psychotherapena* 40.

ammonia, which in a healthy liver is converted into urine—so that the blood-ammonia level is raised appreciably. This is absorbed by the brain, causing foul breath, irritability and confusion, and can even lead to comas. A characteristic sign is a flapping tremor of the hands called asterixis. This condition, if it persists, can lead to permanent brain damage.

3.8.1 The liver

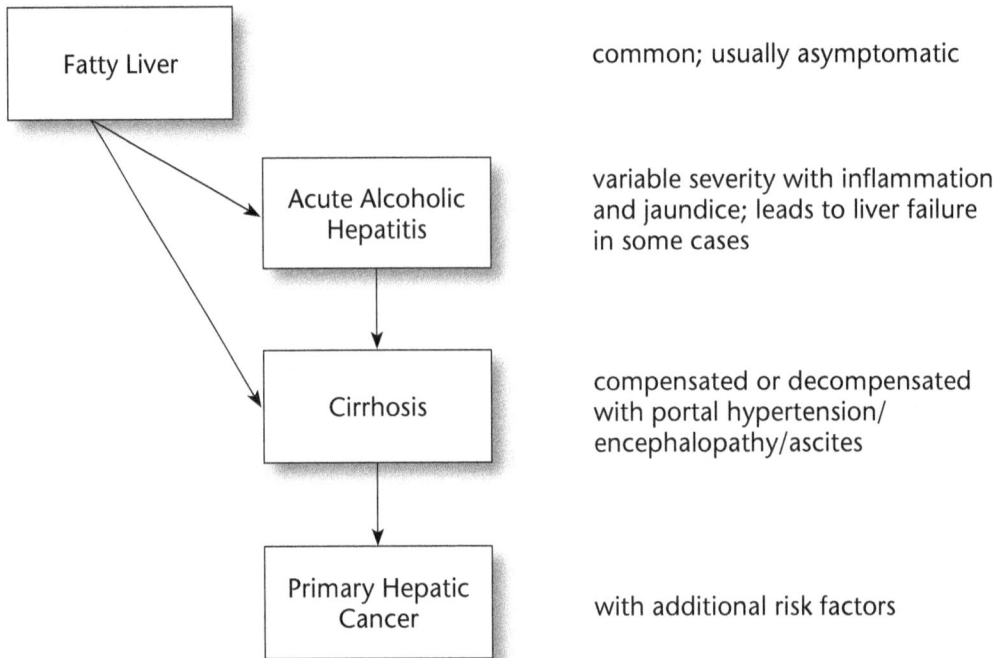

Fatty Liver	common; usually asymptomatic
Acute Alcoholic Hepatitis	variable severity with inflammation and jaundice; leads to liver failure in some cases
Cirrhosis	compensated or decompensated with portal hypertension/ encephalopathy/ascites
Primary Hepatic Cancer	with additional risk factors

Figure 7.3 Types of liver damage caused by chronic alcohol abuse.[39]

Liver damage is generally considered to be the most serious outcome of alcohol abuse, yet it must be remembered that the liver is the only organ of the body that regenerates itself. In assessing hepatoxicity (ie the capacity of a substance to cause damage to the liver) the total amount of alcohol consumed is more relevant than the frequency (continuous or periodic drinking) of consumption or the type(s) of alcohol ingested. Over a short period of time up to 80 g of alcohol daily (approximately one bottle of wine) will not cause damage to the liver, but if this level is maintained on a regular basis, damage will develop. As the level of alcohol increases above 80 g per day, the risk of damage to the liver escalates, so that at 160 g of alcohol a day, the risk is 25 times greater than normal.

Some people's livers are particularly sensitive to alcohol and would not be able to take anything close to 80 g of alcohol daily before liver damage occurs. There may be a genetic predisposition that makes these people more susceptible and thus more likely to experience the after-effects of a heavy drinking episode, such as nausea and vomiting.

---

39 Williams, R 'The Pervading influence of alcohol liver disease' (2008) 43 (4) *Hepatology Alcohol and Alcoholism* 393-397.

However, these unpleasant consequences can act as a powerful disincentive, and will generally prevent 'light drinkers' from becoming heavy drinkers.

25–30% of chronic alcohol abusers develop cirrhosis.

The oxidation of alcohol in the liver takes priority over other metabolic processes and it alters the ability of the liver to carry out those other processes. For example, gluconeogenesis (the formation of blood glucose by the liver) is inhibited and therefore hypoglycaemia or low blood sugar occurs, causing weakness, confusion, dizziness, blackouts and even seizures and fits. Because the liver gives precedence to alcohol metabolism, there is a tendency for fat to accumulate in the liver cells themselves and for excess lipids to form in the blood (hyperlipoproteinaemia). These lipids are triglycerides and can be seen after taking blood from the vein of a heavy drinker, even after fasting, and either centrifuging it or leaving it to stand. The serum, above the red blood cells, is then full of fat and is thick, opaque and milky and not clear and straw-coloured, as it should be. The accumulation of fat in the blood increases the risk of a fat embolus developing and causing a stroke (a cerebrovascular accident) or a thrombus, which in turn can lead to a heart attack (myocardial infarction).

Alcohol abuse invariably produces excessive fat deposits in the liver called 'fatty liver'. As already mentioned, this is due to the liver's prioritising of the alcohol oxidation process (alcohol metabolism).

3.8.2 Fatty liver

Depending on the susceptibility of the individual, some alcohol-abusers continue to accumulate fat in the liver without any further abnormality occurring. In such cases, the liver will enlarge but is rounded and smooth and upon the withdrawal of alcohol will return to its normal state. Fatty liver is present in over 90% of chronic alcohol drinkers. Those with alcoholic fatty liver disease who continue to consume large amounts of alcohol daily have been found to have a 8–30% risk of developing fibrosis or cirrhosis after 10 years. Progression beyond fatty liver requires additional risk factors such as obesity, hepatitis C and genetic susceptibility.[40]

3.8.3 Alcoholic hepatitis

Some individuals who abuse alcohol can go on to develop alcoholic hepatitis, which is an acute inflammatory condition of the liver that gives rise to fever, a raised white-cell count, jaundice, anorexia, nausea and abdominal pain in the region of the liver. Acute alcoholic hepatitis is found more commonly in the younger age groups. This condition can lead to fulminating liver failure in about 10% of cases, with death due to liver failure, gastrointestinal bleeding or infection.[41] In the United States alone, alcoholic liver disease affects more than 2 million people (ie, approximately 1% of the population). The true prevalence of alcoholic hepatitis, and especially of its milder forms, is unknown because patients may be asymptomatic and never seek medical attention. However,

---

40 Cortezo-Pinto, H 'The Role of fatty liver in the development of advanced alcoholic liver disease' ESBRA Symposium 2007.

41 Yu, CH, Xu, C, Ye, H , Li, L & Li, Y'Early Mortality of alcoholic hepatitis' (2010) 16 (19) *World J Gastroenterolgy* 2435-2439.

severe alcoholic hepatitis present in a small fraction of patients who abuse alcohol has a 28-day mortality range of between 30–50%.[42]

3.8.4 Liver cirrhosis

Depending on the severity of the alcoholic hepatitis, the remaining 90% of cases (allowing for the 10% who develop fulminating liver failure) can go on to develop cirrhosis of the liver; an irreversible condition in which scar tissue and haphazard regeneration of non-functioning liver tissue are present. The liver initially enlarges with a rough knobbly surface; it can then shrink with progressive scar tissue, and this action destroys the liver architecture.

Cirrhosis is characterised not only by extensive fat accumulation but also by iron overload in the case of heavy wine drinkers. Between 25 and 30 % of chronic alcohol abusers will develop cirrhosis of the liver, and there is only a 33 % five-year survival rate for cirrhosis patients who continue to drink.[43]

Cirrhosis has two main complications. The first is due to the stricture which the deformed liver architecture places on the hepatic blood supply coming from the gastrointestinal system. This is called the portal circulation. The raised pressure in the intestinal portal circulation that may accompany cirrhosis can lead to the development of ascites (fluid on the abdomen) and an enlarged spleen (splenomegaly). This also encourages blood from the portal circulation to bypass the liver and develop a collateral circulation or pathway such as that into the abdominal wall (varices in the abdomen) or into the oesophagus (oesophageal varices). Because of this, the blood is not detoxified by the liver before passing into the main circulation, with the result that the toxic substances which are usually broken down by the liver can reach the brain, causing hepatic encephalopathy, as mentioned earlier. Bleeding from oesophageal varices can be fatal.

3.8.5 Primary hepatic cancer

The second complication of cirrhosis is primary liver cancer or hepatocellular carcinoma. There are estimated to be 500,000 new cases worldwide each year and the disease is more prevalent in developing countries. Hepatocellular cancer is more predominant in cirrhosis due to the extra growth of haphazard liver cells and has been found in between 2,5 and 7 % of cirrhosis case.[44]

The other causes of primary hepatic cancer are Hepatitis B (HBV) and Hepatitis C (HCV). Chronic alcohol consumption accelerates primary hepatic cancer in Hepatitis B.[45]

Predominantly more males are affected than females (the ratio being 3:1) and the condition occurs more often in those who have abstained since diagnosis, presumably

---

42 Cohen, S & Ahn, J 'The diagnosis and Management of alcoholic hepatitis' (2009) 30 (1) *Alimentary Pharmacology and Therapeutics* 3-13.

43 Royal College of Physicians *A Great and Growing Evil* (1987) 42; Rosalki, S *Clinical Biochemistry of Alcoholism* (1984) 264.

44 Montalto, G, Cervello, M, Giannitrapani, L, Dantona, F, Terranova, A & Castagnetta L 'Epidemiology, risk factors and natural history of hepatocellular Carcinoma' (2002) 963 *Annals of the New York Academy of Sciences* 13-20.

45 Ohnishi, K, Jida, S, Iwama, S, Goto, N, Nomura, F, et al 'The effect of chronic habitual alcohol intake on the development of the cirrhosis and hepatocellular carcinoma: relation to hepatitis B surface antigen carriage' (1982) 49 *Cancer* 672–680.

because they have survived long enough for the disease to have developed. The prognosis for primary liver cancer is very poor and the survival period is usually six months from the time of diagnosis. More is said about primary liver cancer under the section titled 'Cancer' below.

3.8.6 Chronic liver damage

The signs of chronic alcohol liver damage are indicated by the diverse systems that are affected. Firstly, blood is affected by reduced prothrombin levels (prothrombin is a blood-clotting factor produced in the liver) and bruising is seen in the skin or bleeding from the intestine associated with oesophageal varices. Secondly, the abdomen can become swollen due to the increase in size of the liver and the presence of fluid in the abdominal cavity, owing to the increased portal hypertension. For the same reason, the legs often swell. 'Caput medusae' (varices at the umbilicus) can be present owing to the portal circulation bypassing the liver. Thirdly, there are also hormonal changes, which result in gynaecomastia (enlarged breasts), loss of body hair and/or testicular atrophy. 'Spider naevi' (enlarged branching end arterioles) may appear in the skin and, if more than five can be counted below the root of the neck, this is considered to be diagnostic of chronic liver damage.

3.9 Pancreatitis

Alcoholic pancreatitis is often misdiagnosed, owing to the time lag between the bout of drinking and the onset of symptoms. Alcoholic pancreatitis is often a late or an undiagnosed condition that occurs predominantly in young or middle-aged males. It has a tendency to mimic a number of other painful conditions. It is particularly missed if patients are unaware of or deny the true extent of their drinking. It can mimic any condition which causes upper abdominal pain or lower sternal pain, sometimes radiating to the back, from an inferior or posterior myocardial infarction to a peptic ulcer or perinephric abscess, cholecystitis, hepatitis, mesenteric adenitis or spastic colon. The pain is continuous and can occur at any time between 12 and 48 hours after excessive alcohol abuse. The delay in the onset of pain is one of the main reasons why the disease is sometimes incorrectly diagnosed. Progressive attacks result in chronic pancreatitis and can eventually lead to the development of a poorly functioning pancreas and, subsequently, diabetes mellitis and steatorrhoea.

3.10 The gastrointestinal system

The oesophagus can become inflamed, developing an oesophagitis, owing to the reflux of acid from the stomach. The likelihood of cancer of the oesophagus is also increased in heavy drinkers, especially when the drinking is combined with smoking. The oesophagus can also be affected by the development of the Mallory-Weiss Syndrome. This consists of mucosal lacerations which occur due to severe retching caused by excessive alcohol abuse. Oesophageal varices developed as a result of the portal shunting caused by cirrhosis of the liver can begin to bleed. Both conditions can produce haematemesis (vomiting of blood). The stomach can become acutely inflamed by alcohol abuse and symptoms such as nausea, vomiting or dyspepsia will present. Numerous small erosions and petechiae occur, but these can heal within a few days. It is a matter of controversy whether alcohol intake can induce peptic ulceration, but heavy drinking will certainly exacerbate the condition. The effects of alcohol on the intestine must not be overlooked and diarrhoea may be a recurring complaint among chronic alcohol abusers.

4. NUTRITION AND METABOLISM

The fact that alcohol has a high kilojoule content (ie calorific value) but a poor nutritional content explains why alcohol abuse often produces an obese but malnourished individual. The caricature of an alcoholic as someone with a swollen face and huge stomach (the beer drinker's paunch) but wasted arms and spindly legs is, in fact, not far from the medical truth. As alcohol has a high calorific value and the metabolism of alcohol takes precedence over other metabolic processes, considerable dissipation of energy takes place in an individual who drinks heavily. Sweating and a raised body temperature are characteristic and are particularly evident in the early hours of the morning.

> Sweating and a raised body temperature are characteristics of excessive alcohol metabolism and are often seen in very heavy drinkers

Although there is a high calorific intake, loss of weight occurs because the body's metabolic rate is increased. An excessive drinker inevitably has a poor diet and whatever is eaten is not utilised adequately, because of the preoccupation of the liver with metabolising the alcohol. The body lacks the essential nutrients, fats, proteins, vitamins and minerals required for the growth and repair of all body functions. Muscles are wasted due to protein breakdown and a lack of magnesium and zinc. The brain and the peripheral nervous system can be damaged as a result of a lack of thiamine, pyridoxine, nicotinic acid and other vitamins. The bones will lack calcium and demineralisation can develop, producing osteoporosis. When accidents happen, the bones are therefore likely to fracture.

4.1 Endocrine System

The Endocrine system affected are the adrenal glands, which increase the levels of cortisol, producing the characteristic round, red moon face of a pseudo Cushing's disease and obesity with raised blood pressure and abnormal glucose tolerance.

5. THE MUSCLE AND THE HEART

An underestimated effect of excessive alcohol abuse is the effect on the muscle tissue and the heart. Muscle tissue degenerates in consequence of a breakdown of its protein (myopathy) and wasting of the large muscle groups of the arms, legs and shoulder girdle occurs particularly. An inflammatory process called myositis develops and muscle pains and cramps occur. Back pain is increased, owing to poor muscular support and joint pains are frequently present.

The heart is affected in four main ways—cardiac arrhythmias, cardiomyopathy, beri-beri heart, and a high incidence of coronary heart disease.

5.1 Cardiac arrhythmias

Cardiac arrhythmias are symptomatically observed by the patient as palpitations and missed beats with an associated tachycardia (or fast heart rate). The arrhythmias are called 'atrial fibrillation', 'ventricular extrasystoles', and 'tachycardia'. They usually occur after a heavy drinking bout and are not usually associated with permanent damage unless superimposed on existing heart disease, when in some cases they could be fatal. Alcohol cardiomyopathy and arrhythmias are more common than is realised.

5.2 Cardiomyopathy

Alcoholic cardiomyopathy is a chronic condition in which the heart becomes enlarged. It has often been shown at post mortems that the hearts of those who abuse alcohol excessively are enlarged and therefore cardiomyopathy can be considered more recurrent than is diagnosed. The heart becomes dilated as the muscle is not functioning properly, so setting up a progressive degeneration process that leads towards cardiac failure. Eighty per cent of patients with alcoholic cardiomyopathy who continue to drink die within three years of diagnosis.[46]

5.2.1 Beri-beri heart

Beri-beri heart is very similar to cardiomyopathy because the heart goes into failure and there is a tachycardia (fast heart rate); but this is due to thiamine deficiency rather than the direct toxic effects of alcohol on the heart. However, the likelihood exists that the two conditions occur together.

5.2.2 Case history

A white male, aged 31, who worked as a senior chargehand operator, had been employed for 10 years without any work performance problems. There was no history of absenteeism, poor work performance or absence due to sickness. However, he had been drinking for approximately 16 years. Over the last eight years he had been drinking heavily—at least a bottle of brandy a day. He developed angina and later became short of breath and experienced palpitations, particularly at night. Alcoholic cardiomyopathy was diagnosed. He stopped drinking after he was told of the diagnosis and advised to abstain, but soon relapsed and progressively declined until he had a much enlarged heart. The only thing that could have saved him was a heart transplant. He died of heart failure at the age of 32.

5.3 Coronary heart disease

There is an argument that suggests that the consumption of a moderate amount of alcohol helps to prevent coronary heart disease. In the case of excessive alcohol consumption however, research suggests that the reverse is true. Excessive alcohol consumption actively encourages the development of coronary heart disease, owing to the excessive lipids in the blood and possibly the enlarged red blood corpuscles (macrocytosis).

---

46 Royal College of Physicians *A Great and Growing Evil* (1987) 42.

5.4 High blood pressure

Habitual alcohol consumption is known to be a major risk factor for high blood pressure.

Many studies have confirmed that the blood pressure of heavy drinkers is higher than that of non-drinkers (when excluding other medical causes of high blood pressure).[47] The reduction of alcohol intake causes a decrease in blood pressure. The proportion of high blood pressure attributable to alcohol has been estimated to be 5–30%.[48]

A drinking history should always be taken of any patient with increased blood pressure. If a drinking history reveals excessive consumption of alcohol, then, before hypertensive treatment is started, the blood pressure should be monitored while the patient is abstinent. It frequently happens that moderately elevated and sometimes high blood pressure reverts to normal without treatment, but only through abstinence. Care must be taken to monitor the blood pressure in the withdrawal phase as, again, the blood pressure can rise further and treatment for withdrawal may have to be extended.

5.5 Cerebrovascular accidents (strokes)

The high incidence of cerebrovascular accidents (strokes) in excessive drinkers is possibly related to the elevated blood pressure, the hyperlipaemic blood throwing off fat emboli, macrocytosis (enlarged red cells), and haemorrhaging due to a decreased ability to clot blood. Whatever the cause, strokes are possibly one of the most frequent fatal complications of excessive alcohol intake, particularly if associated with smoking.

6. ANAEMIA, DEPRESSED IMMUNE SYSTEM AND HIV

Chronic alcohol abuse can affect the blood, causing anaemia due to nutritional deficiency (particularly vitamin B2 and folic acid) and the inhibition of erythropoiesis (formation of red blood cells). The frequent occurrence of polycythaemia in connection with chronic alcohol abuse is due to hypoxia (low blood oxygen) caused by heavy smoking, because the two conditions often present together. In addition, the immune system can be depressed and this exposes the patient to frequent infections.

The association of alcohol abuse with AIDS must be mentioned here. Alcohol reduces one's inhibitions and therefore increases the likelihood of 'high risk' sexual behaviour and, consequently, exposure to HIV (human immunodeficiency virus).[49]

To date no research has revealed a direct link between the damaging effect of chronic alcohol abuse and the destructive effect of HIV on the immune system.[50]

7. TUBERCULOSIS AND LUNG INFECTIONS

Heavy alcohol use and dependence have long been associated with active tuberculosis (TB).[51] The South African Medical Research Council (SAMRC) hosted a seminar with the WHO in Cape Town, in July, 2008, specifically to look at the link between alcohol consumption, HIV disease and TB. Worldwide data and meta-analysis were prepared

---

47 Wakabayashi, I 'Impact of Body Weight on the Relationship between Alcohol Intake and Blood Pressure' (2009) 44 (2) *Alcohol and Alcoholism* 204-210.

48 Plant 'Alcohol, sex and AIDS' 1990 (25 (2/3)) *Alcohol & Alcoholism* 293–301.

49 Ibid.

50 Ibid.

51 Jacobson, JR 'Alcoholism and Tuberculosis' (1992) 16 *Alcohol Health Research World* 39-45.

for the seminar. It was felt by those at the seminar that there was conclusive evidence of a causal link between heavy drinking patterns, alcohol use disorder (AUD) and the incidence of active TB. These exposures were also linked causally to worsening of the disease for both TB and HIV. The causal pathways leading to active TB were considered to be both biological and social in nature.

The biological link arises via alcohol's capacity to impact on multiple organs and systems, which may manifest in a weakening of the immune system and the protective barriers of specific organs such as the lungs. The second causal link is associated with the social-behavioural consequences of heavy alcohol use or dependence, where there appears to be a connection between heavy alcohol use and the development of multi-drug-resistant TB (MDR-TB).[52]

Public health interventions that target 'the alcohol problem' have been shown to be amongst the most effective in terms of reducing the burden of disease, especially in low- and middle- income countries. In Belarus, for example, a recent research study disclosed that a 1% increase in alcohol sales per capita could cause a 0,49 and 0,36 increase in pulmonary tuberculosis mortality rates in males and females respectively.[53]

Tuberculosis is found in problem drinkers and will invariably recur, due to behavioural and social factors that co-exist with alcohol abuse, and which cause increased susceptibility, malnutrition and the concomitant poor compliance with or default of treatment.[54]

There is an increased likelihood of developing chemical pneumonia as a result of the inhalation of vomit, or even lung abscesses, or bronchiectasis. The majority of heavy drinkers are also heavy smokers; besides having a depleted immune system, they can thus also suffer from chronic bronchitis and emphysema or even lung cancer.

8. CANCER (ORAL, OROPHARYNGEAL, HYPOPHARYNGEAL, LARYNGEAL, OESOPHAGEAL, HEPATOCELLULAR[LIVER], COLORECTAL[COLON], BREAST)

Alcohol is not a carcinogen. However, it is believed to act mainly as a promoter and cocarcinogen although its metabolite acetaldehyde has a more direct effect interacting with environmental carcinogens such as cigarette smoke.[55] Tuyns showed that alcohol consumption of more than 80 grams of alcohol per day (approximately one bottle of wine) increased the Relative Risk (RR) of oesophageal cancer by a factor of 18. Smoking without drinking alcohol increased the RR by a factor of 5 for individuals smoking 20 or more cigarettes a day. Together both factors synergistically increased the RR by 44.[56]

Tuyns also showed that an alcohol intake exceeding 1,5 bottles of wine daily resulted in a 100-fold increased risk of oesophageal cancer.[57]

---

52 Parry, C, Rehm, J, Poznyak, V & Room, R 'Alcohol and Infectious Diseases: an overlooked causal linkage?' paper from the Joint MRC and WHO Seminar (July 2008).

53 Razvodovskii, I 'Alcohol sales and Pulmonary Tuberculosis mortality in the Republic of Belarus between 1981 to 2001' (2006) 9 *Problemy tuberkuleza i boleznei legkikh* 27-31.

54 Kliiman, K, Altraja, A 'Predictors and Mortality associated with treatment default in Pulmonary Tuberculosis' (2010) 14 (4) *Int J Tuberculosis and Lung Disease* 454-463.

55 Poschl, G & Seitz, H, 'Alcohol and Cancer (a review)' (2004) 39 (3) *Alcohol and Alcoholism*.

56 Tuyns, A 'Alcohol and cancer' (1978) 2 *Alcohol: Health and Research World* 20–31.

57 Tuyns, AJ 'Oesophageal cancer in non-smoking drinkers and in non-drinking smokers'(1983) 32 *International Journal of Cancer* 443–444.

However, quitting alcohol (along with tobacco) showed a 70% reduction in oesophageal cancer risk within 5–9 years.[58] Ninety per cent of all patients with head and neck cancer regularly consumed alcohol in quantities twice that of a control group.[59]

If the RR for an individual with a daily alcohol consumption of 25 grams equals 1, then this figure would rise to 32 if his or her alcohol intake exceeded 100 grams per day (1,25 bottles of wine). When daily alcohol consumption rises to 100–159 grams (1–1,5 bottles of wine) then the RR for the following cancers would rise to:

	RR
Oral Cancer	13,5
Oropharngeal Cancer	15,2
Hypopharngeal Cancer	28,6[60]

Cancers of the mouth, tongue and oesophagus are frequently seen in heavy spirit drinkers who also smoke. There is a suggested higher incidence of cancer of the oesophagus in wine-growing countries, particularly France, and areas of Africa where sorghum beer is brewed in iron pots. In the latter case the iron pots are the carcinogen and the alcohol (the beer) acts as a potentiating factor.

Chronic alcohol consumption seems also to be associated with an increase in the occurrence of precancerous adenomatous polyps in the large bowel resulting in an increased RR of between 1,5 and 3,5 for rectal cancer and, to a lesser extent, colon cancer.[61,62]

In South Africa, where there is a high prevalence of both Infective Hepatitis B and C and chronic alcohol consumption, and where the combined effect of these two conditions (alcohol and the hepatitis viruses) accelerates the rate of primary hepatic cancer, the need to confront this threat to public health is urgent.[63,64]

Eighty per cent of cases of primary hepatic cancer from Europe and North America develop from cirrhosis; in Asia, however, nearly 50% of cases are not due to cirrhosis but instead develop from chronic hepatitis B and C.[65]

58 Castellaque, X, Munoz, N, De Stefani, E, Victora, CG, Quintana, MJ & Castelletto, R 'Smoking and drinking cessation and risk of oesophageal cancer' (2000) 11 *Cancer Causes and Control* 813-818.

59 Maier, H, Dietz, A, Zielinski, D, Junemann, K H & Heller, W D 'Risikofaktoren bei Patienten mit Plattenepithelkarzinomen der Mundhöhle, des Oropharynx, des Hypopharynx und des Larynx' (1990) 115 *Deutsche Medizinische Wochenschrift* 843–850.

60 Bruguere, J, Guenel, P, Leclerc, A & Rodriguez, J 'Differential effects of tobacco and alcohol in cancer of the larynx, pharynx and mouth.' (1986) 57 *Cancer* 391–397.

61 Seitz, H K, Pöschl, G & Stickel, F'Alcohol and colorectal cancer' (2003) in Scheppach, W & Scheuerle, M (eds) *Exogenous Factors in Colonic Carcinogenesis* 128–141.

62 Scheppach, W, Bingham, S, Boutron-Ruault, MC, Gerhardsson de Verdier, M, Moreno, V, Nagengast, F M, Reifen, R, Riboli, B, Seitz, HK & Wahrendorf, J 'WHO consensus statement on the role of nutrition in colorectal cancer' (1999) 8*European Journal of Cancer Prevention* 57–62.

63 Poschl, G & Seitz, HK ' Alcohol and Cancer Alcohol and Alcoholism' (2004) 39(3) 155-165.

64 Ohnishi, K, Jida, S, Iwama, S, Goto, N, Nomura, F, Takashi, M, Mistina, A, Kono, K, Kimura, K, Musha, H, Kotota, K & Okuda, K 'The effect of chronic habitual alcohol intake on the development of the cirrhosis and hepatocellular carcinoma: relation to hepatitis B surface antigen carriage' (1982) 49 *Cancer* 672–680.

65 Simonetti, RG, Liberati, A, Angiolini, C & Pagliaro, L 'Treatment of hepatocellular carcinoma: a systemic review of randomized controlled trials' (1997) 8 *Annals of Oncology* 117–136.

A great number of epidemiological studies have clearly identified chronic alcohol consumption even in moderate amounts as a risk factor for breast cancer. This may possibly be due to an alcohol-mediated increase in oestradiols.[66,67,68] There is increasing evidence that acetaldehyde, the breakdown product from alcohol rather than alcohol itself, is responsible for the cocarcinogenic effect of alcohol.[69]

Overall, the risk of chronic alcohol consumption causing one form of cancer or another is quite high, particularly in some types of cancers. Heavy drinkers with additional risk factors should seriously consider a reduction in their alcohol intake to levels below 20 grams twice a week (for men) and no more than 10 grams twice a week (for women). Alcohol should preferably be taken with meals and concentrated alcoholic beverages should be avoided.

9. SKIN CONDITIONS

Various skin conditions can develop as a result of chronic excessive alcohol abuse. Firstly, sores, bruises and fungal infections are often seen on the legs of dependent drinkers. Secondly, acne rosacea are usually seen on a plethoric (red) face; the acne showing pustules as well as raised red spots (papules). Thirdly, the conjunctiva are often red and telangiectasia (small, spider-like arteries) are visible on both cheeks. Fourthly, older men can sometimes develop a reddened, swollen, coarse nose called rhinophyma. Fifthly, pellagra (a deficiency of nicotinic acid) is often seen, particularly in ethnic groups who have malnourished, dependent drinkers with the characteristic rough, thickened brown skin of the hands, arms, chest and face and rickety rosary (small subcutaneous beadlike protrusions around the neck). Sixthly, chronic alcohol abuse has been identified as a risk factor for developing psoriasis (patches of dry, red, scaly skin), and the emotional distress caused by the condition usually leads to the continuation of unhealthy drinking habits. Researchers in Finland found that the daily intake of alcohol in patients before the psoriasis developed was twice that of individuals in the control group.[70]

In another study the prevalence of psoriasis in patients with chronic alcohol abuse and with alcoholic liver disease was 15%, compared to 1–3% in the general population.[71] Furthermore, for women who drink more than 2–3 strong beers a week, psoriasis is 72% more prevalent than it is in the general population.

10. THE REPRODUCTIVE SYSTEM

Both the male and female reproductive systems are affected by chronic alcohol abuse. For men, testicular atrophy, hypospermia and impotence are linked to heavy or excessive drinking habits. Testicular atrophy (shrinking of the testes) occurs because alcohol

---

66 Poschl, G & Seitz, H 'Alcohol and Cancer (a review)' (2004) 39 (3) *Alcohol and Alcoholism* 155-165.

67 Feigelson, HS, Calle, EE, Robertson, AS, Wingo, PA &Thun, MJ 'Alcohol consumption increases the risk of fatal breast cancer' (2001) 12 (10) *Cancer Causes Control* 895-902.

68 Rohan, TE, Jain, M, Howe, GR & Miller, AB 'Alcohol consumption and risk of breast cancer: a cohort study' (2000) 11 (3) *Cancer* Causes & *Control* 239-247.

69 Seitz, H K, Matsuzaki, S, Yokoyama, A, Homann, N, Vakevainen, S & Wang, XD 'Alcohol and cancer' (2001) 25 *Alcoholism Clinical and Experimental Research* 137–143.

70 Poikolainen, K, Reunala, T, Karvonen, J, Lauharanta, J & Kärkkäinen, PI 'Alcohol intake: a risk factor for psoriasis in young and middle aged men?'1990 (300) *BMJ* 780-783.

71 Tobin, A, Higgins, M, Norris, S & Kirby, B 'Prevalence of psoriasis in patients with alcoholic liver disease' (2009) 34 (6) *Clinical and Experimental Dermatology* 698-701.

has a direct inhibitory effect on the production of the male hormone, testosterone. Hypospermia (low semen production) and impotence (the inability to achieve or maintain an erection) can also be caused by alcohol abuse. For women, alcohol diminishes the production of oestrogen (the female hormone), which can cause a coarsening of the features as well as menstrual irregularities.

However the most significant problem under the heading of reproduction is Foetal Alcohol Syndrome (FAS). South Africa has the highest rate of FAS in the world, even when compared against other 'high-risk' indigenous populations in the US and Australia. This condition consists of growth deficiencies in the foetus and newborn child, craniofacial anomalies and central nervous system (CNS) dysfunction. It leads to intellectual disabilities and behaviour problems. Heavy prenatal alcohol exposure has been associated with widespread neuropsychological deficits in children.

In recent years it has become increasingly clear that FAS is not the only outcome of prenatal alcohol exposure; and that there exists a range of physical, behavioural and cognitive defects. This has led to a further suggested condition called Foetal Alcohol Spectrum Disorder (FASD), an umbrella term covering all the birth defects associated with prenatal alcohol abuse. The prevalence of FASD is estimated to be approximately 1% of all births and the average IQ of children with FAS is estimated to be in the low 70s.[72,73]

Foetal Alcohol Syndrome has a disruptive, if indirect, effect on the work environment. Working mothers who have FAS-affected children can anticipate having to care for them when they mature into adults, since they (the children) are unlikely to develop the necessary social skills that will allow them to function as independent members of society. This suggests that the mothers will find it extremely difficult to hold down a regular job if they are repeatedly called away from work to attend to their grown-up children's needs.

11. IT IS NOT ALL BAD NEWS!

Brain damage, and particularly that associated with binge drinking, is due to the death of brain cells (neuronal death) and alcohol inhibits of the formation of new nerve cells (neurogenesis or nerve cell regeneration). After the age of 55 the recommended limits for drinking increase to 28 units per week.[74]

Interestingly, abstinence from alcohol is associated with a recovery of both brain volume and neuropsychological loss. Abstinence improves working memory, visual-spatial abilities and certain motor abilities. Regeneration of the brain during sustained abstinence could improve executive functioning and impulse control. Abstinence over a long period of time has been reported to resolve most neurocognitive loss associated with alcoholism.

Recovery starts even after one day of abstinence and after two days cell growth is increased in both the grey and white matter of cortical regions. Cell growth increases in the first week of abstinence and especially after the first two days of abstinence. After one week a further burst of cell growth occurs in a more regional aspect of the brain.

72 Guerri, C, Bazinet, A & Riley, E 'Foetal Alcohol Spectrum Disorders and Alterations in Brain and Behaviour' (2009) 44 (2) *Alcohol and Alcoholism* 108-114.

73 May, PA & Gossage, JP 'Estimating the prevalence of Foetal Alcohol Syndrome: a summary' (2001) 25 *Alcohol Res Health* 159-167.

74 White, IR et al, *BMJ* 2002, 325. 191–197.

Exercise and environmental enrichment are known to protect the brain from neurodegenerative insults and age-related dysfunction, and to improve learning ability. Exercise can also counteract alcohol inhibition of nerve cell regeneration.[75]

Heavy or excessive drinkers can significantly improve their health by reducing the amount of alcohol they consume to the recommended levels and avoiding concentrated alcohol.

SUMMARY

Health is affected by alcohol both in the acute stage of intoxication and the chronic stages of heavy or dependent drinking. Many of the body's systems are affected; and although the liver is often considered the organ most affected, this is not necessarily the case. It is often the nervous system (an organ system) that suffers the most; from the very beginning of the abuse and during both acute intoxication and chronic abuse. Brain damage is particularly affected by binge drinking. Cardiac effects are often underestimated—high blood pressure being a common indicator of alcohol abuse. The prevalence of several cancers increases as a result of chronic alcohol consumption; some cancers more than others. Alcohol acts as an accelerator and is synergistic with hepatitis B and C. The presentation of pathology caused by alcohol abuse is as varied as the reasons why people abuse alcohol. A summary of all the symptoms and signs is shown in Appendix 11.

III CHEMICALS, THE WORK ENVIRONMENMT AND ALCOHOL AND DRUGS

1. INTRODUCTION

We are, to an increasing extent, identifying more diseases in the workplace, many of which could suggest causation or potentiation by alcohol abuse. It was 45 years ago that smoking began to be considered as a bias when research was done into occupational respiratory diseases.[76]

Today, any research into occupational respiratory or cardiac disease which does not take smoking into account is identified as hopelessly flawed. It is conceivable that the same consideration should be given to alcohol. Too often research into occupational disease does not take into account that 15–30% of the workforce being measured are either heavy or dependent drinkers, that alcohol is a risk factor for every organ system in the body, and that it can be identified as a cause of the problem in just as many occupational diseases.

2. DISEASES AND SYMPTOMS, CHEMICALS AND ALCOHOL

Table 7.1 lists, in the left-hand column, a number of diseases and symptoms. In the right-hand column, against each of the listed diseases/symptoms, the various substances (chemical compounds, metals, gases, and so on) and factors (stress, fatigue, heat, ergonomics) that cause the disease/symptom are recorded. Alcohol, in reaction with these substances, aggravates these diseases/symptoms. In the next section we will look at how this happens.

---

75 Crews, FT & Nixon, K 'Mechanisms of Neurodegeneration and Regeneration in Alcoholism' (2009) 44 (2) *Alcohol and Alcoholism* 115-127.

76 Cornish, HH 'Solvents & vapours'in *Casarett & Doull's Toxicology* 2 ed (1980) 475.

Table 7.1 Alcohol and chemicals as causes of disease
Causes of the following diseases or symptoms could be attributed to alcohol or the relevant chemicals

Diseases and symptoms	Related chemicals
Peripheral neuropathy	Pesticides; organic solvents (styrene, ketones, carbon disulphide); acrylonitrile; radiation; microwaves; metals (arsenic, lead)
Organic psychosis	Carbon disulphide; metals (mercury, organic lead)
Convulsions	Organic solvents (phenol)
Hallucinosis	Organic solvents; ether; methyl alcohol; toluene; xylene
Headaches	Lead; organic solvents; acrylonitrile; toluene; metals (manganese)
Dizziness	Organic solvents; phenol; carbon tetrachloride; toluene; xylene
Decreased cognitive and perceptual skills	Styrene
Sleep problems	Organic solvents
Tremor	Organic solvents; carbon disulphide; metals (manganese, mercury, vanadium)
Mood changes	Organic solvents
Amnesia	Organic solvents
Fatigue/weakness/stress	Heat; organophosphates; organic solvents; styrene; dinitrobenzene; vinyl chloride; metals (lead); stress
Chest pain	Organophosphate; metals (beryllium); irritant gases; stress
Cardiac problems	Organic solvents; carbon disulphide; toluene; stress
Cancers	Organic solvents; bischloromethyl ether; vinyl chloride; acrylonitrile
Gastrointestinal upsets	Organophosphates; organic solvents; carbon tetrachloride; metals (arsenic, cadmium, lead, thallium)
Liver diseases	Organic solvents; carbon tetrachloride; toluene; trinitrotoluene
Blood diseases	Organic solvents; tetrachloroethane; benzene
Skin (acne)	Chlorinated naphthylenes
Posture (backache)	Ergonomics
Accidents	Stress

2.1 Alcohol and chemicals

The effects of alcohol on physical health in the occupational setting can have varied toxic consequences when associated with certain chemicals; consequences that are often unknown to the unwary. Alcohol can react with chemicals by competitive metabolism, by the potentiation of effects, and by the induction or inhibition of enzyme systems that increase the toxic metabolites. Each of these reactions is described below.

2.1.1 Competitive metabolism

Alcohol, like many chemicals, utilises the enzyme known as alcohol dehydrogenase (ADH) for metabolism. The presence of alcohol in the blood when certain chemicals are absorbed into the body can have marked effects on the metabolism and therefore on the elimination of these chemicals. This is due to competitive metabolism. The effect is found particularly with organic solvents, especially those derived from benzene, as their first metabolic step is to an alcohol derived by oxidation. This alcohol is in direct competition with any ethyl alcohol in the blood for the available ADH, which breaks down potentially harmful alcohols. If the quantity of ethyl alcohol is excessive, it will compete successfully against the alcohol derivative of the organic solvent and accumulation of the solvent could develop, with a higher potential for toxic effects. In the case of an alcohol-dependent drinker where the process of continual 'topping up' occurs, this could have critical consequences as toxic exposure to the solvent could become chronic.

An example of competitive metabolism concerns trichloroethylene—one of the group of solvents (called halogenated hydrocarbons) used extensively for degreasing and dewaxing; aerosol propellants; refrigerants; and pesticides. Trichloroethylene has also been used commonly as a dry cleaning agent. The product of the metabolic breakdown competes unsuccessfully with ethyl alcohol, which inhibits any further metabolism and therefore it is further concentrated in the blood and can cause a toxic flushing of the skin due to vasodilation brought on by the exacerbated toxic effects. The characteristic effect is known as 'degreaser's flush'. The long-term effects of exposure to halogenated hydrocarbons are important, particularly those of trichloroethylene, which has a long biological half-life. The cumulative effects must be considered, especially if this metabolism is being hindered by a chronic excessive alcohol intake. The halogenated hydrocarbons have a central nervous system depressant effect that is enhanced in conjunction with alcohol, causing increased central nervous system depression. Individuals recovering from acute alcohol intake are therefore far more susceptible to the damaging properties of halogenated hydrocarbons on the liver since these can cause fatty liver degeneration leading to centrilobular necrosis. Kidney damage has also been reported. In animal studies, researchers have found a highly significant increase in hepatic carcinoma in a long-term oral feeding study involving trichloroethylene.[77]

2.1.2 Potentiation

The effects of alcohol can be enhanced or potentiated by the effects of solvents which produce side effects similar to those of intoxication. Those organic solvents, which are cerebral depressants, potentiate the effects of alcohol. Likewise, alcohol can potentiate the toxic effects of chemicals, for example the hepatotoxic effects of bromotrichloromethane, a halogenated hydrocarbon with a low molecular weight. There may be a link between halogenated hydrocarbons and cancer mortality.

Further examples of organic solvents which have potentiating properties with alcohol are trichloroethylene, benzene, toluene, xylene and styrene. Benzene is used extensively in the chemical industry and as a component of motor fuel; it is also used as a solvent

---

77 Li, J 'Persistent ethanol drinking increases liver injury induced by trinitrotoluene exposure: an in-plant case control study'(1991) 25 (3) *Chung Hua Ya Fung I Hsueh Tsa Chih* 143-145.

in the shoe industry and in printing. Exposure to benzene can be high in these latter two industries.

In cases of acute poisoning benzene potentiates the effects of alcohol and in cases of chronic poisoning benzene can suppress the bone marrow, leading to aplastic anaemia and in some cases even leukaemia. Toluene is used as a solvent in paints and as a component of aviation fuel and glues. It can produce liver and kidney damage and, in cases of acute intoxication (eg glue-sniffing), it produces narcosis, hallucinogenic reactions and occasionally cardiac arrhythmias. Trinitrotoluene workers who are chronic heavy drinkers run the additional risk of liver damage.[78]

Alcohol stimulates intestinal absorption and thus can potentiate the effects of the absorption of certain industrial substances, eg lead, mercury, arsenic and aniline.[79]

An illustration of this is alcohol's interaction with cobalt, which was discovered when cobalt was used to improve the foaming qualities of beer. There was a marked increase in toxic cardiomyopathy (congestive heart failure) attributable to cobalt.[80]

Xylene has similar properties to toluene and is used in adhesives, in varnishes, lacquers and paints as well as in the plastics, textile and pharmaceutical industries. It can produce narcosis, which is potentiated by alcohol, and in chronic cases can lead to aplastic anaemia—most likely due to contamination with benzene. Styrene is used in the manufacture of polystyrene and synthetic rubber and in the glass fibre industry; it can produce lethargy and narcosis, again potentiated by alcohol.

Alcohol and lead both interact on the synthesis of haeme (for haemoglobin) and suppress two enzymes (delta-amino laevulinic acid dehydratase and ferrocheletase) necessary for the synthesis of haemoglobin. This produces an increased urinary excretion of coproporphyrin, one of the chain of precursors of haemoglobin.

The effect of lead or alcohol on haemoglobin synthesis will produce anaemia only in severe cases of lead poisoning or alcohol abuse. But the urine testing for coproporphyrin in monitoring lead workers is masked by the additional effects of excessive alcohol consumption.[81] Most body lead is stored in bone, but alcohol displaces lead absorbed by bone and increases the blood-lead concentration. This makes lead more available to act on other organs. A high consumption of alcohol may impair the body's ability to detoxify lead, pesticides and polychlorinated biphenyls (PCB).

2.1.3 Potentiation of carcinogenic effects

Alcohol is a recognised carcinogenic promoter or co-carcinogen. It can work as a direct promoter—for example, in conjunction with tobacco, alcohol promotes the occurrence of cancer of the oesophagus or the oral cavity. It is suggested that people who smoke and drink excessive amounts of alcohol have a much higher risk of developing cancer of the oral cavity and of the oesophagus. Those who drink more than 10 units (80 g) of alcohol daily have an 18 times increased risk of developing cancer of the oesophagus and if, in addition, they smoke 20 or more cigarettes a day, then the risk is 44 times greater. Alcoholic drinks with a higher concentration of alcohol, eg whisky, cane spirit or vodka, can cause an even greater risk of developing cancer when taken in conjunction with

78 Goddard, J 'Alcohol as a hazard' in ILO *Encyclopedia Occupational Health & Safety* 3 ed (1983) 108.
79 Hammond, PB & Beliles, RP 'Metals' in *Casarett & Doull's Toxicology* 2 ed (1980) 442.
80 Roskali, SB *Clinical Biochemistry of Alcoholism* (1984) 169.
81 Royal College of Physicians *A Great and Growing Evil* (1987) 48.

cigarette smoking. Alcohol can also work as an indirect promoter of cancer by causing a deficiency in essential vitamins and nutrients as well as by affecting the immune system.

2.1.4 Induction or inhibition of enzyme systems

The microsomal oxidizing system required for the metabolism of most cellular processes, in particular, seems to be affected by alcohol and this affects the metabolism of chemicals and drugs. For example, alcohol potentiates the toxicity of carbon tetrachloride, thiacetamide and dimethyl-nitrosamine.

Carbon tetrachloride has been used in the production of freons and was previously used as a solvent in the dry-cleaning industry, in fire extinguishers and as a fumigant. It is highly toxic, causing narcosis, central nervous system disturbances, liver damage and renal damage. Cardiac arrhythmias have been noted and hepatocellular (liver cell) carcinoma has been identified.

Thiacetamide, a food additive, has been found to be hepatotoxic (liver toxic) and thyrotoxic (thyroid toxic).

Dimethylnitrosamine, one of the nitrosamine compounds, has potent carcinogenic activity and can cause cirrhosis of the liver. Nitrosamines are used or found in rocket fuel production, rubber manufacture, as synthetic cutting fluids, as a contamination in leather tanning, where there are particularly high concentrations, and in pesticide production and use. Nitrosamines are also found in environmental exposure, particularly that associated with cigarette smoke, and in the use of nitrites for preserving meat and fish, eg in salami, sausage, bacon and herring. Nitroglycol used in the explosives industry produces severe headaches and alcohol potentiates this effect. Further, 1,1,1-trichloroethane, trichloroethylene and toluene enhance serotonin-3 receptor function in the same way as ethanol.[82]

2.1.5 Increase in toxic metabolites

Some chemicals, for example calcium cyanamide, affect the metabolism of alcohol and can lead to the formation of toxic metabolites.

Thiuram compounds used in the synthetic rubber industry and as a fungicide can cause a disulfiram (antabuse) reaction. This involves an inhibition of the metabolism of alcohol, which causes an increase in the toxic metabolite acetaldehyde as the process of further breakdown of alcohol is inhibited. The reaction produces a pounding headache, a flushing of the face, a red blotchy rash similar to urticaria on the upper body, bronchospasm and palpitations. The blood pressure can be markedly raised, too.

2.2 Alcohol and altitude

The reactions to alcohol are affected by altitude: as the altitude increases, so the effect of the alcohol is increased. It has been subjectively postulated that the effects of alcohol are doubled at the high altitude at which commercial airplanes cruise. This effect is thought to be due to the changes in environmental oxygen tension rather than a direct pressure effect.

---

82 Lopreato, G, Phelan, R, Borghese, C, Beckstead M & Milic J 'Inhaled drugs of abuse enhance serotonin-3 receptor function'(2003) 70 (1) *Drug and Alcohol Dependence* 11-15.

2.3 Alcohol and temperature

2.3.1 Heat and dehydration

Dehydrated men become intoxicated more easily as their total body water is diminished. Looking at it from another perspective, a man who has had a heavy drinking bout will be dehydrated and acidotic. If, in addition, he combines this condition with physical work in a hot environment, he could be placing himself in an extremely dangerous situation, which could potentiate the effects of heat exhaustion and, as a result of dehydration, lead to heat exhaustion or even heat stroke.

2.3.2 Cold temperatures

Alcohol dilates the peripheral blood vessels and in severely cold climates can give rise to the disarming effect of increased warmth as the cold peripheral tissues are warmed by blood from the interior or core of the body. This can have a detrimental effect if the cold exposure continues, as heat, which should be conserved in the core of the body, is dissipated and lost at the periphery and could theoretically further expose a person to the dangers of hypothermia.

SUMMARY

Alcohol has a marked effect on several metabolic systems in the body that we depend upon for the safe metabolism of chemicals absorbed while we are at work. The main concern is potentiation of the toxic properties of organic chemicals and metals. The effects that alcohol has on our ability to adapt physiologically to the environment can also be hazardous. As has been well shown, alcohol also works as a carcinogenic promoter (or cocarcinogen). However acetaldehyde, the metabolic product of alcohol in the body, may be the true culprit and the cocarcinogen. Competitive metabolism with alcohol of other absorbed chemicals in the workplace can compete for the available acetaldehyde dehyrogenase, the enzyme which breaks down acetaldehyde allowing the chemical to accumulate especially in the liver.

When a hazard is identified in the workplace, insufficient consideration is given to alcohol as a direct or indirect complementary cause of the harmful effects. Likewise alcohol could be blamed for a problem that has an occupational origin. Even if alcohol exacerbates an occupational exposure – the disease is still occupational.

Chapter 8

The Effects of Drugs

MIKE MCCANN & NADINE HARKER BURNHAMS

This chapter should be read in conjunction with chapter 3, Drugs and Drug Abuse—an Introduction, which provides further information on this subject. Material from this earlier chapter that is particularly important is, for ease of reference, repeated here.

Drug abuse affects not only the health of the drug taker but also that of his or her family, friends, co-workers and, at least potentially, many others. This chapter begins by considering the role that drug abuse plays in the occurrence of accidents, and especially workplace accidents, and how this undermines the safety of others, notably employees. The second half of the chapter focuses on the health risks associated with drug abuse and how this impacts on the individual. Thus the chapter is divided into two sections:

I   Accidents and safety
II   Health of the individual.

I ACCIDENTS AND SAFETY

1. INTRODUCTION

Workplace accidents caused by drug abuse pose major concerns for industry and remain a risk to the health and safety of the drug user and other employees.[1] National data reported by the 2000 National Household Survey on Drug Abuse[2] in the USA indicate that 15,4% of persons aged 18 or older used illicit drugs during the past year, while 8,8% were current (past month) users.[3] (Office of Applied Studies, Substance Abuse and Mental Health Services Administration 2002). Although comparable statistics are not available in South Africa; of those individuals receiving treatment for drug abuse a percentage are employed either on a part-time or full-time basis. Worldwide there are 10,6 million heroin users yet 26,2 million amphetamine users.[4]

---

1   Spicer, RS & Miller, TR 'Impact of workplace peer focused substance abuse prevention and early intervention program' (2005) 29 (4) *Alcoholism: Clinical and Experimental Research* 609-611.

2   *National Household Survey on Drug Abuse* Office of Applied Studies SAMHSA http://www.oas.samhsa.gov/nhsda.htm (accessed October 2010).

3   Substance Abuse and Mental Health Services Administration. Office of Applied Studies *Drug Abuse Warning Network, 2003: Interim National Estimates of Drug-Related Emergency Department Visits DAWN Series D-26, DHHS Publication No. (SMA) 04-3972 Rockville, MD (2004).*

4   P Menary (Police Inspector Police Service Northern Ireland) presentation at ALAMA Conference (March 2010).

2. THE LINK BETWEEN DRUG USE AND WORKPLACE ACCIDENTS AND INJURIES

Various literature sources highlight the role of alcohol and drugs in the workplace as the cause of major occupational accidents.[5,6,7] A study on working high school students conducted by Shipp et al (2005)[8] found a positive association between increasing rates of current and lifetime use of all substances and injury risk. Similar findings were reported in an earlier study by Holcom et al (1993).[9] Widely publicised reports of accidents in which drug or alcohol use was involved have also become more common in recent years. The catastrophic oil spill in Alaska involving the Exxon Valdez tanker; where it was alleged that the tanker's captain was in charge of the vessel while under the influence of alcohol, ultimately heightened business and public concern about the role of substance abuse in workplace accidents.[10] Injury resulting from workplace accidents is one of the consequences of substance abuse, with costs of occupational injuries in the United States exceeding $100 billion annually.

However, even though a seemingly obvious relationship between substance abuse and resultant injury in the workplace exists, researchers find it difficult to draw a clear association or to quantify the association.[11,12] This is largely due to the fact that research findings up to now have been fairly mixed and the methodologies needed to draw these associations are often complex.[13] In spite of these drawbacks, many companies around the world have adopted various wellness programmes (ranging from Employee Assistance Programmes to universal prevention programmes) as a means of addressing the growing problem of substance abuse and minimising the burden substance abuse can create.

5   Wickizer, TM, Kopjar, B, Franklin, G, Joesch, J, 'Do drug-free workplace programs prevent Occupational Injuries?' (2004) 39 (1) *Health Services Research* 91-110.

6   Spicer, RS & Miller, TR 'Impact of workplace peer focused substance abuse prevention and early intervention program' (2005) 29 (4) *Alcoholism: Clinical and Experimental Research* 609-611.

7   Ramachand, R, Pomeroy, A & Arkes, J 'The Effects of Substance Use on Workplace Injuries' Center for Health and Safety in the Workplace, Occasional Paper (2009).

8   Shipp, EM, Tortolero, SR, Cooper, SP, Baumler, EG & Weller, NF 'Substance use and Occupational Injuries amongst high school students in South Texas' (2005) 31 (2) *The American Journal of Drug and Alcohol Abuse*. 253-265.

9   Holcom, ML, Lehman, WEK & Simpson, DD 'Employee Accidents: Influences of Personal Characteristics, job characteristics and substance use in jobs differing in accident potential' (1993) 24 (4) *Journal of Safety Research* 205-221.

10 Wickizer, TM, Kopjar, B, Franklin, G & Joesch, J 'Do drug-free workplace programs prevent Occupational Injuries?' (2004) 39 *Health Services Research* 91-110.

11 Ramachand, R, Pomeroy, A & Arkes, J 'The Effects of Substance Use on Workplace Injuries' Center for Health and Safety in the Workplace, Occasional Paper (2009).

12 Kaestner, R & Grossman, M 'The Effect of Drug Use on Workplace Accidents'(1998) 5 (3) *Labour Economics* 267-294.

13 Wickizer, TM, Kopjar, B, Franklin, G & Joesch, J 'Do drug-free workplace programs prevent Occupational Injuries?' (2004) 39 *Health Services Research* 91-110.

According to the Center for Disease Control, the majority of occupational injuries in the USA are transportation accidents.[14] Although very little literature on drug-related occupational injuries in the South African context exists, studies conducted by Pick et al (2003) suggest that a number of occupational injuries in South Africa's mining industry are related to substance abuse, and, more particularly, to cannabis use.[15]

At this point, it is important to note that the effect that a drug has will depend on the type of drug, the amount that is taken, the person who is taking it and, sometimes, on the circumstances in which it is taken or administered. For instance, cocaine can be either snorted or injected and the immediate effect on the body will vary depending on which method is chosen. Large doses of drugs may result in an overdose or even death, whereas small doses of, for example, a depressant, may just induce drowsiness and a feeling of wellbeing. Two (or more) drugs could have a synergistic effect; so too could a combination of drugs and alcohol.

In the next section we turn our attention to the main categories and types of drugs there are.

3 CATEGORIES AND TYPES OF DRUGS

Drugs can be placed in three main categories based on the primary effects they have on the central nervous system. These categories are:
- Stimulants
- Hallucinogens
- Depressants or narcotics.

3.1 Stimulants

The types of drugs in this category include amphetamines, cocaine and ecstasy (MDMA, MDA, MDE).

3.1.1 Amphetamines

These are agents that excite the central nervous system. They are often referred to as 'uppers' or 'speed', because they 'rev up' the vital functions of the body and produce a mental state associated with heightened alertness, elevated mood or euphoria, increased activity, excited talkativeness, and a feeling of power.[16,17] Prolonged use or abuse of

14 Jarman, DW, Naimi, TS, Pickard, SP, Daley, WR & De AK 'Binge drinking and occupation, North Dakota, 2004–2005' (2007) 4 (4) *Prev Chronic Dis* at http://www.cdc.gov/pcd/issues/2007/oct/06_0152.htm (accessed November 2010). See also Centers for Disease Control and Prevention 'Fatal Occupational Injuries, 2005' (2007a) 56 (13) *Morbidity and Mortality Weekly Report* 297-301 and http://www.cdc.gov/mmwr/preview/mmwrhtml/mm5613a1.htm (accessed 7 January 2010).

15 Centers for Disease Control and Prevention, 'Fatal Occupational Injuries, 2005' (2007) 56 (13) *Morbidity and Mortality Weekly Report*. 297-301 also at http://www.cdc.gov/mmwr/preview/mmwrhtml/mm5613a1.htm (accessed 7 January 2010).

16 Pidd, K & Roche, A 'Prevention of alcohol-related harm in the workplace' (2009) *Prevention Research Quarterly*. National Centre for Education and Training on Addiction (NCETA), Flinders University, South Australia. www.druginfo.adf.org.au. National Centre for Education and Training on Addiction Australia Fact sheet 4.

17 Cape Town Drug Counselling Centre *Families and Drugs: its closer to home than you think* (2007) published by CTDCC.

stimulants has also been associated with loss of appetite, insomnia, aggressive actions or behaviours and extreme nervousness leading to acute anxiety and even paranoia.

Illegal amphetamines have now been replaced by methamphetamine, which has more side effects and is stronger. The drug is manufactured in illicit laboratories. These laboratories have been discovered in houses, motel rooms, garages, sheds and cellars. The manufacture and use of methamphetamine is a worldwide problem and is reaching epidemic proportions in countries such as the USA, Thailand, Australia, Eastern Europe and the Cape Town area of South Africa. The manufacturing process is quite simple and does not require specialised equipment or facilities. Household products contain many of the ingredients needed. However, the production process is extremely dangerous. Gases given off during manufacture include phosphine, iodine and hydrochloric acid. The fumes these gases emit can kill in high doses. The chances of identifying an illicit laboratory are relatively small; however, explosions are common (occurring in one in six laboratories, and in the US there are between six and eight explosions each week), and the consequences of this are often tragic. It is generally due to one of these incidents that an illicit laboratory is discovered.

The toxic waste generated by the production process is highly carcinogenic and consists of one part methamphetamine to six parts toxic waste. The disposal of the waste is invariably primitive or simply left to those finding the abandoned laboratory. Methamphetamine can be taken orally, injected or even snorted. Amphetamines have no proven physical dependence but do have a high degree of psychological dependence. Psychological dependence occurs when a user develops a powerful mental craving for the pleasurable effects of the drug of abuse. Users begin relying on the drug to produce a state of well-being, and may not be able to engage in daily tasks or face life unless they are using the drug. Psychological dependence is usually associated with an obsession with the drug of choice and the user loses all interest in life outside of obtaining the drug and using it. Such intense and uncontainable craving leads the user to commit anti-social even criminal acts in order to obtain the drug. Despite deterioration of health, family and other relationships users, feel compelled to carry on taking the drug with a disregard for the consequences of their actions.

Methamphetamines can also raise blood pressure significantly or even dangerously. Once the drug is withdrawn after prolonged use, the effect is one of exhaustion, irritability, severe depression and disorientation. The drugs works on the dopamine system; depleting the body's total supply of dopamine by dumping it into the brain to create a high that can last for 15 hours. In some cases users can binge for up to 20 days chasing the first high. The central nervous system then crashes, leading to severe depression, psychosis and disorientation. The withdrawal can take between 30 to 90 days.

Only 10% of people become completely 'clean' of methamphetamine. The craving can easily return. Often the psychosis involves the feeling of things creeping under the skin and then severe scratching develops, particularly of the forearms, leading to open longitudinal deep sores almost to the bone. Grinding of the teeth is another phenomenon, which can result in damaged teeth. The oral cavity is damaged further as the individual's saliva dries up, the level of acidity increases and the condition of 'meth mouth' arises, where the person's teeth fall out and the gums rot with sepsis and degeneration. The toxic unhygienic conditions in which the drug is produced, combined with injecting or snorting, leads inevitably to significant contamination and the development of open sores and abscesses, which can be prolific and can lead to cellulitis and septicaemia.

Identification signs of acute intoxication: Loss of appetite, increased blood pressure, agitation, dilated pupils, increase in body temperature at high doses, weight loss, and high levels of energy and activity. Amphetamine use is associated with disinhibitory behaviour, which manifests in a raised level of sexual awareness. This in turn can lead to promiscuity and the user engaging in unsafe sexual practices over a short period of time. The risks of HIV, HCV and HBV are very prevalent.

Amphetamines can be detected in urine up to 48 hours after absorption (see chapter 3).

The poem 'I am crystal meth.' written by Alicia Van Davis before she died of a meth overdose is very poignant on this subject and can be found at the blog http://somechicksblog.com/meth-poems-art/i-am-crystal-meth.

3.1.2 Cocaine

Cocaine was once used as a mucosal local anaesthetic and has a short half life, which means its effect is not prolonged, lasting for approximately one hour. This produces a very compulsive and frequent use (and abuse) of the drug.

Cocaine is snorted, injected or even smoked. Chronic or prolonged use by snorting can damage the nasal septum. This damage can take the form of erosions of the septum, or even, in extreme cases of abuse, its total destruction. Prolonged use or an overdose can lead to agitation, hallucinations, convulsions and cardiac damage. Once the drug is withdrawn there is apathy or irritability, fatigue, exhaustion, and even depression. As with the use of amphetamines, there is little or no physical dependence but there is extreme psychological dependence .

Identification signs of acute intoxication: Irritability, increased heart rate, high blood pressure and fast pulse, dilated pupils, increase in body temperature, and high levels of energy and activity.

Cocaine can be detected in the urine as a metabolite (see chapter 4 Drugs).

3.1.3 Ecstasy (MDMA)

Worldwide, an estimated 4.5 million people use Ecstasy. In some countries Ecstasy is the second most widely abused illicit substance after cannabis (eg the Netherlands). Although Ecstasy markets are still concentrated in Western Europe, North America and Australia, they are filtering through to Asia and Africa.

Ecstasy is also a central nervous system (CNS) stimulant and has chemical structure similar to the methamphetamine and the hallucinogen mescaline and can produce both stimulant and psychedelic effects. However, the principal active ingredient in Ecstasy is MDMA (3,4 methylenedioxymethamphetamine). MDMA is most often found in tablet form although it is sometimes found in powder and capsule form. Central nervous stimulants that are not illicit include some slimming tablets and products containing caffeine and nicotine.

Identification signs of acute intoxication: MDMA leads to temporary effects such as increased heart rate, raised blood pressure, nausea, dry mouth, heightened energy, decreased appetite, jaw clenching, grinding of teeth, muscle aches, gait disturbance, insomnia, irritability and lack of concentration. Other hallucinatory effects may include perceptual and other visual distortions. There are normally changes in consciousness with strong sensual and emotional overtones, and altered speech.[18] Other side effects include hyponatremia and hyperthermia which in rare cases cause death. Hyponatremia is caused by excessieve water intake, causing a drop in sodium levels and brain swelling. Hyperhtermia is due to loss of the normal thermal balance mechanism, leading to body temperature rising above 42 °C. This can lead to organ failure.

3.2 Hallucinogens

The types of drugs in this category include LSD, mescaline, psilocybin, phencyclidine (PCP) and ketamine (Special K).

Hallucinogens are agents that impact on the vital functions of the central nervous system, creating distortions in thought and perception that range from sensory illusions to outright hallucinations as well as changes in mood. Other drugs such as cannabis and amphetamines, if taken in high enough doses, can induce similar hallucinogenic effects but this is not necessarily the reason why they are taken. Unlike most of the other drugs described, hallucinogens do not induce dependence and they are seldom used frequently. Use of these drugs is usually associated with those under the age of 30. Psychotic reactions can occur and they are associated with flashbacks if large doses have been taken in the past, but generally there are no long-term sequelae (secondary consequences) of developing medical problems.[19]

3.2.1 LSD (acid)

Lysergic acid diethylamide, or LSD, is generally accepted to be the most potent of the hallucinogenic drugs. The effect it has depends upon the psychiatric stability of the person taking it, as well as their personality. Panic attacks can be induced a few hours later and flashbacks can occur many years later.[20]

3.2.2 Mescaline (speed)

Mescaline is thought to have similar effects to LSD, however hallucinations associated with use of Mescaline are alterations of existing objects, sounds and stimuli and not the manifestation of bizarre and imaginary objects, sounds or persons, as in the case of LSD. Mescaline requires a larger dose than LSD for the effect to occur and it then lasts shorter. It has been known to cause withdrawal-type symptoms if taken in high enough doses.

3.2.3 Psilocybin (magic mushroom)

Psilocybin is a substance found in the psilocybe genus of mushrooms, which generates a hallucinogenic effect when taken in large doses and can induce psychosis. It can also have a toxic effect on the heart and central nervous system and there is a risk of poisoning. The effect is similar to LSD, though of shorter duration.

---

18 Ecstasy use in South Africa (2008) factsheet. Prepared by the Alcohol and Drug Research Unit of the Medical Research Council.

19 Hulse, G, White, J, Cape, G (eds) *Management of Alcohol and Drug Problems* (2002) Oxford University Press.

20 Hulse (n 19) at 310–327.

3.2.4 Phencyclidine (PCP; angel dust)

Phencyclidine can be a respiratory depressant at high doses; it can also induce schizophrenic-type symptoms such as depersonalisation, visual or auditory hallucinations and general thought disorders.[21]

3.2.5 Ketamine (Special K)

Ketamine is an anaesthetic used in emergency medical situations. It acts quickly, stimulating the cardiovascular system and can, like LSD, produce hallucinations. Ketamine is similar to PCP in its ability to produce a schizophrenic-type reaction. It can also induce bad 'trips', which can be dangerous and can result in suicide (see chapter 3).

3.3 Depressants or narcotics

Depressants have the primary effect of slowing down the functions of the central nervous system. In small doses depressants cause feelings of well-being, calmness and relaxation.[22,23] For this reason they are sometimes referred to as 'downers'.[24]

Depressants can be used to treat anxiety, stress, panic, and sleep disorders, and to provide relief from physical pain. However, depressants can produce unpleasant side effects, such as tiredness or extreme lethargy, dizziness and loss of libido. Taken in sufficient quantities, they can also induce comas and can even bring about death. The use of depressants can also dull an individual's inhibitions, which could lead to the situation where he or she engages in inappropriate or antisocial behavior. Alcohol, heroin, morphine, Wellconal, barbiturates, tranquilisers, mandrax and solvents are depressants.

3.4 Effects on workers and workplace

It is clear that the use of the drugs just discussed, when considered in the context of the workplace, has serious repercussions for the health and safety of employees and the operability of the workplace. The workplace and workers can be affected in the ways set out below:

3.4.1 Inability to operate machinery or drive a vehicle

In South Africa, driving a vehicle under the influence of alcohol or any drug is illegal and an arrestable offence. The Occupational Health and Safety Act 85 of 1993 also contains clauses which prohibit the use of machinery when under the influence of any substance(s). Employees under the influence of stimulants may exhibit enhanced risk-taking behaviour, for instance by driving more aggressively and disobeying the rules of

---

21 Cape Town Drug Counselling Centre *Families and Drugs: its closer to home than you think* (2007) published by CTDCC.

22 Cape Town Drug Counselling Centre *Families and Drugs: its closer to home than you think* (2007) published by CTDCC.

23 Pidd, K & Roche, A 'Prevention of alcohol-related harm in the workplace' (2009) *Prevention Research Quarterly*. National Centre for Education and Training on Addiction (NCETA), Flinders University, South Australia www.druginfo.adf.org.au.

24 Cape Town Drug Counselling Centre *Families and Drugs: its closer to home than you think* (2007) published by CTDCC.

the road, but they are also less able (or unable) to judge speed and distance accurately.[25] These effects have implications for productivity and worker safety, and may impact negatively on worker relationships.

Employees under the influence of a depressant are likely to have slower reaction times, which will interfere with their perceptions of 'sound, time and space'.[26] Some prescription and over-the-counter medications reduce the user's powers of concentration and/or coordination; they can also have a sedative effect, where the user experiences drowsiness or may even fall asleep. Medications should therefore be used with caution when operating heavy machinery or driving.

3.4.2 Workplace accidents

All illicit drugs can decrease alertness, potentially increasing the risk of accidents occurring. Employees under the influence of large doses of an illicit substance may struggle to complete simple manual tasks, and are at risk of committing serious errors of judgement. The outcome could be that the employee causes injury to him- or herself, colleagues and, depending on the workplace environment, customers and/or members of the general public. The risk of injury through drug use/abuse is not confined to substances taken 'on the job'; in many instances substance abuse may have taken place several hours before the work day (or work shift) begins, but the spillover effects, such as an alcohol-induced hangover or depressant-induced drowsiness, may be present, which increases injury risk.[27] According to Lemon (1993), hangovers affect cognitive skills, resulting in reduced concentration and poor judgement.[28]

3.4.3 Strained relations with customers and other employees

Depending on the type of drug used, employees may impair existing co-worker relationships and relationships with customers. This can manifest in a number of ways. For example, an employee under the influence of a stimulant may appear over-excited, evidenced by his or her tendency to talk rapidly and animatedly. Alternatively, the same employee might exhibit aggressive behaviour towards others, which is then followed by one or more periods of severe depression. For customers and co-workers such erratic behaviour is worrisome, and often results in others distrusting the employee. Depressants, by contrast, may result in withdrawn behaviour and difficulty in holding a sensible conversation,[29] while hallucinogens may cause an employee to appear vacant or stunned, or to appear happy yet exhibit nervous energy.[30]

---

25 Pidd, K & Roche, A 'Prevention of alcohol-related harm in the workplace' (2009) *Prevention Research Quarterly*. National Centre for Education and Training on Addiction (NCETA), Flinders University, South Australia www.druginfo.adf.org.au. National Centre for Education and Training on Addiction Australia Fact sheet 4.

26 Ibid.

27 Ramachand, R, Pomeroy, A & Arkes, J 'The Effects of Substance Use on Workplace Injuries' Center for Health and Safety in the Workplace, Occasional Paper (2009).

28 Lemon, J 'Alcoholic Hangover and Performance: A Review' (1993) 12 (3) *Drug and Alcohol Review* 299-314.

29 Pidd, K & Roche, A 'Prevention of alcohol-related harm in the workplace' (2009) *Prevention Research Quarterly*. National Centre for Education and Training on Addiction (NCETA), Flinders University, South Australia. www.druginfo.adf.org.au. National Centre for Education and Training on Addiction Australia Fact sheet 4.

30 Ibid.

Taking illicit drugs is a hazardous activity. The disruptive effects they cause can severely disrupt the normal behaviour patterns of the user. In the context of the workplace, an employee who takes drugs will almost certainly experience difficulties in performing their jobs effectively and responsibly. The employee-drug user not only endangers their own health but also puts at risk the health and safety of others.

II HEALTH OF THE INDIVIDUAL

4. INTRODUCTION

The short-term and long-term effects of illicit drug use on the central nervous system are many and varied. As noted in the previous section, the factors that determine what effects there are include the type of drug taken, in what quantities and how often it is taken, the chosen method of ingestion, the personality and general health of the individual user, and so on. However, many drugs do produce global body changes—such as dramatic changes in appetite and increases in body temperature—that may impact a variety of health conditions. Withdrawal from drug use can create numerous adverse health effects, including restlessness, mood swings, fatigue, changes in appetite, muscle and bone pain, insomnia, cold flushes, diarrhoea and vomiting.

In addition to these drug-related health problems, there exists a further set of health problems that are aggravated by the use of illicit drugs, namely

- HIV/AIDS, hepatitis and other infectious diseases
- Cardiovascular health problems
- Respiratory health problems
- Mental health problems.

5. HIV/AIDS, HEPATITIS AND OTHER INFECTIOUS DISEASES

Concurrent with substance abuse and associated work effects, the HIV/AIDS epidemic continues to have a major impact on workers' health. According to Adams et al (2007), some mining companies in South Africa report HIV prevalence to be as high as 30% among their workforce.[31] More worryingly, is the growing body of research on the link between substance abuse and HIV worldwide and in South Africa. The role of non-injecting substances of abuse and risky sexual behaviour remains a major concern to public health practitioners in South Africa. While the majority of HIV/AIDS transmissions in Southern Africa occur through heterosexual contact, recent studies indicate that substance use plays a substantial role in this. Studies by Parry and Needle (2006),[32] Morojele et al (2006),[33]

---

31 Adams, S, Morar, R, Kolbe-Alexander, T & Jeebhay, MF *Health and Health Care in the Workplace. Rationing of Medicines and Health Care Technology* (2007) available at www.hst.org.za/uploads/files/content_ack_07 (accessed July 2008).

32 Parry, C & Needle, R *Southern African International Rapid Assessment and Response Evaluation: Executive Summary of Key Findings of Drug Use and Sexual Risk Patterns among Vulnerable Drug Using Populations* (2006) South Africa: Medical Research Council.

33 Morojele, NK, Kachieng'a, MA, Mokoko, E, Nkoko, MA, Parry, CDH, Nkowane, MA, Moshia, KM, & Saxena, S 'Alcohol use and sexual risk behaviour among risky drinkers and bar and shebeen patrons in Gauteng province, South Africa' (2006) 62 *Social Science & Medicine* 217-227.

Parry and Pithey,[34] and Wechsberg et al (2008)[35] examined the link between drug use and sexual risk behaviours and found ample evidence of an association between substance abuse and risky sexual behaviours among men, women and adolescents of both sexes.

Drug intoxication and addiction can compromise judgement and decision-making by minimising inhibitions, and potentially lead to risky sex, needle sharing, or the trading of sex for drugs by both men and women. Drug users, particularly injecting drug users, are at risk of contracting HIV, hepatitis C (HCV), and other infectious disease, through the sharing and reuse of syringes and other injection paraphernalia that have been used by infected individuals.[36] The number of injecting drug users in South Africa is still relatively small—approximately 16 000 according to some estimates[37]—which contrasts sharply with the situation in the United States where injection drug users (IDUs) represent the highest risk group for acquiring HCV infection.[38] Worryingly, there is no vaccine for the hepatitis C virus. However, anyone who has injected drugs should go for testing.

6. CARDIOVASCULAR HEALTH PROBLEMS

Adverse cardiovascular problems and effects associated with drug abuse range from users experiencing elevated or abnormal heart rates to myocardial infarction. The misuse/abuse of stimulants can have several short-term effects, such as an increase in body temperature, heart rate and blood pressure, dilation of the pupils and constriction of blood vessels. The latter condition can cause shooting pains in the area surrounding the heart in users of speed and cocaine. However, when the effect of the drugs has worn off the blood vessels are likely to dilate again and the pain disappears.[39] Neurological effects, such as strokes, seizures, headaches, and even coma are also synonymous with drug use, particularly stimulant abuse. In rare instances, sudden death has been associated with the first use of cocaine.[40,41] It is also important to note that drug abusers with pre-existing medical conditions such as hypertension, irregular heartbeat and other heart conditions are often at a greater risk of developing significant problems.

34 Parry, CDH and Pithey, AL 'Drug Abuse and HIV-Risk Behaviour in South Africa' (2006) 5 (2) *African Journal of Drug and Alcohol Studies* 140–157.

35 Wechsberg, W, Luseno, W K, Riehman, KS, Karg, R, & Parry, C 'Substance use and sexual risk within the context of gender inequality' (2008) 43 *Substance Use and Misuse* 1186-1201.

36 National Institute on Drug Abuse, NIDA Capsules, (Rockville, MD: Press Office of the National Institute on Drug Abuse, 1986).

37 Viviers, P 'Annual Reports Questionnaire: Part II (2007)' Pretoria: Department of Social Development in *Global State of Harm Reduction* (2008) 108.

38 National Institute on Drug Abuse, NIDA Capsules, (Rockville, MD: Press Office of the National Institute on Drug Abuse, 1986).

39 Nunley, KF 'Drug Effects on the Brain' DrugRehabs.Org available at http://www.drug-rehabs.org/sart/drug%20effects (accessed October 2010).

40 National Institute on Drug Abuse, NIDA Capsules, (Rockville, MD: Press Office of the National Institute on Drug Abuse, 1986).

41 Cape Town Drug Counselling Centre *Families and Drugs: its closer to home than you think* (2007) published by CTDCC.

Because of its stimulant properties and the environments in which it is often taken, MDMA is associated with vigorous physical activity for extended periods.[42] This can lead to one of the most significant, although rare, acute adverse effects—hyperthermia, which occurs when the body's temperature control mechanisms fail and a person in effect 'overheats '. [43,44] Treatment of hyperthermia requires prompt medical attention, as it can quickly lead to muscle breakdown, which can in turn result in kidney failure. In addition, dehydration, hypertension, and heart failure may occur in susceptible individuals. MDMA can also reduce the pumping efficiency of the heart,[45]of particular concern during periods of increased physical activity, causing further complications.

7. RESPIRATORY HEALTH PROBLEMS

The use of drugs is linked to a variety of respiratory health problems such as cold symptoms, sinus infections, and pharyngitis, which can cause, according to Brook et al (2002), moderate to severe disruption over a five-year period in both male and female adolescents.[46] The presence of existing lung complications (including various types of pneumonia and tuberculosis) may be worsened by the depressant effects some drugs have on respiration. In addition, street heroin often contains non-soluble substances that have the potential to restrict (through a clogging of blood vessels) the passage of blood to the lungs, liver, kidneys, and brain. This can cause infection or even death of small patches of cells in vital organs.[47] One of heroin's after effects is that it can cause a user's breathing to slow down, sometimes to the point of respiratory failure and death.[48]

Cannabis has been associated with cancer of the lungs and other parts of the respiratory tract because it contains both irritants and carcinogens. Cannabis smoke contains 50–70% more carcinogenic hydrocarbons than tobacco smoke.[49] Cannabis smoke produces high levels of an enzyme that converts certain hydrocarbons into their carcinogenic form, which may accelerate the changes that ultimately produce malignant cells in the body.[50]

---

42 Parrott, AC 'Human psychopharmacology of Ecstasy (MDMA): a review of 15 years of empirical research' (2001)16 *Human Psychopharmacol Clin Exp* 557-577.

43 Lyles, J; and Cadet, JL 'Methylenedioxymethamphetamine (MDMA, Ecstasy) neurotoxicity: cellular and molecular mechanisms'(2003) 42 *Brain Research Reviews* 155-168.

44 Dafters, RI & Lynch, E 'Persistent loss of thermoregulation in the rate induced by 3,4-methylenedioxymethamphetamine (MDMA or "Ecstasy") but not by fenfluramine' (1998) 138 *Psychopharmacology* 207-212.

45 Lester, SJ, Baggott, M, Welm, S, Schiller, NB; Jones, RT, Foster, E, & Mendelson, J 'Cardiovascular effects of 3,4-methylenedioxymethamphetamine: a double-blind, placebo-controlled trial' (2000) 133 *Annals of Internal Medicine* 969-973.

46 Brook, JS, Finch, SJ, Whiteman, M & Brook, DW 'Drug Use and Neurobehavioral, Respiratory and Cognitive Problems: Precursors and Mediators' (2002) 30 *Journal of Adolescent Health* 433-441.

47 National Institute on Drug Abuse, NIDA Capsules, (Rockville, MD: Press Office of the National Institute on Drug Abuse, 1986).

48 National Institute on Drug Abuse, NIDA Capsules, (Rockville, MD: Press Office of the National Institute on Drug Abuse, 1986).

49 National Institute on Drug Abuse, NIDA Capsules, (Rockville, MD: Press Office of the National Institute on Drug Abuse, 1986).

50 Sridhar, KS, Raub, WA, Weatherby, NL Jr, Metsch, LR, Surratt, HL, Inciardi, JA, Duncan, RC, Anwyl, RS & McCoy, CB 'Possible role of marijuana smoking as a carcinogen in the development of lung cancer at a young age' (1994) 26 (3) *Journal of Psychoactive Drugs* 285-288.

8. MENTAL HEALTH PROBLEMS

Drug abuse causes chemical changes in the brain that can make day-to-day functioning difficult. Most drugs of abuse trigger the brain to release more dopamine than normal. Over time, this can affect how the user senses pleasure, and the brain comes to expect the presence of the drug. The absence of the drug may cause depression. As a result, many drug abusers experience extreme difficulty when trying to quit drugs. Chronic use of some drugs of abuse can cause long-lasting changes in the brain, which may lead to paranoia, depression, aggression, and hallucinations.

Some drugs, for example methamphetamine, when chronically abused, can produce symptoms such as anxiety, agitation, confusion, insomnia, mood disturbances, and violent or aggressive behaviour in the user/abuser. Drug abusers may also present with a number of psychotic features, which include paranoia, visual and auditory hallucinations, and delusions. Psychotic symptoms can sometimes last for months or years after abuse has ceased.[51]

It should also be noted that the proportion of persons suffering from co-occurring mental health disorders (co-morbidity) has increased drastically and has been well documented in epidemiologic and clinical studies.[52] Persons with co-occurring disorders (COD) have one or more disorders relating to the use of alcohol and/or other drugs of abuse as well as one or more mental health disorders. For example, a person with an undiagnosed psychiatric or mental health disorder such as anxiety or depression may abuse drugs to alleviate the symptoms of the anxiety or depression. If he or she receives treatment for the drug addiction but not for the depression or anxiety, the depression/anxiety remains. This implies that the need for relief from the condition's symptoms also remains, which could see the individual continuing to use drugs to manage his or her condition. In a National Comorbidity Study (NCS) conducted by Kesslar et al (1996), approximately half the respondents who met criteria for a substance-use disorder at some time in their life also met criteria for one or more lifetime mental disorders. It is therefore important that a full clinical assessment is completed when employees present with any substance-related problem.

9. OTHER HEALTH PROBLEMS

Drug abuse has also been associated with liver complications and other gastrointestinal disorders. Drugs restrict the liver's ability to perform its key functions of filtering and cleansing the blood. Also, the long-term abuse of drugs such as heroin can cause severe liver-tissue damage.

Many drugs of abuse have been known to cause nausea and vomiting soon after ingestion. Gastrointestinal complications such as abdominal pain and nausea have been connected with cocaine and heroin abuse. The chronic misuse of non-narcotic analgesics has also been associated with gastrointestinal problems such as ulcers, analgesic nephropathy (including renal failure and renal cancers), and atherogenesis.[53]

---

51   National Institute on Drug Abuse, NIDA Capsules, (Rockville, MD: Press Office of the National Institute on Drug Abuse, 1986).

52   Harris, K & Edlund, M 'Use of Mental Health Care and Substance Abuse Treatment Among Adults with co-occurring Disorders' (2005) 56 *Psychiatric Services* 954-959.

53   Over the counter and prescription medicine misuse (2008) FACTSHEET prepared by the Alcohol and Drug Research Unit of the Medical Research Council.

Neurological disorders are synonymous with drug abuse. All drugs of abuse act on the brain to produce their euphoric effect but they can also cause seizures, strokes, and brain damage. Drug use can cause brain changes that lead to problems with memory, attention and decision-making, all of which can significantly diminish the individual's quality of life.

SUMMARY

The effects of drugs are varied and depend upon, among other things, the dose taken, the class of drug used and the physiology of the individual drug user. Drugs are used illegally for a number of purposes but the majority of reasons are connected to recreational use. Some drugs will cause significant physical dependence while others will only cause psychological dependence. However, in the case of cocaine and methamphetamine the psychological dependence involved can have particularly severe consequences. The rapid expansion of the methamphetamine market in all regions of the world, and the associated severe toxic reactions the drug produces, is a source of universal concern. Illicit drugs that are administered by injection dramatically increase the risk of developing hepatitis (HCV or HBV) and HIV. Alcohol abuse creates myriad problems; not least in the workplace, where the consequences of an alcohol-induced hangover can jeopardise the performance of the recovering employee, his or her colleagues and the organisation as a whole. Changes in behavior or personality, and the triggering of underlying mental health problems are a constant threat with the use of illegal drugs. The lack of effective treatment for dependence or substance misuse when there is co-morbid mental health illness is commonplace and this provides a challenging and difficult situation to manage. A summary of symptoms and signs of drug abuse can be found in Appendix 11.

Chapter 9

Objective Ways of Identifying Trends of Substance Abuse Problems in the Workplace

Mike McCann & Nadine Harker Burnhams

1. INTRODUCTION

It has been estimated that a company can expect anything between 5–35% of its workforce to have an alcohol problem that in some way affects their work. Drug use has a similar, if often less perceptible effect upon employee performance. The difficulty comes in identifying these problems. The true extent of alcohol and drug abuse usually becomes apparent only when a company makes a conscious effort to uncover it, which usually happens after a serious incident has occurred, such as an accident, a breakdown or a dramatic drop in productivity. This reactive (as opposed to proactive) approach means that the company sees only the observable extent of the problem and not necessarily the actual degree and level of abuse.

In this chapter and the next (chapter 10) we will consider the issue of identifying substance abuse. In the present chapter we will look at the objective methods used to identify trends of substance abuse in the workplace, which will include an examination of the influences and pressures that may lie behind such abuse arising in the first place. In chapter 10 we will look at the objective ways in which it is possible to identify individual employees who suffer from a substance abuse problem.

2. IDENTIFYING THE EXTENT OF SUBSTANCE ABUSE IN THE WORKPLACE

Substance abuse in the workplace creates subjective problems and objective problems.

The subjective problems are those which are identified as being the expressed view of a particular individual and as such are often difficult to measure or quantify and can be distorted by varied perceptions.

The objective problems are those which are measurable and quantifiable. They are invariably discrete and factual. Objective problems can be grouped and tabulated to give statistical data that can help to identify the extent of the problem in the company. Objective problems can be assessed according to the following criteria:

- Health
- Absenteeism and sickness absence
- Accidents
- Disciplinary offences
- Productivity

- Medical tests
- Random testing for intoxication
- Culture.

2.1 HEALTH

The health criteria discussed here involve only those conditions which are commonly and usually present in the form of short-term absence due to sickness. It must be stressed that these criteria identify trends of substance abuse; they do not provide diagnostic evidence of substance abuse problems in particular individuals. Similarly, the various health conditions described below can be caused or aggravated by factors other than alcohol and/or drug abuse. For more information, refer to chapter 7 Effects of Alcohol on the Individual and chapter 8 Effects of Drugs on the Individual.

2.1.1 Blood pressure

One of the basic medical tests is blood-pressure measurement; if a company has a large number of employees suffering from high blood pressure, this could be caused by alcohol problems. Alcohol abuse is the most common cause of raised blood pressure: raised blood pressure is three times more common in heavy drinkers than in the general population.[1] A study examining the relationships between illicit drugs, alcohol and blood pressure, found that men who used alcohol and illicit drugs were more likely to have irregular blood pressure readings and higher systolic blood pressure (SBP).[2] Illegal drugs, and more specifically cocaine, marijuana, amphetamines, and methamphetamine, are probable sources of severe or newly diagnosed hypertension.[3]

2.1.2 Gastric problems

A majority of the recurring unidentified causes of short-term gastrointestinal problems are attributable to alcohol excess.[4] Alcohol-related conditions account for 51% of gastroenterology inpatients.[5]

By far the most common of these complaints is acute gastritis, which is identified by the presence of one or more of the following symptoms: nausea, vomiting, retching and upper abdominal pain, often accompanied by diarrhoea. Since most heavy drinking takes place at weekends and/or after payday, the incidence of gastric complaints among employees is often higher during the period immediately following these occasions. Any assessment of the prevalence of alcohol abuse in the workplace needs to take account of this causal link.

---

1   Royal College of Physicians *A Great and Growing Evil* (1987) 63.
2   Kim, MT, Dennison, CR, Hill, MN, Bone, LR, Levine, DM 'Relationship of alcohol and illicit drug use with high blood pressure care and control among urban hypertensive Black men' (2000) 10 (2) *Ethnicity and Disease* 175-183.
3   Ferdinand, KC 'Substance abuse and Hypertension' (2000) 2 (1) *Journal of clinical hypertension* 37-40.
4   Weintraub, E, Dixon, L, Delahanty, J, Schwartz, R, Johnson, J, Cohen, A, Klecz, M 'Reason for medical hospitalization among adult alcohol and drug abusers' (2001) 10 (2) *American Journal on Addictions* 167-177.
5   Waddell, TS & Hislop, WS 'Analysis of alcohol-related admissions in gastroenterology, cardiology and respiratory medicine' (2003) 48 (1) *Scottish Medical Journal* 114-116.

2.1.3 Musculoskeletal effects

Long-term heavy drinkers often have weak muscles as a result of disuse and myopathy (damage to muscle), particularly those of the abdominal wall, which are important for maintaining posture and lumbar spine support. There is therefore a higher incidence of lower back pains and general musculoskeletal problems in employees who are chronic abusers of alcohol. A trend of periodic musculoskeletal injuries, particularly those to the low back, could thus be an identifiable pointer once ergonomic factors have been excluded. Heavy drinkers are especially prone to low back injuries. Gouty arthritis and muscular pains are further common afflictions, since alcohol raises the levels of uric acid in the blood and can cause myositis (inflammation of muscle) or myopathy.

2.1.4 Respiratory problems

There is a higher incidence of pulmonary tuberculosis (PTB) in heavy drinkers as well as recurring chronic chest infections resulting from an excessive alcohol intake depressing the immune system.[6]

Excessive drinkers have been known to have many recurrences of PTB over a period of years. A high incidence of PTB and recurring chest infections could therefore indicate a trend of excessive alcohol consumption in employees. In addition, cannabis—a drug widely used in South Africa—equally contributes to cumulative respiratory infections amongst users. Cannabis smoke has been found to deliver 50–70% more carcinogens and is therefore more harmful than tobacco smoke.[7]

2.1.5 Nervous system

Dizzy spells, blackouts, fits and drop attacks, particularly in the morning, can indicate severe alcohol problems. Depression is much more prevalent in heavy drinkers, particularly when dependence is present. A general assessment of the central nervous system and affective complaints, other occupational causes having been excluded, can, in conjunction with other indicators, provide a means of assessing the possible existence of substance abuse.

Longitudinal studies on the relationship between substance abuse and psychological stressors suggest that psychological stress is significantly associated with the use of crack cocaine and methamphetamine, and the nonprescription use of prescription painkillers and tranquilisers.[8]

2.2 ABSENTEEISM AND SICKNESS ABSENCE

Identification of the extent of alcohol or drug problems in a company and in individual employees depends upon the maintenance of good records. Employee medical records

---

6   Rehm, J, Samokhvalov, AV, Neuman, MG, Room, R, Parry, C, Lönnroth, K, Patra, J, Poznyak, V, Popova, S 'The association between alcohol use, alcohol use disorders and tuberculosis (TB): A systematic review' (2009) 5 (9) *BMC Public Health* 450.

7   McGuinness, TM 'Update on marijuana' (2009) 47 (10) *Journal of psychosocial nursing and mental health services* 19-22.

8   Booth, BM, Curran, G, Han, X, Wright, P, Frith, S, Leukefeld, C, Falck, R & Carlson, RG 'Longitudinal relationship between psychological distress and multiple substance use: results from a three-year multisite natural-history study of rural stimulant users' (2010) 71 (2) *Journal of studies on alcohol and drugs* 258-267.

and personnel, time-keeping and accident records can be collated; then analysed to see if any trends regarding substance abuse exist within the company. If accurate, up-to-date, computerised records are maintained it will be possible to determine existing and emerging trends for various groups of employees, whether by department, by age, by geographical location, and so on. Close analysis of data may reveal subcultures of alcohol abuse within specific departments, work teams and/or small groups of employees.

Personnel records should enable an employer to monitor not only the disciplinary actions taken, if any, but also all absenteeism, whether due to sickness or otherwise. The time-keeping records should identify all movements into and out of the workplace and not just before and after the work shift. Late arrivals, extended lunch breaks and a shortened work period due to absence from the work station should also be included. Lunchtime movements are particularly important to monitor, but time-keeping records seldom make provision for this.

Employees may be absent from work for a number of reasons. Broadly speaking, absence from work is either permitted or unpermitted (or AWOL: absent without official leave), and absence through sickness is either certified or uncertified.

In the case of certified sickness absence, a sickness certificate must be completed by a doctor on behalf of the employee. The certificate must meet certain minimum requirements, that is, it must stipulate the name and address of the doctor, the date when the certificate was signed, the date when the consultation occurred and the dates when the worker went off and back on duty.

The employer is also entitled to a diagnosis or a reason why the sickness certificate was granted. The certificate should be signed by the doctor or the person who gave the consultation and must bear the registered medical qualifications of the doctor. If the certificate indicates that the consultation occurred after the sickness (ie the off-duty period) started, then the words 'As stated by the patient', or some equivalent expression, should be added.

The impact of random breathalysing on absenteeism statistics indirectly indicates a correlation between alcohol abuse and absenteeism. In one study, after the introduction of random breathalysing, Late for Work (LFW) decreased dramatically and Absence without Leave (AWOL) increased (see Fig 10.1 at page 267).

The use of records to identify trends of alcohol abuse among employees was highlighted in a study of two groups of 48 employees working for the same company (see Table 9.1). One group had been identified as having alcohol problems; the other, the control group, was known not to abuse alcohol. The months worked by both groups averaged to 125,3 months or 10,44 years. Thus the control group and the alcohol problem group each had an aggregate of 480 years' service for the company. Medical personnel and time-keeping records were used to assess differences between the two groups.

Table 9.1 McCann, MG 'The effect and impact of breath analysis in a workplace' MD Thesis 1999. Ch 3. Health and work effects in an alcohol problem group compared with a control group (Average years worked 10,4)

	GIT	Raised BP	PTB	Gout	Depression
Alcohol problem group N-48	1,5	6,5	5,5	2,5	13,8
Control group N-48	1	1	1	0	0
	CNS	Assaults	Periods of absence due to sickness		Days
Alcohol problem group N-48	10,8	13,7	2,6		3,5
Control group N-48	0	1	1		1
	Mon or Fri	AWOL	Lateness		Discipline taken
Alcohol problem group N-48	4,6	4	4		3,26
Control group N-48	1	1	1		1

KEY:

GIT = Gastro Intestinal
PTB = Pulmonary Tuberculosis
Mon = Mondays
AWOL = Absent without leave

BP = Blood Pressure
CNS = Central Nervous System
Fri = Fridays

2.2.1 Sickness absence

Sick certificates are notoriously unreliable in terms of establishing the true nature of a problem when the use of alcohol is involved. A study in Manchester, England,[9] looked at the sick certificates in the previous year of patients attending an alcohol rehabilitation centre. Among those still employed there was, on average, 70 days loss of work, while among those unemployed at the time of admission to the centre 208 days of work were lost. (The average sickness absence rate in the UK in 1976 was 3.81% from the General Household Survey Great Britain 1971-1997.)[10]

The sick certificates showed:

- a psychiatric diagnosis in 36% of cases
- a digestive problem in 14% of cases
- a respiratory problem in 14% of cases
- an accident in 10% of cases.

---

9   Saad, ES & Madden, JS 'Certificated incapacity and unemployment in alcoholics' 1976 (128) *Br J Psychiatry* 340.

10 Barmby, T, Ercolani, M & Treble, J 'Sickness Absence in Great Britain' (1998) *Labour Market Trends* 405-413.

Only 3% of the certificates identified alcohol as the true underlying cause. Although evidence suggests that psychiatric conditions are the most common group of diagnoses, it should be understood that nervous and anxiety disorders are sometimes used as euphemisms for drug- and alcohol-related problems. The abuse of illicit drugs has been associated with considerable morbidity.[11]

Doctors have many reasons for wishing to hide the true nature of the condition, but the fundamental one is to protect their patients, due to the stigma attached to alcoholism and drug abuse and the potential for employees to lose their jobs. It must also be remembered that only a small percentage of patients suffering from alcohol or drug dependence are positively identified by general practitioners. It has been estimated that only about 10% of patients with an alcohol problem are identified by GPs. Quite often, also, the general practitioner is hesitant to involve himself in what is seen to be a laborious and thankless task. A lot of time and effort can be spent on such a patient to no avail. Outside the workplace, attempts to control alcohol problems have a poor record of success. Medical practitioners therefore tend to identify and treat the symptoms and not the cause of the problem drinker's addiction. For instance, 12% of general practitioners in the Cape Town metropole thought that they could effectively help patients reduce their alcohol consumption, while 78% indicated that, given adequate training and support, they could become more effective in addressing their patients' alcohol-related behaviours. The GPs were also asked to comment on possible barriers that hindered their ability to intervene when a patient presented with an alcohol-related problem. Difficulties in getting compensated for treating patients with alcohol problems (often through an unwillingness on the part of medical insurance companies to pay for this type of treatment), insufficient training, lack of screening and counselling materials, perceptions of ineffectiveness, and time constraints were cited as the more common barriers.[12]

2.2.1 (a) Extent of sickness absence

A 1959 American survey of the medical records of 10 000 employees showed that those who abused alcohol had an absenteeism rate 2,5 times greater than that of the controls.[13] In our South African study we showed an absenteeism rate of between 2,6 and 4,6 greater than that of the controls, depending on the parameters used. Pell and D'Alonzo (1970) revealed that of 76 687 employees, 922 (1,2%) were defined as alcoholic and they had an absenteeism frequency rate of twice that of the controls.[14] More recently, employees who drink frequently (at least weekly) and at high risk levels were 26 times more likely than their non-drinking counterparts to miss a work day due to personal alcohol use.[15]

---

11   Morrison, CL & Ruben, SM 'Drug users and sick notes' (1994) 309 *British Medical Journal* 207.

12   Koopman, FA, Parry, CDH, Myers, BJ, Reagon. G 'Addressing alcohol problems in primary care settings: A study of general medical practitioners (GPs) in Cape Town, South Africa' (2008) 36 *Scandinavian Journal of Public Health* 298-302.

13   Maxwell, MA `A study of absenteeism, accidents and sickness payment in problem drinkers in one industry' 1959 (20) *Quart J Studies on Alcoholism* 302-312.

14   Pell, S & D'Alonzo, CA `Sickness absenteeism of alcoholics' 1970 (12) *J Occup Medicine* 198-210.

15   Roche, A & Pidd, K 'Workers' Alcohol Use and Absenteeism' *National Centre for Education and Training on Addiction (NCETA), Flinders University* (2006).

The incidence of heavy drinking over the previous 30 days has also been positively associated with the number of days an employee will be absent in the succeeding 12-month period.[16] Similarly, The National Survey on Drug Use and Health (NSDUH) found that employees abusing opioids miss more than 2,2 days of work monthly, compared with the 0,83 days per month reported for the average person. In addition it has been found that although drug abuse is positively associated with absenteeism, presenteeism is also affected by misuse of and dependence on opioids.[17]

The company must consider the alcohol and drug abuse subculture in the workforce, its prevalence, and the degree to which it is accepted as common practice. Once alcohol and drug problems are addressed by the company, sickness absence could at first increase for a short time as the substance abuse programme starts to make its presence felt, but soon the sickness absence rate will drop rapidly. The reasons for this slight initial increase are due, firstly, to a decrease in 'topping up' with alcohol before and during the work day (which has been alleviating the hangover effects) and, secondly, the avoidance of confrontation with management if severe dependence has occurred.

The most useful parameters for measuring sickness absence arising from alcohol and drug abuse are:
- the annual frequency rate
- the disability rate, and
- the severity rate.

The annual frequency rate is 'the number of periods or episodes of absence due to sickness' there have been in a year per employee.

The disability rate is 'the number of days' sickness in a year per employee.

The severity rate is the 'number of days' sickness that occur 'in a period or episode' of sick leave. The severity rate defines the difference between short-term and long-term absence due to sickness. In the case of alcohol problems we would expect to see a low severity rate but a high disability rate, ie increased levels of short-term sickness absence. In Pell and D'Alonzo's study the authors showed that the frequency of the illness or number of periods of absence was a more important criterion than the length of the periods of absence due to sickness. In this study the alcohol group had increased short *and* long periods of absence, meaning that the overall frequency of periods was increased irrespective of the severity.[18]

This study also identified an increase of sickness absence due to age. As the employee with an alcohol problem became older so his disability rate or number of days sick leave increased appreciably. Thus, early alcohol problems will produce low severity, high disability (or number of days sick) and high frequency of number of sick periods or episodes. Late alcohol problems produce high severity as well as high disability and high frequency rates. As mentioned in the previous section, short-term minor respiratory problems such as colds and 'flu are seen in the earlier stages of an employee's alcohol

---

16 Bacharach, SB, Bamberger, P, Biron, M 'Alcohol consumption and workplace absenteeism: the moderating effect of social support' (2010) 95 (2) *Journal of Applied Psychology* 95(2):334-348.

17 Ruetsch, C 'Empirical view of opioid dependence' (2010) 16 (1) *Journal of Managed Care Pharmacy* S9-13. Presenteeism refers to the loss in productivity caused by a sick employee who attends work but is unable to function properly.

18 Pell & D'Alonzo (n 15).

problem. The more chronic respiratory illnesses, which are due to severe debilitation, are seen in the much later stages of the illness and will often end in medical disability.

In sharp contrast to alcohol and some of the other forms of drugs, the average time lapse between first use of a drug such as crystal methamphetamine and entering a drug treatment programme is 1,5 years.[19] This suggests that morbidity associated to use of crystal methamphetamine becomes more visible more quickly resulting in early high frequency of number of periods sick.

2.3 ACCIDENTS

Accident records should identify all the parameters of the accident: where, how and when it occurred (including the time of day as well as the date), and who was involved. The effects of alcohol and drug abuse on accidents are discussed in chapters 7 and 8.

2.3.1 Identifying the presence of alcohol or drugs in accident cases

In chapter 5 we looked at the issue of workplace injuries from the perspective of one particular company, a pulp mill, where injuries on duty were measured over a two-month period, namely May and June, 1985. All employees who attended the company surgery with an injury sustained while on duty, excluding gassings and eye injuries due to foreign bodies entering the eye, were requested to have confidential blood tests done to identify their probable alcohol intake or whether they were problem drinkers. The tests used consisted of gamma GT (gamma glutamyl transferase), MCV (mean corpuscular volume) and blood-alcohol levels (milligrams per 100 ml of blood). In the two-month period there were 100 injuries to staff on duty who qualified for measurement and one employee who refused the tests; 38, or 38%, had abnormal tests identifying alcohol problems and 18, or 18%, of these were positive for the presence of alcohol in the blood at the time of attending the surgery. This is an example of how prevalent the association between alcohol and accidents is.

Three further studies present a similar picture:

A study that measured blood-alcohol levels in Zambian copper mine workers showed that 30% of a series of accident cases had measurable levels of alcohol in the blood. The average was 0,06 g% (60 mg/100 ml) and 6% had levels over 0,08 g% (80 mg/100 ml). This study concluded that employees with blood-alcohol levels between 0,08 g% and 0,16 g% had a low risk of detection for intoxication but a higher risk of having an accident.[20]

In another study, an engineering company referred 48 of its employees for rehabilitation over a four-year period. It was found that 32 (or 66,6%) of these employees had suffered injuries on duty prior to referral. This was 50% higher than the average.[21]

Third study found that use of marijuana or cocaine increased the probability of reporting a workplace accident over the same time period by 25%.[22]

19 Parry, CD, Myers, B, Plüddemann, A 'Drug policy for methamphetamine use urgently needed' (2004) 94 (12) S.Afr Med J 964-965.

20 Buchanan, DJ 'Studies on blood alcohol in the workers of a Zambian copper mine' 1988 (23) Alcohol & Alcoholism 239-242.

21 Beaumont & Allsop 'The Beverage Report' 1983 (13) Occup Safety & Health 25.

22 Ramchand, R, Pomeray, A & Arkes, J The effects of substance use on workplace injuries. RAND Centre for Health and Safety in the Workplace. Rand Corporation, Santa Monica.

2.3.2 Time of day of accidents

Workplace accidents often happen at certain times of the day. This is particularly noticeable in the case of employees engaged in shift work, where the link between alcohol consumption and accidents has been studied in some depth. In morning shift work, for example, accidents occurring during the first two hours of the shift are more likely to be substance related. Researchers have also discovered that substance-related accidents are common in the first two hours of the afternoon shift and the first two hours of the night shift;[23] and that for day-shift operations there are three one-hour periods—8 am to 9 am; 9 am to 10 am; 1 pm to 2 pm—where alcohol-related accidents predominate.[24]

2.3.3 Type of accident

Another method of assessing the association between alcohol and accidents is to identify the types of accidents.

In a study conducted at an engineering company, of 81% of the accidents related to alcohol 33% were due to falls, 29% were due to handling faults and 19% were due to stepping on or striking against an object.[25] In the company, which instituted random breathalysing, the records of accidents were assessed 18 months prior to the introduction of the breathalyser and again 18 months after. Accidents were divided into different categories: non-disabling accidents, where there was no loss of work time; disabling accidents, where there was a loss of work time of up to 14 shifts; and reportable accidents, where there was a loss of work time of more than 14 shifts. Statistical tests showed that the reduction in the number of non-disabling accidents after the introduction of the breathalyser was highly significant ($p<01$). The reduction in the number of disabling accidents was also highly significant ($p<01$). [26]

2.3.4 Assessing the accident and incident rate

The extent of the number of accidents (or near misses if these are monitored) affected by alcohol can be measured indirectly by the disabling injury frequency rate (DIFR) as well as the incident rate (IR). A higher than average DIFR will almost certainly warrant attention being given to a possible alcohol-related cause. One American company instituted alcohol testing for all incidents which involved a cost or damage to company property of more than $US100 (R7 910).[27] This can be described as 'at cause' alcohol testing.

2.4 DISCIPLINARY OFFENCES

These need to be properly monitored and documented in the personnel files. Too often, individual minor misdemeanours are not investigated or are even overlooked at the time and not put in the context of a developing trend. Matters are further complicated by

23 Argyropoulos-Grisanos, MA & Hawkins, PJL *Alcohol and Industrial Accidents* (1986).
24 Beaumont & Allsop (n 22) at 25.
25 Ibid.
26 McCann, MG 'The effect and impact of breath analysis in a workplace' paper presented at Medichem Conference, London (October 1992).
27 Beaumont and Allsop (n 22).

the existence in many organisations of a 'wash-out period' for employees who infringe company rules, including those prohibiting the use of alcohol and drugs. The 'wash-out period' is the time interval after which a particular disciplinary warning standing against the employee lapses. This means that at the end of every time interval (very often a six-month period) any existing offences are cancelled out and the employee's disciplinary record is in effect 'wiped clean'.

The wash-out period is an important fair labour practice; however, it should not be allowed to interfere with the identification, assessment, and persuasive treatment of a progressive alcohol problem.

In one company, for example, a long-serving employee had managed to earn 14 final warnings, each in a different six-month period, the majority of which were for intoxication at work. This case shows how employees with an alcohol or drug problem can control their behaviour to a degree that the culture and policies of the company allow.

2.5 PRODUCTIVITY

Performance varies for many reasons and is often very difficult to measure, particularly over short periods of time. The performance of all employees should, where possible, be measured on a daily basis and even before and after lunch. This would give useful indicators of an alcohol or drug problem in the company. Examples of such indicators include a drop in productivity on Monday mornings and the morning after payday, or if a large number of staff leave the factory at lunchtime and there is a drop in productivity following their return after lunch.

These factors must be weighed against the type of company as well as the prevailing culture. This can be illustrated by the following case: A particular computer software company was experiencing poor productivity in one of its departments. The company decided to increase the staff contingent in the department to help cope with the perceived increased workload. The actual cause of the problem, however, lay elsewhere. This was something the company realised when it was discovered that the Head of Department had a drinking problem and encouraged members of his department to drink heavily at lunchtime, with little work being done in the afternoon. When the Head of Department resigned and a substance abuse policy was instituted, productivity in the department rose dramatically.

Where there is a subculture of substance abuse, shrinkage (staff pilfering) is frequently a problem and the losses involved can be considerable. Do the salesmen extend their business lunches beyond a reasonable time and indulge in excessive drinking, using the need to entertain the client as an excuse? Are management condoning the practice because they mistakenly believe it is a good way of gaining business?

2.6 MEDICAL TESTS

Perhaps the most definitive way of assessing the extent of an alcohol or drug problem in the company is to conduct medical tests. If certain tests are done at the pre-employment stage and then periodically throughout employment, it is possible to monitor employees' health vis a vis substance abuse and to see what trends have developed or are emerging in the company. If testing is not possible for all employees, then consideration needs to be given to testing job categories where alcohol or drug abuse exists or could develop, or where substance abuse would put the safety and health of employees and others at risk. These tests are discussed in detail under Individual Identification in chapter 10 below.

2.7 RANDOM TESTING FOR INTOXICATION

When companies first institute random testing they are often shocked at the number of employees who arrive at work in an intoxicated state. One South African company measured a sample of one in seven employees intoxicated when random testing was first introduced.[28] In America, an increasing number of companies are looking towards testing for drugs and alcohol abuse. When testing is instituted, often a higher proportion of employees than expected is found to be positive.

If alcohol and drug problems are monitored effectively in the individual employees, then this will give an accurate assessment of the trends throughout the company. It is important to assess all parameters, including the cultural effects and implications for management of random testing, if a true reflection of what is happening is to be gained. Random testing should be implemented in the context of the recommendations made in chapters 10 and 13 below.

2.8 CULTURE

The culture of drinking is dealt with mainly in chapter 5 but also in chapter 15. It is important to emphasise the importance of addressing the cultural issues which could be reinforcing or encouraging the problem. All corporate celebrations at which alcohol is provided should also be reassessed. For example, the production parties, the long service award parties and the Christmas parties should be assessed to determine if these events are being misused. Perhaps they can be organised in a way which does not encourage alcohol abuse, with strict instructions being given to the barmen. The corporate pub is another area which needs proper control. While the pub may foster good relationships among employees and perhaps improve their loyalty to the company, it can also provide the opportunity for employees to engage in inappropriate behaviour as a result of drinking too much.

Informal, rather than formal drinking may also historically have been condoned by management. Lunchtime visits to nearby illegal drinking venues is one example of the sort of 'management-approved' informal drinking that employees may engage in. If this pattern of midday drinking is left unaddressed, the detrimental effect it will have on productivity (as well on the employees' health) will be considerable.

When the process of identifying alcohol problems is initiated, the company must first assess the true extent of management drinking and how far this influences the attitudes of other employees towards alcohol consumption. Management drinking is likely to be at least partly responsible for any subculture of drinking that exists. Whatever management would like to think, the employees are always aware of the extent of management drinking. Word filters not only down but also up the company hierarchy tree. The receptionist at the front desk or the security guards at the entrance gate are perfectly placed to observe late after-lunch arrivals; the car park attendant will notice the manager who walks unsteadily towards his car; and the personal assistant will detect the slurred speech of the executive who telephones to say that he's 'stuck in traffic'. As mentioned in chapter 2, one Scottish company assessed that 14% of its managers

---

28   McCann (n 27).

had a drinking problem, and it is unlikely that their subordinates were unaware of their problems. An accurate assessment of the culture of the company and of the impacts of any subcultures of drinking (as described in chapter 5) is important and cannot be over-emphasised.

SUMMARY

In this chapter we considered the issue of how to detect trends of actual or potential substance abuse in an organisation and how this manifests at different levels of the organisation. We looked at the ways in which substance abuse can be assessed objectively, and did so by examining each of the following indicators: health; absenteeism and sickness absence; accidents; disciplinary offences; productivity; medical tests; random testing for intoxication; and culture. It is important to remember that not all of these indicators necessarily signify substance abuse; for instance, productivity loss may be due to machine failure, poor quality control procedures or high material costs and nothing at all to do with substance abuse. However, employers should not reject the possibility that the presence of one or more of these indicators may point towards the existence of a significant substance abuse problem in their organisation.

Chapter 10

Testing: Identifying Alcohol and Drug Problems and Intoxication in the Employee

Mike McCann & Nadine Harker Burnhams

The criteria for identifying alcohol and drug problems and intoxication in individual employees can be divided into subjective and objective.

1. SUBJECTIVE IDENTIFICATION CRITERIA

It must be remembered that a large number of employees with an alcohol or drug problem can conceal their problem for up to five years.[1] Intoxication clearly signifies that a person has an alcohol or a drug problem. However, this is only true in cases of overt intoxication where the individual's behaviour makes it obvious that he or she has been misusing alcohol or drugs. Even then, judging whether someone is or is not intoxicated based on their behaviour is subjective and can be highly inaccurate since not all drinkers and drug users act the same. The majority of cases involving intoxication at work are missed if only subjective methods are used.[2]

Regarding alcohol intoxication, one series of 51 positive blood alcohol tests performed on employee-patients attending an occupational health clinic during working hours revealed that none of the subjects showed any overt subjective signs of intoxication, yet 14 had a blood-alcohol level over 250 mg/100 ml of which five indicated levels above 300 mg/100 ml and the level of one was 440 mg/100 ml.[3]

Experienced drinkers can hide the effects of alcohol, preventing those effects from showing in their normal behaviour. In hardened drinkers, levels of up to 0,5 g% or 500 mg/100 ml may be present without there being any signs of inebriation.[4] There are many dependent drinkers who have regular employment and are socially acceptable for many years.

In a series of 1 000 cases, blood-alcohol measurements were taken at various blood-alcohol concentrations and independent doctors assessed the level of clinical intoxication without prior knowledge of the amount of alcohol consumed. The techniques used to

---

1   Maxwell, MA 'Early identification of problem drinkers in industry' (1960) 21 *Quart J Studies on Alcoholism* 655-678.

2   Buchanan, DJ 'Studies on blood alcohol in the workers of a Zambian copper mine' (1988) 23 Alcohol and Alcoholism 239-242.

3   McCann, MG 'The effect and impact of breath analysis in a workplace' MD Thesis 1999.

4   Maxwell (n 1) at 655-678.

identify clinically identifiable intoxication missed 5% of cases at levels of intoxication as high as 0,4 g% and 20% of cases as high as 0,2 g% (see Figure 10.1 below).

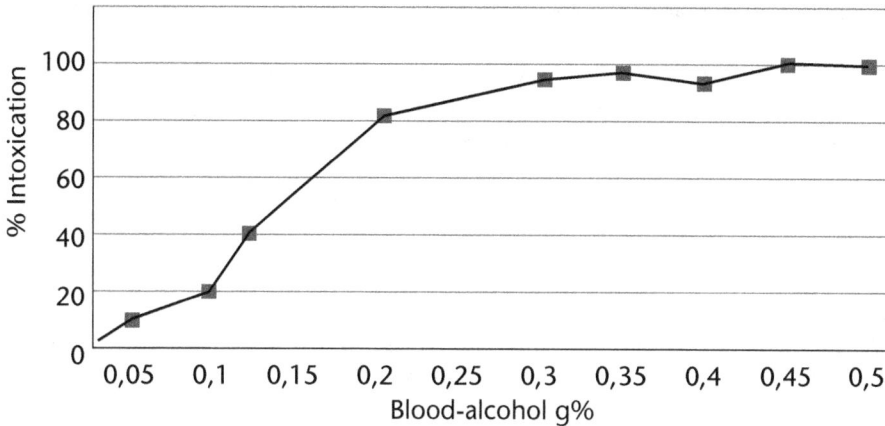

Figure 10.1 Percentage occurrence of clinically identifiable intoxication at various blood alcohol concentrations.[5]

The figures in the graph above are startling. Only 20% of cases with blood alcohol levels of 0,1 g% were identified by clinical observation as being intoxicated, and only 50% at 0,14 g%; 5% were not identified at a level of 0,4 g%!

However, it is instructive to look at the wealth of research which suggests that subjective examination of an individual for intoxication is not accurate.[6] Penner and Coldwell showed how two doctors independently examined a group of individuals who had taken alcohol. One doctor assessed that the driving ability of 58% of them was affected by the alcohol and the other doctor assessed that only 27% were affected in this way by the alcohol. There was, furthermore, also a poor correlation between these subjective assessments and the blood-alcohol levels. Andreson (1950) showed how in a group of 170 drivers examined as being clinically intoxicated, 3% had no alcohol in their blood at all.[7]

As early as 1957, Lofthus concluded that it was almost impossible to diagnose intoxication merely by clinical examination.[8]

The subjective clinical examination for intoxication is such an inexact practice that the majority of countries have replaced this form of diagnosis for drunken drivers with a more scientific method, namely using direct measurement of breath, urine, saliva or blood, and even hair.

While many of the above research studies highlight the weaknesses of using subjective clinical examination to assess levels of intoxication in potential drunken drivers, these same flaws should be expected in subjective assessments of intoxication in employees

---

5   Cooper, WE Schwar, TG and Smith, LS 'Percentage of clinical intoxication at various blood alcohol concentrations' in *Alcohol, Drugs and Road Traffic* (1979) 185, Penner, DW & Coldwell, BB 'Car driving and alcohol consumption' (1958) 7 *Canada MAJ* 93.

6   Penner, DW & Coldwell, BB 'Car driving and alcohol consumption' (1958) 7 *Canada MAJ* 93.

7   Andreson, PH 'Traffic and alcohol'(1950) *Medico-legal J* 104.

8   Lofthus, J 'Blood alcohol test and clinical examination of automobile drivers in Oslo' *Quart J Stud Alcohol* cited in: Cooper, Schwar and Smith *Alcohol, Drugs and Road Traffic* (Juta 1979).

in the workplace. The fact that responsibility for conducting this assessment usually lies with the direct line manager of potential offenders compounds the problem. This is because the direct line manager will be unwilling to antagonise individuals with whom he or she works each day and depends upon to complete work tasks and assignments.

Holt et al (1980) showed how difficult it was to identify intoxication by using subjective criteria.[9] They asked a group of doctors to identify by the usual subjective measures whether groups of people were intoxicated or not. This was followed by a blood-alcohol test to assess objectively the level of intoxication. Of the three main subjective criteria used:

- only smelling subjects' breath missed 14% of those who had been drinking alcohol, of which 7% were over the limit;
- using slurred speech as a criterion, they missed 25% of those who had been drinking, of which 17% were over the limit;
- considering abnormal coordination only, they missed 26%, with 18% over the limit;
- of those found to be not intoxicated, 7% were over the limit;
- 6% were identified as intoxicated when they had not been drinking at all.

From this the conclusion was drawn that the subjective diagnosis of alcohol intoxication—even with a clinical examination by a doctor—is unreliable. For instance, hardened drinkers can compensate for the effects of alcohol on their normal behaviour, particularly when they are aware that they are being scrutinised, but this does not alleviate the already described deterioration in their ability to be productive and to maintain a safe working environment.

Like alcohol, the consumption of illicit drugs has a substantial effect on the workplace, particularly with regard to health, safety and work relationships.[10] Drug abuse that occurs hours before an employee begins work is also hazardous since the effects of consumption may still be present when the employee begins his working day or shift, which has the potential to disrupt workplace activities and cause injury to the employee and/or his co-workers.

Some of the more important work-related subjective criteria are mentioned below.

1.1 Work-related subjective criteria—factors and signs

1.1.1 On-the-job absenteeism (presenteeism)

This is when someone is at work but not fulfilling their effective performance at work due to alcohol or drug abuse either while at work or prior to attending work. More productivity is lost due to on-the-job absenteeism than to any other single factor. Despite its prevalence, however, on-the-job absenteeism is also difficult to define and very difficult to identify. This lack of clarity regarding what does (and does not) constitute on-the-job absenteeism means that the problem is often overlooked or ignored.

Such absenteeism includes employees who come to work when they are sick, which means that they are incapable of performing to their true capabilities. They find it hard

---

9   Holt, S, Stewart, I, Dixon, J, Elton, R, Taylor, T & Little, K 'Alcohol and the emergency service patient' (1980) 281 *BMJ* 638.

10   Bywood, P 'Illicit drugs in the Australian workforce: Prevalence and patterns of use' paper presented to the 24/7: Work-Related Alcohol & Drug Use. A National Forum (Adelaide, South Australia 29–30 June 2006).

to concentrate and so they do easier, less taxing, lower priority work. Because they are confused, these employees struggle to remember important information (for example, the time of a meeting they have to attend) or what it is they have to do (for example, they may find it hard to follow instructions or to recollect what activities they must complete from the previous day). In safety critical tasks and when dealing with precise work this can have serious detrimental effects as quick decisions and reflexes will be affected. In his study, Maxwell identified several other high-ranking indicators of on-the-job absenteeism, namely putting things off, an uneven work pace, and neglect of details.[11] Other factors are absences from the workstation, visiting the rest room, dozing or sleeping on the job, unexplained absences and a general decline in physical capacity to do the work.

1.1.2. Clinical indications

It is important to note that hangovers, red and bleary eyes, hand tremors, a flushed face and morning and lunchtime drinking were all placed within the top 15 high-ranking indicators in Maxwell's study. In the case of cannabis users, bloodshot or glassy eyes and a persistent cough may be present. Emotional indicators such as nervousness or jitteriness and edginess or irritability were within the top three rankings. Mood changes, intolerance, and undue sensitivity to others' opinions ranked within the top 20. Some 30% of men were able to keep any signs of a developing problem from showing for up to three years or more after they themselves had recognised the onset of their problem. A total of 22% managed to conceal all signs or symptoms for at least five years.[12]

The element of concealment is important: it suggests that many problem drinkers and drug users are aware of their condition but lack the confidence and/or are unwilling to confront the issue, or believe that their problem is not severe enough to warrant action. This reluctance or refusal to act means that the employee's work performance continues to deteriorate, and eventually becomes so poor that either the employee or the employer is obliged to do something. By this stage, however, it is often too late to correct the situation and the employee's position becomes untenable. Conversely, if an alcohol or drug problem is detected at or near onset, the employer can take steps to help the employee and minimise the losses due to poor employee performance.

In the work environment, managers, supervisors and fellow workers often see these subjective criteria but are unwilling or lack the confidence to confront, or they assess the problem as being not severe enough to warrant action. Only when objective performance factors are developing is action taken, and by that stage the identification and early detection have been missed, at a cost to the company in terms of poor performance and the potential loss of a trained employee.

1.1.3. Deteriorating job performance

As procrastination occurs and more decisions and work are put off, there is an inevitable deterioration in job performance. Work takes longer to do and more errors are committed, which are sometimes identified only much later if they have been covered up or hidden. Details are overlooked, strange excuses are given for absence from the workplace or for

---

11   Maxwell (n 1).
12   Maxwell (n 1).

work delays, and the employee is found to be unreliable. Also, customers will complain of poor service.

Short-term deficiencies in work performance may not appear unduly alarming. For instance, if an employee's performance deteriorates at the start and the end of the week but is stable in the days in between, the manager or supervisor may not notice this since some fluctuation in employee performance is to be expected. However, if this situation is allowed to continue, over months or perhaps even years, the employee's overall work performance will decline.

An issue which is relevant under the heading of deteriorating job performance is the amotivational syndrome. Although the amotivational syndrome remains controversial, it is a good way of describing the effect of significant substance abuse on an employee's behaviour and performance. It is associated particularly with chronic cannabis use and consists of a group of behaviours involving apathy, introversion, passivity, lethargy and reduced concentration. These symptoms have also been associated with cocaine, organic solvent, and a residual effect of methamphetamine abuse.[13] It is important to mention these under this heading in this chapter as it is a significant problem of deteriorating job performance. It must not be forgotten that these symptoms are also typical of a significant depression which may also be part of the effects of chronic substance abuse.

1.1.4. Employee relations

An aggressive or argumentative attitude can be the first identifying sign of an alcohol or drug problem developing in an employee and such an attitude can seriously affect the efficiency and performance of a work group. Overtly, the employee is irritable, over-sensitive to criticism, has paranoid tendencies, and is unpredictable, with mood swings occurring particularly after lunch (see the discussion of the rating study by Maxwell under On-the-job absenteeism above).

1.1.5. Appearance

Finally, changes in the employee's physical appearance can signify that he or she is experiencing drink or drug problems. An employee with a puffy face, red and bleary eyes and a generally unkempt appearance may look like this because he or she is struggling to control his or her alcohol or drug habit. Hand tremors, shivering, sweating and other medically related signs, both acute and chronic, may also be present. Problem drinkers can be identified by the smell of alcohol on their breath, particularly in the period following a lunch or tea break; a telltale sign they may try to cover up by brushing their teeth or taking breath mints. Similarly, cannabis users often use scent or deodorant to mask the pungent smell that burning hemp emits. The subjective signs are often difficult to interpret and can be overlooked without a second thought, but documenting them over a period of time builds up a picture that is much easier to respond to.

In the Appendices of this book you will find a 'Verification of Alcohol Intoxication Form' and a 'Verification of Drug Intoxication Form' (see Appendix 9). These documents

---

13 Ashizawa, T, Saito, T, Yamamoto, M, Schichinohe, S, Ishikawa, H, Maeda, H, Toki, S, Ozawa, H, Watanabe, M, Takahata, N. 'A case of amotivational syndrome as a residual effect symptom after methamphetamine abuse' (1996) 31 (5) *Japanese journal of alcohol studies & drug dependence.* 451-461.

list the subjective identifying features that may be present in an employee who is intoxicated. The form, once completed, presents a reasonable (though still subjective) indication of an employee's possible intoxication. Management can use the information obtained to evaluate what action is needed to bring about a change in the employee's behaviour, and/or to assess what sanctions are appropriate.

2. MEASURABLE OBJECTIVE IDENTIFICATION CRITERIA

2.1 Direct objective testing for alcohol and drugs

The direct objective methods used to test for the presence of alcohol or drugs in the human body are:
- the blood-alcohol test;
- the urine-alcohol test;
- the saliva-alcohol test;
- the alcohol-breathalyser test.

The urine, saliva and breathalyser tests can be administered by trained non-medical personnel such as police officers, security officers, supervisors and personnel officers. By contrast, the invasive nature of the blood-alcohol test means that it can only be performed by medical personnel or by persons who have received suitable training, such as phlebotomists.

Alcohol measurements undoubtedly prove alcohol absorption. The *American Annals of Internal Medicine*[14] has recommended that a blood-alcohol level above 100 mg/dll (0,1 g%) at a routine medical examination, or above 150 mg/dl (0,15 g%) without signs of intoxication, or above 300 mg/dl (0,3 g%) at any time should be considered highly suggestive of dependence.

Reporting for work in an intoxicated state should be treated as misconduct (see chapter 20 below, Alcohol and Drug Policy). This intoxication should be identified by an objective measure such as a breathalyser test, a urine test or a saliva/oral fluid test (see Tools used for identification, below in this chapter). These tests, or screening measures, can be implemented in the following ways:
- Pre-employment testing
- Random testing
- Testing 'for cause'
- Return to duty testing
- Follow up testing
- Periodic testing.

2.1.1 Pre-employment testing

Employers do not want to hire individuals who are addicted to or dependent upon alcohol or drugs, which is why many request job candidates to undergo a pre-employment test to establish whether such an addiction or dependency exists. However, there are numerous ethical and legal issues attached to this form of testing and it is not something that can be done in all circumstances by all employers. We do not propose to address these issues here, since the concept of testing for alcohol and drug misuse

---

14 'Criteria for the diagnosis of alcoholism' (1972) 77 *American Annals of Int Medicine* 249-258.

has already been looked at in chapter 9 section 2.7, and will be looked at later in chapter 12 Legal aspects of pre-employment screening and chapter 13 Legal aspects of testing employees. We suggest you revisit these chapters for more on pre-employment testing.

2.1.2 Random testing

This form of testing is also considered in some detail in chapters 9, 10 and 13 and can be referred to again if necessary.

Here, we can note that the advantage of this alternative is that the test works as a physical deterrent and helps to identify 95% of cases of intoxication that would otherwise go unidentified. It also produces a direct, objective measure of intoxication and consumption. This would otherwise be a subjective assessment, easily manipulated and difficult to confront, particularly if the behavioural signs of aggression and argumentativeness are present.

There are proponents both for and against random testing or screening. In particular, questions must be asked about corporate liabilities, on the one hand, and encroachment on civil liberties on the other. The company has a responsibility to maintain a safe working environment not only for the employees but for any members of the public who could be affected by an unsafe act, and the employer must take all reasonable precautions to prevent foreseeable risks. In this regard, the Exxon Valdez environmental pollution of Alaska and the New York subway train crash in August 1991 (when five people were killed and some 200 injured—see chapter 6) perhaps speak for themselves. Were all precautions taken to avoid unnecessary risk as far as alcohol consumption was concerned? The answer is 'no' and the use of simple screening tests to identify intoxicated employees could in both cases have averted a disaster. Significantly Exxon has now implemented a stringent programme of alcohol and drug monitoring on all its ships.

2.1.3 Testing 'for cause'

As the name indicates, this form of testing is based on the reasons why an employer might want to test employees for drug and/or alcohol use. This method is extremely popular with employers since it gives them the opportunity to establish how and why a workplace accident or incident occurred and who may have been involved. Testing 'for cause' may arise in the following situations:

- following a work-related incident in which the use of alcohol or drugs may have been a cause or contributing factor
- when circumstances suggest the possibility of impairment by drugs or alcohol
- when ad hoc testing forms part of the entry requirements for certain types of work (This would include, for example, a contractor installing electrical equipment on a client's premises, or a chemical engineer hired to remove hazardous waste from a construction site.)
- if an individual's performance is affected through dependency on alcohol or drugs.

Despite difference in interpretation of the term 'for cause', the four scenarios just described are generally accepted to be justifiable reasons for insisting that an employee/worker takes an alcohol or drug test. 'For cause' testing is typically used when a workplace accident or adverse incident has occurred, especially when this event has led to personal injury or damage to property. 'For cause' testing, in common with the other forms of alcohol and drug testing, must be completed in accordance with a strict protocol and performed by suitably trained personnel.

2.1.4 Return to duty testing

This form of testing screens employees coming back to work after a period of absence. It is mainly used for employees engaged in high-risk work, where any impairment through drug or alcohol use could result in serious injury, loss or damage. In these circumstances it may be reasonable for the employer to institute alcohol and drug testing to ensure that employees are fit to resume their duties. An example of return to duty testing can be found in the oil rig industry. Here, many employees work for two weeks and then have two weeks' leave (the most common shift pattern, though there are others). On coming back to the rig the employees might have to undergo a return to duty test before they are allowed to recommence their work.

2.1.5 Follow up testing

Follow up testing is used when someone has already been identified as having a problem and has signed a contract that they agree to be tested as and when chosen by the testing agency or management. Employees who have undergone a drug and/ or alcohol rehabilitation programme may also be tested in this way; here the process is usually conducted in confidence by the organisation's occupational health professional or in some cases by the Health and Safety Officer.

2.1.6 Periodic testing

The reasons for introducing periodic testing are similar to those used for random testing (see above), although periodic testing is conducted on a regular (every six months, for example) and not random basis.

Whatever method of testing an employer uses or contemplates using, there are a number of important points to take into account, namely:

(a) The implications of the testing process. (As we have noted previously in this chapter, the use of alcohol and drug tests is a highly contentious issue. The ethical and legal implications of introducing testing procedures need to be fully considered before any action is taken.)

(b) The need for an evidence-based approach. (Testing employees without good cause is unwarranted and can lead to legal sanctions. An employer must show that it has a valid reason (or reasons) for introducing alcohol and drug testing of employees.)

(c) Using USA Food and Drug Administration (FDA) approved apparatus

(d) The latest research and information on drug and alcohol testing must be available.

Direct objective testing is used mainly in situations of actual or suspected alcohol misuse, although it can also be of use where drug dependency or addiction is the issue. For example, in a study of oil-rig workers, the results of a drug test revealed that 9,2% of these employees tested positive for THC (tetrahydrocannabinol—cannabis). The US National Petroleum Refiners Association[15] averaged 5% positive pre-employment testing of urine for drugs. Although these figures do not relate to alcohol, they are an example of how the prevalence of a drug problem can be identified.

---

15   US National Petroleum Refiners Association *Substance Abuse Policy Questionnaire Report* (1989).

Alcohol studies include those of Buchanan,[16] who discovered that 30% of accident cases in a Zambian copper mine had measurable alcohol levels. Of a selected group of employees randomly breathalysed prior to work, 33% had measurable blood alcohol; 9% of these employees had a blood-alcohol level greater than 0,08 g%. Of the employees identified subjectively and referred for testing, 66% registered over 0,16 g%. McCann[17] looked at the direct and indirect objective testing of a chemical company's workforce and showed that in direct and indirect testing of accident cases over a two-month period in 1985 (May and June), 38% (38 cases) were positive for direct and indirect testing, and 22% (22 cases) were positive for alcohol in the blood (direct testing). Upon the direct and indirect testing of 1 265 male employees in a company, 33,7% were identified as excessive alcohol users. Upon direct `random' testing (using a breathalyser) by security officers at the entrance to a chemical company, one in seven employees tested positive for alcohol in their blood on the first day of testing, and the mean reading was 0,134 g%.

In the following five weeks, one in 28,8 randomly chosen employees were over the prescribed level of 0,08 g% and the mean reading was 137,7 mg/100 ml or 0,137 g% BAC. With continuous random daily breathalysing, the number of intoxicated (0,08 g% or higher) employees dropped to one in 144,47 after 6 months and to one in 169 after 12 months.

The first month's readings in Figure 10.2 show that 40,34% of the subjects chosen had alcohol present in their blood when coming on shift, of which 29,61% were designated low-level alcohol content and 10,73% were designated intoxicated or over the limit of BAC (0,08 g%). By the end of the fourth month, the percentage of workers who tested positive for alcohol was 7,50%, of which 0,84% were designated `intoxicated'. By the end of the twelfth month the percentages were 4,2% positive for alcohol and 0,58% for intoxication. The numbers chosen for testing increased dramatically from the first month to a fairly consistent figure by the fourth month. Of the 1 285 subjects chosen for testing in the second month, the number identified as intoxicated was the same as that for the fourth month, when 4 744 were chosen. The progressively declining trend of positive intoxication tests was shown to be consistent. The comparable trend of those with positive but low alcohol levels (ie below 0,08 g%) is also shown in Figure 10.2.[18]

---

16 Buchanan (n2) at 239—242.
17 McCann (n 3) at 71.
18 *American Annals of Int Medicine* (n 14) at 13.

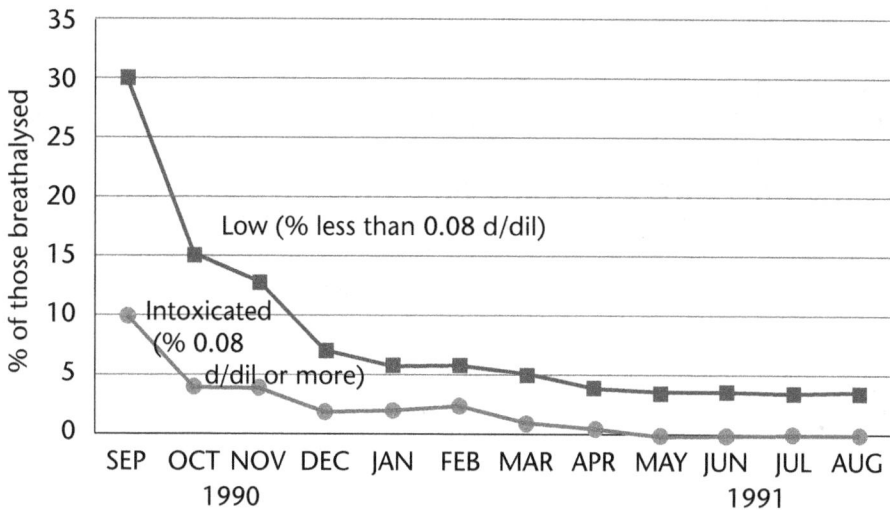

Figure 10.2 *Reduction in number of employees identified with low and intoxicated levels of blood alcohol after random breathalysing over a period of one year*

3. TOOLS FOR IDENTIFICATION

3.1 Direct testing for alcohol and drug consumption[19]

Blood, breath, urine and oral fluids (saliva) can be tested for assessing the presence of alcohol or drugs in the body. They are useful tests for identifying individuals with alcohol or drug problems and for evaluating the level of intoxication of these individuals. Occupational health professionals can use these tests to monitor employees on a rehabilitation programme.

For example, tests done in the morning can reveal evidence of early-morning drinking or, by extrapolation, of heavy drinking the previous night. If a man has a blood-alcohol level of 80 mg/dl (0,08 g%) at 10.00am and finished drinking the night before at 10.00 pm then his blood-alcohol level at 11.00 pm would have been approximately 0,260 g% (15 x 12 + 80 = 260 mg/dl or 0,260 g%).

If the same man's blood-alcohol level was 320 mg/dl (0,32 g%) at 10.00 am, then it would be highly likely that he had taken a drink before coming to work as his extrapolated level would be over 500 mg/dl (0,5 g%), which is close to a lethal level, although tolerance does play a significant part. It should be noted, however, that these extrapolations can only be rough guides as other factors are involved (see chapter 1 above).

In one American study of patients who convincingly denied drinking on joining a rehabilitation programme, 52% were shown to have alcohol in their urine. As previously mentioned, these alcohol levels can be used to gauge the level of dependence.[20]

Direct testing can be a violation of personal liberty if not performed correctly. However, this consideration must be weighed against the harm which individuals can inflict upon co-workers, employers or the general public as a consequence of their abuse. It is usually insufficient to wait for voluntary referrals, since denial is a primary symptom

---

19   See Appendices 1, 2, 3 of this book for Protocols of Testing.
20   McCann (n 3) at 71.

of alcohol or drug abuse and the enabling or dependency behaviour of friends, co-workers and family may hinder voluntary acceptance of treatment.

Employers have a duty to maintain a safe environment, which is something that can be achieved if a properly designed occupational health and safety programme (OHSP) is introduced. The early identification, prevention and treatment of substance abuse should form part of the programme; the programme should also make provision for the education of employees on the issue of alcohol and drug abuse, describe the intervention measures used, and summarise the help available to employees experiencing problems of substance abuse. (See chapter 6 for the risk assessment and management of problems, chapter 9 for identifying trends, chapters 11 and 14 for legal implications and chapter 18 for prevention initiatives).

3.1.1 Venous blood test for blood alcohol[21]

When a person's intoxication level is measured, testing venous blood is often considered to be definitive. Invariably this is the case, but there is one occasion when venous blood does not give a reliable result, and that is when the test is performed within 30 and 60 minutes of the last drink.

This is because the distribution of alcohol throughout the body takes time and takes longer to reach the blood on the body's periphery, that is, the venous blood supply, than it does to reach the arterial or pulmonary blood supply. Therefore, during the absorption phase of alcohol the blood alcohol content (BAC) of arterial blood will always be greater than the BAC of venous blood. A sample of venous blood taken during the absorption phase of alcohol, that is, during the 30–60 minute time period referred to, will thus not give an accurate indication of a person's level of intoxication.

The state of intoxication occurs in the brain. The brain, like the liver, kidneys and lungs, is an organ that has a rich arterial blood supply. As just mentioned, in the absorption phase of alcohol the arterial blood receives a higher concentration of alcohol than venous blood, which is why taking a blood sample from the cubital vein of the arm during this phase is likely to yield inaccurate results. Thus, during the absorption of alcohol from the gut, the breath-alcohol concentration is a more sensitive test of impairment.[22]

While the breathalyser test might be suited to the absorption phase of alcohol, other tests may be preferable in the distribution and elimination phases. Because alcohol is distributed throughout the body in relation to the water content of the relevant body tissues, higher levels of alcohol are recorded in a person's body fluids, that is, in his or her urine or saliva. Thus if whole blood is 1,00, then the ratio to other tissues will be: urine 1,33, saliva 1,18, alveolar breath 0,000476, and the brain 0,85.[23]

Despite the higher BAC of urine (1,33) and saliva (1,18) and the observations made regarding the limitations of the venous blood test during the absorption phase of alcohol, the level of alcohol *in the blood* is generally taken to be the definitive test for intoxication. This being the case, it is usual to relate the other body fluid measurements to the standard of blood alcohol via a process of conversion.

---

21 See Appendices 1, 2 and 4 for Protocols of Testing.
22 Jones, AW 'Enforcement of drink driving laws by use of "per se" legal alcohol limits: blood and/or breath concentrations as evidence of impairment' 1989(4) Alcohol, Drugs and Driving 99.
23 Denney, RC 'Measuring alcohol' in Rosalki, SB (ed) *Clinical Biochemistry of Alcoholism* (1984) 51-55.

The conversion ratio between blood alcohol and that of breath, urine and saliva is generally constant for a particular individual but may vary between the absorption, distribution and elimination phases.

The choice of conversion factor (the absorption phase ratio, the distribution phase ratio or the elimination phase ratio) will govern to a limited extent the accuracy of the test in cases of borderline intoxication. For example, the blood–breath conversion factor of 0,000476 shows that one volume of blood contains the same amount of alcohol as does 2 100 volumes of alveolar air.[24] This conversion factor is more constant with the absorption phase of alcohol than the elimination phase. Usually, the conversion factor is reversed to that of breath-to-blood, giving a conversion factor of 2 100:1. In some American states 2 100:1 has been chosen for medico-legal purposes.[25]

In Britain and the Netherlands a conversion factor of 2 300:1 has been chosen for medico-legal purposes, which links the factor more closely to the elimination phase of blood alcohol than the absorption phase. The importance of the conversion factor works on the assumption that the venous blood alcohol test is the best way to evaluate a person's level of intoxication, but it has been shown that this is not necessarily the case. In some countries (eg Britain and South Africa) the legal limit for driving is now defined as a breath-alcohol level as well as a blood-alcohol level, thus eliminating the pitfalls associated with the use of conversion factors.[26]

If a conversion factor has to be used, one which correlates more effectively with the absorption phase, rather than the elimination phase, is in our view to be preferred, because intoxication is more pronounced during the absorption phase (see Mellanby effect, chapter 1 above).

How this relates to the workplace is important, because more emphasis is generally placed on the breathalyser, urine or saliva test (or that of an equivalent measuring instrument) than on a blood-alcohol test.

The breathalyser test will be more accurate than the venous blood test during the absorption phase; this implies that employees who have consumed alcohol just prior to coming to work are more likely to test positive with the breathalyser test than with the venous blood test. As already mentioned, this is due to the delay between the appearance of arterial or pulmonary blood alcohol and the appearance of venous blood alcohol.

3.1.2 Breathalyser

There are two basic types of apparatus in use, the electronic breathalyser and the alcolyser.

(a) Electronic breathalyser

The electronic breathalyser is a fuel-cell apparatus which works by the oxidation of breath alcohol to acetic acid on a platinum electrode. This produces a current in proportion to the concentration of alcohol in the sample. The regular calibration of the electronic fuel-cell apparatus is vitally important, particularly if the tests are being used

---

24 Ibid.

25 One volume of blood contains the same amount of alcohol as does 2100 volumes of alveolar breath. This conversion factor has been used to determine the breath alcohol limit (0.38 mg per 1 litre of breath).

26 Jones (n22).

for disciplinary purposes. There is a 5–7% error which usually under-reads, although this can be eliminated by proper calibration. Discrepancies or errors which could constitute inconsistent use of the breathalyser can be eliminated in two ways. Firstly, the breathalyser can be calibrated to read below the level recommended, which ensuring that the test results err on the side of the employee. This adjustment will give an error factor of at least 6,25% in favour of the employee. For example, at an actual blood-alcohol level of 0,08% the reading would be 0,075%, which clearly benefits the employee being tested. Secondly, the employee can be given the choice of having a blood-alcohol test after he or she has undergone the breathalyser test. This gives the employee the opportunity to check the accuracy of one set of test results by comparing them against the results of another. However, given that a properly calibrated breathalyser test is as accurate, if not more so, than a venous blood test, it is not likely that the second test would give significantly different results. Should an employee still elect to have a blood-alcohol test, the test should be delayed for 20 to 30 minutes to allow sufficient time for the alcohol in the blood to reach the periphery of the body, that is, to reach the vein in the arm from which a (venous) blood sample will be drawn.

Recent developments in breathalyser technology have led to the creation of a breathalyser that does not need a mouthpiece. Using BluFire® sensor technology, the new apparatus allows subjects to blow from half an inch away, thus reducing the risk of contamination that occurs if mouthpieces are shared. The BluFire® technology provides extremely accurate test results by steadying airflow and requiring a deep lung air sample for each test. The device does require calibration on a regular basis.

(b) Crystal dichromate breathalyser (the Alcolyser or Redline breathalyser)

In contrast to the electronic breathalyser, the potassium dichromate crystal tube breathalyser is not a reliable piece of measuring apparatus. It has an error factor of 25%, which means that it is not particularly accurate.[27] Because it cannot provide reliable quantitative data it is generally used only for screening purposes. The U-tube section of the equipment is packed with silica gel beads that change colour as alcohol passes over them. The person being tested blows into a glass pipe that is inserted into the U tube and the observer notes the colour change in the crystals. The existence of more sophisticated, reasonably priced digital breathalysing equipment means that the crystal dichromate version is seldom used today.

For procedures on how to implement the tests, see Appendix 1.

3.1.3 Urine testing

Testing for alcohol in the urine occurs during the elimination phase of alcohol. Thus, during the absorption phase of alcohol the urine-alcohol level lags behind that of breath alcohol and blood alcohol. This lag period lasts approximately 20-30 minutes.[28]

Like the blood-alcohol test, the urine test must be administered under a strict protocol (see Appendix 4). Ideally, the first urine specimen should be voided and only the second specimen taken for measurement of urine alcohol. This is because the first urine specimen could have been stored in the bladder for some appreciable time, whereas the second specimen is urine produced at the time of the test. The urine can be tested

---

27 Denney (n 23).
28 Cooper, Schwar & Smith (n 5) at 185.

by head space gas chromatography, enzymatic biochemical procedures or head space analysis using a fuel cell (as in the alcolmeters 400, 500 and 600) for reasonably accurate quantitative results.

A dipstick test is available which will measure the presence of alcohol, but it is not accurately quantitative.

3.1.4 Oral fluid testing

The alcohol concentration in oral fluid (saliva) is not significantly different from that in blood or breath;[29] it also shares a similarly short period of time of identification—up to a few days (see Table 10.2 and page 162 section 3.5.2 Oral Fluid Tests). However, an oral test for alcohol is less invasive, which is one of its main advantages. Another advantage is the test's simplicity—collecting a sample of saliva is a straightforward procedure. There is also a correlation between drug concentration and impairment when assessing very recent use of drugs. However the oral test also has a number of disadvantages. First, the amount of saliva produced varies from individual to individual, which can lead to inconsistency. Second, drugs ingested orally or smoked can contaminate the result. Certain drugs cause a dry mouth so that there is very little oral fluid to test. There is also a narrow window of detection, as mentioned above.

Inexpensive dipstick tests that measure the level of alcohol in oral fluid are useful screening devices. They do not, however, measure the exact level of alcohol, particularly at high alcohol levels. This means that at a workplace inquiry into suspected alcohol abuse, the test results are unlikely to be accepted as evidence of intoxication, although they could point to the need for more accurate, quantitative testing should alcohol be detected.

The fact that the apparatus is portable is useful in workplaces where employees are spread out over a large area: the supervisor can move from work area to work area with the test kit in his pocket and perform however many tests are needed. The same advantage applies to situations where there is a lack of adequate supervision, since a single supervisor can oversee the testing of a great many employees. If an employee tests positive he or she could be taken to the room or place designated for testing purposes, where a quantitative test could be done (eg a fuel-cell breathalyser) by a qualified member of staff or an independent service provider, as the case may be.

Oral fluid alcohol or drug tests are also useful for identifying the degree of cooperation of an employee patient on an alcohol or drug rehabilitation programme, where quantitative measurement is not required.

As mentioned above (see also page 162 section 3.5.2 Oral Fluid Tests) oral testing for alcohol or drugs is not the most accurate of measuring techniques. For example, using oral fluid to test for THC (tetrahydrocannabinol—the main intoxicant in cannabis) is considered to be only between 66–70% accurate. Even so, a recently completed European project highlighted the usefulness of oral testing in the area of road safety. The Rosita project evaluated police roadside testing procedures and techniques in several European countries between 2002 and 2005.[30] A key finding of the research team was that oral fluid testing

---

29 Mancinelli, R & Ceccanti, M 'Biomarkers in Alcohol Misuse: Their Role in the Prevention and Detection of Thiamine Deficiency' (2009) 44 (2) *Alcohol and Alcoholism* 177-182.

30 Verstraete, AG Roadside Testing Assessment (ROSITA): A European Union Project on Roadside Drug Testing. Ghent University Hospital. JCADTS proceedings 2000. (assessed at www.druid-project.eu)

is the most promising alternative to blood testing. The study concluded that oral fluid testing in the field offers practical advantages over other types of screening for cannabis though further evaluation studies are required. Further work in Victoria Australia shows that a two-test process is highly specific and sensitive.

Oral testing is currently being researched globally and it is reasonable to think that it will feature in alcohol and drug programmes of the future. At the time of writing of this book, however, questions still remain regarding the issue of accuracy, which suggests that for the meantime we should refer to the potential, rather than the actual benefits attached to this form of testing.

3.2 Indirect objective testing or biochemical tests

Indirect objective testing is done by measuring the effects of alcohol and drugs that have occurred in the body. These tests are used by medical personnel to identify the extent of harm or potential harm that a person has caused or is likely to cause to him- or herself. The indirect tests require medical interpretation and should therefore be administered by medical personnel only. They are very useful in identifying a developing or hidden alcohol and drug problem, whether for pre-employment purposes, for routine or random testing of employees, or for monitoring employees on a rehabilitation programme. Some indirect alcohol tests (eg serum acetate) can identify alcohol present at the time of the test and others (eg GGT, MCV and CDT) can identify a progressive abuse problem with or without alcohol being present at the time of the test.

Indirect biochemical tests can help in the recognition of alcohol and drug problems, even if the problems or the test results are denied by the individual. They can help to identify an alcohol and drug problem before it becomes overt and affects the individual's physical health and his or her objective work performance.

These tests can identify a progressive problem concerning alcohol or drug abuse in much the same way as other medical tests can reveal evidence of other progressive disorders—the tests for blood cholesterol, blood uric acid, blood pressure (BP) and lung function, for example. They are particularly useful as serial markers for the progressive monitoring of patients on a rehabilitation programme and are therefore an important tool of the medical alcohol and drug programme. The patient acts as his own control as you observe the tests reverting to normal; a subsequent sudden rise denoting a relapse.

3.2.1 Gamma glutamyl transferase (GGT)

Gamma glutamyl transferase is a liver enzyme that is also the most widely used biochemical indicator for excessive alcohol intake. At an early stage of chronic alcohol abuse, this liver enzyme is almost always induced by the existence of persistent alcohol that is presented to the liver for metabolism.

The test is a simple, inexpensive method of identifying excessive alcohol.[31] The level of GGT is raised in between 75% and 85% of chronic alcohol abusers. A raised GGT is more likely in excessive regular daily drinkers than in binge or bout drinkers, who can have periods of total abstinence between the episodes of drinking. In longstanding severe cases of over 20 years' alcohol abuse, when cirrhosis of the liver is well developed, the ability to induce the liver enzyme is lost. This usually coincides with a sudden loss of tolerance and the long-time drinker becomes intoxicated on smaller amounts of alcohol.

---

31   Rosalki, S (ed) *Clinical Biochemistry of Alcoholism* (1984) 68-77 and also see Mancinelli ibid.

Younger patients (under 30 years) generally do not have significantly raised levels until they are much older or unless they have had a previous liver infection or are particularly sensitive to alcohol. However, alcohol abuse in this age group has increased dramatically in recent years and cases of alcohol hepatitis and cirrhosis among young people are increasingly common. The number of young people with AAH (acute alcoholic hepatitis) is also on the rise. This is a disease that frequent binge drinkers are particularly prone to, which suggests that this practice is prevalent among the young. It is also possible for AAH to follow a period of unusually heavy drinking. (See chapter 7 section II 3.8.1 to 3.8.6).

In social and moderate drinkers the GGT levels are unlikely to rise above the normal reference values. To produce a probable indicative rise in GGT, the individual must exceed five weeks of daily heavy consumption of more than 60 g of alcohol (ie approximately one bottle of wine, a quarter bottle of spirits, two quarts of lager, or four and a half 'dumpies' of lager).

In dependent drinkers the level of GGT can be expected to rise to two or three times the maximum normal reference level, and in heavy chronic drinkers at least one-and-a-half times. On a successful rehabilitation programme the GGT levels can drop by as much as 50% within two weeks and return to normal within six weeks unless chronic hepatitis or obstruction due to cirrhosis has developed. In these cases a raised level will often persist, but seldom as high as for alcohol induction. Gamma glutamyl transferase can also be induced by drugs such as phenobarbiturates and phenytoin. This is a factor that must be taken into account in the treatment of epileptic patients since these drugs often form part of the treatment regimen, although the levels of induction will be increased according to alcohol excess.

If the normal maximum reference value is 37, then it can be expected that a level of 55 is indicative of early abuse or excessive drinking. However consideration must be taken of the individual laboratory normal reference values, which are calculated from their particular normal population group. At levels around 100 there is definitive alcohol abuse and at levels around 200, dependence is most likely to be well established. Levels as high as 1,000 are often seen in protracted cases of alcohol dependency and levels of 4,500 have been identified in some alcohol-dependent patients, but this inevitably leads to liver failure.

3.2.2 Mean corpuscular volume (MCV)

Mean corpuscular volume refers to the size of an individual's red blood cells, which can be established by means of an MCV test. When chronic alcohol abuse prevails over a period of time, the MCV is enlarged. The red cells in alcohol abusers tend to be round rather than oval. The enlargement occurs in the developed red blood cell and is seen in about 60% of chronic excessive drinkers. Even a small rise, when it occurs in isolation from any other abnormal red blood cell indices, is indicative. With abstinence the MCV takes longer to return to normal—about two to three months. This test often reveals a raised MCV in younger alcohol-abuse patients (those under the age of 30) when the GGT is not affected.[32] Another study has shown that females (86%) are more susceptible than males (63%) to the rise in MCV[33]

---

32 Morgan, MY, Camilo, ME, Luck, W, Sherlock, S & Hoffbrand, AV 'Macrocytosis in alcohol related liver disease: its value in screening' (1981) 3 *Clin Lab Haematol* 35-44.

33 Fauske, S & Haver, B 'Women with alcohol Problems' (2009) 44 (2) *Alcohol and Alcoholism* 177-182.

3.2.3 Uric acid

The serum uric acid is often raised in excessive drinkers. Whereas the uric acid test is neither sensitive nor specific, it does add an extra diagnostic tool to the identification process.

3.2.4 Triglycerides

Because alcoholic beverages have such a high carbohydrate content (and little else of nutritional value); the serum triglyceride levels will rise in cases of excessive consumption. A fasting serum triglyceride is a useful additional test, particularly if the blood is lipaemic. If the blood cells in a test tube are allowed to settle, the usually clear serum appears opaque or thick creamy white. It is useful to show the patient this in comparison to a normal specimen of serum.

Other liver enzymes found in the serum which help to improve the confirmatory diagnosis of alcohol abuse are glutamate dehydrogenase (GDH), aspartate transaminase (AST), and alanine transaminase (ALT). When liver damage occurs as a result of alcohol toxicity, the serum level of AST is inevitably higher than that of ALT as is explained in para 3.2.6 below.

3.2.5 Carbohydrate deficient transferrin (CDT)

In 1993, when this book was first published, carbohydrate deficient transferrin (CDT) was a newly developed test for alcohol abuse about which little was known. Research conducted in the intervening period has shown the test to be a more effective marker for males than females because females have a higher normal level of CDT than males. Also CDT rises during pregnancy. CD Transferrin is an isoform of transferrin, a protein used for transporting iron molecules in the blood. It appears after a regular intake of 50–80 g of ethanol daily for a week,[34] which is approximately the same as 6 units of alcohol or 1/5 of a bottle of spirits, a bottle of white wine, or over 3½ pints of lager or 4 dumpies (340 ml). This individual would have consumed a minimum of 44 units (or 350 g) of alcohol per week and could therefore be classified as a 'heavy drinker'. This test is claimed to be at least 82% sensitive and 97% specific to ethyl alcohol. It takes at least 30 days (half-life 15 days) for the test to return to normal.

3.2.6 Transaminases AST and ALT

The AST and ALT transaminases are liver enzymes involved in protein synthesis. Alanine transaminase (ALT) is more specific as it is only found in the liver whereas aspartate transaminase (AST) can be found in many organs, as well as muscle. An ALT blood test, if it reveals high levels of these enzymes, may indicate alcoholic liver disease. Different causes of liver damage can be established by comparing the two enzymes (the AST/ALT ratio): if the ratio is greater than one then alcohol related hepatitis is probably responsible for the rise; if the ratio is less than one, viral hepatitis or drug damage is probably the cause. This test is less effective for those under the age of 30 and over the age of 70.[35] The alcohol related liver damage can be shown within 2–3 days.

---

34   Stibler, H 'Carbohydrate deficient transferrin in serum: a new marker of potentially harmful alcohol consumption reveiwed' (1991) 37 (12) *Clinical Chemistry* 2029.

35   Conigrave, KM, Saunders, JB & Whitfield, JB 'Diagnostic tests for alcohol consumption' (1995) 30 (1) *Alcohol & Alcoholism* 13-26.

3.2.7 Ferritin and albumin

The ferritin blood test measures the amount of iron in the body. High levels of ferritin (too much iron in the blood) indicate damage to one or more organs that store blood, which includes the liver. The link between liver disease and alcohol abuse is well proven, which is why the ferritin test is useful. Albumin is an essential protein that helps to repair damaged body tissues and to maintain the body's growth. Albumin is found in the blood and if a blood test shows low levels of the protein, liver damage may be the cause.

In a large population study, the combination of GGT, AST, ALT, ferritin and albumin was shown to help differentiate between abstainers, moderate drinkers and heavy drinkers. Even moderate drinkers showed elevated levels of ferritin. Experiments on animals have shown that iron and alcohol act synergistically to enhance lipid peroxidation (which leads to cell damage) and liver injury. Heavy drinking has been shown to increase ferritin levels and secondary hepatic iron overload is a typical characteristic of patients who are alcoholics.[36]

3.2.8 Hair testing

Hair testing is a recently developed non-invasive method used to test for alcohol and drugs. The test is reasonably well established, despite its newness, but the costs involved mean that it is not yet in general use.

In respect of alcohol, hair testing is *indirect* as it depends on the interaction of alcohol with fatty acids producing fatty acid ethyl esters (FAEEs), which are deposited on the hair. In the case of drugs this is a *direct* test of the actual drug that is deposited on the hair. (Note: FAEEs can also be found in blood and urine.)

As hair grows from the root (at approximately 1 cm per month), these deposits are delayed to a certain extent, which means that they cannot be detected until the hair grows out (2–4 weeks). The distance from the scalp of the hair portion containing drugs allows an estimate to be made of the approximate time of drug consumption. The deposited substances are relatively stable in the face of external influences such as hair treatments, cosmetics and sunlight. Due to the way in which drugs are deposited in the hair, hair analysis provides a detailed view of drug consumption over the past weeks or months. For considering day-to-day consumption, blood or urine testing would be necessary.

The sum of the concentrations of four of these FAEEs (ethyl myristate, ethyl palmitate, ethyl oleate and ethyl stearate) are used as indicators of an individual's alcohol consumption. The amounts found in hair are measured in nanograms (one nanogram equals one billionth of a gram), and with the benefit of modern technology, it is possible to detect such small amounts. A positive result is always associated with recent alcohol consumption.[37]

---

36 Fletcher, LM 'Alcohol and Iron: one glass of red or more?' (1996) 11 *J Gastroenterol Hepatol* 1039-1041 and Whitfield et al 2001 'Effects of alcohol consumption on indices of iron stores and of iron stores on alcohol intake markers' 25 *Alcohol Clin Exp Res* 1037-1045 in (2009) 44 (2) *Alcohol and Alcoholism* 199-203.

37 Auwarter, V, Sporkert, F, Hartwig, S, Pragst, F, Vater, H & Diefenbacher, A 'Fatty Acid Ethyl Esters in Hair as markers of alcohol consumption. Segmented hair analysis of alcoholics, social drinkers and teetotallers' (2001) 47 (12) *Clin Chem* 2114-2123. See also Laposata, M 'Fatty Acid Ethyl Esters: Short term and long term serum markers of ethanol intake' (1997) 43 *Clinical Chem* 1527-1534; Skopp, G, Schmitt, G, Potsch, L, Dronner, P, Aderjan, R and Mattern, R 'Ethyl Glucuronide in human hair' (2000) 35 *Alcohol Alcohol* 283-285.

The way in which alcohol metabolites (FAEEs) enter into the hair affects the amount of alcohol or drugs recorded during the hair analysis test. Like other drugs, FAEEs enter into the hair via the ceratinocytes, the cells responsible for hair growth. These cells form in the root of the hair (that is, they are subcutaneous) and then grow through the surface of the skin taking any substances with them. However, the sebaceous glands also produce FAEEs in the scalp (that is, they are cutaneous) and these migrate together with the sebum along the hair shaft.[38] These glands lubricate not only the part of the hair on the surface of the skin that grows at 0,3 mm per day but also the more mature hair growth, providing it with a protective layer of fat.

This means the sebaceous glands supply the whole length of hair with sebum, which in turn carries FAEEs into the hair, resulting in an accumulative increase of FAEEs from proximal (closest to the scalp) to distal (farthest from the scalp) hair sections.

However there is a significant correlation between the intensity of the alcohol intake and the concentrations of the FAEEs in hair. Results between 0,05 and 30 ng/mg were found in hair.[39]

Because of the increasing FAEE concentrations from proximal to distal it is preferable to always consider analysis of a standard length of hair. For example, analysis of a 1cm hair sample taken close to the scalp of an individual will give a much lower result than the analysis of a 6 cm long sample also taken close to the scalp from the same person. The closer the conditions (ie hair length) are to the standard procedure, the more certain one can be of the accuracy of the result.

However, a recent preliminary investigation of the AUDIT and DUDIT versus biomarkers of alcohol and drug use highlighted challenges unique to the South African context.[40] Researchers on the study were unable to obtain hair samples from some of the African and coloured participants in the study. In some cases participant hair was shorter than 1 cm and quite curly. This immediately compromises the validity of the findings considering that analysis is performed on a standard length of hair, as described above. In addition, a proportion of women had their hair plaited in braids or weaved, which meant that a natural strand of head hair could not be obtained. These findings demonstrate the need to pay attention to the realities of the existing situation before deciding upon a particular test.

A 6 cm long hair sample can be used to analyse alcohol and drug consumption of the previous 6 to 12 months (this is commonly used in Germany to test drivers). If head hair is not available or is too short (minimum: 2 cm), underarm, chest, leg and pubic hair may be analysed as markers of chronic alcohol abuse. Body hair gives a picture going back up to twelve months.[41]

The incorporation of FAEE into hair does not appear to be affected by hair pigment, which is contrary to what is known about the chemistry of drug and melanin interactions.

38 Auwarter et al Ibid.

39 Pragst, F & Balikova, MA 'State of the art in hair analysis for detection of drug and alcohol abuse' (2006) 370 Clinica Chimica Acta 17-49.

40 Kader, R 'A preliminary investigation of the AUDIT and DUDIT versus biomarkers of alcohol and drug use among HIV infected clinic attendees in Cape Town, South Africa' (2010) unpublished data, Medical Research Council, Cape Town.

41 Hartweg, S Auwarter, V & Pragst, F 'Fatty Acid Ethyl Esters in Scalp, Pubic, Axillary, Beard and Body hair as markers for Alcohol misuse.' (2003) 38 (2) Alcohol and Alcoholism 163-167.

This should avoid any bias and discrimination in the interpretation of alcohol abuse based on hair colour.[42]

Recent studies have shown FAEEs to be specific markers for distinguishing social drinkers from heavy drinkers or alcohol dependent drinkers.[43]

In summary, FAEE is found in hair, blood and urine and when present is suggestive of heavy alcohol consumption.

3.2.9 Hair and ethyl glucoronide (EtG)

Ethyl glucoronide (EtG) can be identified in body fluid and hair and remains in the blood for up to 36 hours and in urine for up to five days after heavy alcohol use. Ethyl glucoronide is not found in non drinkers.[44]

An EtG test is effective for detecting heavy drinking even when other tests have yielded negative results. There is a significant correlation between the intensity of the alcohol intake and the concentrations of the FAEEs in hair. Results between 0,05 and 30 ng/mg were found in hair.[45]

As mentioned above, in the absence of head hair it is possible to use hair taken from the face (beard), chest, armpit, stomach, pubis or legs. In one study, samples of hair were collected from different parts of the body, including the head, and compared for the standard depicted for head or scalp hair. In some cases when head hair tested negative positive results were identified with pubic hair. When positive for head hair all the other types of hair were also positive. Thus if non head hair is used care must be taken to ensure a standardised interpretation of the results and particularly for pubic hair, which could show significantly higher concentrations.[46] Ethyl glucuronide concentration in hair is not influenced by hair pigmentation.[47]

---

42 Kulaga, V, Velazquez-Annenta, Y, Aleksa, K, Vergee, Z & Koren, G 'The effect of hair pigment on the incorporation of Fatty Acid Ethyl Esters (FAEE)' (2009) 44 (3) *Alcohol and Alcoholism* 287-292.

43 Salem, R, Refaai, M, Cluett-Brown, J, Russo, JW & Laposata M 'Fatty acid ethyl esters in liver and adipose tissues as postmortem markers for ethanol intake' (2001) 47 (4) *Clinical Chemistry* 722-725.

44 Wurst, FM, Alexson, S, Wolfersdorf, M, Bechtel, G, Forster, S, Alling ,C, Aradóttir, S, Jachau, K, Huber, P, Allen, JP, Auwärter, V & Pragst, F 'Concentration of fatty acid ethyl esters in hair of alcoholics: Comparison to other biological state markers and self-reported ethanol intake' (2004) 39 (1) *Alcohol and Alcoholism* 33-38. See also Wurst, FM, Kempter, C, Seidl, S & Alt, A 'Ethyl Glucoronide-a marker of alcohol consumption and a relapse marker with clinical and forensic implications' (1999) 34 *Alcohol and Alcoholism* 71-77 and Jurado,C, Soriano, T, Giminez, MP & Mendez, M ' Diagnosis of Chronic Alcohol Consumption: Hair Analysis for Ethyl Glucuronide' (2004) 145 *Forensic Science International* 161-166.

45 Pragst (n38). See also Yegles, M, Labarthe, Auwarter, AV, Hartwig, S, Vater, H, Wennig, R & Pragst, F 'Comparison of Ethyl Glucuronide and Fatty Acid Ethyl Ester concentrations in hair of alcoholics, social drinkers and teetotallers' (2004) 145 *Forensic Science International* 167-173 and Alt, A, Janda, I, Seidl, S & Wurst, F 'Determination of Ethyl Glucuronide in Hair Samples' (2000) 35 *Alcohol and Alcoholism* 313-314.

46   Kerekes, I, Yegles, M, Grimm, U & Wenning, R 'Ethyl Glucuronide Determination: Head Hair versus Non-Head Hair' (2009) 44 (1) *Alcohol and Alcoholism* 62-66.

47 Appenzeller, B, Schuman, M, Yegles, M & Wennig, R 'Ethyl glucuronide concentration in hair is not influenced by pigmentation' (2007) 42 *Alcohol and Alcoholism* 326-327. See also Kulaga, V, Velazquez-Annenta, Y, Aleksa, K, Vergee, Z & Koren, G 'The effect of hair pigment on the incorporation of Fatty Acid Ethyl Esters (FAEE)' (2009) 44 *Alcohol and Alcoholism* 287-292.

In summary, hair testing gives a longer period of detection; it is also highly specific and sensitive, non-invasive and tamper-proof. However, the technology is new, expensive and not sufficiently available in South Africa at present.

3.2.10 Urine and ethyl glucoronide (EtG) and ethyl sulphate (EtS)

Ethyl glucoronide (EtG) is found in urine as well as hair. It is excreted in small amounts together with ethyl sulphate (EtS) after alcohol consumption; it is not excreted or found in non drinkers or abstainers. Compared with urine alcohol, EtG and EtS are excreted in urine for a more prolonged time making them useful as sensitive alcohol biomarkers. A study comparing breath alcohol levels with urine EtG and EtS levels showed that EtG and EtS remained in the urine for several days longer (48–130 hours after the alcohol was eliminated). This test has been utilised in the United States for clinical and medico-legal testing. However caution has been advised with respect to EtG as it should not be used as a single test to prove a positive evidential result. False positives due to urine infection have occurred for EtG but not for EtS; EtS is therefore used as a confirmatory test. At the present time these tests can only identify alcohol qualitatively and not quantitatively.[48]

3.2.11 Alcohol and Phosphatidylethanol (PEth)

Alcohol forms a phospholipid in the blood erythrocytes and develops a specific and sensitive marker for alcohol abuse. PEth can be detected in the blood of an alcohol-dependant person for up to 14 days after abstinence. It is considered both sensitive and specific to alcohol (ethanol) abuse.

3.2.12 Questionnaires (Please see also Appendix 3 on questionnaires and screening tools)

Questionnaires are used for screening alcohol or drug addiction, dependency or other problems. The questionnaires can be completed via an interview or by the subject him- or herself (self-completed questionnaires). The questions asked are usually about either the interviewee's overall experience of alcohol and drugs or about the quantity and frequency of his or her alcohol and drug consumption. The choice of less specific or more specific questions will depend upon the circumstances. Whatever type of questionnaire is selected it needs to be scored and administered in a consistent manner. Questions need to be capable of being understood by all interviewees, by the health professional or other staff member conducting the interviews, and by those individuals with authorised access to the questionnaires, such as human resources personnel.

How the employee responds to the questions is also context-dependent. For instance, employees occupying safety critical positions will be particularly sensitive to questions concerning their alcohol and/or drug habits, given that their answers will almost inevitably be subjected to particularly close scrutiny. In workplaces where a 'zero-tolerance' policy towards alcohol or drug abuse exists, *all* employees are likely to feel ambivalent about the question-and-answer process. By contrast, organisations that have a more sympathetic approach to the issue of substance misuse may find that employees are less wary of the interview procedure.

---

48 Helander, A, Bottcher, M, Fehr, C, Dahmen, N & Beck O 'Detection times for Urinary Ethyl Glucoronide and Ethyl Sulphate in Heavy Drinkers during Alcohol Detoxication' (2009) 44 (1) *Alcohol and Alcoholism* 55-61.

The fact that the validity of questionnaires is determined by the truthfulness of the answers given is, of course, the most significant problem. This is something we will look at in a moment. Despite their limitations, however, questionnaires are an inexpensive, non-invasive means of providing managers, human resource personnel and occupational health professionals with valuable insights regarding the existence and severity of substance abuse problems in the workplace. But it must be remembered that questionnaires are for screening purposes only; they do not provide conclusive proof of alcohol or drug misuse. Any positive results identified must be followed up by an in-depth assessment of the problems presented, which will require the use of legitimate diagnostic tools and the input of suitably qualified personnel.

Frequently used questionnaires relating to alcohol abuse are the Brief Michigan Alcoholism Screening Test (BMAST), where a score of more than five points indicates dependency, or the CAGE questionnaire, a four-question test where two or more positive replies suggest dependency. The CAGE questionnaire is more appropriate in a clinical setting as a self-completed questionnaire.

The World Health Organization's AUDIT screens for the quantity of alcohol consumed as well as the effects of alcohol abuse. The AUDIT (the acronym stands for 'Alcohol Use Disorders Identification Test') is a robust, simple method of screening for excessive drinking and can help in identifying excessive drinking as the cause of the presenting illness. The AUDIT, which is widely accepted as the best screening tool of its kind, is commonly used by clinicians in South Africa as a screening device. It also provides a framework for intervention to help at-risk and harmful drinkers reduce or cease alcohol consumption and thereby avoid the harmful consequences of their drinking. The AUDIT was designed to assist health care practitioners in a range of health settings, but with suitable instructions and training it can be self-administered or used by non-health professionals.[49]

A development from the AUDIT questionnaire is FAST (Fast Alcohol Screening Test), which as its name implies is designed for busy medical settings such as an Accident & Emergency (A&E) department or a GP's consulting room. It consists of a cut-down version of the AUDIT and on trialling was shown to be very effective, with a sensitivity index of over 90%.[50] The Drug Use Disorders Identification Test (DUDIT) was developed as a parallel instrument to the AUDIT. The DUDIT serves as a valuable instrument that can identify individuals who appear to have a drug problem or are drug dependent, as well as screening out those who do not have such problems.[51]

3.2.12(a) Validity of questionnaires in a workplace setting

The problem presented by the alcohol and drug questionnaires is that they are dependent on frank and honest answers. Actual consumption can be underreported due either to the denial of the existence of a problem or to subconscious guilt, which is reinforced in

49 Babor, T, Higgins-Biddle, JC, Saunders, JB & Monteiro MG *Alcohol Use Disorders Identification Test (AUDIT) Guidelines for Use in Primary Care* 2ed World Health Organisation Department of Mental Health and Substance Dependence.

50 Hodgson, R, Alwyn, T, John, B, Thom B & Smith, A 'The FAST Alcohol Screening Test' (2002) 37 (1) *Alcohol and Alcoholism* 61-66.

51 Berman, A, Bergman, H, Palmstierna, T, Schlyter, F 'Evaluation of the Drug Use Disorders Identification Test (DUDIT) in Criminal Justice and Detoxification Settings and in a Swedish Population Sample' (2005) 11 (1) *European Addiction Research* 22-31.

the workplace setting. Denial, particularly at the pre-employment stage,[52] has shown the low reliability and poor validity of questionnaires and interviewing in relation to actual alcohol intake. As suggested above, employees will only feel comfortable providing truthful answers if they know that they have the support of their peers and superiors; conversely, employees will offer evasive or fictitious replies if they believe the workplace culture to be intolerant towards or unsupportive of employees with alcohol or drug difficulties.

3.3 Direct drug testing to determine whether an employee is under the influence of intoxicating drugs

Drug testing has become commonplace in many countries across the world and is used in many contexts ranging from crime investigations to workplace surveillance;[53] and is even used as an indicator for treatment adherence. Drug testing is a technical and scientific method used to detect the presence of specified drugs or their metabolised traces in urine, blood, sweat, hair or oral fluid samples. Workplace testing primarily uses blood and urine specimens to determine the presence of drugs. However the use of alternate biological specimens such as oral fluid testing and hair testing is increasing in some countries and is considered to be more accessible and less invasive to collect in comparison to collecting a urine specimen. Hair testing is useful when assessing the progress (or indeed regression) of an individual on a drug rehabilitation programme since evidence of drug use is detectable in the hair for up to a year.

Although the urine test for drug(s) is the preferred method of testing for many employers, its main disadvantage (from the employer's point of view) is that it cannot show whether the employee being tested is actually intoxicated at the time the test is performed. Furthermore, the urine test cannot be used to determine the amount of drugs consumed or the time of consumption.

Blood testing, on the other hand, may provide more suitable information about whether or not an individual is 'under the influence'. The same can be said of oral testing: a specimen of oral fluid can disclose a significant correlation between drug concentrations and behavioural effects if tested shortly after absorption. However, oral testing also presents difficulties, which is something we considered earlier. Variations in the amount of saliva produced from person to person, the risk of contamination posed by drugs swallowed or smoked, and outstanding concerns regarding the accuracy of the results obtained, suggest that further research is needed on this method of testing.

It is important to remember that under the provisions of section 7 of the Employment Equity Act 55 of 1998:

> (1) *Medical testing of an employee is prohibited, unless—*
> > (a) *legislation permits or requires the testing; or*
> > (b) *it is justifiable in the light of medical facts, employment conditions, social policy, the fair distribution of employee benefits or the inherent requirements of a job.*

---

52 Midanik, L 'The validity of self-reported alcohol consumption and alcohol problems. A literature review' (1982) 77 *Br J Addictions* 357.

53 Cone, EJ 'Legal, workplace, and treatment drug testing with alternate biological matrices on a global scale' (2001) 121 *Forensic Science International* 7-15.

Table 10.1 The chart below gives approximate detection periods for each substance by test type:

Substance of abuse	Urine**	Hair***	Blood*	Oral Fluid*	Comments
Amphetamines (excluding meth-amphetamine)	1–3 days	Up to 90 days	12 hours	3 days	Amphetamine is metabolised by a number of pathways. In general, acid urine promotes excretion whereas alkaline urine retards it. In 24 hours, approximately 79% of the amphetamine dose is excreted in acid urine and about 45% in alkaline urine. Typically, about 20% is excreted as unaffected amphetamine. Unaffected amphetamine can be detected up to 1–2 days after use.
Methamphe-tamine (Tik)	3–5 days	Up to 90 days	1–3 days	Up to 5–13 days	Methamphetamine is excreted in the urine as amphetamine and oxidized and deaminated derivatives. However, 10–40% of methamphetamine is excreted unchanged. Methamphetamine is generally detectable in the urine for 3 to 5 days after use.
MDMA (Ecstasy)	4 days	Up to 90 days	25 hours	Up to 5–13 days	
Barbiturates (except phenobarbital)	2–3 days	Up to 90 days	1–2 days	1–2 days	Short-acting barbiturates are normally traceable in urine for 4 to 6 days, while long-acting barbiturates can be traced for up to 30 days. Barbiturates are excreted in the urine in unchanged forms, hydroxylated derivatives, carboxylated derivatives and glucuronide conjugates.
Phenobarbital	2–3 weeks	Up to 90 days	4–7 days	4–7 days	
Benzodiazepines	Thera-peutic use: 3 days Chronic use: 4–6 weeks	Up to 90 days	6–48 hours	From time of ingestion for up to 2–3 days	Many of the benzodiazepines share a common metabolic route, and are excreted as oxazepam and its glucuronide in urine. Oxazepam is detectable in the urine for up to 7 days after drug use.

Substance of abuse	Urine**	Hair***	Blood*	Oral Fluid*	Comments
Cannabis	Single use: 1–6 days Weekly use: 3–9 days Daily use 7–30 days	Up to 90 days	2–3 days after infrequent use, up to 2 weeks after frequent use	THC may only be detectable in oral fluid for between 6 hours and 12 hours.	Cannabis is detected in the urine 2–3 days after infrequent use, up to 2 weeks if used frequently.
Cocaine	2–4 days	Up to 90 days	24 hours	1 day	Cocaine is excreted in the urine primarily as benzoylecgonine in a short period. Benzoylecgonine has a biological half-life of 5–8 hours, which is much longer than that of cocaine (0,5–1,5 hours), and can generally be detected for 12 – 72 hours after cocaine use.
Codeine	1 day	Up to 90 days	12 hours	1–3 days	
Morphine	2 days	Up to 90 days	6 hours	1–3 days	Morphine is excreted unmetabolised and is the marker metabolic product of opiates. Morphine and morphine glucuronide are detectable in urine for several days after the use of opiates.
Heroin	3–4 days	Up to 90 days	6 hours	1–2 days	

Source: US Department of Transportation: National Highway Traffic Safety Administration. 2004

* Oral fluid and saliva testing results mimic that of blood, with the exception of THC and benzodiazepines. Oral fluid detects THC from ingestion 6–12 hours after ingestion.
** Urine can only detect drug use 6–8 hours or more after ingestion. It takes 6–8 hours for the drug to be metabolised and excreted in urine.
*** It takes 2 weeks for the drug to be metabolised and to show on the hair follicle.

Detection times are subject to weight, age, sex, metabolism and the quantity ingested.

3.4 Rapid drug testing and laboratory analysis

3.4.1 Qualitative screening: Rapid drug testing

Rapid drug testing devices provide a qualitative indication of drugs in urine and in oral fluids. But these tests do not determine how much of the drug is present in the system and thus only provide initial results. Rapid drug screening tests use immunoassay screening to detect the presence of a certain type of drug. If the qualitative screening test is negative the donor is cleared. If not, a second quantitative confirmatory test is required. This test must be conducted in a certified laboratory that contains all the necessary equipment. Another portion of the primary sample is tested, using a different methodology, namely gas chromatography/mass spectrometry (GC/MS), which we will look at in the following section.

Rapid drug testing often takes place onsite, and is fairly easy to administer with proper training. It should also be noted that an onsite drug test cannot accurately determine if the drug detected is an illicit or a prescribed drug, as many prescribed drugs contain alcohol, opioids or amphetamine-like substances.[54] In the event of an onsite test being positive, a further confirmatory test will be needed.

The use of good quality, FDA-approved tests is paramount. This is not yet standard practice in South Africa where at present there are no quality control measures governing the supply of drug testing equipment. This unfortunate state of affairs has led to the widespread distribution of cheap kits producing questionable results.

3.4.2 Quantitative Confirmation Laboratory Testing

Confirmation testing in South Africa is done by gas chromatography-mass spectrometry (GS-MS) methodology. The purpose of the confirmation test is to reduce the probability of a false-positive result and to provide additional information and assurance about the identity of the detected compound. Gas chromatography/mass spectrometry (GC/MS) is widely accepted in both scientific and legal arenas as one of the most powerful diagnostic techniques for the separation, quantification, and identification of drug analytics, especially at low concentrations; it is also considered to be the gold standard for confirmation testing.

3.5 Specimen comparisons

3.5.1 Urine testing as an indicator of drug abuse

Urine and breath analysis are the most common methods of testing for drugs and alcohol in the workplace. However breath analysis can only accurately determine alcohol intoxication and impairment levels. Urine analysis is used to measure alcohol and to detect traces of drugs. The majority of tests can measure only the urinary metabolite of the drug that is excreted. It should be noted that urine metabolite drug testing does not identify immediate intoxication—it measures only previous absorption. Alcohol and amphetamines are the two main exceptions in that they are excreted unchanged. No scientific study has proven a level of urine drug metabolite which is generally accepted as a level presumed to induce impairment or provide knowledge of the time of absorption. This has been proclaimed in court: *Anable v Ford, AFGE v Weinberger, Jones v Mackenzie.*[55] Urine samples are often collected in a specially designed tamper-proof cup, which is then sealed. As a golden rule, screening and confirmation testing must be performed using the same specimen. This is achievable in urine testing if the collecting cup separates the specimen in two distinct chambers. One portion of the specimen will be used during the initial screen, while another portion will be reserved if further confirmation testing is needed.

There are many variables which influence the level of metabolite identified in the urine. Not least of all is the human variation, which in the case of metabolites can be substantial. It has been demonstrated, for example, that someone under observation

---

54 Pidd, K, & Roche, A *'Workplaces: A Greenfield site for AOD prevention and intervention'* (2006) 30 *ADCA News* 10-11.

55 Zeese, KB 'Technological problems with testing' *Drug Testing Legal Manual* (1990) chapter 3 at 29.

can test positive for cannabis in the morning, negative in the afternoon and positive again the next morning.[56] This has considerable implications when assessing the results of recent absorption or serial testing. A rising assay in serial testing is not categorically due to recent absorption and may indicate only an increasing excretion of metabolite in a previously heavy abuser. In the case of cannabis, this increase could be due to the leaching of THC out of fatty tissues: a fluctuating result of between 20 and 60 ng/dl could be due to this process. On the other hand, a jump from 50 ng/dl to over 150 ng/dl in a week is much more likely to be consistent with very recent absorption; assays of 600 ng/dl are commonplace with heavy absorbers who are still smoking cannabis; readings of up to 50 ng/dl could also be indicative of passive smoking.[57] Immediate heavy absorption can still provide a negative urine result as metabolites are still impending.

Urine metabolite drug testing should not be used to identify intoxication. It can be used in periodic medicals to counsel employees or even suspend them from hazardous work if heavy use is identified and in serial testing during counselling and rehabilitation to determine whether use of the drug is continuing, as long as the practitioner takes cognisance of the reasonable fluctuations which can occur between samples.

3.5.2 Oral fluid tests

Drug testing has undergone considerable expansion over the last decade.[58] The use of alternate specimens such as oral fluid for establishing exposure to drugs has become significant in the field of toxicology, though the academic community continues to query the effectiveness of oral testing. An oral fluid test has been seen as a non-invasive alternative to testing urine or blood, particularly by police engaged in roadside testing of drivers (see the discussion of the Rosita project from earlier in this chapter). In addition, oral fluid has been found to be useful in detecting drug use within the previous hour. Urine can only detect drug use 6–8 hours or more after ingestion because it takes this long for the drug to be metabolised and excreted in urine. The detection window for oral fluid is dependent on the drug used, the dose taken, and the route of administration. A drug may be detected in oral fluid in less than one hour and remain detectable 5–24 hours after last use. Oral fluid is therefore a useful option for post-accident testing or where there is a reasonable suspicion that the person is presently under the influence,[59] but also as an alternative to urine when substitution or adulteration is suspected.[60]

Oral fluids consist primarily of saliva, containing both residual substances in the mouth after smoking or snorting and substances that pass from the plasma through infiltration (these refer to substances that are not heavily bound to plasma proteins, antibodies and proteins, for example cocaine, amphetamines, opiates and PCP). The active ingredient of cannabis, tetrahydrocannabinol (THC), however, is trapped in the lipid cells of the buccul mucosa and can be detected by immunoassay and confirmed by mass spectrometry/mass spectrometry (MS/MS) and liquid chromatography/mass spectrometry (LC/MS) technology. At the time of publication of this book these technologies are not yet available in South Africa.

---

56 Zeese (n 17) 28.
57 Zeese (n 17) 28.
58 Drummer, O 'Drug testing in Oral Fluid' (2006) 27 (3) *Clinical Biochem Rev* 146–159.
59 Drug Testing Africa–Testing Officer Manual, 2010.
60 Drummer (n 57) at 146–159.

Although oral fluid testing documents numerous advantages, it is important to emphasise that because this method cannot be used as conclusive evidence of intoxication it should not be regarded as a substitute for urine or blood testing.[61] (See Table 10.2 below for further information on the advantages and disadvantages of various tests.)

3.5.3 Blood tests

The use of blood testing to establish the presence of drugs is invasive and expensive; however, it can also be an important definitive test. The testing of blood specimens can be used to infer the degree of impairment because the drug and/or metabolite in blood correlate with the concentration in the brain, which is where intoxication/impairment occurs.

3.5.4 Sweat testing

In the United States, sweat testing is almost exclusively used by child protection services and parole departments, and to monitor illicit drug use in court-ordered surveillance programmes as well as drug rehabilitation programmes. Although research has shown that drugs are indeed excreted in sweat,[62] the incorporation of drugs into the body's sweat glands is a process that is poorly understood.[63] Some drugs and drug metabolites that have been detected in sweat include THC, amphetamine, methamphetamine, codeine, morphine, heroin, PCP and cocaine, benzoylecgonine, egonine methylester, nicotine and alcohol. Concentrations of drugs found in sweat are generally low, resulting in a high variability in detection capabilities across individuals. Contamination of sweat specimens is a concern, making sweat testing highly unreliable.[64]

For instance, if sweat is collected from skin that has surface contamination with a drug or if hands that have been contaminated with drugs touch the sample of sweat to be analysed, the drug can be easily absorbed (Drug Testing Africa, 2010). For these reasons, it is essential that drug testing is undertaken by trained screen testing officers only.

4. CHAIN OF CUSTODY AND TESTING PROTOCOL

The protocol for testing must be carefully assessed and the 'chain of custody'—the security system devised to ensure safe handling of the specimen and reduce human error—must be monitored (see Appendix 4). Chain of custody describes the process of documenting the handling and storage of a specimen from the time a donor gives the specimen to a screen testing officer, to the subsequent screen test, to the disposition of the specimen and, finally, to the release of the report.[65]

Errors in the testing protocol may be due to the following factors:
- a badly designed and/or monitored chain of custody

---

61 Crouch, D, Walsh, JM, Flegal, R et al 'An evaluation of selected oral fluid point-of-collection drug-testing devices'. (2005) 29 Jnl of Analytical Toxiology.

62 Karch, SB (ed) Workplace Drug Testing (2007) CRC Press USA. See also Barnes et al 'Excretion of Methamphetamine and Amphetamine in human sweat following controlled oral Methamphetamine administration' (2008) 54 Clinical Chemistry 172-180.

63 Karch, SB Workplace Drug Testing (2007) CRC Press USA.

64 Pidd (n 53). Drug Testing South Africa-Testing Officer Manual, 2008.

65 Drug Testing South Africa.

- poorly maintained and/or unhygienic equipment
- cross-reaction with metabolites of other drugs (eg anti-inflammatory)
- intermittent metabolic processes
- concentration or dilution of urine (urine should be voided from the bladder, then the next excretion is tested)
- storage of urine in the bladder (see above point).

Any drug testing which does not use a chain of custody and does not adhere to testing protocols is fraught with hazards.

Personnel used as screen testing officers in the workplace should be trained individuals, preferably with a medical background. Screen testing officers should receive training in urine testing and other methods. They should be identifiable in the workplace as the company's screen testing officers and should maintain and follow standard operating procedures and adhere to a code of ethical conduct. These precautions are necessary if a company wishes to avoid the risk of non-compliance.

5. NON BIOLOGICAL TESTS

Non biological tests measure performance; they do not measure intoxication. We will consider two of these tests: the Eye Check™ pupillometer and the Stroop test. Note that non biological tests measure performance as it appears at the time of the test and not a developing intoxication problem.

5.1 Eye Check™ pupillometer

The Eye Check™ pupillometer is a non-invasive direct test of performance yet an indirect test of impairment due to a developing alcohol or drug problem. This biometric test measures the reaction of the pupil of the eye to a light source. The subject looks into the pupillometer (the apparatus resembles a pair of binoculars) after the eyes have adapted to a dark environment. The light source is a flash of light onto the pupils of the eyes and the pupil reflex reaction to the flash of light is measured. The reaction of the pupils to the light can determine the possibility of drug or alcohol impairment or fatigue. The changes in pupil size are correlated with the level of alertness. One advantage of this test is that it measures the direct impairment rather than the cause of the impairment. A further advantage is its simplicity: learning how to use the pupillometer requires minimal training. There is unlikely to be any legal barrier to its use in areas of work involving detailed reaction and concentration particularly of a safety critical nature. There are various groups who would be contraindicated from using the test, such as those with a previous head injury or eye damage (however, if only one eye is damaged, the other eye can be used—the device only uses one eye to perform a test), those over the age of 65, and pregnant women. The test is a pre-screening test which if identifying a positive result would need to be confirmed by alternative tests (see above). It would have a useful role in addressing the difficult issue of the hangover effect.[66]

---

66 Richman, J 'The sensitivity and specificity of Infrared Pupillometry Measurements in identifying drug impairment in a County Probation Program' December 2002 Presented Scientific Program American Academy of Optometry (December 2002).

5.2 The Stroop Test

The Stroop Test measures cognitive disinhibition via an assessment of the time taken to perform a number of simple tasks. The individual is shown a series of cards and on each card the name of a colour appears—'Blue', 'Green', 'Red', 'Yellow', and so on. The word shown is printed in either a matching-colour ink (the word 'Blue' is printed in blue ink) or a non-matching colour ink (the word 'Blue' is printed in red ink). The individual has to read out the ink colour shown ignoring the printed word, thus for the word 'Blue' printed in red ink the correct answer would be 'Red'. The cards are shown in a random sequence. The latency period and error rate is noted. Any weakening of performance in error rate or latency represents the Stroop effect. The words can be changed by substituting the word 'alcohol' or any other drug which is likely to have been taken. This test has been used to observe the cognitive differences in someone intoxicated.[67]

6. ADVANTAGES AND DISADVANTAGES OF VARIOUS TESTS

Table 10.2 summarises the advantages and disadvantages of the various tests discussed in this chapter. The method(s) of collection and the limitations of each test are also presented.

Table 10.2 Advantages and disadvantages of various tests for alcohol and drugs

Type of test	Advantages	Disadvantages	Collection methods	Limitations
Breath Testing	an onsite test that does not require subsequent confirmatory testing non-intrusive can detect recent alcohol intoxication and impairment levels comparatively as accurate as blood testing	can only detect alcohol use expensive measure of testing and also requires ongoing maintenance/calibration cannot detect hangover effects result not admissible as evidence in court unless apparatus is able to provide a printout of result	breathalyser oral fluid alcohol test	screen test calibration is imperative after 300/1 000 tests depending on the type of device device must be approved by relevant drug administration agency short detection time

---

67   Rose, A & Duka, T 'The influence of Alcohol on basic motoric and Cognitive disinhibition' (2007) 42 (6) *Alcohol and Alcoholism* 544-551. See also Mintzer, M Z, Stitzer, ML 'Cognitive impairment in methadone maintenance patients' (2002) 67 *Drug and Alcohol Dependence* 41–51.

Type of test	Advantages	Disadvantages	Collection methods	Limitations
Blood Testing	can be used to infer impairment and intoxication difficult to contaminate admissible as evidence in court	unreliable indicator of intoxication during absorption stage of alcohol half life of drugs in blood is short, making blood specimens less useful for routine drug screening invasive process	laboratory tests only	only trained medical personnel can take blood short detection period results not instant
Oral Fluid Testing	non-intrusive can detect recent use (use within 24 hours) simple collection process minimal risk of tampering	low drug concentrations on-site testing is not a definitive test result not admissible as evidence in court at this point in time	Laboratory/ confirmatory testing 100% accuracy Onsite testing methods 68% accuracy	no on-site screen test kits available with FDA approval laboratory/ confirmatory testing not available in South Africa (specimens sent overseas for testing but this is expensive) rapid oral fluid drug tests in the workplace not allowed in many parts of USA
Urine testing	least expensive of all testing methods non-scientific trained staff can initiate tests or do on-site immunoassay test (followed by lab testing) extensive scientific basis for testing methodologies confirmatory tests 100% accurate laboratory test results are admissible as evidence in court	intrusive positive result requires laboratory confirmation testing cannot detect very recent use quality of screening kits not always uniform susceptible to adulteration on-site test results not admissible as evidence in court	Onsite screen tests Laboratory collection containers (specimens to be collected by a qualified screen testing officer or collection officer).	device must be approved by relevant drug administration agency results compromised if correct chain of custody not adhered to

Type of test	Advantages	Disadvantages	Collection methods	Limitations
Hair Testing	provides potential for long-term assessment of drug use non-invasive not easily contaminated convenient storage specimens can be collected on-site	laboratory testing required easily evaded by shaving head and body hair may not detect recent drug use costly no on-site test result	laboratory-based test samples must be collected by trained collecting officer	This testing method does not indicate current impairment but provides a history of usage and is therefore not recommended for use in the workplace. laboratory testing not available in South Africa (specimens sent overseas for testing but this is expensive)
Sweat Testing	relatively non-intrusive provides cumulative measure of drug exposure collection device is relatively tamper proof	sweat patch cannot be worn over excessive hair or cuts variations in sweat production risk of contamination laboratory-based test only results not admissible as evidence in court	plaster patch worn by the individual	device must be approved by relevant drug administration agency

Type of test	Advantages	Disadvantages	Collection methods	Limitations
Pupillo-metery	non-invasive direct test measures direct impairment not cause of impairment results in approx 5 mins cost effective: only those failing the test need further testing with immunoassey devices and/ or laboratory confirmation testing one-off purchase and the operator can calibrate the device on-site	some people contraindicated from use (those with previous head injury; those with damage to both eyes; those over 65; pregnant women) positive result requires laboratory confirmation testing	on-site testing	device must be approved by relevant drug administration agency The operator must have received training.

This table is based on Pidd & Roche, 2006; *Drug Testing Africa, 2010* Medical Device Link

7. LIMITATIONS TO TESTING

Workplace alcohol and drug testing is considered by many to be the logical response to the problem of alcohol and drug abuse in the workplace. Proponents argue that the introduction of random testing of employees is the best and swiftest way to discourage alcohol- and drug-related behaviour at work. This theory—that testing acts as an effective deterrent to behaviour of this type—has been the subject of several research studies, which found that the evidence to substantiate the theory was inconclusive. The studies reviewed have highlighted many methodological flaws including weak study designs.[68]

However a common thread visible in all studies is the emphasis placed on alcohol and drug testing forming a part of a complete substance abuse programme that includes a substance abuse policy, an awareness and prevention component, drug and alcohol testing, and a treatment and referral component. This suggests that even when testing is extremely accurate, reliable and properly conducted, it should not be regarded as a panacea for all substance abuse problems in the workplace. Some studies suggest that drug testing in isolation could have an unexpected negative effect on employee morale and motivation resulting in reduced productivity levels. Employees may consider on-the-job testing unfair, its main purpose being to get rid of employees as swiftly as possible. On the other hand, employers may argue that they have the right to screen

---

68   Pidd & Roche (n 53)10—11.

potential employees via pre-employment testing since this is the best way to ensure the continued health and safety of the existing workforce.

Other limitations to drug testing are linked to procedural problems. This is particularly true for biological tests performed by individuals who have not received proper training on chain of custody procedures, specimen management procedures, and other aspects of training protocol. Under these circumstances inaccurate and misleading test results are possible. Drug testing is only reliable when employees are briefed on testing protocols and when trained screen testing officers administer the test.

Finally, although reference has been made to this in previous chapters, it is nevertheless important to re-emphasise the following: introducing random testing to a company in isolation and without an education and awareness programme, a substance abuse policy, or a treatment and referral programme may not achieve the desired behaviour change. Drug testing therefore plays only one role in the workplace, and is best used as part of a comprehensive and integrated approach.[69]

At the same time, however, it must also be stressed that in a safety critical workplace a zero tolerance approach is required, which needs to be supported by testing. A policy which depends on proof of impairment without testing is never likely to work successfully.

SUMMARY

The identification of alcohol and/or drug problems in an employee relying solely on subjective clinical assessment has been well documented as being both inaccurate and lacking in sensitivity. The problems of substance abuse differ from any other medical condition; the patient will usually deny the existence of a problem or refuse to cooperate with the medical history-taking that is fundamental to any subjective clinical assessment. This denial is exacerbated in an occupational setting. The subjective clinical assessment, due to its poor sensitivity, will pick up only cases of severe abuse and thus the ability to solve the abuse problem in the early stages is often lost.

Griffiths Edwards stresses the reasons why the diagnosis is often missed: not knowing what you are looking for, a lack of vigilance, embarrassment at asking questions, an inadequate knowledge of what to do if the case is identified, and, most importantly, the patient's denial or evasion.

In addition, purely subjective clinical observation and identification is inherently unreliable. Objective testing, whether direct (measuring alcohol and drug levels in body fluids or tissues) or indirect (measuring biochemical changes in the body), provides more sensitive and specific identification of an alcohol or drug problem. New and more sensitive tests are being utilised now; these tests can be less invasive and can provide a picture of the alcohol or drug abuse that has occurred over the previous days or weeks. These tests are particularly useful for the follow up of rehabilitating employees back at work after treatment and can identify if there have been any relapses. In safety sensitive and/or high risk work areas where substance abuse among employees is suspected, these tests are also likely to prove invaluable. The only difficulty at present is the high costs involved, although these should fall significantly once the tests (hopefully) become more mainstream.

---

69   Pidd & Roche (n 53) 10-11; SANCA 2005.

Hair analysis is identified as a test for the future. The test's advantages are that it is highly specific and sensitive, non-invasive, tamper proof, and that it provides a longer period of detection. One test can provide a picture of alcohol or drug consumption over several months. In most situations, however, a single test is unlikely to be sufficient and a combination of several is needed (though one specific test might 'lead the way').

Questionnaires regarding alcohol and drug abuse must be treated with caution when they are used in a workplace setting. Employees feeling embarrassed or threatened at having to complete a questionnaire may provide dishonest or evasive answers; an intolerant organisational culture vis-a-vis substance abuse may also have the same effect.

Testing in the workplace should form part of an integrated approach towards alcohol and drug abuse; an approach that addresses issues of policy, prevention, education and treatment. Testing in isolation is unlikely to change alcohol- and drug-related behaviours in the workplace. It is also absolutely essential for testing protocols and procedures to be standardised and for testing procedures to be free from hazards. Non biological tests (the EyeCheck™ pupillometer, for example) focus on how alcohol or drug consumption affects performance, which may merit their use in safety sensitive and/or high risk work areas where substandard performance could lead to serious injury, loss or damage.

Chapter 11

Legal Obligations of Employees, Employers & Trade Unions

Christopher Albertyn & Urmila Bhoola

1. THE EMPLOYEES' OBLIGATIONS

The legal obligations of employees arise from the employment relationship, from common law and from statute.

The common-law position is as follows. The employee has a legal obligation to perform work as required under the contract of employment.[1] If the employee does not, they are in breach of that contract and the employer may act against the employee on account of that breach. If the breach is serious or if it amounts to a repudiation[2] of the contract, then the employer may terminate the contract of employment and claim damages; alternatively, the employer may claim damages and enforce specific performance of the terms of the contract.

This means that an employee must perform his or her duties diligently and as efficiently and effectively as the employee is capable of doing. If the employee presents for duty or is at work when impaired, the employee is in breach of the contract and the employer has certain remedies. These are:

- the employer may send the employee away from the workplace and deny payment of the employee's wages for that day, because the employee has not tendered the performance of duties in terms of the employment contract;
- the employer may take disciplinary action against the employee on grounds of the employee's impairment because the employee has not met the employer's reasonable expectations of the employee's conduct, viz that the employee will present at work fit and ready to perform the work safely and competently; the employer may terminate the employment contract if the employee's breach is sufficiently serious or if it constitutes a repudiation[2], and the employer may claim damages from the employee.[3]

---

1   These obligations are the following: 'a duty of obedience to the employer's lawful instructions, a duty of fidelity, a duty of care and a duty of reasonable efficiency or competence' Rycroft, A & Jordaan, B *A Guide to South African Labour Law* (Juta 1992) 34.

2   A repudiation occurs where the employee makes clear (usually by conduct) to the employer that the employee refuses or will refuse to carry out the obligations undertaken by the employee as part of the employment contract: *White and Carter (Councils) Ltd v McGregor* [1962] AC 413; [1961] 3 All ER 178. 'The test as to whether conduct amounts to . . . a repudiation [which the other party can accept] is whether fairly interpreted it exhibits a deliberate and unequivocal intention no longer to be bound': Williamson J in *Street v Dublin* 1961 (2) SA 4 (W).

3   This will seldom be of value to an employer and will normally be restricted to the period of notice in the employment contract, but there are circumstances when an employer could claim damages for consequential loss arising from the employee's breach of contract.

If an employee is not intoxicated at work, but has reached such a state of physical or mental deterioration as a consequence of an alcohol or drug dependence that the employee is unable to perform duties to the requisite standard under the employment contract, the employee repudiates that contract. In these circumstances the employer has the remedies available in common law referred to above.

Intoxication at work without justification constitutes an unfair labour practice by an employee in relation to the employer.

1.1 The common-law relationship of employment is supplemented by statute

An employee is subject to the obligations contained in the following statutory sources: the Labour Relations Act 66 of 1995 (LRA), the Occupational Health & Safety Act 85 of 1993 (OHSA), and the new Prevention of and Treatment for Substance Abuse Act 70 of 2008. A discussion of the last-named act now follows.

1.2 The Prevention of and Treatment for Substance Abuse Act 70 of 2008[4]

The act was assented to by Parliament in 2009 but its proclamation is still pending. Although not directly applicable to the workplace it is based on the recognition that substance abuse has become a pervasive problem in South Africa as a result of the global drug trade and that a comprehensive response is needed to address the issue. The Act establishes a central drug authority and provincial abuse forums as well as structures at local authority level to address alcohol and drug abuse; it also provides for norms and standards to be developed.

The HIV/AIDS pandemic in South Africa is inextricably linked to substance abuse, and requires an evidence-based approach to issues of substance abuse. In this context, the non-governmental organisations ARASA[5], the Aids Law Project and the Treatment Action Campaign[6] have endorsed the legislation as advancing a set of medically sound interventions regarding substance use. ARASA had expressed concerns that the Bill on which the Act was based failed to acknowledge that substance use is a chronic and relapsing medical condition, and to sufficiently recognise the links between substance use, HIV/AIDS and other infectious diseases, as well as to include key interventions to prevent and treat substance use and its associated harms. ARASA emphasised that the link between HIV and hepatitis C as well as viral hepatitis (HCV) and the rise in heroin and injection drug use—as well as the abuse of other substances—in South Africa require the establishment and wide availability of interventions that specifically address syringe exchange, substitution therapy and other harm reduction programmes.

ARASA reinforce that substance use is a disease of the human brain, with all addictive substances having specific physical effects on the brain itself. These effects, which keep drug users taking drugs, last for long periods of time—even after the cessation of drug use. Thus the biological nature of substance use, and the long-lasting changes in the brain that it causes, makes substance use for most people, a chronic, relapsing disorder, with total abstinence a relatively rare outcome. Because of this, ARASA submits that interventions for addiction must be more like the interventions used to address other

---

4 Published by the Presidency for general information in GG 32150 on 21 April 2009, but not yet promulgated.
5 AIDS & Rights Alliance for Southern Africa.
6 ARASA report Cape Town 26 February 2007.

chronic illnesses, such as diabetes and heart disease, and less like those used to deal with acute conditions such as bacterial infections or broken bones.

ARASA highlights the fact that viral hepatitis is extremely common amongst injecting drug users (IDUs) where up to 98% of the population, the report points out, can be infected despite a low prevalence of HIV. In particular, between 5–10% of all HIV infections globally can be attributed to injection drug use. By 2003, injection drug use had been reported in 136 countries, of which 93 also identified HIV infections among drug injectors. Particularly noteworthy is that the emergence of HIV infection in IDU populations is often explosive, with the establishment of 30–40% prevalence in the first year.

The Act provides for community-based services which can be accessed by persons who abuse or are dependent on substances and to persons affected by substance abuse while remaining within their families and communities. It also makes provision for detoxification which is defined as a 'medically supervised process by which physical withdrawal from a substance is managed through administration of individually prescribed medicines by a medical practitioner in a health establishment, including a treatment centre authorised to provide such a service under the National Health Act'.

Some other key definitions used in the Act:

> 'abuse' means the sustained or sporadic excessive use of substances and includes any use of illicit substances and the unlawful use of substances;
> 'substances' means chemical, psychoactive substances that are prone to be abused, including tobacco, alcohol, over the counter drugs, prescription drugs and substances defined in the Drugs and Drug Trafficking Act 140 of 1992, or prescribed by the Minister after consultation with the Medicines Control Council established by section 2 of the Medicines and Related Substances Control Act 101 of 1965, and 'drugs' in the context of this Act has a similar meaning.
> 'persons affected by substance abuse' means any member of a family or community not abusing or dependent on substances but who requires services related to substance abuse. It also makes provision for both in- and out-patient treatment as well as voluntary submission for treatment or involuntary/ compulsory submission following a court order.

The Act also makes provision for the establishment of one or more 'halfway houses', either public or private, to provide a sober living environment for service users who have completed a formal treatment programme for substance abuse and require a protected living environment in order to prepare them for reintegration into society.

The objects of the Act are to—

(a) combat substance abuse in a coordinated manner;
(b) provide for the registration and establishment of all programmes and services, including community-based services and those provided in treatment centres and halfway houses;
(c) create conditions and procedures for the admission and release of persons to or from treatment centres;
(d) provide prevention, early intervention, treatment, reintegration and after care services to deter the onset of and mitigate the impact of substance abuse;
(e) establish a Central Drug Authority to monitor and oversee the implementation of the National Drug Master Plan;

(f) promote a collaborative approach amongst government departments and other stakeholders involved in combating substance abuse; and

(g) provide for the registration, establishment, deregistration and disestablishment of halfway houses and treatment centres.

It requires ministers and organs of state to provide for the following measures as part of a coordinated and multifaceted strategy:

(a) demand reduction—which is concerned with services aimed at discouraging the abuse of substances by members of the public;

(b) harm reduction—which for the purposes of this Act is limited to the holistic treatment of service users and their families, and mitigating the social, psychological and health impact of substance abuse; and

(c) supply reduction—which refers to efforts aimed at stopping the production and distribution of illicit substances and associated crimes through law enforcement strategies as provided for in the applicable laws.[7]

It is envisaged that the objects and measures just outlined will be aligned to a Drug Master Plan, to be developed by Cabinet, and which will contain the national drug strategy and set out the processes needed to control and manage the supply of and demand for drugs in South Africa.

The statutory obligations upon an employee concerning alcohol abuse are similar to those which apply to employers. One such obligation appears in the General Safety Regulations of the Machinery and Occupational Safety Act 6 of 1983 (MOSA) and reads as follows:[8]

> At a workplace or on premises where machinery is used, no person shall have in his possession or partake of or offer any other person intoxicating liquor or drugs, expect with the express permission of the employer...

Although MOSA has been repealed, the regulations issued under it remain applicable if it was in force prior to the promulgation of OHSA (section 43(5) of OHSA).

Regulation 6 of the General Administrative Regulations promulgated in terms of MOSA provides that:

> Subject to the provisions of section 28(1)(*m*), (*n*) and (*o*) of the Act, and without derogating from any other specific duty imposed on an employee by the Act or the regulations, every employee shall—
>
> (*a*)   carry out any lawful order given to him and shall obey the safety rules and procedures laid down by his employer or by anyone authorised thereto by his employer, in accordance with or for the proper observance of the provisions of the Act or the regulations or in the interest of safety; and
>
> (*b*)   where a situation which is unsafe at or near his workplace comes to his attention, as soon as possible report such situation to a safety representative or to his employer.

---

7   Section 3(1).
8   Regulation 12(2).

If an employer were to require that an employee undergo an alcohol test or leave the workstation on account of the employer's suspicion that the employee is under the influence of alcohol, the employee would be obliged to comply if the employer had reasonable cause for doing so.

If the employer believes an employee to be under the influence of alcohol, the statutory obligation[9] upon that employee towards the employer is to:

> carry out any lawful order given to him [eg to cease work and to leave the workplace] and [he] shall obey the health and safety rules and procedures laid down by his employer or by anyone authorised thereto by his employer....[10]

In the regulations published under the OHSA the obligation of the employer is stated as follows :

> 2A. Intoxication.—(1) Subject to the provisions of subregulation (3), an employer or a user, as the case may be, shall not permit any person who is or who appears to be under the influence of intoxicating liquor or drugs, to enter or remain at a workplace.
>
> (2) Subject to the provisions of subregulation (3), no person at a workplace shall be under the influence of or have in his or her possession or partake of or offer any other person intoxicating liquor or drugs.
>
> (3) An employer or user, as the case may be, shall, in the case where a person is taking medicines, only allow such person to perform duties at the workplace if the side effects of such medicine do not constitute a threat to the health or safety of the person concerned or other persons at such workplace.[11]

An equivalent provision is contained in the General Administrative regulations published under OSHA[12] and in addition the following provision exists regulating access to the workplace :

> Admittance of persons
> 11. (1) Subject to the provisions of section 8 of the Act an employer or user, as the case may be, shall not permit a person to enter a workplace where the health or safety of such person is at risk or may be at risk, unless such person enters such workplace with the express or implied permission of and subject to the conditions laid down by such employer or user:
> Provided that only the express or implied permission shall not apply in respect of a person entitled by law to enter such workplace or premises.
> (2) An employer or user, as the case may be, shall, if he or she deems it necessary in the interests of health or safety, post up a notice at every entrance to a workplace prohibiting the entry of unauthorised persons to such workplace and no person shall enter or remain at such workplace without the permission of the employer or user, as the case may be.

---

9   Regulation 6(a).
10 Section 14(c) Occupational Health & Safety Act 85 of 1993.
11 See GNR.1031 of 30 May 1986: General safety regulations R2A inserted by GNR 928 of 2003.
12 GG 17403 R1449 of 6 September 1996.

Hence, if an employer were to require, as part of its safety rules and procedures, that an employee undergo a non-invasive alcohol or drug test or leave the workstation on account of the employer's reasonable suspicion that the employee is under the influence of drugs or alcohol, the employee is obliged by the statutory regulation to comply with those requirements.

The caveat to this description of employee obligations is that the employer must have reasonable cause for taking such steps. The employee would be entitled to challenge the employer's decision on the basis that the employer did not have reasonable cause.

The employee has a duty of care towards fellow employees. If an employee negligently causes harm to a fellow employee, the employee incurs a delictual liability towards the fellow employee. The offending employee has no indemnity[13] from a claim for damages arising from delictual behaviour at work. If a fellow employee or a contractor visiting the site of work or a customer of the employer or a member of the public suffers harm and/or loss as a consequence of the negligence of the employee (who ought not to have been under the influence of drugs or alcohol at work), the employee is liable to compensate them.

In terms of the Compensation for Occupational Injuries Act 130 of 1993 (the COIDA) 'serious and wilful misconduct' includes at section 1 'being under the influence of intoxicating liquor or a drug having a narcotic effect'. The COIDA provides[14] that no compensation is payable if the accident is attributable to the serious and wilful misconduct of the worker, unless the accident results in serious disablement or the worker leaves a dependant who is wholly dependent on him or her. Thus employees may vitiate the worker's compensation benefits to which they would otherwise be entitled if they were to be injured in an accident caused by their own intoxication.

If an employee is suffering from drug or alcohol dependence, the employee needs to cooperate with the employer and with the trade union to find an appropriate way in which the dependence will be addressed within the workplace. Each of the parties—employer, trade union and employee—needs to cooperate to find suitable accommodation of an employee who is suffering from a drug- or alcohol- dependence problem. The accommodation should be reasonable.

2. THE EMPLOYER'S OBLIGATIONS

The common-law obligations of the employer are fourfold: to the substance abusing employee, to other employees, to contractors and their employees, and to the public. These obligations arise in common law and by operation of statute.

2.1 Obligations to the substance abusing employee

The employer should make every reasonable effort to ensure that its employees, including substance abusing employees, are not likely to harm or injure themselves while at work. If the employer has good cause to believe that an employee may harm or injure themselves, the employer may request the at-risk employee to undertake

---

13 Such as was possessed by the employer in terms of section 7 of the Workmen's Compensation Act 30 of 1941 (WCA). On 1 March 1994 the COIDA repealed and replaced the WCA. Section 35 of COIDA provides that a claim for compensation under the Act precludes any other action for damages for any injury resulting in disability or death of an employee. An injury caused by negligence of the employer can lead to increased compensation in terms of section 56 of COIDA.

14 Section 22(3)(a).

whatever tests are needed to establish to the employer's reasonable satisfaction that the employee is not under the influence of drugs or alcohol.

It is important to note that the employer's obligations at common law to the employee remain in place after the employer has satisfactorily established that the employee is unfit for work on account of intoxication. This means, therefore, that the employer should not allow the intoxicated employee to work or to remain in the workplace if it is reasonably likely that the employee's impairment could lead to self-injury or self-harm.

The employer should also prevent the employee from travelling home until in a fit state to do so;[15] alternatively, the employer is entitled (at the employee's cost)[16] to arrange for the employee's transport home.

The statutory obligations of the employer towards the intoxicated employee are similar. They arise from two provisions in the General Administrative Regulations of MOSA, which read:

> *Without derogating from any specific duty imposed on employers ... every employer ... shall—*
>
> *...*
>
> *(c) in the interests of safety, enforce discipline at the workplace, or on premises where machinery is used;*
>
> *. . .*
>
> *(g) take such steps as may be necessary to remove any threat or potential threat to the safety of persons as far as is practicable;*
>
> *. . .*
>
> *(i) as far as is reasonable, not permit any employee to do any work or to process, use, handle, store or transport any article or to operate any machinery unless the precautionary measures established in terms of paragraph ... (g), or any other precautionary measures which may be prescribed, are complied with.[17]*

The regulation dealing specifically with intoxication[18] contains the following provision:

> *An employer ... shall not permit any person who is or who appears to be drunk or under the influence of drugs, to enter or remain at a workplace or on premises where machinery is used if such person's presence constitutes a threat to the safety of himself or other persons at such workplace or on such premises.*

Thus an employer has a statutory duty to prevent an employee it suspects of being impaired from working or being at the workplace. If the worker is unfit to work, the worker is likely not fit to drive home so the employer should keep the employee on the premises away from the production area until the employee has recovered sufficiently to

---

15 In an English case (reported in the Morning Advertiser of 9 May 1989) a publican licensee was prosecuted for and found guilty of aiding and abetting a customer to commit a criminal offence—driving over the legal limit—after he failed to attempt to restrain the customer from driving in a drunken state. The licensee was fined for doing nothing when, in the court's view, he ought to have sought to prevent the customer from driving. It is unlikely that our courts would regard an employer as being contributorily negligent for permitting an intoxicated employee to drive his car from the company's premises, but the English case is none the less instructive and cautionary.

16 The employer acts as the employee's negotiorum gestor.

17 Regulation 5, General Duties of Employers and Users of Machinery.

18 Regulation 12.

proceed home, or the employer should arrange transport home for the worker (subject to the employer's right to claim a refund of the cost incurred on the negotiorum gestor principle).

If an employee establishes that he or she suffers from substance addiction or dependency, he or she may require some reasonable accommodation from the employer to address the situation. So, for example, the employee may need time off (whether paid or unpaid is a matter for negotiation between the two parties) to attend an in-house treatment facility and the employer may need to accommodate the employee with such time off. The employer should be alert to its obligation to act reasonably and to provide reasonable accommodation short of undue hardship. If the employee is represented by a trade union, the employee's union representative should be involved in the process of developing the accommodation arrangements for the employee. The trade union equally has an obligation to act reasonably in developing the accommodation arrangements.

2.2 The obligations of employers towards fellow employees of the impaired employee

The employer must ensure that employees work in a safe environment. An impaired employee may cause harm to fellow employees and the employer therefore has a duty, both in common law and in terms of OHSA, to ensure that this does not occur. If the employer is in breach of the obligation, it incurs a statutory liability. In terms of the COIDA a third party may be held liable for damages arising from an occupational injury or disease and the employee may also claim compensation under COIDA[19] A fellow employee's normal common-law remedy of damages against the employer is, however, eliminated. The employee injured at work as a result of some wrongful act by an intoxicated co-worker has no direct claim against the employer for allowing an inebriated employee to work. The claim for compensation (direct loss of earnings and compensation for permanent injury) must be directed against the Compensation Commissioner. The COIDA removes the employee's common-law right to claim damages from his employer. The quid pro quo to the employee for this loss of remedy is the no-fault liability of the commissioner. The injured employee need not prove negligence on the part of the impaired colleague or the employer to obtain compensation. The only requirements are that the injury resulted from an accident and that the accident arose out of the employee's work. However, if an injured employee is able to prove employer negligence (that is, demonstrate that the employer allowed an impaired employee to work or to remain on the workplace premises), the injured employee may claim additional compensation from the commissioner on account of such negligence.[20]

An employer suffers indirectly from claims made against the commissioner by its employees. The loss the employer experiences is in the form of an increased premium it may be required to pay into the state fund used to compensate employees injured at work. The commissioner will reassess the risk rating of the employer and will raise the premium if it is established that the employer has attracted a sufficiently high number of claims.[21]

---

19 Section 36(1).
20 Section 56.
21 Section 85 provides for variation of the employer's tariff of assessment.

Employees whose health and safety is at risk because of the presence of an intoxicated worker have the right to seek help from the court. If there is a real and substantial risk to the employees' safety, the court can order the employer to ensure that the impaired employee is not permitted in the workplace and to take all reasonable precautions to this effect. In the absence of a suitable alternative remedy employees may refuse to work with an impaired worker provided that such impairment represents a genuine threat to their safety.

2.3 The obligations of employers to contractors and their employees

An employer has an obligation to ensure a safe working environment for all people who come into the workplace, including contract workers. There are two categories of contract employees: those employed by a labour broker yet working effectively under the employer's supervision and control, and those employed by an independent contractor performing work on the employer's premises. There is no direct contractual nexus between the employer and such employees. Their contract is with the third-party intermediary, the independent contractor.

Subject to the provisions of section 9 of the OHSA, if a contractor's employee is injured at work on account of the employer's negligence (eg allowing an impaired employee in the workplace); the employer is liable to the contractor's employee in delict.

2.4 The obligations of employers to the public

The employer's obligations to members of the public are not restricted by the occupational safety legislation. The normal common-law rules of contract and delict apply. If members of the public enter the employer's premises with the employer's consent, the employer has an obligation to ensure that such visitors are not injured or subject to harm while in the employer's workplace. If the employer fails to fulfil this obligation, it faces liability to the visitors for the loss or injury they sustain. This liability arises in delict, and possibly also in contract on the basis that the visitors enter the employer's premises on the implied term that the employer will provide a safe environment.

Most employers try to circumvent this obligation through the use of a disclaimer. The disclaimer, whether displayed in the form of a notice or poster or signed by visitors entering the employer's premises, absolves the employer of any responsibility for any loss, injury or damage sustained by members of the public while on the employer's premises, regardless of whether the loss, injury or damage was caused by the employer's negligence. In essence, the disclaimer negates the individual's right to claim damages against the employer should he or she be harmed in some way while on the employer's premises.

The enforceability of the disclaimer is open to question, however. In particularly hazardous environments, for example a factory, a visitor is unlikely to appreciate or recognise every source of potential danger and the employer cannot point to the disclaimer should the visitor be injured because of this lack of knowledge. The OHSA imposes a statutory duty upon employers to maintain a safe workplace and provides that any agreement which limits the employer's liability to provide a safe workplace environment is void.[22] This provision and the existence of the general statutory

---

22 Section 41.

requirement to provide a safe workplace are likely to be regarded as being sufficient, on grounds of public policy, to vitiate any contractual waiver of the obligation.

An employer may also be liable for loss or injury sustained by members of the public 'off site'. Thus, a company that employs a number of delivery drivers may be held responsible if one of these employees causes a road accident through careless or reckless driving. Alternatively, a firm that has employees whose work is performed outside of the firm's premises (for example, a computer services company that employs technicians to work in the homes of its clients) may face a claim for damages should one of these employees cause injury to people or property while off-site (the computer technician's incompetence leads to the destruction of a client's computer, for example).

The clear purpose of the common law and the statutory provisions is to make certain that alcohol and drugs are not consumed at work, and that those workers whose capacity to work efficiently and safely is debilitated by sustained alcohol or drug abuse, are not permitted to enter their place of work.

The employer's vicarious liability for personal injury is largely removed by the statutory provisions concerning third-party insurance. A person injured in a motor vehicle collision as a result of the negligence of an intoxicated driver has no direct claim against the employer of the driver, unless the statutory compensation in respect of that collision is insufficient to meet the claimant's damages. In that event some residual liability may remain.

The employer's liability for damage to property is, however, not restricted. In the above example of the intoxicated driver, this means that the injured party's claim for the cost of repairs to his vehicle—the property that was damaged— would lie against the employer for permitting an intoxicated employee to drive one of its vehicles, and this is so even if the employer had taken out insurance to guard against this possibility.

The employer may also be charged under criminal law for negligently or recklessly allowing a driver-employee to use a vehicle while under the influence of alcohol. These are consequences which a prudent employer would seek to avoid by ensuring that its drivers do not make use of the vehicles while they are under the influence of alcohol.

3. THE OBLIGATIONS OF TRADE UNIONS

Trade unions, as the spokespersons and representatives of the employees, have obligations to ensure that the workplace is safe and healthy and that the risk of harm to workers is diminished. Part of that obligation is to ensure that impaired employees are not permitted to work and to put their fellow employees and the public at risk. To fulfil this obligation, trade unions often work with employers to develop policies and procedures regarding the issue of impairment at work. But trade unions also have a responsibility towards their members, which means that they work on behalf of employees who have been accused of working under the influence of alcohol or drugs. Thus the trade union will look for and present whatever exonerating information there may be; it will also make sure that the employer follows the correct investigative and/or disciplinary procedures and that the employee is given a fair hearing.

The second broad area of trade union involvement is with employees who suffer from an addiction and whose continued employment depends upon their appropriately managing their addiction. The union is likely to represent the employee to negotiate the terms of an accommodation that the employer will make to keep the employee employed, while enabling the employee to address the addiction. The union's duty here is to make sure that whatever arrangements are concluded between the employer and the employee are fair and reasonable to the latter. If the union considers any of the employer's proposals unrealistic or unfeasible, in other words, if it appears to the union that the suggested accommodation arrangement is destined to fail, it will raise these concerns during the negotiation process.

SUMMARY

An employee, an employer and a trade union have various obligations towards one another, to other employees of the employer and to members of the public. All of these obligations stem from the basic common law and the statutory obligation upon the employer to ensure that no employee is permitted to work while inebriated. If the employer fails in this regard, and if as a result of this failure a third party suffers damage or loss, the employer may be held variously liable. Similarly, an employee incurs various liabilities as a consequence of damages suffered by any person as a direct consequence of the employee's intoxication while at work. Both employers and employees have a common law and statutory duty to make sure that there is no intoxication in the workplace.

Chapter 12

Legal Aspects of Pre-employment Screening

Christopher Albertyn & Urmila Bhoola

1. INTRODUCTION

In the course of this chapter, and in the legal chapters that follow, there is quite detailed discussion of the comparative law in Canada. This is partly fortuitous, in that one of the authors now works within the Canadian jurisdiction, and partly intentional. The purpose for such a large inclusion of Canadian comparative information is to provide an international reference point against which the South African jurisprudence can be compared. The inclusion of the Canadian material will enable the reader to see how another society has dealt with the same issues.

2. GENERAL CONSIDERATIONS

Persons may be excluded from employment on medical grounds, only if, without reasonable accommodation to the point of undue hardship, their infirmity is such as to make them unfit to perform the work for which they are to be employed.

It is reasonable for employers to try to ensure that they do not take people into their employment who are not fit to perform the work for which they are to be employed. However, there are certain requirements of fairness and legality that must be complied with.

Some employers use pre-employment medical screening to determine whether or not a person is fit for duty. If these tests include measures to determine whether a prospective employee has a drug or alcohol addiction, or whether there is evidence of substance abuse, certain ethical and legal considerations apply. In particular, the medical testing cannot result in discrimination against prospective employees because of their disability. This is because human rights legislation prohibits discrimination on grounds of disability.

Medical testing has reached such a state of sophistication and complexity that virtually every inherent physical defect or propensity can be determined. Notionally, an employer could create a regime in which only people who show no physical defects may be employed, with the result that persons with imperfections quite irrelevant to their proposed employment would be excluded. Such pre-employment medical screening would serve an irrelevant and illegitimate purpose. This is because medical testing may be used only to establish whether the prospective employee satisfies a bona fide occupational requirement for the job in question. If the test discloses medical information that is not germane to a bona fide occupational requirement of the position, then the test will likely be found to be an unreasonable barrier to the prospective employee. A prospective employee, who is not hired as a consequence of the medical testing, can claim discrimination on a prohibited ground if they can establish that that they were not hired because of a disability.

Pre-employment medical testing for substance abuse or dependence may be a bona fide occupational requirement in high risk industries or occupations. For job applicants in these industries or occupations, the prospective employees should be informed that such testing will be done prior to their being asked to submit to the tests. They should be entitled to have the results revealed to the fewest number of people who must know the information. They should themselves be entitled to the results. If they are excluded from employment on account of the test results, the exclusion should not be on account of a disability that does not relate to a bona fide job requirement and it should be objectively justifiable, given the nature of the work to be performed by the prospective employee.

3. NON-DISCLOSURE BY JOB APPLICANT

The failure by an employee to make a frank disclosure to an employer at the time of employment may be sufficient cause for termination of employment if the true state of affairs subsequently comes to the attention of the employer and the information withheld is germane to the employee's employment. The employer must be able to show that, if the relevant information had been disclosed, the employee would not have been employed, and the employer would have acted reasonably to have excluded the employee on account of that information.[1] In a South African case involving a cabin attendant employed by the national airline, his failure to disclose his addiction to cocaine during a routine medical was held to constitute gross dishonesty.[2] The arbitrator referred to the requirements laid down by the Civil Aviation Authority and the airline policy regarding medical requirements for cabin crew, and found that it was clearly stipulated that persons with a history of drug dependency were not suitable for employment as cabin crew. Moreover, the symptoms and effects of cocaine use were so significant that the airline could, in the interests of public safety, not afford to show any tolerance in this regard. In these circumstances, it was found that had the employee disclosed the dependency at the time of his employment application, he would not have qualified for appointment.

4. THE INHERENT REQUIREMENTS OF THE JOB

The nature of the job is also relevant in determining whether testing for substances will be justified as a precursor to employment, and whether the operational considerations of the business can impinge on the right of an employee to privacy. The courts may be more inclined to permit this where public safety is of consideration, although in Hoffman[3] the South African Constitutional Court found that each case should be treated on its merits and blanket exclusion of HIV-positive employees would not be justified by safety concerns, as contended by SAA. In the United States, for instance, drug testing is considered to be a legitimate condition of employment for government positions

---

1   Walton v TAC Construction Materials Ltd (1981) IRLR 357.
2   SALSTAFF on behalf of Govender v S A Airways (2001) 22 ILJ 2366.
3   Hoffmann v South African Airways 2000 (1) SA 1 (CC).

involving public safety. For example, where involvement in, and enforcement of drug offences is involved; where it is a job requirement to carry a firearm; or where it was a job requirement to handle classified material which might fall into the hands of smugglers. The interests of government were considered to outweigh the privacy interests of job applicants for these types of positions.[4]

5. INTERNATIONAL STANDARDS

In recognition of privacy rights, and to prevent unreasonable limitations on employment opportunities, industrialised societies have sought to limit the application of pre-employment screening. In the United States, persons may be excluded from employment on medical grounds only if their infirmity is such as to make them unfit to perform the work for which they are to be employed, and their limitations are beyond the capacity of the employer to accommodate.

In Germany, virtually every employer must employ a certain percentage of disabled people.[5] The purpose of the statutory provision is to prevent disabled people from being excluded from employment. The objective is to ensure that reasonable opportunities for employment are given to people who, on grounds of capacity alone, would normally be overlooked in the selection of new employees.

In Italy, as in the United States, an employer may exclude a prospective employee from employment on medical grounds only if the employee is unfit to perform the work for which they are to be employed. The employer receives no details of the medical condition of the prospective employee concerned, only the bland report, 'fit for duty' or 'not fit for duty'. The protection of the confidentiality of the prospective employee's medical history and status is rated more highly than the employer's interest to know the nature of any infirmity.

6. SOUTH AFRICA

In South Africa medical testing in the pre-employment context is permitted, although restrictions are placed on testing to determine whether employees are HIV positive or living with AIDS. Medical testing is broadly defined in the Employment Equity Act (the EEA)[6] as including 'any test, question, inquiry or other means designed to ascertain, or which has the effect of enabling the employer to ascertain, whether an employee has any medical condition'. This testing is thus prohibited unless it is justifiably aimed at determining whether the job applicant meets the inherent job requirements. Otherwise, the testing must be justified by medical facts, employment conditions, social policy, and the fair distribution of employee benefits. The Employment Equity Act considers job applicants to be employees for testing purposes and having similar rights against

---

4   Dupper et al *Essential Employment Discrimination Law* (Juta 2004) 195.

5   Weiss *Labour Law and Industrial Relations in the Federal Republic of Germany* (Kluwer 1987) explains this as follows:
     'The main goals of the Act [on Handicapped Persons of 1974] are the integration of handicapped persons in employment relationships, special assistance during employment and special protection against dismissals...Employers in both the private and public sectors who employ more than 16 workers are obliged to employ at least 6% handicapped persons. When this obligation is fulfilled the employer has to pay a certain sum of money to the administrative agency with which handicapped workers must register to benefit under the Act. This sum of money has to be spent exclusively on supporting the situation of handicapped workers: para 104 p 53.'

6   Act 55 of 1998 at s 7.

discrimination or having their dignity, privacy and bodily integrity violated.[7] If another law authorises the test—as does the occupational health and safety legislation—then it is justified as legal. The employer may exclude a job applicant on medical grounds if they are found not to meet the 'inherent requirements' of the job. The legislation does not define what constitutes an inherent requirement, but this is similar to the Canadian bona fide occupational requirement. The Labour Court has defined an inherent job requirement as an 'indispensable attribute' which 'must relate in an inescapable way to the performing of the job'.[8]

The employment equity legislation therefore allows medical testing in the pre-employment context provided certain requirements are met. If these requirements are not met the testing would fall foul of the EEA and be considered unfair discrimination. However, discrimination can be legally valid if it is done for the purpose of affirmative action (in other words, positive or fair discrimination). Thus, since the purpose of the medical testing provision, set out above, is to regulate unfair discrimination, an employer can use medical screening to identify employees who have a medical condition if it wants to consciously overcome stereotyping of such employees. This has been a policy, for instance, among some mines, to employ people who are HIV-positive in certain job grades to reduce the stigma of living with HIV/AIDS and make a positive social commitment. This approach, using medical testing for the purposes of affirmative action, would be considered valid as it is legally considered to be fair discrimination. The social purpose, similar to that used in Germany and the UK, is to ensure that a reasonable proportion of the workforce is made up of persons with disabilities, to promote their entitlement to employment. Since the purpose of the testing is to prevent discrimination against employees, an employer can screen any employee who volunteers. However, although the South African provision permitting medical testing appears to give carte blanche to employers to test in the pre-employment context, there are numerous ethical and constitutional issues that arise. The Constitution of South Africa entrenches the right of every person to equality and the right not to be unfairly discriminated against, as well as the right to privacy, dignity and personal security. In the context of testing for HIV status, provided it is voluntary and safeguards of confidentiality and anonymity are met (for instance through random saliva sampling), the Labour Court in South Africa held that this was not discriminatory.[9] Similar safeguards apply to testing for alcohol and substance use in the employment context as we discuss in chapter 13.

In general therefore, although South African law permits certain types of medical testing (including testing for drug and alcohol use) in the pre-employment context, the testing must be justified. The most common reason for testing, to determine if a job applicant meets the inherent job requirements, would be justifiable if it can be shown that without the requirement the person will not be capable of performing the job or the business interests of the operation or public safety will be affected. At the most trite level, testing for drug and alcohol use for employment as an airline pilot differs vastly from that of an applicant for a job packing shoes. In *Esau & Qakaza v Wynland Boerdery Belange t/a Zetler Bros*, the court referred to the old 'tot' system where agricultural workers were often paid in alcohol and where alcohol dependency was seen

---

7   Section 9 of the EEA.
8   *Woolworths (Pty) Ltd v Whitehead* (2000) 21 *ILJ* 571 (LAC).
9   *Irvin and Johnson Ltd v Trawler Line Fishing Union and others* (2003) 24 *ILJ* 565 (LC) at para 26.

as desirable by the employer.[10] However, as discussed above, the Constitutional Court in *Hoffman* held that an inherent requirement has to be strictly construed.

7. CANADA

In Canada, under the various federal and provincial statutes, any discrimination on grounds of disability is prima facie unlawful. Subject to the bona fide requirements of the position and the employer's duty to accommodate the prospective employee to the point of undue hardship, the law requires that disability not be a factor in the decision to employ someone. Employment may be denied if the disability is such that the employer cannot accommodate the employee's disability without undue hardship. Undue hardship is assessed on a case by case basis. The tribunal considering the matter will consider what the employer can do to assist the employee to perform the job, by modifying the job itself, by re-arranging the work, yet without incurring extensive costs or detrimentally affecting other employees or the business operations.[11] Since dependence on drugs or alcohol, an addiction, is treated as a disability, testing which results in a finding of such dependency will require the prospective employer to accommodate the employee's disability in employment, unless there are other bona fide reasons for not hiring the employee.

In Canada, there are two streams of jurisprudential thought on pre-employment drug and alcohol screening. These two streams are colloquially referred to as 'the Ontario approach' and 'the Alberta approach', following the leading cases from those provinces. In rough terms, the Ontario approach sees random drug testing (and, by implication, pre-employment screening) as being in violation of rights of privacy and human rights legislation; while in Alberta, pre-employment screening is not necessarily in violation of human rights legislation.[12] The Supreme Court of Canada has yet to issue a decision that resolves the contrary approaches.

The Ontario approach, followed as well in Quebec,[13] is that pre-employment drug screening is prima facie discriminatory.[14] In contrast, the Alberta Court of Appeal has decided that there are circumstances in which pre-employment screening is legitimate. In *Alberta (Human Rights and Citizenship Commission) v Kellogg, Brown & Root (Canada) Co*, the Court accepted the Ontario standard that pre-employment screening that results, from the screening alone, in a refusal to hire the employee, is prima facie discriminatory

---

10   (1994) 1 ICJ 8.11.3.

11   *See British Columbia (Public Service Employee Relations Commission) v British Columbia G.S.E.U.*, 1999 CanLII 652 (S.C.C.), [1999] 3 S.C.R. 3 (Meiorin), the seminal Canadian case on the relationship between discrimination, bona fide occupational requirements, and the duty to accommodate to the point of undue hardship.

12   *United Association of Journeymen and Apprentices of the Plumbing and Pipefitting Industry of the United States and Canada, Local 488 v Bantrel Constructors Co.* [2007] A.J. No 1330.

13   Local 143 of the *Communications, Energy and Paperworks Union of Canada v Goodyear Canada Inc.* [2007] Q.J. No 13701.

14   *Alberta (Human Rights and Citizenship Commission) v Kellogg, Brown & Root (Canada) Co.*, 2007 ABCA 426 (CanLII); *Entrop v Imperial Oil Ltd.*, [2000] O.J. No. 2689 at 89; *Elizabeth Metis Settlement; Browning v Saskatchewan* 2002 SKQB 501 (CanLII), (2002), C.C.E.L. (3d) 91, 2002 SKQB 501; *Fraser Lake Sawmills v IWA, Local I-424* (B.C. Labour Relations Board December 16, 2002) and *Millazzo and Canadian Human Rights Commission v Autocar Connaisseur Inc. and Motor Coach Canada*, [2003] C.H.R.D. No 24, 2003 C.H.R.T. 37 (MacTavish).

on grounds of disability.[15] The Court said that the exclusion from employment of those suffering from the disability of drug dependency, without exploring their possible accommodation in employment, is discriminatory. However, on the specific facts of the case, the Alberta Court of Appeal found that the policy of pre-employment drug use screening did not discriminate against the prospective employee because he was not, in fact, drug dependent, but a recreational user. Consequently, because the prospective employee was not suffering from a disability, there could be no question of discrimination against him contrary to the human rights legislation. The Alberta Court of Appeal found that the employer could apply its pre-employment screening policy to not hire him because of his drug use. The screening was sufficient for the employer to reasonably conclude that the prospective employee might constitute a risk were he to be employed in a safety-sensitive position. Accordingly, the pre-employment drug screening, with respect to the particular employee, was found not to violate the Alberta Human Rights, Citizenship and Multiculturalism Act, R.S.A. 2000, c. H-14.

The following portions of the Alberta Court of Appeal decision explain the rationale for its conclusions:

> Although it might be argued that this analysis really deals with the issue of bona fide occupational requirement we conclude that it also has a role to play in whether a workplace policy is discriminatory under the Act. The Act prohibits certain, but not all, treatment based on human characteristics as discriminatory. The jurisprudence has extended the prohibited grounds to include instances where an employer incorrectly perceives that an employee has a prescribed disability. In this case [the employer's] policy does not perceive [the employee] to be an addict. Rather it perceives that persons who use drugs at all are a safety risk in an already dangerous workplace.

> [The employee] testified that what he did on his own time was his business. He did not at any time suggest that he would cease his recreational use of drugs while employed by [the employer]. As we have already stated the evidence established that effects of cannabis use lingers for days particularly given that the concentration of active ingredients is now many times higher than it was in the past. Given these concerns the policy's effects are not misdirected in their application to[the employee].

---

15 *In Canada (Human Rights Commission) v Toronto-Dominion Bank (C.A.)* [1998] 4 F.C. 205, the Federal Court of Appeal found that an immediate post-employment drug testing policy did not discriminate against drug addicts on grounds of disability because of the accommodation policy that accompanied the test.

The other line of authority,[16] from Ontario, while not directly addressing pre-employment drug screening, finds that random drug testing is unlawful and in violation of the Ontario Human Rights Code. The rationale for this approach is discussed elsewhere.

Most jurisdictions permit pre-employment medical screening, subject to some protection for employees, but the question remains whether medical screening includes screening for drug and alcohol use.

---

16   *Entrop v Imperial Oil Ltd.*, [2000], O.J. No. 2689, July 21, 2000, but cf. *Weyerhaeuser Co (c.o.b. Trus Joist) v Ontario (Human Rights Commission)* [2007] O.J. No. 640, which followed the Alberta approach that the pre-screening was not discriminatory because the individual had not established a disability.

Chapter 13

Legal Aspects of Testing Employees

Christopher Albertyn & Urmila Bhoola

Medical screening for alcohol and substance abuse is legal and valid in some contexts in most jurisdictions. What are the considerations for determining the appropriate circumstances for an employer to test?

Testing employees for drug or alcohol use or abuse involves balancing two competing interests: the employer's interest to ensure a safe and healthy workplace and the worker's entitlement to the privacy of his or her recreational activity.

1. EMPLOYEE CONSIDERATIONS AFFECTING THE NATURE AND CONDUCT OF TESTING

1.1 Confidentiality

If the information obtained from testing reveals that an employee has an addiction or a dependency, then that information resides with the employee and with the employer's occupational health unit or its medical practitioner, who has a responsibility of confidentiality towards the worker. The worker's medical information does not belong to the employer; an employee is entitled to medical confidentiality[1] unless he or she explicitly waives it.

The testing and the information retention should be the responsibility of independent health care consultants or of arm's length occupational health units of the employer, who guarantee the confidentiality and privacy of the worker's medical information. The employer is entitled, though, to know if the employee's alcohol or drug consumption is reasonably likely to have an impact on work performance or on the health and safety of other employees and the public. The employee should know of this consequence in advance of undergoing the testing. The employer is not entitled to the details of the worker's medical condition, only whether that condition is reasonably likely to have an impact upon the worker's performance at work or on the health and safety of other employees and the public.

If the information gathered from the testing reveals that the employee has an alcohol or drug consumption problem that is likely to impact on that worker's performance or on the health or safety of other employees or the public, then the occupational health unit or medical practitioner has a responsibility to disclose to management, not the

---

1   The International Labour Organisation Code on the Protection of Workers' Data provides guidelines for employers to ensure that personal private information, obtained for instance through medical testing, is safeguarded.

detail of the worker's medical condition, but the nature of the appropriate restrictions on the worker's employment. The employee may give permission for the details of the medical condition to be disclosed to the employer. If the employee is not fit for duty, the occupational health unit is required to advise management of this. If the employee is fit for duty, but certain restrictions or accommodations are necessary, then the occupational health unit should inform management of the nature of these restrictions or accommodations. Employee consent is not required for disclosure of this information.

The occupational health unit or consultant may—and should—take steps to help the employee confront and combat drug or alcohol problems, through counselling and treatment or through appropriate referral of the employee for treatment and rehabilitation. If the employee does not co-operate with the occupational health unit, and the evidence suggests that the employee is not fit for work, or that fellow employees or the public may be put at risk by the employee's substance abuse, then the employee should know that this information will be conveyed to management.

1.2 Dignity and personal security

The South African Constitution protects the right to human dignity as well as security of the person. Section 12 provides that everyone has the right to bodily and psychological integrity which includes, among others, the right to security in and control over their body. Testing should accordingly be in conformity with these rights. In *Chetty v Kaymac Rotomoulders (Pty) Ltd*,[2] the fact that testing was done in full view of other employees was an indication that the employer had scant regard for the dignity of its employees. In the *Metrorail v Satawu*[3] matter it was argued that compulsory testing is an invasion of an employee's right to privacy. These basic rights are derived from the common law and are currently protected by the Constitution. The court held that an employer is not justified to invade the basic rights of its employees. The fact that legislation informed the introduction of a new policy requiring compulsory testing did not justify the employer unilaterally changing the terms and conditions of employment of the employees.

2. EMPLOYER CONSIDERATIONS REGARDING TESTING

2.1 Safety standards

Employers in most countries are obliged to comply with safety standards prescribed in legislation and regulations. In South Africa this is regulated by the Occupational Health and Safety Act (the OHSA) and regulations[4] made in terms of this Act to set standards for different jobs and industries. It may be justifiable to exclude persons with a dependency problem for their failure to comply with safety standards that are essential to the job.

---

2   (2004) 25 *ILJ* 2391 (BCA).

3   Unreported judgment of Revelas J (J4561/2001).

4   Act 85 of 1993. The legislation requires medical testing and surveillance in various industries and prescribes clear roles for the occupational health nurse and medical practitioner. OHSA requires medical surveillance in various jobs and industries and this is defined to include ongoing systematic collection, analysis and interpretation of heath related data. This is performed at various stages including pre-employment, post-incident, return from absence as well as on exit. A medical certificate is provided as proof of the employee's ability to perform the job or on any limitations to employment. Testing for alcohol and substance use may be useful to assess the psychological requirement component of these regulations as their application to construction jobs include a wide range of jobs ie crane operators, maintenance workers, service artisans.

However, in a case involving an insulin-dependent diabetic excluded from a job as a firefighter because of safety considerations, the Labour Court in South Africa held that a blanket ban on employees with diabetes was unjustified. In *Independent Municipal and Allied Trade Union & another v City of Cape Town*[5] the employer argued that the medical condition rendered the person unfit for employment as a firefighter because he could not meet the safety standards inherent in the job. The court held that the minimal risk of a severe diabetic attack in a hazardous situation should not disable the employee from carrying out the inherent requirements of the job. This followed a Constitutional Court decision (*Hoffman v South African Airways*)[6] in which the blanket exclusion of all persons with HIV/AIDS, as stipulated in the airline's policy for reasons of public safety, was held to discriminate against persons who were asymptomatic and thus able to carry out the cabin crew duties.

2.2 Discipline

Employers have an interest in ensuring workplace discipline. Where a policy proscribes alcohol or substance use at work as serious misconduct, the employer would be entitled to initiate disciplinary action for breach thereof. However, fairness is a key criterion regulating the treatment of the employee in the context of discipline, and prior to disciplinary measures, the employer should consider measures to treat and support the employee. In various instances in South Africa it was found justifiable to dismiss the employee for misconduct (being drunk at work) or incapacity (being unable to perform work) provided they were treated fairly in the process and the reason for the conduct had been objectively determined by testing. However the misconduct that the employee is charged with, has to be consistent with the conduct prohibited in the policy or disciplinary code. In *Hotel Liquor Commercial & Allied Workers Union of SA v Fedics Group (Pty) Ltd t/a Fedics Food Services*[7] the employee had been dismissed for possession of marijuana. The court held that, at the risk of being overly technical, the policy did not prohibit mere possession and the charge had to be couched in terms of the conduct prohibited. The employee had admitted possession but claimed that he smoked the marijuana after work.

In *NUMSA obo Davids/Bosal Africa (Pty) Ltd*[8] the arbitrator held that dismissal was not a punishment; it was the exercise by the employer of its contractual right to terminate the services of an employee in response to the latter's breach. The ultimate test was whether the continuation of the employment relationship had been rendered intolerable or whether the relationship of trust between the employer and the employee had been broken. The interests of both employer and employee had to be taken into account. From the employer's perspective, the deterrent function of dismissal could not be disregarded. Just as employers could deter their employees from being dishonest by dismissing culprits, so could they dismiss for acts not involving moral turpitude. Working under the influence of alcohol was such an offence, especially where the work was inherently dangerous. The arbitrator held as follows:

---

5   (2005) 26 *ILJ* 1404 (LC).
6   *Hoffman v South African Airways* 2000 (1) SA 1 (CC).
7   (1993) 2 LCD 150 (IC).
8   [1999] 10 BALR 1240 (IMSSA) at para 14 p1245.

> *The test is, in my view, whether the consequences of a repetition of the misconduct (either by the same employee or by others) will adversely affect the operation of the employer's business, the safety of the workplace, and/or the employer's trading reputation.*

The only circumstance in which such an offence can be condoned, was when the employee had a dependency problem. The employee in the abovementioned case had not pleaded that he had such a problem at the time. He had been aware of the rule that he had broken and of the potential consequences of his action. The commissioner accordingly upheld the dismissal as justified and fair in the circumstances.

The consistent application of discipline is a key requirement. An employer was held to be entitled to set standards of conduct for its employees and a court or arbitrator should not lightly interfere in such standards, unless they lead to unfairness or were applied inconsistently.[9]

In the chapter dealing with discipline at work, (chapter 14), we address the remedies available to an employee faced with substance abuse that has, or is likely to have, an impact on discipline in the workplace and on worker and customer safety.

2.3 Nature of the work

The nature of the job is relevant in determining whether testing for substances will be justified, and whether this outweighs the right of an employee to privacy. The courts may be more inclined to permit this where the nature of the job puts public safety at risk, although in the seminal case of *Hoffman*,[10] the Constitutional Court found that each case should be treated on its merits and blanket exclusion of HIV-positive employees would not be justified on the grounds of safety to customers, as contended by the national airways. In the US, for instance, drug testing is considered to be a legitimate condition of employment for government positions involving public safety. For example, where involvement in and enforcement of drug offences is involved; where it is a job requirement to carry a firearm; or where it was a job requirement to handle classified material which might fall into the hands of smugglers. The interests of government were held to outweigh the privacy interests of job applicants for these types of positions.[11] In the *Fedics* case discussed above the employer provided catering services at the client's premises and argued that the dismissal was justified because the conduct of employees would prejudice good order and discipline at the client's premises and affect the employer's reputation.

3. LEGAL CONSIDERATIONS FOR TESTING

3.1 Reasonable cause, mandatory and random testing

Employers have the right to impose mandatory drug and alcohol testing where reasonable cause exists or in response to workplace incidents where the circumstances are such

---

9   *National Union of Metalworkers of SA obo Motsele v Haggie Wire & Strand* (2006) 27 ILJ 871 (BCA). See, however, *Phalaborwa Mining v Cheetham* (2008) 29 ILJ 306 (LAC) where the LAC held, per Willis J, that in some instances inconsistent treatment was justified depending on the nature of the work and that dismissal of a manager for having drinks during business lunches had to be distinguished from the conduct of other employees.

10 Supra (n 6).

11 See Dupper et al Essential *Employment Discrimination Law* (Juta 2004) 195.

that the tests constitute a reasonable line of inquiry. The protection for employees is the requirement for employers to establish in every case that it had just cause to impose the mandatory testing, including the question of whether the requirement was reasonable in the circumstances.[12]

3.1.1 South Africa

3.1.1(a) The Employment Equity Act 55 of 1998

Various statutory and common law rules regulate when an employer would be entitled to test employees either for reasonable cause or randomly. Of key importance in assessing the legitimacy of the testing, are the provisions of any collective agreement with a trade union regarding the circumstances in which testing may be conducted, and the terms applicable. Some agreements provide for a shop steward to be present during a test for alcohol or substance use. This is discussed in the chapter on policy formulation. Testing can also be a term of an employee's contract of employment. However, the testing would first have to be legal and valid in terms of the applicable statutory and common law. In certain instances testing would be discriminatory. For instance, discrimination on the grounds of disability is unfair under the Employment Equity Act 55 of 1998 (the EEA). The Act defines people with disabilities as those who have a 'long term or recurring physical or mental impairment which substantially limits their prospects of entry into, or advancement in employment'.

In certain circumstances employees who use alcohol and substances may be considered to have a disability, which requires the employer to assist and support them and make reasonable accommodation of their needs at work. The Code on the Treatment of People with Disabilities, promulgated under the EEA, applies to all employees with clinically recognised 'impairments' that are regarded as 'substantially limiting', but excludes, among others, disorders relating to drug or alcohol abuse (unless the employee is undergoing a recognised treatment programme). Medical testing to determine the extent of the employee's disability is justified provided certain criteria have been met. The following criteria are said to be applicable to testing in compliance with this provision: the physical activity involved in the job, whether the test relates to actual and reasonable job requirements, whether the needs of persons with disabilities are reasonably accommodated in conducting the tests, whether applicants have been informed about the nature and purpose of the tests and the fact that the results will be confidential.[13]

3.1.1(b) The inherent requirements of the job

The EEA accords the same treatment to both employees and job applicants in regard to medical testing. The Act also prohibits unfair discrimination, but provides that where an employee is excluded or preferred due to the inherent requirements of the job, this would not be unfair discrimination. This would be because the inherent requirements of the job reflect a genuine operational need rather than discrimination. This is equivalent to the bona fide occupational requirement in the UK Sex Discrimination Act of 1975 and the Race Relations Act of 1976. An inherent requirement is one that attaches to

---

12 *Canadian National Railway and CAW-Canada*, (2001) 95 L.A.C. (4th) 341 (Picher); *Fording Coal Ltd. v United Steelworkers of America*, Local 7884, [2002] B.C.C.A.A.A. No 9 (Hope).

13 D du Toit et al *Labour Relations Law* 5 ed (2006) 618.

an immutable physical characteristic (like race or gender) which enables the person to perform the essential characteristics of the job. In the context of pregnancy discrimination the Labour Court defined an inherent job requirement as an 'indispensable attribute' which 'must relate in an inescapable way to the performing of the job'.[14]

That the inherent requirement defence must be strictly construed was confirmed by the Constitutional Court.[15] Although the issue was whether an employee can exclude HIV-positive persons as cabin crew, prior to the enactment of the EEA, the court made some observations on testing. Its relevance to substance abuse is that, in defining the medical condition of HIV/AIDS the Constitutional Court noted that transmission also occurs through mother-to-child routes, through transfusion of blood products, and through needle sharing by intravenous drug users. The court also referred to the reasons for pre-employment testing of employees and potential employees for any medical condition as being, in general:

- to see whether they are fit for the inherent requirements of the job;
- to protect them from hazards inherent in the job;
- to protect others (clients, third parties etc) from hazards; and
- to promote and maintain the health of employees.

3.1.1(c) The Labour Court and testing

The Labour Court[16] has imposed specific conditions relating to testing for HIV/AIDS in order to prevent discrimination against employees who are living with HIV/AIDS. These include pre- and post-test counselling; ensuring the confidentiality of results; limitations on the period within which the tests can be conducted; and categories of employees who can be tested. The Labour Court has approved testing that is voluntary; random; anonymous or confidential, provided that the test is not a condition of employment, promotion or other benefits, that test samples are received and processed by someone independent of the employer, and that no employee is discriminated against or otherwise prejudiced for refusing to take the test.[17] It is arguable that some of these conditions should apply to testing for drug and alcohol use, since the possibility for stereotyping and discrimination against employees exists as in the case of HIV/AIDS.[18] However the rights of employees to equality and fairness in recognition of their constitutional and statutory rights must be balanced against the operational needs of the business and the employer's right to enforce discipline and safety.

3.1.1(d) Other statutory provisions relating to testing :

(i) The Prevention and Treatment for Substance Abuse Act, 70 of 2008

This legislation has been approved by Parliament and is pending promulgation which revises the earlier approach to substance use under the old Drug Abuse Act and provides

---

14   *Whitehead v Woolworths (Pty) Ltd* (2000) 21 *ILJ* 2647 (LAC).

15   *Hoffman v South African Airways* 2001 (1) SA 1 (CC).

16   The court has a discretion to approve the testing and impose conditions under section 50 (4) of the Employment Equity Act.

17   Joy Mining Machinery v NUMSA (2002) 23 *ILJ* 391 (LC).

18   In *Moleveld and De La Rey v 1001 Building Material (Pty) Ltd* (2006) 27 *ILJ* 1237 (CCMA) the arbitrator found no factual basis for the employee's allegation that he had been tested and dismissed simply because he was 'a coloured person'.

for medically sound interventions regarding substance use. The new Act acknowledges that substance use is a chronic and relapsing medical condition. However, concerns have been raised that[19] it fails to sufficiently recognise the links between substance use, HIV/AIDS and other infectious diseases. This Act forms the subject of chapter 11 in which its implications for the workplace are discussed.

(ii) The Tobacco Products Control Act

This Act requires an employer to set rules prohibiting smoking in the workplace in order to protect public safety. This arose in *NUMSA on behalf of Bhulwana v Boardman Brothers (Pty) Ltd*.[20] The applicant union referred a dispute to arbitration, claiming that the imposition of a rule prohibiting smoking, alcohol and drug use in the workplace, without union consultation amounted to a unilateral change to terms and conditions of employment. The employer argued that the right to prohibit the use of tobacco, alcohol or any other habit forming drugs vested in the owner of any premises and was entrenched in section 9 of the Tobacco Products Control Act 83 of 1999. The employer had a responsibility to ensure the health of its workers and was not required to consult on the issue.

(iii) Occupational injuries and illness

Testing for substance use is also legitimate in the occupational health and safety context, given the exclusion of liability of the Department of Labour for workplace accidents in circumstances where the accident is attributable to the 'serious and wilful misconduct' of an employee. In this context section 22(3)(a) of the Compensation for Occupational Injuries and Diseases Act[21] (COIDA), provides that where a workplace accident is attributable to the 'serious and wilful misconduct' of the employee, that employee is not entitled to compensation unless the accident results in serious disablement; or the employee dies in consequence thereof leaving a dependant wholly financially dependent upon him or her. The COIDA defines 'serious and wilful misconduct' as, inter alia, 'being under the influence of intoxicating liquor or a drug having a narcotic effect'.[22] Under OHSA the employer is required to maintain, as far as is reasonably practicable, a working environment that is safe and without risk to the health of its employees. There is a concomitant duty on employees to act in the interests of safety and report incidents. Performing work under the influence of alcohol has in some instances been held to be a serious risk

OHSA also requires medical testing and surveillance in various industries and prescribes clear roles for the occupational health nurse and medical practitioner. The Act requires medical surveillance in various jobs and industries and this is defined to include ongoing systematic collection, analysis and interpretation of health-related data. This is performed at various stages including pre-employment, post-incident, return from absence as well as on exit from employment. A medical certificate is provided as proof of the employee's ability to perform the job or on any limitations to employment. Testing for alcohol and substance use may be useful to assess the psychological requirement

---

19   See for example, submissions to Parliament by ARASA, discussed in chapter 11.
20   (2004) 25 *ILJ* 2258 (BCA).
21   Act 130 of 1993.
22   Section 1 (xlii)(a).

component of these regulations as their application to construction jobs includes a wide range of jobs ie crane operators, maintenance workers and service artisans.[23]

The preamble sets out the purpose of OHSA as being

> to provide for the health and safety of persons at work and for the health and safety of persons in connection with the use of plant and machinery; the protection of persons other than persons at work against hazards to health and safety arising out of or in connection with the activities of persons at work and the establishment of a health and safety council.

The Act defines 'biological monitoring' as a planned programme of periodic collection and analysis of body fluid, tissues, excreta or exhaled air in order to detect and quantify the exposure to or absorption of any substance or organism by persons. It requires 'medical surveillance' which means 'a planned programme or periodic examination (which may include clinical examinations, biological monitoring or medical tests) of employees by an occupational health practitioner or, in prescribed cases, by an occupational medicine practitioner'.

Section 8 of OHSA sets out the general duties of employers to their employees. It requires employers to 'provide and maintain a safe working environment as far as is reasonably practicable'. The specific duties imposed on the employer by section 8(2) are, inter alia, as follows:

> (a) the provision and maintenance of systems of work, plant and machinery that, as far as is reasonably practicable, are safe and without risks to health;
>
> (b) taking such steps as may be reasonably practicable to eliminate or mitigate any hazard or potential hazard to the safety or health of employees, before resorting to personal protective equipment;...
>
> (h) enforcing such measures as may be necessary in the interest of health and safety;
>
> (i) ensuring that work is performed and that plant or machinery is used under the general supervision of a person trained to understand the hazards associated with it and who have the authority to ensure that precautionary measures taken by the employer are implemented.

Employer's also have duties and obligations toward members of the public under section 9 of OHSA. This includes conducting the business in a manner that ensures, as far as is reasonably practicable, that members of the public are not exposed to hazards to their health or safety.

The employer is also required in terms of section 7 to develop a health and safety policy, which must be signed by the chief executive officer and displayed prominently in the workplace.

The following obligations and duties of employees are set out in section 14 of OHSA :

> Every employee shall at work-
>
> (a) take reasonable care for the health and safety of himself and of other persons who may be affected by his acts or omissions;

---

23 Kew,G & Deacon,CH (2006) *The construction regulations of the Occupational Health and Safety Act No. 85 of 1993: a review and discussion of the current medical surveillance requirements.* ACOCSA Conference Abstract, June 19–20, Johannesburg, South Africa..

(b) *as regards any duty or requirement imposed on his employer or any other person by this Act, co-operate with such employer or person to enable that duty or requirement to be performed or complied with;*

(c) *carry out any lawful order given to him, and obey the health and safety rules and procedures laid down by his employer or by anyone authorized thereto by his employer, in the interest of health or safety;*

(d) *if any situation which is unsafe or unhealthy comes to his attention, as soon as practicable report such situation to his employer or to the health and safety representative for his workplace or section thereof, as the case may be, who shall report it to the employer; and*

(e) *if he is involved in any incident which may affect his health or which has caused an injury to himself, report such incident to his employer or to anyone authorized thereto by the employer, or to his health and safety representative, as soon as practicable but not later than the end of the particular shift during which the incident occurred, unless the circumstances were such that the reporting of the incident was not possible, in which case he shall report the incident as soon as practicable thereafter.*

The Act provides for regulations to be issued for safety and health issues. The construction regulations of OHSA provide for medical testing as part of medical surveillance in hazardous work in the construction industry.[24] The regulations also provide for alcohol and drug testing.

Regulations promulgated under the Unemployment Insurance Act[25] provide that in terms of section 20(1)(b) of the Act illness benefits may be paid 'in cases of alcoholism or drug dependence for the period during which a person is admitted to and undergoes treatment at a registered rehabilitation centre or psychiatric hospital'.

3.1.1(e) Random testing in South Africa

In South Africa testing for alcohol and substance use among employees has been permitted where it is random, voluntary and confidential, and is not motivated by victimisation or unfair discrimination. The balance between an employee's right to privacy, dignity, bodily and psychological integrity and fair labour practices and an employer's right to maintain discipline, ensure employee and general safety and conduct its business operations always has to be maintained. In regard to random testing it is important to eliminate any doubt that employees selected for testing as being victimized or discriminated against and the employer may have to monitor testing patterns where such allegations are made, or in workplaces where relations are fraught with conflict. It is clear that various considerations apply to introducing random testing and an employer has to take these into account in developing a legitimate approach to testing. In addition, an employer seeking to introduce a random testing policy would

---

24 The Construction Regulations (CRs) of OHSA were promulgated on 18 July 2003. In terms of the regulations, employers are obliged to ensure that employees, in certain occupations, are in possession of medical certificates of fitness for their occupations, namely:
   • Employees on supported or suspended platforms, 15(12)(a);
   • Crane operators, (20)(g), and
   • Operators of all construction vehicles and mobile plant, (21)(1)(d)(i).

25 Regulation 4(8), GN 400 of 28 March 2002 of the Unemployment Insurance Act 63 of 2001.

have to consult with trade unions representing its workforce, and it would be ideal that the parties reach consensus on the need for a policy as well as its specific provisions. A policy imposed on the workforce or without the sanction of the representative trade union is likely to meet with resistance and even industrial action.

Random drug and alcohol testing is fairly common although there was an instance where the employer's attempt to introduce compulsory drug and alcohol testing and make non-compliance a disciplinary offence, was held by the Labour Court in *Metrorail v Satawu* to be a unilateral alteration of the terms and conditions of employment of employees.[26] The trade union had argued that compulsory testing would be an invasion of the right to privacy in the sense of the acquisition of private information about the employee. The court in essence held that the employer, irrespective of its rationale for introducing the policy, could not infringe the constitutional rights to bodily and psychological integrity of employees.

Random testing has also been criticised as a means of discriminating against employees. In *Chetty v Kaymac Rotomoulders (Pty) Ltd*[27] the arbitrator criticised the manner of the testing – the facts that testing was done in full view of the workforce and that no criteria were provided for selection were considered to be problematic, given that the employee disputed that the selection was random. In another matter an employee was unfairly subjected to a random breathalyser test when he arrived at work intoxicated. He had consumed alcohol at home but was unexpectedly summoned to work overtime due to a staff shortage. He was dismissed after being found to be 'considerably under the influence of alcohol but not completely intoxicated'.[28]

Although no specific common law rules exist to regulate random testing, the rules held by the Labour Court to be applicable to testing for HIV in order to ensure non-discrimination can be usefully applied as they are based on similar considerations of confidentiality, anonymity and fairness. This has been dealt with in chapter 13.

3.1.1(f) Reasonable cause testing in South Africa

In *Arangie v CCMA & Aberdare Cables*[29] in a review of an arbitration ruling, the Labour Court held that a proper reading of the security procedure in operation at the company suggested that the employer could only subject an employee to testing if they were suspected of being under the influence of alcohol. In this case there was nothing to suggest that the employer suspected this and it had therefore not been appropriate to subject the employee to a test. The employee had refused to take an Alco scan breathlyser test on the basis that he considered it to be unreliable. He was charged with '[r]efusing to comply with a reasonable request to undertake an Alco Scan when reporting for duty which is viewed very seriously by the company.' The arbitrator however focused on whether he had 'contravened the rule or practice of the company by refusing to blow into an alcohol scanner and to leave the company site after he had refused to blow into the alcohol testing instrument.' The Commissioner proceeded to find that the gravity of the offence made the employment relationship intolerable and justified the sanction of dismissal in the circumstances. The Court found that the

---

26 See (n)3.
27 (2004) 25 *ILJ* 2391 (BCA).
28 *Goodyear SA (Pty) Ltd v CCMA* [2003] ZALC 11 (11 September 2003).
29 [2008] ZALC 155 (18 December 2008).

decision of the Commissioner did not properly take account of the company policy, the relevant provisions of which stated:

> No employee will be obligated to take such a test, however the company reserves its right to refuse entry to the premises to such an employee suspected to be under the influence of alcohol or other substances.

'This was critical for the determination of the question of whether a refusal to undergo the test constituted misconduct' and justified the employee's dismissal. The court found that 'the rule that the Commissioner was concerned with was not what led to the dismissal of the Applicant'. He focused on the practice at the company that an employee who refused to take the test was obliged to leave the premises. The matter was referred back to the CCMA.

In *Mayer v Mind Pearl AG*[30] an employee was dismissed for possession and use of drugs in the workplace after a fellow employee reported finding him 'snorting' a white powder in his work cubicle. He denied the incident and maintained that he did not use drugs.

> At the arbitration the employer called an expert witness who explained the symptoms associated with the use of a drug similar to cocaine known as CAT. Other employees gave evidence of changes which they had observed in the employee's behaviour and performance which were similar to those described by the expert. The fact that the employer had not sent him for a blood test, although he had been willing to take one, was not considered significant. The arbitrator held that it was open to the employee to take a test himself if he thought the result would clear him and, in any event, it was likely that the outcome would have been inconclusive after a five-day period. His dismissal was upheld as fair.

In *Carolissen v International Brokers and Credit Control (Pty) Ltd*[31] the dismissal of a car salesman was held to be justified without the necessity for testing because it was a specific term of his employment contract that alcohol abuse would give rise to instant dismissal. Evidence was led by witnesses about his behaviour but he claimed that:

> the employer had no proof against him as no breathalyzer test had been taken and the witnesses had all lied. The arbitrator found that although the employee stated that he did not drink at the office -- and it was probable that he did not -- his behaviour during working hours was indicative of being under the influence of alcohol. It was not necessary for the employer to administer breathalyzer tests or take blood tests. It was sufficient to have an eye witness account of someone who knew him well and could tell the difference between the employee when sober and when under the influence of alcohol. The employee had been counselled and warned and was aware of the rule against alcohol abuse. His contract made it clear that he could be summarily dismissed. His behaviour had an adverse impact on the employer's operational requirements and the sanction of dismissal was appropriate. The dismissal was substantively fair.

Although in general, reasonable cause testing is permissible provided it is performed according to the procedure stipulated in a policy, rule or collective agreement, or is

---

30   (2005) 26 *ILJ* 382 (CCMA).

31   (2004) 25 *ILJ* 2076 (BCA).

required by statute, in some instances the Labour Court has cautioned against testing when reasonable cause is assumed too easily. In *AASA v Govender NO & others*[32] it was found to be an overdose of medication that led the employee to engage in uncharacteristic behavior. The general rule however is that testing is permissible depending on the nature of the work. In *Tanker Services (Pty) Ltd v Magudulela*, although evidence was led that the employee smelt of alcohol, spoke with a slur and was unsteady on his feet, in short had all the symptoms of someone who had consumed alcohol, the Court held that:

> a farm labourer may still be able to work in the fields although he is too drunk
> to operate a tractor. Consumption of alcohol would make an airline pilot unfit
> for his job before it made him unfit to ride a bicycle.[33]

The approach in *Tanker Services* was applied in an arbitration in which the safety risk was significant. In *Le Roy v SA Express Airways:*[34]

> an employee [an airline pilot] was charged at a disciplinary hearing with
> having operated as a pilot in command of an aircraft while under the influence
> of intoxicating liquor, and of having contravened various rules and standards
> regulating his conduct in the workplace. He was dismissed and in arbitration
> proceedings claimed that his dismissal was unfair. The charges were levelled after
> complaints by other members of the crew regarding the employee's conduct on
> the flight and his smelling of alcohol . The employee admitted to drinking eight
> beers between 21:45 and 03:00 but denied that he had drunk excessively or been
> under the influence of alcohol at the time he signed on for duty and flew the
> plane. The employer contended that the dismissal was fair because the employee
> had knowingly breached the employer's rules that a flight crew member shall not
> consume alcoholic beverages within eight hours of flight or standby duties, and
> shall avoid excessive alcohol intake as of 24 hours before flight.

The arbitrator examined the evidence and concluded that:

> the employer had no absolute proof of the employee's movements on the night
> in question, nor could it prove what the employee drank, how much he drank,
> when he stopped drinking or when he went to sleep. To prove that he had
> breached the two rules the employer was dependent on the allegations by the
> crew, the opinion of an expert witness who advised the company prior to the
> enquiry, and the employee himself.

The arbitrator had regard to *Tanker Services* (supra) in dealing with the meaning of 'being under the influence of alcohol' where:

> the court held in that case that intoxication is a matter of degree and stated
> that an individual could be said to be under the influence of alcohol if he was
> no longer able to perform the tasks entrusted to him with the skill expected of a
> sober person. The court made the point that an evaluation of whether a person is
> unable to perform such a task is dependent on the nature of the task.

---

32 (1999) 20 *ILJ* 2854 (LC).
33 (1999) 20 *ILJ* 431 (CCMA).
34 (1999) 20 *ILJ* 431 (CCMA).

Inconsistent application of a rule prohibiting alcohol and substance use can be detrimental to an employer's efforts to deal with the problem. In *United National Breweries v CCMA & others*[35] a forklift driver was dismissed for being drunk on duty. He was questioned by his co-workers who observed that he 'was smelling of liquor'. The evidence was that his breathalyser reading was at the maximum, and the charge was serious because there were a number of other employees at the same workstation who could have been injured and company property could have been damaged. He did not dispute at his disciplinary enquiry that he was under the influence of alcohol, and knew this was a serious offence that could lead to his dismissal, particularly since he was employed as a driver. He led evidence of another employee to show that the company was inconsistent in the application of its rule. The arbitrator found:

> It is common cause that there is a rule regarding the use or the abuse of alcohol at the workplace. There is also no question as to the validity and or reasonableness of this rule, especially when it comes to forklift drivers as they move material from one point to another and expose other workers and company to potential harm and damage if they are not in full control of their physical and mental abilities. It is also common cause that the employee was aware of this rule.

The dismissal was held to be unjustified on the grounds that the employer had inconsistently applied the rule.

It is clear from the above case law that testing is not a controversial issue in South Africa, provided it is done in compliance with the employer's policy, rules or a collective agreement. The issue is rather when discipline, and more importantly dismissal, is justified. Testing is therefore generally justified where reasonable cause exists by way of observation of the employee's conduct; where acceptable testing methods are used and the test is conducted by the occupational health practitioner; and where other employees have complained about the conduct of the employee. The nature of the work and the safety risk are paramount considerations in justifying testing.

3.1.1(g) Discipline for alcohol abuse versus counselling and support

When is it justified for an employer to treat alcohol abuse as misconduct compared to incapacity when the employee is not an alcoholic?

Steenkamp J considered the issues in the Labour Court in a well-reasoned judgment dealing extensively with the issues and legal authorities. In *Transnet Freight Rail v Transnet Bargaining Council*[36] the court found that it was common cause that the employee was not an alcoholic and that the misconduct she committed was reporting for work under the influence of alcohol, and rendering herself incapable of performing her duties. The court found that an employee who was not afflicted by alcoholism as a disease did not have to be subjected to rehabilitation or other requirements of the employee wellness programme, and should be dealt with in terms of the provisions of the LRA regulating discipline for misconduct.

The Labour Court confirmed this principle:

> When an employee, who is not an alcoholic and does not claim to be one, reports for duty under the influence of alcohol, she will be guilty of misconduct

---

35 P539/02 unreported 15 March 2006.
36 (2011) 32 *ILJ* 1766 (LC).

and not incapacity. Once an arbitrator finds that an employee is not an alcoholic, he/she is required to consider whether a finding of guilt is fair and whether the sanction applied by the employer is reasonable and justified in the circumstances. In order to do this the commissioner is required to continue to apply the law relating to misconduct and not that relating to incapacity.[37]

3.1.2 Canadian approaches

Reasonable cause testing is based on a reasonable observation or belief that the employee may be impaired by alcohol or drugs while at work, or be in possession of a substance in contravention of a company policy.

The arbitral jurisprudence confirms that if the employer has reasonable and probable cause to suspect that an employee is impaired while on duty at work, the employer may require that the employee undergo a test.[38] This is particularly true when the employee is employed in a safety sensitive position. Examples of circumstances that have been upheld are: a nurse on a construction site overhead an employee say he used marijuana every night,[39] *Fluor Constructors Canada Ltd and I.B.E.W.*, Loc. 424 (Re) (2001), 100 L.A.C. (4th) 391; police had found marijuana at the home of an employee in a safety sensitive position.[40]

If an employee refuses to undergo the test where there is reasonable cause, he or she does so at their own risk. This means, barring other mitigating factors, the employee faces dismissal for such a refusal.

The Canadian model has been described in *Imperial Oil Ltd v Communications, Energy and Paperworkers Union of Canada*, Local 900 (Policy Grievance) (2006), 157 L.A.C. (4th) 225 (M. Picher), [2006] O.L.A.A. No. 721[41] as follows:

At the risk of oversimplification, the Canadian model for alcohol or drug testing in a safety sensitive workplace as developed in the arbitral jurisprudence generally contains a number of elements as summarized below:
- *No employee can be subjected to random, unannounced alcohol or drug testing, save as part of an agreed rehabilitative program.*
- *An employer may require alcohol or drug testing of an individual where the facts give the employer reasonable cause to do so.*

It is within the prerogatives of management's rights under a collective agreement to also require alcohol or drug testing following a significant incident, accident or near miss, where it may be important to identify the root cause of what occurred.

---

37 http://www.worklaw.co.za.

38 See *Imperial Oil and C.E.P.U.C.*, Loc. 900 (Re), [2006] O.L.A.A. No. 721, 157 L.A.C. (4th) 225 (M. Picher); *Esso Petroleum Canada and C.E.P.U.*, Loc. 614 (Re) (1994), 56 L.A.C. (4th) 440 (McAlpine), [1994] B.C.C.A.A.A. No 244; *International Association of Heat and Frost Insulators and Asbestos Workers, Loc.* 110 v Trace Canada Co. (2001), 96 L.A.C. (4th) 343 (Beattie).

39 *Brotherhood of Locomotive Engineers v Canadian Pacific Railway Co* upheld [2003] A.J. No 513 (Alta. Q.B.).

40 *Re Canadian Pacific Ltd. and United Transportation Union,* (1987) 31 L.A.C. (3d) 179 (M.G. Picher); but cf. *International Association of Heat and Frost Insulators and Asbestos Workers, Local 110 v Trace Canada,* [2004] A.C.A.A. No. 68 (Beattie) where reasonable cause was found to be absent.

41 This award was upheld on review: *Imperial Oil Ltd. v Communications, Energy & Paperworkers Union of Canada,* Local 900 [2009] 96 O.R. (3d) 668; [2009] O.J. No 2037 (O.C.A.).

Drug and alcohol testing is a legitimate part of continuing contracts of employment for individuals found to have a problem of alcohol or drug use. As part of an employee's program of rehabilitation, such agreements or policies requiring such agreements may properly involve random, unannounced alcohol or drug testing generally for a limited period of time, most commonly two years. In a unionized workplace the Union must be involved in the agreement which establishes the terms of a recovering employee's ongoing employment, including random, unannounced testing. This is the only exceptional circumstance in which the otherwise protected employee interest in privacy and dignity of the person must yield to the interests of safety and rehabilitation, to allow for random and unannounced alcohol or drug testing.

The cases generally recognise that an employee's refusal or failure to undergo an alcohol or drug test in the three circumstances described above may properly be viewed as a serious violation of the employer's drug and alcohol policy, and may itself be grounds for serious discipline...

As set out above, a key feature of the jurisprudence in the area of alcohol or drug testing in Canada is that arbitrators have overwhelmingly rejected mandatory, random and unannounced drug testing for all employees in a safety sensitive workplace as being an implied right of management under the terms of a collective agreement. Arbitrators have concluded that to subject employees to an alcohol or drug test when there is no reasonable cause to do so, or in the absence of an accident or near miss and outside of the context of a rehabilitation plan for an employee with an acknowledged problem is an unjustified affront to the dignity and privacy of employees which falls beyond the balancing of any legitimate employer interest, inlcuding deferrence and the enforcement of safe practices. In a unionized workplace, such an extraordinary incursion into the rights of employees must be expressly and clearly negotiated. It is not to be inferred solely from general language describing management rights or from language in a collective agreement which enshrines safety and safe practices.

As mentioned in chapter 14, there is dichotomy in the jurisprudence as between Alberta and Ontario in its approach to random drug testing.[42] In Ontario the issue at stake is the interest of the employer to provide a safe and productive work environment as against the interest of the employees to protect their privacy rights. The matter was analysed as follows in *Trimac Transportation Services - Bulk Systems v Transportation Communications Union* (1999), 88 L.A.C. (4th) 237 (Burkett); [1999] C.L.A.D. No 750:

... the shared expectation of the parties to collective bargaining, shaped by the jurisprudence, is that an employer has the right under its general right to manage to make rules relating to the safe operation of the workplace and that the union can challenge these rules under the just cause provision as not reasonably related to the business objective or as otherwise in contravention of the collective agreement...

In circumstances where these rights are competing, such that employees may be disciplined for noncompliance, resolution is achieved by weighing

---

42   *Alberta (Human Rights and Citizenship Commission) v Elizabeth Metis Settlement* [2003] A.J. No 484.

or balancing the competing impacts. In respect of drug and alcohol testing of employees the balance has been struck in favour of protecting individual privacy rights, except where reasonable and probable grounds exist to suspect the drug and alcohol impairment or addiction of an employee in the workplace and except where there is no less intrusive means of confirming the suspicion. Conversely, the balance has been struck in favour of management's right (as part of its general right to manage) to require drug or alcohol testing, where the two aforementioned conditions exist. It follows that each case must be decided on its own facts.

On the facts of that particular case, the arbitrator found that the random drug testing was not justified because there were less intrusive methods available to the employer to confirm any reasonable suspicion it might have of drug or alcohol abuse. The outcome of this case is that random drug testing is justified only if there is no less intrusive method to accomplish the employer's objective of achieving a safe workplace and if the circumstances of the workplace had reached such a state that random drug testing had become a necessity. In other words, the drug or alcohol usage and abuse must have reached such a stage that the employer had no other reasonable alternative to combat the problem.

As regards the importance of employee privacy rights, the arbitrator said the following:

…As importantly, the express right to make rules for the promotion of safety, while it pertains to the subject matter at hand, cannot be read as constituting a grant of authority to invade employee privacy to the extent caused by mandatory random drug testing…Absent an express grant of authority to management to impose mandatory random drug testing, the employer acts on the basis of an implied right that is subject to challenge under the just cause provision as an unwarranted invasion of employee privacy.

…

The onus is upon the Company, as the party seeking to force employees to submit to mandatory random drug testing, to establish that the risk threshold necessary to validate its initiative is met.

The leading authority on random drug testing is *Imperial Oil Ltd v Communications, Energy and Paperworkers Union of Canada*, Local 900 (Policy Grievance), above.[43] The board of arbitration found that the company's policy of random drug testing by means of the buccal swab method violated the collective agreement and the employees' rights to individual privacy and dignity. The following portion of that decision sets out the considerations that weigh against a random drug testing policy:

For reasons which are apparent in the jurisprudence reviewed above, arbitrators have not held to the narrow line of characterizing an alcohol or drug test as a form of coerced assault in considering the legitimacy of alcohol and drug testing in the workplace, as regards employees who work in safety sensitive positions under a collective bargaining regime. Rather, they have consistently adopted a balancing of interests approach, seeking fairly to allow employers that margin necessary to ensure safety while preserving to employees, particularly to

---

43   See also: *Sarnia Cranes Ltd* [1999] OLRB Rep. May/June 479, [1999] O.L.R.D. No 1282; *Entrop v Imperial Oil Ltd* [2000] O.J. No 2689 (O.C.A.).

employees who have given no reason for suspicion of impairment, a modicum of dignity and privacy..

...Imperial Oil believes, in good faith, that randomly drug testing all of its employees will have a deterrent effect. The expert testimony, largely unchallenged, tends to affirm that view. But the value of deterrence is but one element to be weighed in the balancing of interests. No doubt corporal punishment would also have a deterrent effect, but a free and civilized society puts limits on the value of deterrence. In a safety sensitive workplace, the assessment of the legitimacy of the random drug testing of all employees, including innocent employees, must involve some balancing of the employer's interest in deterrence against the countervailing interest of employees in being treated with dignity and respect.

... In the final analysis, in balancing the interests of the parties, a question to be considered is not merely whether the extreme approach of random drug testing for all employees is effective, but also whether it is necessary or justified. The experience of other employers in a variety of safety sensitive industries would appear to suggest that it is not.

The lessons from these cases are that the factual circumstances inform whether a random drug and alcohol testing program will be sustainable. The following factors will be considered: the reasons for the testing (is there a particular problem that needs addressing?); the safety sensitive nature of the operation or of the tasks performed by those being tested; the methods used in conducting the tests (how intrusive and personal are they?); the availability of other less intrusive, though equally effective, methods for testing impairment; the accuracy of the results in determining impairment. The employer must meet a high threshold to justify a random drug testing programme. Assuming reasonable cause, accurate, prompt results regarding impairment and minimal or insignificant intrusion into workers' privacy rights, a random drug testing program may be upheld. This was contemplated in the *Imperial Oil* case, above, as follows:

It may well be that the balancing of interests approach, which we favour, would allow for general random, unannounced drug testing in some extreme circumstances. If, for example, an employer could marshal evidence which compellingly demonstrates an out-of-control drug culture taking hold in a safety sensitive workplace, such a measure might well be shown to be necessary for a time to ensure workplace safety. That might well constitute a form of 'for cause' justification. In the case at hand, however, the evidence is manifestly to the contrary...In these particular circumstances we are compelled to conclude that the employer has not discharged the onus of justifying its policy and to find that subjecting innocent employees to mandatory, unannounced, random drug testing is an unwarranted intrusion on their privacy and is an unjustifiable affront to their dignity.

3.2 Post-incident Testing

3.2.1 South Africa

Testing is permitted and even required pre-and post-incident in terms of OHSA.

In *NUMSA on behalf of Williams v Robertson & Caine (Pty) Ltd*[44] the employee's supervisor smelt alcohol on his breath, requested him to take a breathalyser test which showed the presence of alcohol, and sent him home. In an arbitration in which he contested the substantive fairness of his dismissal, the arbitrator first considered whether the employee was under the influence of alcohol. The arbitrator referred to OHSA and its General Safety Regulations before finding that dismissal was an appropriate sanction. The arbitrator stated (at 2081) that:

> The Act does not define what it is to be under the influence. The Act merely stipulates that an employer may not allow an employee to remain at the workplace if that employee is or appears to be under the influence.'

> The arbitrator relied on:

> Regulation 2A(1) of the General Safety Regulations, inserted by GN R928 of 25 June 2003, and issued in terms of OHSA provides that an employer 'shall not permit any person who is or who appears to be under the influence of intoxicating liquor or drugs, to enter or remain at the workplace'. According to Reg 2A(2) 'no person at a workplace shall be under the influence of or have in his possession or partake of or offer any person intoxicating liquor or drugs.

The applicant in the abovenamed case worked with machines and table saws and the risk of injury was severe. The arbitrator found that the applicant would be under the influence of alcohol if he were no longer able to perform the tasks entrusted to him with the skill expected of a sober person. He found the employer's conduct to be justified in that

> [t]he evidence before me indicates that the applicant's job required a high degree of skill, was technically complex and given the nature of the tools he used, his job was extremely dangerous. The applicant had in fact lost a finger at his previous job and this happened while he was sober. I am of the view that if one applies the abovementioned test to the facts of this case, the applicant was under the influence of alcohol.

The dismissal was found to be fair.

In *Odayar v Compensation Commissioner*[45] the employee succeeded in an appeal to the High Court in terms of section91(5)(a)(i) of COIDA after his claim for compensation for post-traumatic stress disorder arising out of and in the course of his employment as a police officer was repudiated. The Compensation Commissioner had found that the employee was not injured in an 'accident' as defined in the Act, in that he could not show that his illness arose 'out of and in the course of his or her employment'. He had testified that during the course of his work he had been exposed to numerous violent incidents and 'exposure to these incidents adversely affected his health', and had forced him to 'turn to alcohol in order to drown his sorrows'.

'The court was satisfied that the evidence established overwhelmingly that the appellant's disease, namely post-traumatic stress disorder [including his alcohol abuse], arose as a result of and in the course of his employment. As such, he was entitled to claim compensation for an occupational disease.'

---

44 (2005) 26 ILJ 2074 (BCA).
45 (2006) 27 ILJ 1477 (N).

3.2.2 Canadian approaches

After an incident or 'near miss' an employer is entitled to require a worker to be tested for alcohol or drugs to eliminate impairment as a contributing factor. Any injury to a worker is regarded as an incident and the employer may require the employee to be tested.[46] This principle was expressed as follows in *SHP 530* on July 18, 2000 (M Picher):

> In respect of drug and alcohol testing of employees the balance has been struck in favour of protecting individual privacy rights, except where reasonable and probable grounds exist to suspect the drug and alcohol impairment or addiction of an employee in the workplace and except where there is no less intrusive means of confirming the suspicion. Conversely, the balance has been struck in favour of management's right (as part of its general right to manage) to require drug or alcohol testing, where the two aforementioned conditions exist. It follows that each case must be decided on its own facts.[47]

The contentious issue is the extent to which, after a very minor injury, the employer can require the employee to undergo a test for drug or alcohol use. In our view, if there is some possibility that impairment could have played a part in the accident or near miss, the employer is entitled to require a test to discount these possibilities, irrespective of how minor the injury.

The refusal to undergo a test when it was reasonable for the employer to require a test is grounds for discipline and, in appropriate cases, for dismissal.[48]

3.3 Testing as part of a programme of treatment or as a term of continuing employment

Frequently, a term of reinstatement of an employee who has acknowledged to have a drug or alcohol addiction is to agree that periodic or random testing will be done to confirm that the employee is cooperating with treatment and rehabilitation, and not abusing drugs or alcohol. Such terms can be part of 'last chance' agreements that the employee will comply with attendance and other requirements of employment.[49]

In Canada, a last chance agreement will usually provide that if the employee is alleged to breach the last chance agreement, the employer need only prove the breach. The result will be defined in the agreement, viz the employee's dismissal. So, if, for example, the employee agrees not to be impaired at work, or not to exceed the workplace absenteeism average, or that random testing will prove negative, and the employer is able to show that one or other of these conditions has not been satisfied, then the employee will be automatically dismissed. Usually a last chance agreement will be for a specific period of time, normally 2 years.

In the South African case of *Yende v Cobra Watertech*:[50]

---

46 *Construction Labour Relations v United Brotherhood of Carpenters and Joiners of America*, Locals 1325 and 2103 (Hewitt Grievance), [2001] A.G.A.A. No 29, 96 L.A.C. (4th) 343.

47 See also *Canadian National Railway Company v National Automobile, Aerospace, Transportation and General Workers Union of Canada (CAW-Canada)*, 2007 CanLII 43492 (ON L.A.) (Albertyn).

48 *Suncor Energy Inc. v C.E.P.U.*, Local 707 (Pearson), [2004] A.G.A.A. No 35 (Jones).

49 See *Imperial Oil Limited v C.E.P.U.*, Local 777 (Parsons) [2001] A.G.A.A. No 102 in which a discharge was upheld arising from a post-reinstatement random test.

50 (2004) 25 *ILJ* 2412 (BCA).

the employee tested positive for cannabis in two drug tests conducted by the employer and held a month apart. He was charged with being under the influence of drugs whilst on duty and was dismissed after a disciplinary enquiry. The employer had a zero tolerance policy relating to being under the influence of drugs at work. In arbitration proceedings the arbitrator found it was clear that the employee had a dependency on cannabis, and that the employer had taken acceptable measures to rehabilitate him when it could probably have dismissed him for a first offence in terms of its policy. For this reason the employer chose to have him tested over a period of time, to see whether the dependency decreased. However, the test did not show that the employee was performing his duties under the influence of cannabis, but rather that his habit had not diminished. The charge had been of taking and being under the influence of drugs whilst on duty, and this had not been proved. The dismissal was accordingly held to be unfair. Reinstatement was ordered. When considering the issue of compensation however, the arbitrator took into account that, although the employer had no clear policy that employees should not test positive for drugs during the period of their employment, as opposed to while on duty, it was clearly concerned about the employee. The employee would have known this, but made no attempt to reduce or terminate his habit. Compensation of three months' salary [instead of reinstatement] was awarded.

4. VOLUNTARY SUBMISSION FOR TREATMENT AND COUNSELLING

An employer should create a conducive and confidential environment in which a problem or dependent drinker or drug abuser can comfortably come forward to seek assistance to overcome a substance abuse problem without fear of prejudice to job or promotion prospects. Such openness enables problem drinkers or drug users to voluntarily submit to counselling and treatment.

In *Chetty v Kaymac Rotomoulders (Pty) Ltd* [51] the employee argued in his unfair dismissal arbitration that 'he had confided in his superiors and sought help for his drug problem, and it was therefore unfair to dismiss him without trying to assist him.' The arbitrator found that the employer 'seemed not really interested in assisting the employee with his addiction', despite its professed supportive attitude. The employee, in view of a pending audit of all employees for drugs (of which it gave employees two weeks' notice), had approached his superior and informed him of his addiction and requested assistance in an effort to 'get clean'. The manager had undertaken to contact the South African National Council for Alcohol Abuse (SANCA) but had not done so at the time the random audit was conducted. The employee testified that on the day of the testing he had been cooperative, despite his frustration at not being offered assistance despite his voluntary disclosure of his addiction. The arbitrator found for this reason that the dismissal was substantively unfair and ordered financial compensation.

Ideally the employer will have a separation between its operational/human resources divisions and its occupational health unit. Employees should have the opportunity to provide confidential information and concerns to the employer's occupational health unit, without that information passing to the operational units of the employer. So treatment and counselling can occur without the operational divisions of the enterprise

---

51 (2004) 25 *ILJ* 2391 (BCA).

being informed, unless some work accommodation is required for the employee. The accommodation would then be arranged by the occupational health unit, and the employee's departmental manager would know only what type of accommodation was required for the employee, not the reason for the accommodation. This protects the employee's privacy.

5. REFERRAL BY CO-WORKERS

If the problem of alcohol or drug abuse and dependence is admitted, understood, and discussed sympathetically within the workplace, and if employees feel comfortable that they will not be prejudiced if they admit to having a substance abuse problem, then fellow workers may urge such an employee to seek counselling and treatment. Co-workers may, in such circumstances, request the counsellor, or a person from the occupational health unit of the employer, to meet with a fellow worker whom they know to have a drinking or substance abuse problem. Workers can take responsibility for the welfare of their fellows if they feel satisfied that no prejudice may be caused to those referred for counselling.

We recognise that co-workers are unlikely to refer their fellow employees for treatment or assessment. Typically co-workers tend to protect intoxicated employees from detection and they go to considerable lengths to conceal the existence of a drinking or drug abuse problem in fellow employees for fear that the truth may prejudice the worker's employment security. However, if a supportive environment is created in the workplace, and if workers know that their jobs will not necessarily be jeopardised if they admit to an addiction or dependency, the extent of concealment and covering-up of alcohol and drug abuse problems can diminish.

The role of co-employees in securing discipline for use at work was demonstrated in a South African arbitration ruling in *Mayer v Mind Pearl AG*.[52] The applicant was dismissed after a disciplinary enquiry for possession and use of drugs in the workplace after a fellow employee reported finding him 'snorting' a white powder in his work cubicle. The employee denied the incident entirely and maintained that he did not use drugs. He claimed that there was no evidence against him and that his dismissal was substantively unfair. At arbitration, the employer called an expert witness who explained the symptoms associated with the use of a drug similar to cocaine known as CAT, and other employees gave evidence of changes which they had observed in the employee's behaviour and performance which were similar to those described by the expert. The commissioner found the corroborative evidence to be acceptable and that the applicant was guilty of the possession and use of drugs at work.

6. PERIODIC TESTS

There are medical methods described above for determining, at a relatively early stage, whether a worker is becoming a problem or dependent drinker or a drug abuser. There are several possible tests, which complement each other, and they tell relatively accurately the amount of alcohol the person is consuming and whether, as compared to an earlier test, there has been a reduction or increase in the volume of consumption. They are extremely valuable sources of information because they reveal to the drinker

---

52 (2005) 26 *ILJ* 382 (CCMA). Also discussed earlier in this chapter. See (n) 31.

and the medical practitioner that there may be excessive alcohol consumption well before the overt medical or behavioural signs of problem drinking present themselves.

The periodic tests are designed to monitor alcohol and drug use or dependence. They are valuable both to the affected employee and to the employer. The employer is not entitled to the confidential information regarding the employee's treatment, but the employer knows that problems of dependent drinking are being identified at an early stage, when the prospects of influencing the worker's consumption pattern are relatively good, and the company's medical or occupational health department is involved with the worker concerned in an attempt to improve consumption habits. The employee and the employer benefit from procedures and tests which make possible the early identification of problem drinking or drug use.

The information obtained from the periodic tests should be confidential between the worker concerned and the company's medical practitioner or occupational health unit. The medical practitioner would be charged with the responsibility of guiding the employee concerned to counselling and, if necessary, treatment.

A company's substance abuse policy, or a procedural agreement between management and a union, may provide for periodic medical check-ups for the company's employees. Normally such examinations involve an assessment of the state of the lungs, heart and other bodily organs. We suggest the examinations may include tests from the perspective of alcohol or drug abuse. These tests can give valuable early warning to the individual workers of whether they should consider their drinking or drug use to be a problem and whether they should change their recreational habits. Clearly, the information gained from such tests is for the workers' benefit to evaluate the state of their health. The information should be confidential to the employee and to the occupational health unit of the employer. The information should not be available to line management and human resources, unless it is part of an agreed substance abuse review, as part of the accommodation of the employee.

If an employee has been disciplined for substance abuse problems – such as frequent absenteeism, or other neglect of work responsibility – either as a 'last chance' or as part of an effort to overcome the substance abuse – the employee may agree with the employer (usually with the assistance of the employee's union representative) to undergo a programme of treatment and review. The monitoring of the success of the treatment programme may involve periodic or random testing for substance use to determine whether the employee is cooperating with the treatment. The programme of testing should be arranged so that there is scope for improvement within each period between the tests, and the tests should be appropriate and accurate.

The tests may also be used to monitor the progress of a problem or dependent drinker or drug addict who, as a condition of the suspension of discipline, is undergoing counselling and/or treatment in terms of a progressive disciplinary policy concerning alcohol or drug abuse. The disciplinary procedure would provide that management is entitled to be informed of whether or not the employee is co-operating with the counselling and/or treatment. Management need not know the details of the periodic test results, but an improvement in these test results would be clear evidence to the medical department and the counsellor that the employee is co-operating, and a failure to cooperate would justify reviewing the employee's accommodation and, depending on the circumstances, his or her continued employment.

SUMMARY

Every workplace should have clear policy and procedures in place to identify substance abuse and substance dependence, as each involves separate considerations. Substance abuse is addressed primarily through discipline; substance dependence or addiction is addressed primarily through appropriate accommodation. While random drug or alcohol testing is problematic and has been held in some jurisdictions to be unlawful, reasonable cause, post-incident and post-reinstatement testing are permissible. Testing should, however, be subject to the safeguarding of employee interests (ie privacy, dignity, confidentiality) and fair labour practices, while taking account of the employer's interest in maintaining discipline and ensuring the safety of workplace. The rules must be clearly understood and applied consistently to all employees.

Chapter 14

Fair Discipline:
The South African Approach

Christopher Albertyn & Urmila Bhoola

1. INTRODUCTION

The South African Bill of Rights in the Constitution guarantees all persons the right to equality, which includes the right not to be unfairly discriminated against, as well as the right to privacy, dignity and bodily integrity.[1] Section 23 of the Constitution entrenches the right to fair labour practices. The right to fair labour practices in section 23 requires that disciplinary action has to be carried out in the context of equality, equal respect, dignity and privacy. In practice the employee is likely to be disciplined for absenteeism, although, in general, disciplinary codes would define alcohol or substance abuse as serious misconduct.

An employer is entitled to take disciplinary action for misconduct against an employees who contravene a workplace rule prohibiting alcohol or substance abuse or who are unable to perform their duties for this reason. In certain instances dismissal for incapacity may be more appropriate but this requires the employer first to take steps to make reasonable accommodation of the needs of the employee and to provide counselling, treatment and support. Although the dividing line between misconduct and incapacity may not always be clear, the courts have emphasised the need for empathy and have held dismissal for alcohol-related offences to be justified only where the offence is serious, in that the employee is incapable of performing the required duties. The legal position on dismissals for intoxication as expressed by the Labour Appeal Court is that for an employee to be dismissed for being under the influence of liquor or for drunkenness, they must, depending on the nature of the job, be so intoxicated as to be unable to render services in accordance with the minimum standards expected in the contract of employment as held in *Mondi Paper Co v Dlamini*.[2]

2. THE CODES OF GOOD PRACTICE

Discipline arising from alcohol and substance abuse is regulated by the Labour Relations Act 66 of 1995 and good practice guidelines issued under the various labour statutes.[3]

---

1 At sections 9, 14, 10 and 12 of the Constitution respectively.
2 [1996] 9 BLLR 1109 (LAC).
3 The Employment Equity Act 55 of 1998, Basic Conditions of Employment Act 75 of 1997, Occupation Health and Safety Act 85 of 1993, Unemployment Insurance Act 63 of 2001 and Compensation for Occupational Injuries and Diseases Act 130 of 1993 are the relevant labour statutes.

In particular, at Schedule 8 to the LRA, the Code of Good Practice on Dismissal and the Code of Good Practice on the Employment of People with Disabilities[4] are important in addressing the rights and obligations of employers and employees in the context of alcohol and substance abuse.

3. MISCONDUCT OR INCAPACITY

Under South African law, an employee who consumes alcohol or drugs in the workplace can either be disciplined for misconduct or incapacity. The approach taken by the employer would depend on the circumstances of each case and would be determined by:
- the provisions and procedures of a disciplinary code;
- the nature of the business and the work performed by the employee;
- the extent to which awareness exists in the workplace about general wellness;
- safety issues; and
- the extent to which the employer is able to assist with reasonable accommodation, employee assistance programme (EAP) support and rehabilitation of the employee.

The extent to which the employer can enforce discipline is to a large extent dependent on the legitimacy and validity of its policy regulating alcohol and substance abuse. The question then arises whether this should be a separate policy or encompassed within a general employee wellness policy.[5]

4. FAIR DISMISSAL

The Labour Relations Act 66 of 1995 (the LRA) requires dismissals to be substantively and procedurally fair. The requirements of the LRA are supplemented by the Code of Good Practice : Dismissal which sets out specific guidelines to be followed by employers to ensure fair dismissal for incapacity or misconduct. The LRA also defines a dismissal to be automatically unfair where it is based on various personal characteristics, including disability, religion and culture.[6]

Despite the prohibition on automatically unfair dismissals (defined as, among others, dismissal based on a discriminatory factor like race, gender, pregnancy), the LRA contemplates that the dismissal may be fair if the reason for the dismissal is based on an inherent requirement of a particular job (section 187(2)(a)). It is therefore possible that pre-employment testing may determine that an employee is alcohol or drug dependent and cannot satisfy essential job requirements.

---

4   Issued in terms of section 54(1) of the Employment Equity Act.
5   In South Africa, given the epidemic proportions of employees who are HIV positive, the concern about further stigmatising HIV positive employees has led to some employers preferring to deal with the issues of testing, counselling, support and other relevant issues in a general wellness policy instead of an HIV/AIDS policy. The same considerations may be relevant to alcohol and substance abuse and it may be useful for some of the relevant issues to be encompassed in a chronic illness policy rather than a self-standing alcohol and drug abuse policy. See the policy chapter for further discussion.
6   Section 187 of the LRA.

5. SUBSTANTIAL AND PROCEDURAL FAIRNESS

The requirements of the LRA and the Dismissal Code regarding substantial and procedural fairness must be complied with. In order to prove that the dismissal was substantively fair, the employer would have to show that there was a valid reason for the dismissal. This would be a breach of a workplace rule such as one prohibiting the use of alcohol and certain prohibited substances. The consequences of the breach must also be clearly understood by the employee. The second requirement is that the discipline must be effected in terms of a fair procedure where the employee's rights to natural justice are observed – this would require proper notice of the disciplinary hearing, the opportunity to challenge and lead evidence, the right to representation and the right to appeal.

6. CASE LAW

A number of cases summarised in the following pages have dealt with the nature of the rule that was breached, and the consequences of a lack of clarity about the rules relating to alcohol and substances in the workplace.

6.1 Misconduct

In order to discipline an employee for misconduct, the rule against alcohol and drug use in the workplace must be reasonable and must clearly set out the conduct prohibited. There are various types of rules that prohibit the use of alcohol and substances in the workplace that could be considered reasonable. These could include:

- an absolute prohibition on the possession of alcoholic beverages in the workplace;
- a prohibition on being under the influence of alcohol during working hours;
- a prohibition on being under the influence to the extent that work performance is impaired; and
- a rule precluding the alcohol level in employees' blood from exceeding a certain level.

6.1.1 Nature of the misconduct

In *Tanker Services (Pty) Ltd v Magudulela*[7] the employee was dismissed for being under the influence of alcohol while driving a 32-ton articulated vehicle belonging to the employer. The court held that an employee is 'under the influence of alcohol' if unable to perform the tasks entrusted, with the skill expected of a sober person. The evidence required to prove that a person has infringed a rule relating to consumption of alcohol or drugs depends on the offence with which the employee is charged. If employees are charged with being 'under the influence', evidence must be led to prove that their faculties were impaired to the extent that they were incapable of working properly. This may be done by administering blood or breathalyser tests, but if such equipment is not available, evidence of physical observations made by the employer may be sufficient.

Whether employees are unable to perform their work depends to some extent on nature of the work. The question in the *Tanker Services* case was whether Mr Magudelela's faculties had been impaired to the extent that he could no longer perform the skilled, technically complex and highly responsible task of driving an extraordinarily

---

7   [1997] 12 BLLR 1552 (LAC). Discussed in Grogan, J *Dismissal* (Juta 2010) 190-192.

heavy vehicle transporting a hazardous substance. Having found that Magudulela could not safely do so in his condition, the court concluded that Magudelela's behaviour amounted to an offence sufficiently serious to justify dismissal.

The following extract from *Tanker Services (Pty) Ltd v Magudulela* is instructive:[8]

> Whether an employee is, by reason of the consumption of intoxicating liquor, unable to perform a task entrusted to him by an employer must depend on the nature of the task. A farm labourer may still be able to work in the fields although he is too drunk to operate a tractor. Consumption of alcohol would make an airline pilot unfit for his job long before it made him unfit to ride a bicycle. The question which I should ask myself is, whether the respondent's faculties were shown in all probability to have been impaired to the extent that he could no longer properly perform the skilled, technically complex and highly responsible task of driving an extraordinarily heavy vehicle carrying a hazardous substance.

6.1.2 Nature of the charge

In *Mondi Paper v Dlamini* a computer operator was charged with 'drunkenness'. The court found that the employer had placed exclusive reliance on the result of a breathalyser test, and had failed to prove that the employee was actually drunk. The manner in which the charge is formulated is therefore of significance in proving misconduct. Despite this decision, given the information provided in the medical chapter on testing (chapter 10), if the equipment used for testing is reliable and the test definitive, technical results should be sufficient to establish the intoxication. Whether that conclusion will justify dismissal or other discipline depends on all the surrounding circumstances.

6.1.3 Failure to disclose dependence on substances

Failure to disclose an addiction can constitute misconduct. This was the ruling in a case involving a cabin attendant employed by the national airline, his failure to disclose his addiction to cocaine during a routine medical examination was held to constitute gross dishonesty.[9] The arbitrator referred to the requirements laid down by the Civil Aviation Authority and the airline policy regarding medical requirements for cabin crew, and found that it was clearly stipulated that persons with a history of drug dependency were not suitable for employment as cabin crew. Moreover, the symptoms and effects of cocaine use were so significant that the airline could, in the interests of public safety, not afford to show any tolerance in this regard. In these circumstances it was found that had he disclosed the dependency at the time of his employment application, he would not have qualified for appointment.

6.1.4 The charge should mirror the nature of the prohibition

In *Hotel Liquor Commercial & Allied Workers Union of SA v Fedics Group (Pty) Ltd t/a Fedics Food Services*[10] the employee had been dismissed for possession of marijuana. He admitted possession but contended that he smoked it before and after work. The

---

8   At 1554.

9   *SALSTAFF obo Govender v S A Airways* (2001) 22 *ILJ* 2366 (ARB).

10   (1993) 2 LCD 150 (IC).

employer provided catering facilities to clients and its employees did their work on the premises of these clients. It was important for the employer to ensure that its employees conducted themselves appropriately at the clients' premises. The employee had been charged with being in possession of drugs at work, ostensibly in breach of the employer's disciplinary code. An examination of the disciplinary code revealed that possession of marijuana was not listed as an offence. The employer argued that it was entitled to rely on two general provisions in the code, one concerning conduct prejudicial to the good order and discipline of the employer and another concerned with the commission of a criminal act where there is sufficient evidence to prosecute.

The court held that the failure of the code to deal with the possession of drugs was a crucial omission:

> Once an employer has set a standard of conduct in the work place, the penalty for a breach of which is in excess of that which is likely to be imposed in the ordinary course of events, then it is for the employer to ensure that his workforce is aware of it.

Although the court was satisfied that the conduct of the employee was such that it was likely to prejudice the good order and discipline of the employer, it noted that this was not the charge that had been put to the employee. It went on to hold—

> [A]lthough this court should be wary of being unduly technical I do not consider it unfair that respondent should be expected to bring a charge properly couched in terms of its own code and rules, more especially when that offence carries the penalty of dismissal.

6.1.5 The disciplinary code is a guideline

In *Riekert v CCMA & others*[11] the court was in agreement with the proposition that disciplinary codes are guidelines and that an employer will not necessarily be regarded as having acted procedurally unfairly if it has not complied with certain specific parts of its code. The court did not believe, however:

> [T]hat the fact that there is clear case law to the effect that disciplinary codes are guidelines can not under any circumstance be understood by employers as meaning that they may chop and change the disciplinary procedures they have themselves set, as and when they wish to. Employees (and employers) are entitled to expect that their employers (and employees) will comply with the prescribed rules of the game as far as disciplinary enquiries go (and for that matter, as far as all rules set in the workplace, for both employers and employees, are concerned). When an employer does not comply with aspects of its own disciplinary procedures, there must be good reasons shown for its failure to comply with its own set of rules. An employer must justify the non-compliance with its own code, and having regard to all the relevant circumstances, the employer bears the onus to satisfy the objective requirement that its conduct was substantially fair, reasonable and equitable.

---

11   (2006) 27 *ILJ* 1706 (LC).

National Union of Mineworkers v Black Mountain Mineral Development Company (Pty) Ltd[12] involved the application of the employer's standard procedure for alcohol and drug-related behaviour policy. The employer argued that the status of a disciplinary code was that of a guideline not requiring slavish adherence. Murphy AJ commented that the matters referred to all dealt with relatively minor departures from procedural aspects of the prevailing disciplinary code such as the failure of the chairperson to appoint a prosecutor on appeal or the appointment of a presiding officer not strictly in accordance with the prescribed guidelines. Murphy AJ went on to hold that:

> Where the employer's disciplinary code and policy provide for a particular approach it will generally be considered unfair to follow a different approach without legitimate justification. Justice requires that employers should be held to the standards they have adopted (see Changula v Bell Equipment (1992) 13 ILJ 101 (LAC) and SA Clothing and Textiles Workers Union & another v Martin Johnson (Pty) Ltd (1993) 14 ILJ 1033 (LAC)).

6.1.6 When is alcohol or drug use serious enough?

In considering whether alcohol and drug use is a serious offence justifying discipline for misconduct, the Labour Court in *Minister of Correctional Services v Mthembu NO & others*[13] considered a case where a prison warder was charged with contravening the disciplinary code of the employer in that he permitted prisoners to use alcohol in his presence without taking any action. He admitted his guilt and was dismissed. The dispute was referred to arbitration and the arbitrator ordered that he be re-employed with a final warning. On review to the Labour Court, the court considered Item 7 of the Code of Good Practice: Dismissal, which requires an arbitrator or other functionary who determines whether a dismissal for misconduct is unfair, to consider the following:

> (a) Whether or not the employee contravened a rule or standard regulating conduct in, or of relevance to, the workplace; and
> (b) if a rule or standard was contravened, whether or not –
> (i) the rule was a valid or reasonable rule or standard;
> (ii) the employee was aware, or could reasonably be expected to have been aware, of the rule or standard;
> (iii) the rule or standard has been consistently applied by the employer; and
> (iv) dismissal was an appropriate sanction for the contravention of the rule or standard.

The generous interpretation given to the level of intoxication and its relation to the nature of the job was apparent in another arbitration ruling in *National Union of Metalworkers of SA obo Mbali and Schrader Automotive SA (Pty) Ltd.*[14]

The arbitrator said the following:

> The charge of drunkenness or of being under the influence of intoxicating liquor implies that the applicant's faculties were substantially impaired to the extent that the ability to perform his job was impaired or that his state presented a

---

12 1997 (4) SA 51 (SCA).
13 (2006) 27 ILJ 2115 (LC).
14 (2006) 27 ILJ 865 (BCA).

danger to himself or others. In general, it is not enough for the respondent to rely solely on the results of a breathalyzer. The results revealed by the breathalyser test merely indicated the presence of alcohol in the applicant's bloodstream. The applicant was not charged with the presence of alcohol in his bloodstream, a fact that was common cause. He, however, denied that he was drunk. The respondent who is obliged to prove drunkenness, has in my view, only merely succeeded to prove the presence of alcohol in the applicant's bloodstream.

The clinical proof of drunkenness is evidenced by the presence of the classic tell-tale signs such as the smell of alcohol, slurred speech, aggression, staggering (unsteady feet), blood shot eyes, passing out, disorientation, etc.

There is also no evidence that the applicant was disorientated or that he had acted strangely. He cooperated during the test and his appearance was, according to respondent's witnesses, normal.

The employer was ordered to reinstate the employee. The decision in this case runs counter to the medical conclusions set out in the chapters above, where, the subjective factors relied on so heavily in this decision have been established to be of doubtful authenticity. Contrary to the approach in this decision, the objective tests are much more reliable indicators of impairment and intoxication for the reasons explained in the medical chapters above. Certainly, the subjective factors relied on in the decision as the decisive indicators of intoxication provide a basis for reasonable suspicion, but they cannot reliably be the basis for determining intoxication.

6.1.7 Must work be impaired?

Is it necessary to prove that an employee's work performance is impaired by alcohol or drugs or just that use has taken place? This will depend on the actual rule as well as the nature of the work involved. It may also be advisable to distinguish between the offences of being drunk at work and the use of alcohol at work or simply being in possession of alcohol or substances at work. Employers have often condoned management's use of alcohol, especially at business lunches, but there is no reason that, outside this context, consistency should not be insisted upon for offences involving the consumption of alcohol or bringing of alcohol onto company premises. These factors were distinguished in *Palaborwa Mining Company Limited v Cheetham & others*[15] where the dismissal of an employee was set aside by the Labour Court on grounds that the arbitrator had adopted an inflexible approach and that the employee did not behave in a fashion which endangered others. His job description did not place him in a category where he could harm others. Furthermore, his demeanour could not be described by anyone as being any one of those listed in the code. It would appear that if he was not tested for alcohol nobody would have noticed that he had consumed alcohol. Furthermore, the applicant is 58 years old and a first offender. These are all factors which should have been taken into account but were not. ...The employer operated a mine and its policy stipulated that any employee found to have more than 0,05 grams of alcohol per 100 millilitres of blood while on duty could be dismissed for a first offence. ...The arbitrator found that the employer had justified its strict policy by relying on its duty to ensure the safety of its employees working at the mine, and that his dismissal was fair on the basis

---

15   (2008) 29 *ILJ* 306 (LAC).

that, although he was a first offender, in view of his senior and responsible position he should have been above reproach.

6.1.8 Nature of proof required

Exactics-Pet (Pty) Ltd v Patelia NO & others [16] dealt with the level of proof required to prove intoxication.

> The employee had been dismissed following charges of being intoxicated at work. The arbitrator found his dismissal to have been substantively unfair and reinstated the employee retrospectively. It appeared that, when the employee had reported for work, his manager had noticed that he was inebriated—he smelt of alcohol, swore and was incoherent. The manager instructed that the employee be taken to his workstation under supervision until a breathalyser test could be conducted. The test was done some two hours later, when it was found that the level of alcohol in his bloodstream was well above the permissible statutory limit. On review the court found that the arbitrator had been prepared to accept that the crystals in the breathalyser test used had changed colour and since there was no evidence to suggest that the test was defective or inaccurate, he ought to have accepted that, on the strength of the test, there had been a presence of alcohol in the employee's system at the time of testing The arbitrator set the standard of proof too high. ... This was reinforced by the physical observations of the employer's witnesses that the employee had been under the influence of alcohol.

Evidence of a technical nature is often required by the employer, who bears the onus of proving that dismissal in the circumstances of intoxication was fair. In *National Union of Mineworkers obo Thuke and Palaborwa Mining Co Ltd*[17] an occupational doctor who was the medical superintendent of the mine, testified about readings on the relevant intoxication report and explained how alcohol is metabolised in the body:

> This means that either the alcohol was taken two hours before the alcohol test was conducted or that a lot of alcohol units were taken and that during the first test, the alcohol level in the body was still rising. In the case of the applicant, this would mean that he had either consumed alcohol closer to the time of the test or had consumed a large number of alcohol units. It is not abnormal that there could be two different sets of readings resulting from two tests conducted on the same person. This means that it does not necessarily imply that if one stops drinking alcohol, the alcohol level in the body drops.

The employee had stated in his defence that he took Tim Jan[18] medication but the witness testified that the medication did not contain 16.05% alcohol. The one spoonful the employee claimed in his disciplinary hearing that he took would have been about twelve millilitres of juice. Applying Widmark's Formula, which takes into account the alcohol volume, body weight and the two hours elapsed before testing, the witness testified that the alcohol level in the employee's body, if indeed his version were correct, would have been below 0.05 mg%.

---

16   (2006) 27 *ILJ* 1126 (LC).
17   (2010) 31 *ILJ* 1270 (CCMA).
18   A type of aloe juice containing fermented grapes.

6.1.9 Interference in standards set by employer should be limited

A further general principle is that the arbitrator should be reluctant to interfere in the standard of conduct set by the employer. This principle is set out in *National Union of Metalworkers of SA obo Motsele v Haggie Wire & Strand.*[19]

> The applicant, a store assistant employed by the respondent, was dismissed after having been found, at a disciplinary enquiry, to have been under the influence of alcohol on the company premises whilst on duty. The charge was based on the findings of two breathalyser tests administered to the employee, which showed the presence of 0,115 and 0,116 grams of alcohol per 100 millilitres of blood in his body. The employee claimed that, although he had been drinking the previous night he was not drunk at work, did not feel that he had been under the influence of alcohol, and that his dismissal was unfair. The arbitrator noted that the employer's disciplinary code stated that if an employee's blood alcohol level exceeded 0,03 he would be deemed to be intoxicated, and that anyone found to be intoxicated at work could be dismissed without prior warning. The employee was aware of the rule and had previously been disciplined for the same offence. Dismissal was not a punishment but the exercise of an employer's contractual right to terminate the employee's services in response to his breach of contract. The ultimate test was whether the employment relationship had been rendered intolerable, or whether the relationship of trust had been broken. The arbitrator found that the employee had refused to accept that he was under the influence of alcohol or that he had a dependency problem for which he needed help. An employer was entitled to set standards of conduct for its employees and a court or arbitrator should not lightly interfere in such standards, unless they were unreasonable or were applied inconsistently. The dismissal of the employee was held to be substantively and procedurally fair.

6.1.10 The test is whether the continued employment relationship is rendered intolerable

In the matter of *NUMSA obo Davids and Bosal Africa (Pty) Ltd*[20] the employee, a crane driver, reported for work with 0,015% alcohol in his bloodstream and operated a heavy crane for about three hours before his condition was detected. The union contended that dismissal was too harsh a penalty in the circumstances, because the amount of alcohol in the employee's bloodstream had not prevented him from discharging his duties. The arbitrator found that, while discipline had generally to be applied progressively, employers were permitted to dismiss employees after a first offence in appropriate circumstances. Dismissal was not a punishment; it was the exercise by the employer of its contractual right to terminate the services of an employee in response to the latter's breach. The ultimate test was whether the continuation of the employment relationship had been rendered intolerable or whether the relationship of trust between the employer and the employee had been broken. The interests of both employer and employee had to be taken into account. From the employer's perspective, the deterrent function of dismissal could not be disregarded. Just as employers could deter their employees from being dishonest by dismissing culprits, so could they dismiss for acts involving moral turpitude. Working under the influence of alcohol was such an offence, especially where the work was inherently dangerous. The only circumstance in

---

19 (2006) 27 *ILJ* 871 (BCA).
20 [1999] 11 BLLR 1327 (IMSSA).

which such an offence could be condoned, was when the employee had a dependency problem. The employee in the abovementioned case had not pleaded that he had such a problem at the time. He had been aware of the rule that he had broken and of the potential consequences of his action. The arbitrator accordingly upheld the dismissal as justified and fair in the circumstances.

6.2 Incapacity

Drug and alcohol abuse that results in an inability to perform the work which the employee is employed to do would be a valid reason for an incapacity dismissal, provided it is done in compliance with the LRA. The code regulating fair dismissals requires an arbitrator determining the fairness of an incapacity dismissal to determine:[21]

    (a) whether or not the employee is capable of performing the work;

    (b) if the employee is not capable–

        (i) the extent to which the employee is able to perform the work;

        (ii) the extent to which the employee's work circumstances might be adapted to accommodate the disability, or, where this is not possible, the extent to which the employee's duties might be adapted; and

        (iii) the availability of any suitable alternative work.

The cause of the incapacity is also relevant to the fairness of the dismissal. The Code requires that for certain kinds of incapacity, for example alcoholism or drug abuse, counselling and rehabilitation may be appropriate steps for an employer to consider.

In addition, the Disability Code[22] also contains specific guidelines for rehabilitation and reasonable accommodation. This Code applies to all employees with clinically recognised 'impairments' that are regarded as 'substantially limiting', but excludes, among others, disorders relating to drug or alcohol abuse (unless the employee is undergoing a recognised treatment programme).[23]

---

21 At para 11 of the Code.

22 LRA Code of Good Practice: Key Aspects on the Employment of People with Disabilities (2003) *Gazette* 23702 of 19 August 2002.

23 The code contains the following definition of disability:

    '(i) An impairment may either be physical or mental or a combination of both.

    (ii) "Physical" impairment means a partial loss of a bodily function or part of the body. It includes sensory impairment such as being deaf, hearing impaired or visually impaired.

    (iii) "Mental" impairment means a clinically recognised condition or illness that affects a person's thought processes, judgment or emotions.'

  The code reiterates the approach of the Employment Equity Act in that impairment must be of a physical or mental nature. This emulates the medical definition used for example by the World Health Organization (WHO) which defines impairment as 'any loss or abnormality of a psychological, physical or anatomical function'. Substance abuse would fall within the definition. However, paragraph 5.1.3 (iv) excludes, for public policy considerations, certain conditions or impairments from the definition of disabilities. These include but are not limited to:

    (a) sexual behaviour disorders that are against public policy,

    (b) self-imposed body adornments such as tattoos and body piercing,

    (c) compulsive gambling, tendency to steal or light fires,

    (d) disorders that affect a person's mental and physical state if they are caused by current use of illegal drugs or alcohol, unless a person affected is participating in a recognised programme of treatment,

    (e) normal deviations in height and strength; and conventional physical and mental characteristics and common personality traits.'

6.2.1 When is alcohol use an incapacity?

In *Mahlangu v Minister of Sport & Recreation*[24] the employee was deemed to have discharged himself from the service of his employer in terms of the public sector legislation, after an absence of more than 30 days from work. After he made representations to the effect that he was an alcoholic, the employer arranged for him to be rehabilitated and for a medical investigation into his condition to be conducted. Thereafter he was invited to attend an evaluation of his application for reinstatement. At the evaluation, the medical doctor appointed to evaluate his health recommended that he should be sent to a rehabilitation centre at government expense, which he could be required to repay later. He stated: 'If successfully rehabilitated, all the physical complications he has will improve and even disappear. His psychological problems will also ease considerably. He will also be able to resume his duties without problems.'

The Minister, applying his mind to the report, nevertheless confirmed the decision to dismiss the employee, and his decision was upheld by the Labour Court on a technical point. In his judgment, Molahlehi J held

> It is an established approach of our law that a distinction should be drawn between a case of a person abusing alcohol and that of one who is an alcoholic. In the case of alcohol abuse such conduct in general is regarded as misconduct and depending on the circumstances of a given case the employment relationship may be terminated for that reason. An alcoholic person is regarded as being ill and therefore his or her employment can be terminated on the basis of incapacity due to ill health. Different considerations apply in terminating employment due to misconduct and incapacity due to ill health. Termination for misconduct has to do with the fault of the employee whilst termination for incapacity is based on the principle of no fault on the part of the employee.

In *Reckitt & Colman SA (Pty) Limited v CCMA & others*,[25] the employee's dismissal on the grounds of incapacity was held to be justified. He was constantly ill and absent from work, which the employer found out was due to alcohol use. He received counselling and medical treatment for this condition and was informed that the excessive sick leave he was taking had brought about an intolerable situation. If it continued his employment would be terminated. There was a temporary improvement, but he then lapsed into his old ways. The employer attempted to accommodate him over an extended period of time, and eventually terminated his services. The dispute came before an arbitrator who rendered an award in favour of the employee. The basis of the award was that he was dismissed for incapacity arising from ill-health. The arbitrator concluded that the employer did not follow the Code of Good Practice and did not investigate possible alternatives short of dismissal, and whether or not the employee was capable of performing the work. However the Labour Court, in a review of the decision, found that in the light of all the evidence, the arbitrator had come to the conclusion that the employer had tried to do all that was possible in the circumstances. Although this case was viewed by the arbitrator as one relating to incapacity, it could just as well have been a case of misconduct. He should therefore have, on the material before him,

24 (2010) 31 *ILJ* 1907 (LC).
25 [2001] ZALC 163.

concluded that the necessary steps were taken by the employer and were justified in the circumstances.

Where an employer is to some extent responsible for creating the situation, there is more of an obligation to treat the conduct as incapacity and to assist the employee. In *Esau & Another v Wynland Boerdery Belange (Pty) Ltd t/a Zetler Bros*[26] it was noted that where an employee is dismissed for being drunk on duty in the agricultural sector, the court will investigate the extent to which the employer encourages and promotes the misuse of alcohol and whether it still makes use of the 'dop' system on its farm. This is a system based on remunerating employees in the form of alcohol which is still prevalent in some rural agricultural areas. The employer must take into account the possibility of rehabilitation of an employee when determining the appropriate sanction for alcohol abuse. This is especially so where the employer shares responsibility for the employee's alcohol addiction.

Eskom and National Union of Mineworkers obo Fillisen[27] was another example of the empathetic approach taken in a private arbitration which advocated the incapacity dismissal.

Incapacity dismissals are 'no fault' terminations of employment. Since the employee is not at fault, these dismissals require a special procedure to be followed. In a leading English law case (*Lynock v Cereal Packaging Ltd*)[28] the tribunal stated that 'the approach of the employer is ... to be based on ... sympathy, understanding and compassion'. One has to look at the 'whole history and the whole picture'. And further, the employer must make clear to the employee the position after a full enquiry and investigation, 'so that the employee realizes that the point of no return, the moment of the decision' has arrived, and that dismissal is now imminent unless there are other alternatives.

The test which is to be applied is as follows:
- The employer is obliged to ascertain the capability of the employee to perform the work for which he or she was employed.
- If unable to do so, the extent to which the employee can perform functions.
- If so, whether the duties can be adapted.
- If not, whether an alternative post can accommodate the employee.

The process to be followed is not of a disciplinary nature, but is more an all-encompassing enquiry, including counselling and medical assessment. There are essentially two parts to the enquiry: a medical examination to ascertain the correct prognosis, and an internal enquiry into the possible alternative placement or dismissal of the employee.

It is clear that the procedural and substantive guidelines for a dismissal based on misconduct are quite different from those for a dismissal based on incapacity due to ill health. So it is important to establish whether intoxication at work should be dealt with as misconduct or as a possible ground for dismissal based on incapacity due to ill health. These questions were addressed in a recent arbitration matter at the Commission for Conciliation, Mediation and Arbitration ('the CCMA'), in *Naik v Telkom SA*.[29]

---

26 (1995) 16 *ILJ* 237 (ALC).
27 (2002) 23 *ILJ* 1666 (ARB).
28 (1988) IRLR 510.
29 (2001) 21 *ILJ* 1266 (CCMA).

The applicant employee was dismissed from his employment on 9 July 1999 for being under the influence of alcohol whilst on duty'. The applicant had 17 years' service with his employer, had been a heavy drinker for years but had no alcohol-related problems at work until he was appointed to an administrative position. He had voluntarily undergone rehabilitation until his dismissal following an incident of violence and later being found intoxicated and passed out in his car when he was supposed to be attending an important meeting.

The arbitrator emphasised that alcoholism should be treated as an illness in the employment context, to be dealt with like other species of incapacity.

In distinction to the sanction of dismissal which may be applied in misconduct matters even if suitable alternative positions are available that remove, for example, a thieving employee from access to money, the 'no-fault' basis of incapacity hearings imposes upon employers an obligation to attempt to accommodate ill or disabled employees. An alcoholic ought to be afforded the same consideration before dismissal as any other ill employee.

The commissioner accepted that some conduct in the workplace involving the use of alcohol could correctly be described as misconduct, but reiterated that misconduct and incapacity should not be confused, and that alcohol abuse was a species of incapacity.

The employer's disciplinary code which defined the state of being 'incapable of performing duties whilst under the influence of alcohol' as an offence attracting progressive discipline, was held to be inapplicable. The arbitrator held that:

the employee was dependent on alcohol and his being incapable of working on the day in question was a symptom of physical and psychological dependence. While it was appropriate to discipline non-alcoholics, or even, arguably, alcoholics who acted dishonestly in attempting to drink at work, it was not appropriate to deal with the employee's conduct under the rubric of discipline.

When considering how to deal with incapacity due to alcoholism, the commissioner said that:

thought must be given to the nature of the job; the extent to which the illness incapacitated the employee; the length of time that the employee would have to be away from work to rehabilitate; and the possibility of securing a temporary replacement. Before dismissal could be effected the extent of the disability suffered as well as to the availability of alternative work must be considered.

The commissioner found that the employer 'probably had sufficient cause to want the employee out of his administrative position' but was not satisfied that it had sufficient cause to dismiss him, 'especially if there was the possibility of assigning him alternative work, even at a lower grade, where the consequences of a relapse would be less keenly felt'. The arbitrator took into account that, 'although a problem drinker for years, the employee had only actually caused problems at work on two occasions since he began rehabilitation. Furthermore, he had submitted to treatment for his alcohol dependence and was still in treatment'. The employer was ordered to reinstate him with a strong recommendation that the parties enter into consultations regarding a suitable alternative position for the employee.

6.2.2 Impossibility of performance

In *United Association of SA on behalf of Fortuin and Golden Arrow Bus Services (Pty) Ltd*[30] the employee, a diesel mechanic, had as a contractual term, that he should hold a professional driving permit.

> He obtained a licence in January 2001, but when it expired in 2003 he was advised that it could not be renewed because he had a previous conviction for drunken driving and that he had to wait until May 2004 before reapplying. He advised his employer accordingly. He was not aware that in terms of the relevant regulations he could apply to the local Member of the Executive Council (MEC) for Transport to reconsider his application. At a number of meetings the employer stressed to the applicant that it was essential for him to obtain a valid licence. In August 2003 his employment was terminated for incapacity. He challenged the fairness of his dismissal.
>
> The arbitrator noted that the LRA did not define incapacity but that it had been described as 'a species of supervening impossibility of performance'. The arbitrator was not persuaded that the employer's conduct was reasonable or that dismissal was the appropriate sanction. While accepting that the onus was on employees to renew their licences, the employer could have done more to assist the employee to refer his application to the MEC for a decision. The employer was aware that this option was available to the employee but did not mention it. This was not justifiable. The appropriate sanction was suspension without pay for a reasonable period to enable him to attempt to obtain a licence. The dismissal was found to be substantively unfair. The employer was ordered to reinstate the employee, with no backpay and without pay, to give him a reasonable opportunity to obtain his licence, and to pay the usual costs borne by the employer in assisting employees in this respect.

In another arbitration, the empathy with which alcoholism at work is viewed, was again manifest. Where a security guard was dismissed for incapacity in the form of impossibility of performance following a complaint from a client that he was under the influence of alcohol whilst on duty, the employer's decision to dismiss was set aside as substantively and procedurally unfair on the grounds that it could not be said that he was incapable of performing his duties at another client: *Zondi and PPM Security Services* (Pty) Ltd.[31]

6.2.3 Reasonable accommodation

The employer's duty to assist the employee and accommodate his needs was described in *Jansen and Pressure Concepts*.[32]

The arbitrator in considering whether dismissal was an appropriate sanction for the employee's poor time-keeping which he explained was due to an alcohol-related problem, found that the employer had a duty to manage the disciplining of the

---

30 (2004) 25 *ILJ* 1142 (BCA).
31 (2009) 30 *ILJ* 981 (CCMA).
32 (2005) 26 *ILJ* 2064 (BCA).

employee on the basis of incapacity. Proper consideration had not been given to this problem, and the employer had failed in its duty of accommodation in the light of the employee's alcohol problem.

The arbitrator held that:

> however slight the duty on the employer was, however, the employer certainly had a duty to at least give due weight and consideration to the problem, and to make some attempt, however small, to assist the employee. The employer can be expected to have attempted to seek out and provide some form of counselling for the applicant, once it had been made aware that his problem was alcohol-related.

The arbitrator found that although the applicant was not faultless, the employer made three serious errors:

- it failed to apply the important principle of progressive discipline;
- it failed to apply workplace rules consistently; and
- it failed in its duty of accommodation in light of the applicant's alcohol problem.

The issue of the extent to which the employer is expected to provide support arose in *Portnet (Cape Town) and SA Transport & Allied Workers Union on behalf of Lesch.*[33]

> The employee pleaded guilty to charges of serious misconduct, namely being under the influence of alcohol while on duty and verbally abusing his supervisor and was dismissed. It was common cause that both the company and the union had been aware of the employee's alcoholism. ...Company representatives offered help to the employee on numerous occasions over a long period and still he continued to deny the extent of his problems. The employee was well aware of the rule prohibiting working under the influence of alcohol and the intrinsic consequences for his fellow workers. The arbitrator was of the view that, when a person had received numerous warnings regarding his conduct and continued to flout the rules knowingly in the way that the employee had done, the dismissal was justified. Here considerations of incapacity were clearly distinguishable and irrelevant because of the facts. Incapacity procedures would not have had any utility because of the employee's disposition. The arbitrator therefore regarded the company as having done all that it reasonably could to assist the employee and found that the dismissal was justified in terms of the employee's misconduct.

In considering the appropriateness of the sanction, the arbitrator disagreed with the union that the company had assisted the employee to become more alcohol friendly or that it had sent out the wrong signal that his conduct was acceptable.

SUMMARY

The employer must have a clear policy on the possession and use of alcohol and drugs at work. It must have a clear policy on being at work under the influence of drugs or alcohol. The employer will have to prove intoxication if it wishes to discipline

---

33 (2002) 23 *ILJ* 1675 (ARB).

employees for being impaired at work. The courts and arbitrators have held that this requires subjective confirmation, although, in our view, the objective tests, properly done, are much more reliable. The subjective observations should lead to the objective confirmation rather than vice-versa.

The discipline must be appropriate to the situation, depending on all the relevant factors:

- the length of service of the employee,
- past misconduct,
- previous discipline,
- the nature of the work,
- the circumstances of the employee.

The nature of the employee's occupation is an important consideration. If the employee's work is of a safety-sensitive nature, any intoxication at work will necessarily be serious misconduct.

If the employee's intoxication or alcohol or drug use is the result of an underlying dependence, the employee should be treated as suffering from a disability. In this circumstance, the employee should be given a reasonable opportunity of rehabilitation. If the employee does not co-operate with his or her own rehabilitation, this may give cause to the employer to terminate the employment on grounds of the employee's incapacity to reliably perform the work.

Chapter 15

Treatment of the Organisation

Mike McCann & Nadine Harker Burnhams

1. INTRODUCTION

Treatment has been divided into 5 chapters as this will give emphasis to each of the important aspects of treatment:

- Treatment of the Organisation
- Treatment of the Employee Patient
- The role of the Occupational Health Professional (OHP)
- Workplace Substance Abuse Prevention
- Employee Assistance Programmes.

After this chapter the following four chapters deal with further equally important aspects of treatment within the organisation. Chapter 16 focuses on the treatment of the individual employee who has a drink or drug problem, chapter 17 deals with the Occupational Health Professional's role in assessing, treatment and support, chapter 18 provides information on prevention initiatives and chapter 19 describes the Employee Assistance Programme. All these chapters provide an overall structure for the work environment.

This chapter considers the treatment needed to address the problem of institutionalised substance abuse or where a significant culture of abuse is present in a company.

Before discussing the treatment of the individual employee, consideration must be given to changing the working environment if it encourages or condones alcohol abuse (drug abuse is generally considered unacceptable in most working environments), since collective preventive action is always to be preferred to individual treatment.

Treatment of substance abuse can take several forms. Each form is usually connected to a specific theory of substance abuse (see chapter 1) and each theory has its followers and its critics. In the authors' opinion, all of these theories have value and there is little or nothing to be gained by endorsing one and discrediting the rest. Too often a rigid all-or-nothing approach towards treatment makes it a narrowly conceived fixed entity. Alcohol and drug problems are multifaceted, having more than one cause, and are best described as a continuum with varying degrees of dependence. As far as the workplace is concerned, the broader the definition the more treatable the problem will be.

2. CHANGING WORKPLACE CULTURE

Research has consistently shown that education is not enough to change the behaviour of individuals regarding the use of alcohol and/or drugs. In other words, simply by telling someone that a particular practice is bad for them, and why, is unlikely to get them to change their behaviour. Education remains important, of course, but it needs to be supported by other techniques and approaches. Most importantly, it will be necessary to affect cultural changes in the social and work environments in which people interact and influence one another. Peer pressure and established codes of conduct have a strong bearing on how an individual acts. In terms of the present discussion, this means that individual employees may adopt accepted group and/or organisational practices despite the potential hazards to health that these practices hold. Collective preventative action is always to be preferred to individual treatment.

Motivating employees to discard or modify these practices is therefore essential. However, this cannot be done unless all employees, including management, accept that a problem exists.

3. THE PROCESS FROM ACCEPTANCE TO CHANGE

For a company to accept there is a problem, it has to be able to identify objective criteria which signify that the problem exists. The acceptance of a problem of alcohol abuse goes through various stages and culminates, one would hope, in an attitude change and therefore a cultural change. Resistance to change is a common phenomenon in workplace environments, however, and any number of defence mechanisms may be used to block, rationalise or externalise a problem and thus avoid the need for change.

The process of acceptance to change is called a 'cognitive shift' of perception and it comprises three well-defined stages, namely pre-contemplation, contemplation and action as described previously for the individual employee patient. These three stages should each be followed up by reinforcement and maintenance.[1]

3.1 The pre-contemplation stage

At the pre-contemplation stage information is projected to the group, whether they be managers, union representatives or employees. It is important that the information is direct and factual, objectively stating that a problem exists and the implications for the organisation. The information disseminated in the pre-contemplation stage seeks to confront prejudices and correct misunderstandings surrounding the issue of alcohol use and misuse. It is therefore important that the information relayed is factual, evidence-based and concise and that the material is delivered in an authoritative manner. Internal noise, often referred to as 'psychological noise', often blocks the transmission of ideas and information. Here, 'noise' refers to the preconceived, and often biased or misguided attitudes and thoughts an individual holds on the subject of alcohol abuse and the hazards associated with such abuse.

Care should be taken to restrict the amount of information given at this stage; overloading an audience with facts, figures, advice, and so on, can also be detrimental (important items of information may not be absorbed or may be quickly forgotten, for example). It is unlikely that acceptance will be established at this stage and time will be required for the information to be fully assimilated.

Education should be undertaken in a manner agreed upon between management and the union(s). Preferably the information should be imparted in combined seminars of workers and management and endorsed by union and management leaders in the

---

1   Prochaska, JO & Diclemente, CC 'Transtheoretical therapy: toward a more integrative model of change' (1982) 19 *Psychotherapy: Theory, Research and Practice* 276-288; Bennett, JB, Patterson, CR, Reynolds, GS, Wyndy, MS, Wiitala, WL & Lehman, WEK 'Team Awareness, Problem Drinking, and Drinking Climate: Workplace Social Health Promotion in a Policy Context' (2004) 19 (2) *American Journal of Health Promotion*.

company. The seminar (or meeting, workshop, etc) should be led by an expert in the handling of alcohol and drug abuse.

3.2 The contemplative stage

The contemplative stage requires accessibility to further information, such as that relating to hazards and risks; this is also when questioning of individual and corporate values, corporate culture, organisational climate and practices occurs.[2] Individuals could now be perceptive and open; they may be ready to accept and make the required change in attitude.

Substance abuse policy objectives are formulated during this stage. Risk assessment can be used in the design of these objectives (see chapter 6). If a collective agreement on the issue of substance abuse in the workplace is to be implemented, management and trade union leaders will finalise details of this.

3.3 The action phase

The action phase consists of the implementation of the policy and procedures as well as the appointment of an alcohol and drug counsellor. This phase should be undertaken only once there is agreement between management and the union(s) as to the objectives, the methods for achieving them, and the process of implementation.

4. RESISTANCE TO CHANGE

Employees may resist changing their harmful or potentially harmful drinking or drug use behaviours for several reasons, co-dependency or enablement among them. The two terms are essentially the same (if not synonymous) in that they describe a situation in which the inappropriate drinking or drug use behaviour of an individual is condoned, encouraged, ignored or disguised by family members, friends, co-workers, or others. The co-dependent person (wife, colleague, supervisor, etc) does not question the abuse nor does he or she seek help on behalf of the problem user, which means that the abuse is enabled and allowed to continue.

A company with a hard-line approach to the misuse of alcohol and drugs in the workplace may reinforce co-dependent behaviour in co-workers of alcohol- or drug-dependent employees. In these circumstances the non-abusing employees may adopt whatever measures are needed to protect their colleagues from detection and probable disciplinary action. The inverse is also true: a supportive, tolerant organisational culture vis a vis substance abuse may see a reduction in co-dependent behaviour in its workforce.

While an organisation should do all it can to help its substance-abusing employees; this should not be interpreted to mean that the company in any way condones or approves of such abuse. The fundamental aim of any rehabilitation treatment programme is to eradicate or minimise substance abuse in the workplace. Employees must be made aware that substance abuse is unacceptable in a workplace environment and that the company is committed to its elimination. Since the environment plays a key role in the

---

2   Bennet, J, Patterson, C & Reynolds, G et al 'Team awareness, problem drinking & drinking climate' (2004) *American Journal & Health Promotion*.

development of individual behaviour,[3] the need to shape the workplace environment in the right way is crucial.

5. OVERCOMING RESISTANCE TO CHANGE

The success or failure of a corporate substance abuse programme rests upon the degree of employee commitment invested in it. Senior management and trade union representatives must demonstrate their unequivocal support for the programme; so too the managers and supervisors who will be tasked with implementing the programme in the company's divisions, departments and other units of operation. If this support is not secured it is very difficult to change behaviour throughout the company.

Trade unions and management should be, and should be seen to be, in complete agreement on this issue. A joint management-union response to the problem of substance abuse in the workplace has a much better chance of being accepted by employees and the credibility of the corporate substance abuse programme will be enhanced.

A series of alcohol and drug education packages inform employees of the contents of the substance abuse programme; each package tailored to meet the information requirement needs of a different type of employee (see the following section on education of employees). The education packages should be marketed using whatever communication channels are available. Employees must also be given the opportunity to question the information they receive. This is crucial to the contemplative stage, during which employees reflect on and ask questions about what they have heard or seen.

6. EDUCATING EMPLOYEES ON THE SUBJECT OF SUBSTANCE ABUSE

We introduced this subject in the previous chapter, where we suggested that education on substance abuse had to be differentiated according to the needs of three employee groups:
- management and union leadership (education will focus on the implications of alcohol abuse on personal, group and company performance; formation of alcohol policy; disciplinary procedures, and so on)
- employees (education will focus on safe, unsafe and dangerous drinking; health risks [to self and others]; disciplinary procedures; treatment, and so on)
- supervisors, managers and shop stewards (education will focus on how to implement testing procedures; how to manage intoxicated employees; disciplinary procedures, and so on).

'Most people do not know the full extent of the damage caused by alcohol or drug abuse.' Chapter 7 and appendix 11 (The effects of alcohol on the individual) will help to provide some knowledge of accidents, health and the metabolic interaction of alcohol in the workplace. Chapter 8 and appendix 11 (the effects of drugs on the individual) will provide some knowledge of accidents and health with drug abuse.

---

3   Hershon, H 'The disease concept of alcoholism – a reappraisal' a paper presented at 8th International Conference on Alcoholism (Liverpool, April 1990) quotes Heather, N & Robertson, *I Controlled Drinking* (1981), who discuss Mendelson's experiments done in 1966 and 1972 relating to the environmental factors associated with the response of alcohol abuse. In the operant learning of alcohol abuse the idea is to identify those variables which contribute to (or encourage) the maintenance of abusive drinking.

6.1 Package 1: Educating management and union leadership

This package initiates the education programme and includes a wide range of information on a variety of subjects, all of which are discussed elsewhere in this book. The subjects (cross-referenced to the appropriate chapter(s)) are as follows:
- general education on alcohol and drugs (chapters 1 and 3)
- the extent of the alcohol and drug abuse problem (chapters 2 and 4)
- the effects of alcohol and drug abuse on the individual employee (chapters 7 and 8)
- the problems that alcohol and drugs cause in an organisation—accidents, productivity losses, absence, sickness absence, behaviour (chapters 6 and 9)
- how to identify alcohol and drug problems (chapters 9 and 10)
- how to deal with problems of alcohol and drug abuse—constructive persuasion, rehabilitation, post-treatment detoxification, and so on (chapters 15, 16 and 17)
- the role of the occupational health professional (chapter 17)
- organisational risk assessment in respect of alcohol and drug use (chapter 6).

6.2 Package 2: Educating employees

New employees and apprentices are particularly vulnerable to modelling their behaviour on existing employees.

The second package should occur in conjunction with the negotiation and conclusion of the substance abuse policy and procedures. The package should deal with the following topics:
- the alcohol content of different drinks; the recommended limits for maintaining good health
- alcohol metabolism—how the body breaks down alcohol; how alcohol accumulates in the body; how the effects of alcohol can last for many hours
- the impact of tolerance—what tolerance to alcohol means; how tolerance levels vary from person to person; how a high tolerance level can lead to dependence
- recommended drinking habits—drinking with meals, avoiding drinking alone, drinking slowly, not drinking while at work, and so on
- the problems that alcohol may cause in an organisation—accidents, productivity losses, absence, sickness absence, behaviour (as in the first education package)
- the effects of alcohol abuse on the family and community; how to help a family member who is alcohol-dependent
- the implications of on-the-job drinking; what help is available for co-workers
- the education of new employees and apprentices on the dangers of alcohol abuse—modelling of inappropriate behaviour is likely if they perceive substance abuse to be an acceptable element of organisational culture
- reasons for the introduction of the alcohol abuse policy; policy principles; how the policy will be implemented; details of the employee assistance programme (EAP); description of treatment(s) available; disciplinary measures and processes (see chapter 19).

Education on the hazards associated with drug abuse will deal with the same or very similar issues. However, the section on drugs should also make it clear that the use of any drug in South Africa is considered illegal and is therefore punishable by law. While the use of alcohol may be considered safe in some circumstances; the same cannot be said of drugs.

6.3 Package 3: Educating managers, supervisors and shop stewards

The third education package provides information on how to handle employees with an alcohol or drug problem. The package should explain how an employee assistance programme (EAP) functions and what its purpose is (see chapter 19).

Managers, supervisors and shop stewards also need to know the correct procedure to follow should an inquiry into suspected alcohol or drug misuse be necessary. Strict protocols apply to the testing of employees for alcohol or drug use and these must be adhered to at all times.

7. AUDIT OF THE PROBLEM, POSSIBLE CAUSES AND SOME SOLUTIONS

For the audit of the extent of the problem, see chapters 2, 4, 5 and 6 for background information and 9 and 10 for specific information on identification of alcohol and drug problems.[4]

As alcohol is most likely to be the main problem and is the socially and legally acceptable drug, the audit should include a consideration of the alcohol-promoting practices found in the company. A corporate culture that encourages employees to abuse alcohol will exacerbate any co-dependency problems that already exist. Changing the drinking culture of a company presents a huge challenge, especially if this culture is embedded at a structural level. However, there are ways in which positive change can be effected and these include the following:

- **Review the availability and accessibility of alcohol on the premises**
For example, suppose that a company has an on-site bar for employees, a senior management hospitality bar and a licensed staff canteen. In such an 'alcohol-friendly' environment some employees may be tempted, or indeed tacitly encouraged, to engage in harmful (excessive) drinking.

- **Provision of low- or non-alcoholic drinks**
A complete prohibition of on-site drinking may not be possible, and even if it is, it will almost certainly have to be phased in gradually. In both situations, the introduction of low- or non-alcoholic drinks would be advantageous (to employees and to the company); especially if these drinks are marketed effectively (low calorific value, affordability, and so on).

- **Review the availability of alcohol at corporate functions**
Corporate hospitality is an established practice in most industries and generally accepted as 'money well spent' by the host company. The potential financial gains to be made from treating clients, customers and suppliers to a fine dining experience are not to be underestimated. Too often, however, the 'dining' element of the event is neglected in favour of buying large (and often excessive) quantities of alcohol.

- **Implement an intensive advertising campaign**
The extent to which an intensive advertising campaign will affect drinking patterns should be assessed, particularly one which emphasises the negative aspects and antisocial dimension of alcohol abuse and fosters the positive advantages of responsible

---

4   Note that the audit occurs during the pre-contemplative stage.

drinking. The campaign could include the use of videos, posters, newsletters, and statements from senior management and trade union members.

- **Improve workplace practices concerning alcohol abuse**

This includes improving supervision in jobs and/or work areas where there is poor supervision; identifying jobs/work areas where alcohol abuse is likely to develop and taking corrective action; avoiding the placement of previously alcohol-dependent individuals in high-risk positions through the use of screening procedures; identifying underlying problems in the workplace that can lead to stress (frustration, job dissatisfaction, anger, resentment, etc) and addressing these problems.

- **Inconsistency or inconsistencies in the handling of alcohol and drug problems**

Inconsistencies breed doubt among employees regarding the true meaning and value of the programme. These inconsistencies should be reviewed and recommendations for their removal made.

It is worth mentioning at this juncture that the company should not be considered in isolation from the surrounding community. Alcohol and drug dependency is not confined to the workplace; it is a social problem that requires the involvement of all community members. Community leaders, doctors, nurses, social workers, and other health professionals need to be provided with details of the corporate alcohol and drug programme, which they can use to raise community awareness of the dangers of substance abuse. Civic leaders can use the programme information to put forward or support plans for the development of recreational and cultural activities that provide a healthy alternative to the harmful practice of excessive drink or drug use, such as youth clubs, craft centres, IT workshops and literacy groups.

In summary, the total programme should contain a nine-point plan of action:

- An alcohol and drug education programme for management and union leadership (first education package) needs to be developed. Preconceived ideas are ironed out and consistencies of knowledge are developed on the subject. The different methods of identification are introduced. A risk assessment of the impact on the organisation is planned.
- An audit of the extent of the problem in the company should be carried out and presented to the management and union leadership. Employees, or their trade union representatives, must be consulted regarding the purpose, form and scope of the audit.

The two points above can be referred to as the pre-contemplative stage.

- Alcohol and drug policy objectives must be formulated by management and the union(s). These objectives form the basis for further management-union negotiations on the correct procedure(s) for handling alcohol and drug abuse and dependence (see next point below).
- A procedural agreement to deal with alcohol and drug abuse and dependence in the company should be negotiated.
- An education programme for employees (including management) should be presented (second education package). This programme provides details of the new alcohol and drug policy as well as general information on alcohol and drug misuse. This programme needs to start at least four weeks prior to the implementation of any new procedures and rules. The information campaign should comprise

(a) intensive in-house advertising consisting of video advertisements, posters, notices at the gate and letters in pay packets, and

(b) general seminars or meetings addressed by experts and members of management and the union(s).

- An education programme for supervisors, managers and shop stewards on how to handle employees with an alcohol or drug problem should be initiated (third education package).
- A part-time or full-time counsellor should be employed or contracted in and an employee assistance programme (EAP) implemented.
- The procedures for dealing with alcohol or drug abuse and dependence should be implemented.
- Alternative recreational and cultural activities should be encouraged and developed and local community leaders, doctors and community nurses should be educated about the programme to help develop community awareness.

8. THE USE OF DISCIPLINARY MEASURES TO ADDRESS PROBLEMS OF SUBSTANCE ABUSE

Discipline is a quick, effective way of stamping out unacceptable behaviour.[5] Problem drinkers will usually avoid coming to work intoxicated if the prospect of disciplinary action is present. However, in chapters 2 and 10 we noted the impact of random breathalysing on employees reporting for work at a factory. The introduction of random testing produced a relatively quick response in the form of a change in employee behaviour but as is shown this effective and fast response to limit alcohol abuse at work does need to be linked to a positive campaign of education and the corporate reasons for the Alcohol and Drug Policy and programme. Without it the immediate results probably mask the real situation.

Figure 15.1 describes the number of cases of employees reporting late for work (LFW) and of those recorded as absent without leave (AWOL) before and after the introduction of random breath tests. The graph shows a dramatic decline in the number of LFW incidents on the introduction of testing, yet a sudden increase in AWOL incidents followed by a drop to pre-testing levels within six months.

These findings suggest that random breathalysing of employees is not in itself sufficient to eliminate alcohol abuse, although it may curtail it during working hours. A reduction in the number of employees reporting for work in an intoxicated condition is clearly a step in the right direction. However, when we consider that this improvement came about as a result of *negative* reinforcement (in simple terms, 'Employees reporting for work in an intoxicated condition will be disciplined'), the picture becomes clearer. Because the factory workers knew they risked disciplinary action if they arrived at work drunk, they made sure that they were not intoxicated *at the time they reported for duty.* In other words, employees only moderated their alcohol consumption when negative reinforcement of their inappropriate behaviour (in the form of disciplinary action) was a threat. The fact that *more* employees were reported as being AWOL following the introduction of random testing suggests that the actual level of alcohol abuse post-testing was the same as, or close to, the pre-testing level. For both LFW and AWOL

---

5   McCann, MG *The effect and Impact of breath analysis in a workplace and the development of indicators to identify employees at risk of alcohol abuse* (MDThesis, Trinity College Dublin 1999) chapter 7, 90-97).

employees, the need to avoid detection and disciplinary action conditioned their response. Random breathalysing of employees who are starting work can therefore be considered negative (inhibitory) reinforcement of the conditioned responses of alcohol abuse. Conditioning due to avoidance is a powerful form of reinforcement and does not easily disappear.[6] Furthermore, people often feel hostile towards discipline because it nurtures anxiety.[7] To minimise a hostile reaction, it is therefore imperative to link the reinforcement programme of breathalysing with the education campaign to instruct and explain why the company is promoting the alcohol and drug policy and programme. It is considered more advantageous to promote the positive aspects of responsible drinking as well as the negative aspects of alcohol abuse.

These findings suggest that positive reinforcement, that is, the promotion of the benefits of responsible drinking, has an important role to play. Positive reinforcement can take many forms. By selecting respected achievers in a company, management could emphasise the association of success and respect with responsible drinking. This can be a powerful message, particularly in an in-house advertisement video. A similar or even stronger impact could be achieved if an ex-problem drinker but now successful employee features in the advertising campaign.

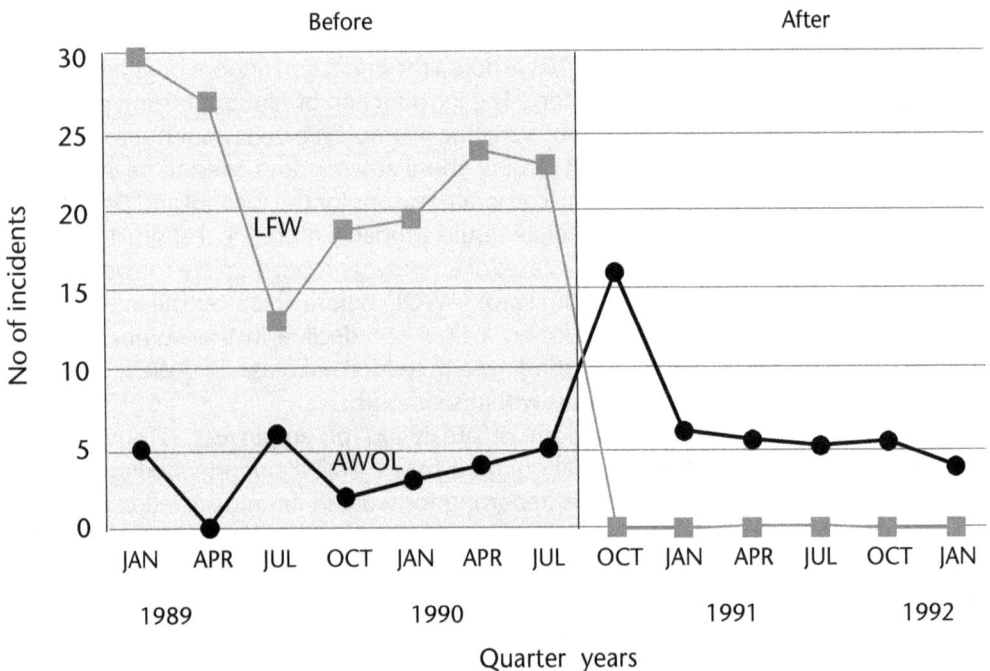

Figure 15.1 Comparison of late for work (LFW) and absent without leave (AWOL) before and after breathalysing was instituted (employees only).[8]

---

6   McKenna,EF 'Learning and memory', in *Psychology in Business* (1987) 171.
7   McCann, MG 'The effect and impact of breath analysis in a workplace and the development of indicators to identify employees at risk of alcohol abuse' (Trinity College Dublin MDThesis, 1999) chapter 7, 90-97.
8   McCann (n 6).

SUMMARY

Before addressing the treatment of the individual employee, we should look at the treatment of the company. Serious consideration should be given to changing the culture of the working environment if it encourages or condones alcohol or drug abuse. Education is not enough to change behaviour: a change in attitude must also occur. This can be blocked by prejudice or self-interest.

The working environment exerts a powerful influence on the learning process and the ability to bring about change. Resistance to change can take several forms.

Alcohol and drug education should be divided into three packages: (i) education of management and union leadership, (ii) education of employees and (iii) education of supervisors, managers and shop stewards.

A nine-point plan of action is indicated for the total programme:
1. education of management and union leadership
2. audit of extent of substance abuse problem in company
3. alcohol and drug policy objectives formulated
4. alcohol and drug procedural agreement formulated
5. education of employees
6. education of supervisors, managers and shop stewards
7. counsellor employed or contracted in; EAP implemented
8. alcohol and drug procedures implemented
9. alternative recreational and cultural activities developed; involvement of community leaders, doctors, nurses, social workers and other health professionals.

Chapter 16

Treatment: The Employee Patient

Mike McCann & Nadine Harker Burnhams

This chapter sets out the theoretical approach of why and how treatments should be provided whilst the chapter on the role of the occupational health professional (OHP) provides a practical approach to treatment. To understand the process of treatment, both chapters should be read, as the two chapters complement each other. This chapter should be read to provide an in-depth understanding. However if time is of the essence then go straight to the chapter on the role of the occupational health professional. (see chapter 17). It must be remembered that the psychiatrist, specialist in addiction treatment is the ideal person to address the assessment and treatment of someone who is dependant. Unfortunately experienced and capable psychiatric addiction specialists are few and far between and it would be in the interests of the employee patient if the OHP has some knowledge of the treatments available so as to influence or advise the GP on the treatment plan. In some rural areas the OHP may also be the GP and any practical possibility of referral to an addiction specialist is remote.

1. INTRODUCTION

Treating employees for alcohol or drug abuse presents a great many challenges. As we discovered in the previous chapter, the occupational health professional (OHP) must try to satisfy both employees and management; and to do so despite the obvious dissimilarities between the sets of needs of the two groups. An OHP must try to determine the correct form of intervention needed; a difficult task given that the employee may be in denial, there may be trade union resistance to some forms of testing, and the OHP may not be able to provide an accurate diagnosis. The fact that no two employees are alike further complicates matters, since the OHP is required to develop a new, unique treatment programme for each employee-patient he or she meets. The decision of what type of treatment is required may be the decision of the OHP or other health care worker who is trained to do alcohol or drug assessments. Some form of knowledge of what is required in an individual case is of value for the OHP to ensure there is all reasonable possibility for effective and cost efficient treatment.

Despite these difficulties the OHP is still required to help at-risk employees to the best of his or her ability. In this chapter we will look at how this can be achieved. We will discuss the stages in the rehabilitation process and the range of available treatments.

However, we first need to outline a few basic principles of treatment that apply in all cases of actual or suspected alcohol or drug misuse.[1] These are set out in the next section.

2. PRINCIPLES OF TREATMENT

It is a myth that an abuser must hit rock bottom to accept that they have a problem. The point of insight occurs at different stages of alcohol and drug abuse and varies from person to person.

A fundamental principle of treatment is to develop a cognitive shift of perception. There are three stages of perceptual shift that lead to acceptance: the precontemplative stage, the contemplative stage, and the action stage. In the precontemplative stage there is little change in the perceived reality, but information is being assimilated. In the contemplative stage the cognitive shift of perception or understanding occurs and culminates in action (the third and final stage), which is acceptance of the treatment.[2]

There are four main features of treatment. These are listed below in order of use with subsections.

Assessment

- Rationalisation or denial
- Questionnaires
- The point of insight into the problem
- The Alcohol History
- Alcohol Dependence Syndrome
- General Medical History
- Medical Examination and Tests
- Identifying Treatment Requirements
- Assessment and Treatment of the Senior Manager or Executive

Detoxification

- Pharmaceutical Treatment of Detoxification

Treatment

- Constuctive Persuasion
- Rehabilitation Facilities
- Pharmaceutical treatment after detoxification
- Role of counselling and Psychotherapy
  - Education
  - Counselling
    - Individual Counselling
    - Group Counselling
    - Self help Groups

---

1   Note that in this chapter the focus is again on problems of *alcohol* abuse in the workplace. The reasons for adopting this approach have been outlined in other chapters (see for example p1 of chapter 17).

2   Prochaska, JO & Diclemente, CC 'The transtheoretical approach: crossing traditional boundaries of therapy' (1990) 83 *J Royal Soc Medicine* 232-236.

- Family Counselling
- Reinforcement Counselling.

Monitoring and maintenance

- objective tests
- inquiry into relapses.

2.1 Assessment

Whether the employee is referred by management or he or she has come voluntarily, it is important to assess the patient judiciously. This first meeting should be handled carefully as it will set the tone for future interactions and can really be considered the first stage of treatment and counselling. If the employee has been referred by management, an unbiased assessment must be made to ensure that alcohol abuse is the true cause of the problem. Perhaps assumptions have been made and the reality is that another problem, or even no problem, exists. The employee could have been coerced into a heavy drinking bout by social and peer-group pressures in unusual circumstances, such as a stag or bulls party. Perhaps there was a significant celebration that got out of hand. This would be particularly true of younger employees. Excessive alcohol consumption is hazardous but instituting a complete ban on alcohol is inadvisable; a prohibition policy is generally unenforceable and will therefore be ridiculed by drinkers.

2.1.1 Rationalisation or denial

During the assessment, a detailed history needs to be obtained. This should be performed in a sensitive, empathetic manner; adopting a moralistic or judgemental attitude or tone will derail the process. Implicit criticism will only heighten the rationalisation or denial that is almost always present in the dependent drinker. Rationalisation will occur in both the volunteer and the coerced dependent drinker, and either may attempt to explain or justify his excessive drinking. This could include 'projecting': the employee blames other people, situations or circumstances for the onset of the problem and claims that if these factors had not existed then the abuse would never have arisen in the first place. There might be an element of truth in this statement, but it is also an inappropriate coping mechanism for a stressful situation and can at best be considered a predependent state. Denial manifests itself either in the belief that an alcohol-abuse problem does not exist (`I can stop if I want to') or by the person not admitting the true extent of the quantities being drunk. It is the main problem to combat in treatment and focusing on it is a prerequisite for moving forward.

2.1.2 Questionnaires

As mentioned in chapter 10, using questionnaires in the workplace has several disadvantages. It is interesting to compare the original drinking history of a patient prior to treatment with the same history recounted six months later, after treatment has been successfully proceeding. The true extent of the patient's substance problem is to be found in the later history after treatment has been successful, since the patient invariably needs time to accept the truth regarding his or her level of consumption. However, questionnaires come to the fore when used in a confidential setting either for treatment or through an Occupational Health assessment. If the employee works for an organisation that has a sound substance abuse policy and if he or she trusts the support that is available, then a more honest response is likely, as long as denial is not a factor.

2.1.3 The point of insight to the problem

To repeat what we said a little earlier: it is a myth that a drinker has to reach rock bottom before being able to accept that they have a drink problem. Like all myths, this one has no factual basis. Rather, it is a matter of reaching 'the point of insight', which can occur at different levels in different people. Most researchers agree that there is no true volunteer. Usually, some pressure or crisis has brought the employee-patient to seek treatment and counselling.[3] The employee could be experiencing financial or relationship problems, for example.

Alternatively, an employee facing a charge of drunk driving or alcohol-related abuse may seek treatment in the hope that the Courts will view this voluntary action as a mitigating factor. Likewise in the workplace the intoxicated employee could face dismissal but often this threat is identified only via a management referral to Occupational Health. They still could be seeking an opportunity for clemency and the question is whether this is a true acknowledgement of a problem of abuse. Management will need to consider this very carefully. Alcohol abuse sometimes co-exists with some form of psychiatric disorder, such as depression, bipolar disorder, schizophrenia or psychotic behaviour. The possibility of there being a dual pathology is something that the assessor should take into account when investigating cases of substance dependency or addiction.

2.1.4 Substance abuse history

The history should detail the quantities and types of substance consumed daily and over a weekend (or on a day off work for shift workers), taking into account the rules of the 'unit' (see chapter 1 above) as this is where rationalisation as a defence mechanism most frequently occurs.

Rationalisation can involve the employee giving vague answers to straightforward questions in an attempt to avoid confronting his or her problem. For example, when the OHP asks the employee 'How much did you drink last night?' he or she may reply `I had a couple of whiskies' or `I had a couple of beers'. These answers are too imprecise to be helpful. Specific details should be sought. The reason for this is that the definition of `a beer' or `a whisky' is open to interpretation. One person could take 'two whiskies' to mean two glasses of neat whisky; another person that it refers to two glasses of diluted whisky. Likewise, person A may consider 'two beers' to mean two quarts (1,5 l) and person B that it means two 'dumpies' (680 ml).

In respect of alcohol, the patient cannot or does not want to remember how much was drunk, so questioning them about the times of day when drinking occurs and for how long will help with this estimate. Information about where the drinking takes place gives an insight into the context of the patient's drinking behaviour or of any possible underlying problems. A gregarious person, for example, will do most of his or her drinking in the company of others in the pub, club or shebeen, while an introverted or depressed individual will often drink alone at home. A drinking history should include the age at which the person started to drink and when the heavy drinking started, and for what reasons.

---

3   Jensen, K 'Why does an alcohol abuser seek treatment?' in *A Danish Approach to the Treatment of Alcoholism* (1983) section 4.

2.1.5 Alcohol or substance dependence syndrome

Knowing the seven criteria for the alcohol dependence syndrome (as described in chapter 1) should guide the questions. The seven criteria are:

1. Narrowing of repertoire
2. Drinking or substance use becoming of prime importance
3. An increased tolerance developing
4. Repeated withdrawals occurring
5. Relieving withdrawals by further drinking
6. Subjective awareness of a compulsion to use/drink
7. Reinstatement after abstinence.[4] (A note should also be made of the periods of abstinence and for how long they lasted.)

2.1.6 General medical history

For a detailed description of the medical history with symptoms and signs relating to alcohol problems please see Appendix 11—Table of History, Signs and Diseases of Alcohol and Drugs relating to Alcohol Problems. A general medical history should be taken, including a family history, childhood history and medical illness history.[5]

Emphasis should also be placed on the number, type, and time and date of previous accidents. An employee's workplace personnel history, particularly relating to absence from work or previous disciplinary circumstances should be included.

2.1.7 The medical examination and tests

The next part of the assessment involves the medical examination and tests. The medical examination must seek to identify the criteria discussed in the earlier chapters on health related problems (chapters 7 and 8) and testing (chapter 10) and Role of Occupational Health Professional (chapter 17). Put together, the history and the test results should provide a picture of the overall problem, the extent of the drinking, the possible underlying behavioural problems and the degree of abuse or dependency, if present.

In summary, the assessment must be both sensitive and empathetic, thorough and objective. It is, in reality, the first stage of counselling; if assessment is handled incorrectly it can undermine the effectiveness of the entire substance abuse rehabilitation programme.

2.1.8 Identifying the treatment requirements

Treatment must not be narrowly construed; an eclectic approach is required.

The assessment fulfils the requirement of identifying the extent of the individual problem and its possible causes. It should also be able to provide indicators of where the emphasis should be placed in treatment. The eclectic approach to treatment not only gives flexibility but also enables emphasis to be placed on particular issues identified in the assessment. Alcohol and drug problems are multidimensional and the treatment must not be narrowly constructed.[6]

---

4 Edwards, G *The Treatment of Drinking Problems* (1982) 23-44, 224.
5 The relevance of a personal social and medical history is exceptionally well-argued in Edwards (above); a source that the authors strongly recommend.
6 Drummond, DC in Lader, M, Edwards, G & Drummond, DC (eds) *The Nature of Alcohol and Drug Related Problems* (1992) 186.6.

The initial treatment provides the opportunity to try out a number of different remedies and to establish which one (or which combination) best suits the specific needs of the individual patient.

The first and most acute decision which must be made regards detoxification: Will the patient require hospitalisation for detoxification or is out-patient treatment all that is needed? Is detoxification really necessary? These questions are the first and most important ones requiring answers.

Some researchers contend that there is a rule of threes—a third of patients will respond to the initial assessment, acknowledge the health hazards identified and either stop completely or control their drinking thereafter. The self-awareness of this group of patients, coupled with the fact that they are usually in the early stages of abuse, means that they can control their problem relatively easily. Another third of patients who respond to direct counselling sessions, will perhaps suffer the occasional relapse, but will eventually control their drinking behaviour. Both of these groups are unlikely to be fully dependent abusers and can move down the continuum away from the triangle (see chapter 1). The third group will probably need detoxification and possibly in-patient treatment, regular monitoring and reinforcement. Such people will always be at risk of reverting to a pattern of self-abuse through alcohol or drugs.

All employee-patients will need education about alcohol/drugs—the tolerable quantities and strengths of alcohol, the impacts on health, signs of dependence, and so on. With this information they will have a better understanding of their own circumstances.

A re-evaluation of the employee's job may be one of the suggested requirements. This is generally recommended for employees who occupy safety-sensitive positions within an organisation. In these circumstances management must decide whether allowing the employee to return to the identical work situation is an advisable course of action. If such a return is likely to endanger the health and safety of others, the employee's duties and responsibilities will need to be reviewed.

The assessment should be capable of determining whether the emphasis should be on individual therapy or group therapy; whether behavioural or psychoanalytical therapy should be the main thrust. In some cases, and particularly those involving dual pathology, in-depth psychiatric treatment may be required. External pressures, both cultural and social, play a large role in the development of the problem, particularly in individuals with inappropriate or inadequate coping mechanisms. For these patients, behavioural therapy is effective.[7] Patients undergoing behavioural therapy develop the skills needed to cope with social and peer-group pressure and with stress, and cognitive skills for acknowledging, understanding, challenging and modifying their feelings and values. Assertiveness training helps those with inadequate confrontational skills. Relaxation techniques enable others to limit the impact of a stressful job.

Treatment might include transactional analysis, which enables individuals to identify the 'games' that they play with respect to alcohol and their social and work relationships. This method may encourage them to develop adult-adult modes of interacting.[8]

---

7   Lader, M, Edwards, G & Drummond, C *The Nature of Alcohol & Drug-related Problems* (Oxford 1992).

8   Steiner, CM *Games Alcoholics Play* (1971).

Desensitisation techniques can sometimes be useful. Alan Marlatt[9] describes, as part of a behavioural approach, a behavioural-maintenance (or relapse-prevention) programme that can be used in the treatment of problem drinkers. He argues that the goal of replacing excessive drinking with abstinence tends to reinforce the oscillation of dependent behaviour from one extreme (loss of control) to the other (absolute control) and forces the individual to adopt one or other of these extreme roles. Marlatt contends that self-control and the choice of moderation or abstinence based on a balanced lifestyle should instead be the goal.

The picture of oscillation between excessive (or dependent) drinking and abstinence would complement the triangle (see chapter 1), the difference being the cause of the oscillation. On the one hand, it could be due to the state of dependence and on the other it could be due to the treatment, namely abstinence or absolute control. Marlatt's insight that the goal should be moderate drinking and not abstinence applies to heavy and problem drinkers. It does not, in our view, apply to dependent drinkers within the triangle as depicted by Edwards et al (see chapter 1), because the prospect of them becoming successful moderate or social drinkers is minimal.

Marlatt's comments concerning treatment deserve emphasis: if a problem or heavy drinker is unrealistically encouraged to become abstinent, he or she will tend to move into the triangle and oscillate between dependence and abstinence. Marlatt's main point is that a balanced lifestyle is the key to successful treatment and not the alcohol itself.

We can think of this balanced lifestyle in terms of Maslow's hierarchy of needs, where balance is achieved through the individual's successive realisation of the following categories or layers of needs: physiological, safety, love, esteem, and self-actualisation.[10]

The problems associated with alcohol abuse in women may be different from those in men and special consideration should be given to their treatment. The inability to handle bereavement is an often-cited cause of excessive drinking in women; as is the social pressures on women in the workplace. Workplace discrimination is another.

The majority of these techniques do not require the sophisticated training of a psychologist; they can be put to good use by an adequately trained health care professional. The good counsellor will have received appropriate training in a variety of techniques; this will mean that he or she will be more capable of identifying the correct, that is, most beneficial, technique for the patient. (See below in this chapter; also, the role of the occupational health care professional as counsellor in chapter 17).

Psychoanalytical therapy requires specialist commitment. It is appropriate once the patient becomes stable and had been abstinent for a period of time. Care should be taken that the therapy is well structured and has direction, with specific goals being set for each patient.

2.1.9 Assessment and Treatment of the senior manager or executive

The senior manager or executive is, without doubt, the most difficult employee to assess or treat for several reasons. Firstly, there is every possibility that such an employee's assessment will be done superficially in the face of real or perceived intimidation. Often the senior manager will offer convincing excuses as to why answering certain

---

9   Marlatt, GA & Gordon, JR *Relapse Prevention* (1985) 4, 17, 35.
10   'Farther Reaches of Human Nature' in Coleman, JC, Butcher, JN & Carson, RC *Abnormal Psychology and Modern Life* 6 ed (1980) 102-103.

parts of the assessment is inconvenient. Secondly, this problem is compounded by the common belief that substance abuse occurs only in blue-collar workers or lower-status employees. These factors undoubtedly place the counsellor conducting the assessment in an unenviable position, and in these circumstances perhaps the assessment is best handled by referring the executive to an outside agency. Then, once treatment has commenced, the counsellor should make frequent contact with that agency so that they are kept informed of the progress of the senior employee. Such knowledge can help in the follow-up or after-care. Fortunately, agencies that will assess and treat the senior executive with sensitivity are now available.

There are generally too many barriers in the way of the senior executive for them to identify the extent of their problem, which is why referral to an agency is often the best option.

In an external environment the senior manager or executive is not subject to the scrutiny and possible criticism of colleagues and subordinates, which makes it more likely that they will divulge details of their problem. They are also more likely to agree to and cooperate in further treatment. (See also 'Dealings with management' in chapter 17 The Role of the Occupational Health Professional).

2.2 Detoxification

The process of detoxification has three main objectives:
- to address the imbalance in bodily functions that will have occurred
- to alleviate the toxicity due to alcohol substance abuse
- to start the weaning of the nervous system from its dependence.

The effects of alcohol/drug withdrawal can vary from minor tremulousness to full-blown convulsions associated with delirium tremens ('the DTs'). This latter condition can be a life-threatening illness and must not be treated lightly. Managing withdrawal depends upon the severity of the condition. However, correct procedural investigations should always be carried out, bearing in mind the following factors:
- Blood should be taken for urea, electrolytes and glucose.
- As electrolyte and osmolarity imbalance are common findings, an osmolarity of greater than 320 mm/kg is indicative of alcohol intoxication.
- Low blood sodium and low blood potassium combined with dehydration due to the diuretic effect of alcohol are often identified.
- Care must be taken in using intravenous fluids even if signs of dehydration are observed because cerebral oedema can occur as a result of dehydration due to alcohol intoxication.
- Hypoglycaemia due to the suppression of gluconeogenesis by the liver is often present and the urine can show signs of ketones without the presence of glucose.
- If there is damage to the liver or alcoholic hepatitis, the serum ammonia level may be raised.
- If the protein intake has been low, which is often the case with an associated malnourishment; a negative nitrogen balance may be present.
- The blood triglyceride and blood urate levels could be considerably raised.
- Some researchers believe that blood magnesium can be lowered in the process of the alcohol withdrawal syndrome, and deficiencies of magnesium and calcium have been found to cause muscular irritability and even seizures. It is therefore recommended

that magnesium sulphate and calcium should be administered during the process of alcohol withdrawal.[11]

- The cardiovascular system must not be ignored, because cardiac conduction abnormalities may develop and/or a toxic alcohol cardiomyopathy may be present.
- Blood pressure must be watched carefully, because alcohol significantly increases blood pressure and also because blood pressure is raised in the state of withdrawal.

Mild, uncomplicated alcohol withdrawal usually consists of tremulousness, sweating, nausea, agitation, insomnia and depression. These symptoms normally occur within 12 hours of commencement of the alcohol withdrawal, but they can also occur in individuals who have had persistently raised levels of alcohol and in whom the level of alcohol has fallen below a certain threshold to which they have become accustomed. There is a characteristic time sequence for the events of severe withdrawal, starting with the tremulousness, then hallucinations, followed by seizures, and ending with delirium tremens. It is claimed that delirium tremens follows in 97% of seizure cases due to alcohol withdrawal. The hallucinations occur within 48 hours, the convulsions between 7 and 48 hours, and the delirium tremens usually 72 hours after the commencement of withdrawal of alcohol. If convulsions occur after 48 hours, they are possibly unlikely to be due to the alcohol withdrawal and another reason should be sought.

2.2.1 Pharmaceutical treatment for detoxification

(a) Mild symptoms

Mild symptoms of alcohol withdrawal such as tremulousness need not necessarily require any treatment as long as the basic investigations have been done. Here it is often advisable to introduce a course of sedation such as chlormethiazole (Heminevrin) at a dosage of two capsules four-hourly for the first 24 hours and gradually reducing it over five days. Chlormethiazole is useful for its dual role as a sedative anxiolytic and an anti-seizure drug. Benzodiazepines such as Diazepam are useful in the acute stages, particularly if intravenous infusion is required, but they are not recommended for prolonged use due to the potential for dependence. If there is liver damage, then lorazepam (Ativan) is advised as it is not metabolised by the liver.

(b) Seizures

It is important to protect against the possible occurrence of seizures, which means that an anti-epileptic drug such as Garoin containing phenytoin and phenobarbitone as anticonvulsants is useful.

(c) Thiamine deficiency

Owing to the likelihood of thiamine deficiency, vitamin B1 should be given with a loading dose of 100 mg intravenously followed by 50–100 mg daily for several days. Evidence indicates that parenteral thiamine should be given to any patient who shows signs presumptive of Wernicke's encephalopathy, eg ataxia, nystagmus, confusion, memory disturbance, delirium tremens, or opthalmoplegia. So there should be a low threshold for administering this drug to any patient with liver disease, peripheral neuritis or a confusional state.

---

11   Rosalki, SB *Clinical Biochemistry of Alcoholism* (1984) 111.

(d) Insomnia

This is a common sequela and it is important to avoid precipitating the further depression that a lack of sleep could produce; the use of a sleeping tablet for 10 to 14 days should therefore be considered.

(e) Hallucinations

The withdrawal of alcohol may precipitate hallucinations. If these occur the patient should be hospitalised and antipsychotic drugs such as phenothiazine or haloperidol (Serenace) or clothiapine (Etomine) should be administered. These have a sedative and antipsychotic effect and are major tranquillisers. If depression is precipitated, then an antidepressant should be used for at least two months.

(f) Slow withdrawal

Other methods of detoxification such as the gradual reduction of alcohol intake over a period of time may be used. This weaning process can be very effective when done under close supervision, especially when carried out together with mild sedation.

(g) Nitrous Oxide and Oxygen

The use of nitrous oxide and oxygen as a method of detoxification has also been advocated. The inhalation of pure oxygen for 20 minutes followed by a mixture of nitrous oxide and oxygen for another 20 minutes and then a further 20 minutes of pure oxygen is supposed to have the unique ability not only to detoxify the patient but also to help suppress his or her craving for alcohol.[12]

(h) The use of Hyperbaric Oxygen Therapy

The patient inhales pure oxygen while enclosed in a pressurized chamber—as a method of detoxification, this could, logically, offer similar benefits, but this has yet to be proved.

As mentioned at the beginning of this section, the detoxification process can be completed on an out-patient basis if the condition is mild, but it will always require hospitalisation in severe cases as the condition can be life-threatening. The treatment of detoxification has been highlighted not to instruct the reader in how to detoxify the patient but to show that it is often a complex, acute problem that requires a systematic medical approach. Detoxification treatment should also be led by an addiction specialist if possible.

2.3 Treatment

2.3.1. Constructive Persuasion

Linking employee disciplinary inquiry to medical treatment—constructive coercion/persuasion. Successful treatment should be the aim, not the punishment

The linking of the disciplinary inquiry to medical treatment is an exercise in 'constructive persuasion'. The advantages of this method are that it maintains an increased pressure on both the treatment-provider and the employee-patient and that it is a form of ongoing

---

12 Gillman, MA 'Analgesic nitrous oxide and oxygen, a safe and rational treatment of the alcohol withdrawal state' 1988 (December) *Forum J* (SANCA national newsletters) 7-90; Daynes 'The initial management of alcoholism using oxygen and nitrous oxide: a transcultural study' (1989) 49 *Int J Neuroscience* 83-86.

re-evaluation of the treatment. If the treatment failure rate is high, a reassessment of the treatment programme should be made. Disciplinary sanctions should be linked to failure of medical treatment in order to increase the employee's commitment to the treatment. If the employee successfully completes the entire treatment programme, he or she might be rewarded with a completely clean personnel record in respect of disciplinary offences relating to alcohol. Partial completion of the treatment programme may attract lower-level rewards; the exact nature of the reward being based upon the degree of success achieved.

The main point we wish to emphasise is that the ultimate aim of constructive persuasion should be successful treatment, not punishment.

2.3.2 Rehabilitation facilities

There are various types of rehabilitation facilities. We consider some of these facilities below.

The choice of which facility to use depends upon a number of factors, cost perhaps being the most important. Facilities vary in the charges they levy; therefore one of the first matters that a company must consider is the cost implications of treatment not only for the company but also for the employee. Moreover, the geographical availability of resources will also affect the decision. Large companies may decide to have their own facilities, especially if there is widespread alcohol and/or drug abuse among employees. Besides cost and geographical availability, the type of treatment programme must be consistent with the tested approaches to alcohol and drug treatment.

2.3.2(a) Referral to in-patient centre

In-patient treatment centres have both advantages and disadvantages. The advantages are that:

- The in-patient environment is geared towards treating the alcohol- or drug-dependent person in a controlled environment where it is easier to observe and assess the individual's progress.
- The treatment can be more intensive and more individualised towards the needs of the patient.
- The patient is away from the stresses or triggers which can stimulate the abuse or craving.
- It is easier to relate to peers with the same problems when living in the same environment.
- In-patient centres are probably the most effective environment for treating severe cases.
- The time period required is usually a minimum of 28 days and can be extended up to three months. In cases of very severe dependency, state institutions will keep some patients for two to three years.

The disadvantages of in-patient treatment are that:

- The institutionalised environment may not be amenable to some employees, particularly as they are away from their family and workplace for a protracted period of time.
- Treatment takes place in a simulated environment, which can make it difficult for patients to relate the therapy to their normal daily existence.

- Patients who feel safe and secure in the facility may experience a heightened sense of vulnerability when they have to return to 'normal life'.
- Direct and indirect costs are higher. The direct costs of this type of treatment are not always paid for by an employee's medical aid provider (medical insurance), which means that the employee or his or her employer will have to bear the expense. The indirect costs arise from the employee-patient's periods of absence from the workplace, and from the employment of a temporary replacement to perform his or her duties during this absence. However, these indirect costs need to be balanced against the costs of losing an employee (because his or her condition deteriorates to the extent that he or she can no longer work) and having to recruit and retrain someone else.

The treatment programme will often differ from one centre to another. However, the two main treatment types are (i) the Minnesota model, which is based on the AA programme with all the support modalities that the AA programme can bring to bear, particularly in the after-care phase and (ii) the behavioural model, which is based on the relapse prevention programme of Marlatt.[13]

2.3.2(b) Referral to out-patient centres

These centres are often found in urbanised industrial environments and usually provide assessment facilities together with counselling and group therapy. Participation in the programme will typically consist of a day or half-day session for an allotted number of days in a two- to four-month period. Thereafter the number of sessions will diminish to about two half-sessions a week for a further number of weeks depending upon the severity of the case. The principal advantage of out-patient treatment centres is the smaller cost factors, both direct and indirect. The direct costs will be less as there would be no boarding. The indirect costs will be reduced since the employee would only be absent from work intermittently; in other words, he or she *would* be able to work on the days when no treatment is needed. The main disadvantage to out-patient treatment is that the individual will still be confronting the pressures that put them on the programme in the first place, which raises the question of whether the programme will be influential enough in its effects on the individual to overcome these existing pressures. If the out-patient treatment is successful, there is no concern about weaning the employee-patient from the protection of the institutionalised environment.

2.3.2(c) Corporate in-house facility

In certain very large companies it is possible to provide a corporate in-house facility, which might also provide an in-patient centre, too. Most moderately large companies with a few well-trained health care workers should be able to develop an assessment and counselling facility with the unique advantages that this type of development provides.

Larger companies might have the resources available to provide a corporate in-house facility for the treatment of employees with drink and/or drug problems. This facility might also include an in-patient service. This option is likely to cost less than the use of in-patient and/or out-patient facilities, at least in the long run. The fact that the company is prepared to devote resources to an initiative of this nature clearly demonstrates its commitment to the welfare of its employees. As we have noted in other chapters, an

---

13   In Marlatt & Gordon (n 9) at 4,17,35.

employer that adopts a proactive, supportive attitude towards the issue of drink and drug abuse is far more likely to gain the respect and trust of its workforce.

Some employees may think that by using the in-house facility they run a greater risk of their colleagues finding out and ridiculing them. However, this risk would also apply if they were to attend an in-patient and/or out-patient facility; furthermore, a responsible in-house service would have made explicit provision for the confidentiality of employee information and the standards of conduct required of other members of staff.

2.3.2(d) Half-way house facility

The half-way house facility is used particularly for the reintegration of in-patient centre employees who are returning from this type of protected environment. It provides a facility where they can gradually involve themselves with the pressures which they found at work but return to the protected environment at night. This facility is also useful not only for maintaining control but furthermore because it removes the patients from their community or home pressures. This is particularly important when individuals do not have a supportive family environment or live on their own.

As the name suggests, a half-way house is a place where recovering patients can receive support during their reintegration into society. This type of facility will typically be used by in-patient centre employees who are gradually reacquainting themselves with the pressures of everyday life but who need a safe place to return to when necessary. Patients often use the house as a place to spend the evening and night because these are the times when the pressure to engage in harmful drinking or drug use is acute; a problem made worse should employees lack a supportive family environment or live on their own. It is important to remember that a half-way house is not a treatment centre; it is a drink- and drug-free environment that offers a temporary safe haven for recovering alcohol and/or drug abusers.

Companies are encouraged to only use registered rehabilitation centres.

2.3.3 Pharmaceutical treatment after detoxification

2.3.3(a) Role of Antabuse (Disulfiram)

Antabuse (Disulfiram) blocks the breakdown of acetaldehyde in the body metabolised from ethyl alcohol. The accumulating acetaldehyde is toxic and produces an unpleasant reaction that could in some cases be dangerous. Antabuse has its place in treatment, but it must never be dissociated from a counselling programme. Too often Antabuse is thought of as the magic treatment that will rid the employer of a frustrating problem. Some employers have been known to demand that occupational health professionals (OHPs) ensure that certain employees are treated with Antabuse. What must be remembered with alcohol dependence is that at the end stage of the condition often the only thing that is driving the patient is alcohol and that to remove the alcohol without replacing it with something else (ie counselling) is akin to leaving the individual like an empty shell.

Antabuse is a useful tool in the alcohol rehabilitation of some employees,[14] but it must be properly supervised and administered. Ideally, the employee should report daily or on alternate days to the clinic and receive the Antabuse from the OHP. It should

---

14   Jensen (n 3).

be documented as regards time of arrival and date. The Antabuse should be dissolved in water and drunk in the presence of the nurse. If an occupational nurse is not available for this supervisory role, then the charge-hand or a manager could become involved in the procedure. It is also possible for the employee's spouse or relatives, and even his or her friends to take part. However, the spouse is often reluctant to participate as it may affect the marital relationship; often this approach is not as successful as when workplace personnel are involved.

Employees must have no alcohol in their blood prior to the first administration of Antabuse and to ensure this they should be breathalysed prior to being given the treatment. It is important that the individual be counselled about the implications of drinking alcohol when on Antabuse treatment. They should be advised of the symptoms that they could encounter, namely a pounding headache, flushed face, urticarial-type rash (especially on the neck and chest), wheezing, tight chest, raised blood pressure, palpitations, nausea and vomiting. The length of the half-life is important to mention: this varies from individual to individual, but can last as long as a week. Owing to the long half-life, it is possible that patients need only take the treatment twice a week; however, the routine of taking the treatment daily also acts as a reinforcement of the therapy. The recommended dosage of the Antabuse is one tablet of 200 mg daily. Some employees are able to drink through the Antabuse reaction and in this case it is advised that the treatment be stepped up to a maximum of 500 mg daily. The treatment is contraindicated for those with a history of heart failure, liver disease or strokes. It must be given with strict advice and information. The liver function blood tests need to be checked before and during treatment. There is no substantial evidence for the unsupervised use of Disulfiram and this approach to treatment should not be encouraged.

Some side effects of Antabuse are frequently anecdotal and fictitious. Claims of impotence are common: such cases have been known but are rare. Usually the alleged side effects will have been caused by the alcohol itself. Rare cases of liver failure have been known to occur as a consequence of Antabuse, but generally the drug has a low toxicity except for those contraindicated for its use.

We suggest that Antabuse be used for relatively short-term treatment, that is, for up to six months. In certain rare cases it can be used for up to a year. Longer use becomes a futile exercise because of the real likelihood of alienating the patient as then there is obvious resistance to therapy. Patients must eventually be given the opportunity to control their own destinies.

Some therapists argue that Antabuse interferes with the cognitive process of perceptual shift if used for a long time. Yet, used for a short period, it can actually improve the perceptual shift as the patient is able to see, possibly for the first time for many years, a dramatic improvement in his or her well-being.

Counselling therapy and Antabuse cannot work until the patient has stopped drinking. Treatment to stop the drinking must occur first; once they are abstinent, they will have the resources to benefit from therapy, of which the Antabuse may be a feature.

The use of Antabuse as an implant is not recommended, because the blood levels produced by the implanted Antabuse are unreliable and may produce only a placebo effect.[15]

---

15   Brewer, C 'Supervised disulfiram in alcoholism' 1986 *Br J Hospital Medicine* 116.

The implant can also be removed by the patient, and fibrosis or infection can isolate the drug from the rest of the body.

Recent research from Germany has shown that supervised Antabuse (Disulfiram) use appears to be more effective than Acamprosate. Longer duration of alcohol dependence predicted a more favourable outcome but with a shorter duration of alcohol dependence Acamprosate gave a more favourable outcome. One possible explanation for these results is that the element of supervision attached to the use of Antabuse is a requirement more likely to be accepted by patients who have been alcohol-dependent for a longer (as opposed to shorter) period of time.[16]

2.3.3(b) Role of Naltrexone and other opiate antagonists in relapse prevention

These pharmaceutical agents are thought to work by limiting the craving for alcohol by their effect on the opiate receptors in the brain.

Naltrexone, an opiate receptor antagonist, has an effect on drinking behaviour in some specific cases but is contraindicated in those still taking opiates. Thirty per cent of patients will experience some mild side effects such as gastrointestinal problems. In high doses there can be some hepatotoxicity, particularly in obese patients.

2.3.3(c) Role of Acamprosate in relapse prevention

Acamprosate, a glutamate antagonist, also has an effect on drinking behaviour though this is considered to be relatively modest. The greatest benefit is seen if treatment is started just before the employee-patient is completely withdrawn from alcohol.[17] Withdrawal from alcohol induces a surge in release of excitatory neurotransmitters like glutamate. Acamprosate reduces this glutamate surge and therefore the craving for alcohol that may occur. There is also some evidence that Acamprosate has a neuroprotective effect.[18]

2.3.4 Role of counselling and psychotherapy

The first and foremost purpose of counselling and psychotherapy is to assess the patient and to understand the dynamics of the patient's problem. Are there long- standing mental health problems associated with a dual pathology, for example, depression, bipolar disorder, schizophrenia? A dual pathology will need specialist psychiatric support. A family history of alcohol or drug abuse or a family history of childhood abuse may have played an important role in the development of the problem. Whatever the outcome of the assessment, the counsellor needs to build a relationship with the patient. The relationship should be empathetic, yet with an ability to confront. The dynamics of the alcohol or drug abuse problem need to be explored; once this has been achieved, the next step is to educate the patient about alcohol or drugs.

---

16 Diehl, A, Umer, L, Mutschler, J et al 'Why is Disulfiram superior to Acamposate in the routine clinical setting? A retrospective long-term study on 353 alcohol-dependent patients' (2010) 45 (3) *Alcohol and Alcoholism* 271-277.

17 Morgan, M & Ritson, B *The management of Alcohol misuse in Alcohol and Health* (2010) chapter 6 at 57.

18 De Witte, P, Littleton, J, Parot, P & Koob, G 'Neuroprotective and abstinence-promoting effects of acamprosate: elucidating the mechanism of action' (2005) 19 (6) *CNS Drugs* 517-537.

2.3.4(a) Education

It must never be assumed that the patients fully understand the connection between alcohol, drugs and their problems, whether these are related to health, work, finances or family. As already mentioned (see chapter 1), the education of the patient must include all the basic information relating to alcohol, such as the alcoholic strength of different types of drink, what constitutes safe, unsafe and dangerous drinking behaviour, how long the body takes to break down alcohol and, of course, the effects of alcohol on health.

Education should be tailored to the needs of the following three groups:
- management and union leadership (education will focus on the implications of alcohol abuse on personal, group and company performance; formation of alcohol policy; disciplinary procedures, and so on)
- employees (education will focus on safe, unsafe and dangerous drinking; health risks [to self and others]; disciplinary procedures; treatment, and so on)
- supervisors, managers and shop stewards (education will focus on how to implement testing procedures; how to manage intoxicated employees; disciplinary procedures, and so on).

2.3.4(b) Counselling

The counselling must be able to develop a cognitive perceptual shift in thinking so that the patient is receptive towards the treatment. Responsibility for action must be accepted by the patient and nurtured by the counsellor and too much direction on the part of the latter must be avoided. Realistic goals must be set and these should be specific. This is aptly shown by the phrase 'take one day at a time', which is used extensively in the AA approach to therapy. Treatment needs to be structured and the goals linked to this structure. Besides structure, the counselling or psychotherapy must have continuity of purpose and a sense of movement.[19] Counselling should provide the basic life skills and coping mechanisms described earlier (see 'Identifying the treatment requirements' above), and could take one of the following forms depending upon circumstances.

2.3.4.(b)(i) Individual counselling and Best Practice Treatment approaches

Individual counselling is used for assessing and building a relationship with the patient and for identifying and treating specific psychiatric, psychological and social problems underlying the alcohol or drug abuse. Patients are referred for or enrolled into counselling based on the outcomes of a clinical and comprehensive assessment.

A comprehensive assessment should address the following key domains:[20]
- nature of the problem, including severity
- co-occurring health and medical problems
- co-occurring psychiatric disorders
- co-existing social and interpersonal problems (among family members or friends or within the workplace)
- co-existing legal or financial problems

---

19 Edwards (n 4) at 23–44,224.
20 Myers, B, Harker, N, Fakier, N, Kader, R & Mazok, C 'A review of evidence-based interventions for the prevention and treatment of substance use disorders' (2008) Technical Report, Medical Research Council, South Africa.

- environmental and developmental factors
- family history and relationships
- social and cultural circumstances
- previous substance abuse treatment history.

Although employee-patients are referred to external agencies for rehabilitation, companies should know about the broad range of treatment services for alcohol and drug abuse that are available. This knowledge can be put to good use in the design of employee assistance programmes (EAPs). More importantly, it is imperative that companies only select treatment services that adhere to strict evidence-based practices. Irrespective of whether treatment occurs in an in-patient/out-patient- or a community-based setting, services should provide specialised medical, psychiatric and social services to individuals presenting with alcohol or drug problems. The focus of treatment should be on stopping or reducing the damage caused by substance abuse and on preventing further health and social harms related to continued substance abuse. Treatment should always be goal-directed and comply with human rights obligations.

Several examples of well used evidence-based treatment approaches are outlined below.

- **Motivational Enhancement Therapy (MET)** is a structured therapeutic approach that is largely based on the techniques of motivational interviewing.[21] Motivational Enhancement Therapy is a client-centred approach for initiating behaviour change; it helps clients to resolve their ambivalence about engaging in treatment and stopping the use of alcohol or drugs. In an empathetic, non-confrontational environment, the client is encouraged to use his or her personal resources to promote change and to take control of a harmful or potentially harmful situation. Core elements are reflective listening, paraphrasing, listening to what is the unsaid meaning, and working with the patient's ambivalence. Several evaluations of MET have demonstrated that individuals treated with MET are more likely to be retained in treatment.[22]
- **Cognitive Behavioural Therapy (CBT)** is a psychotherapeutic approach that aims to solve problems concerning dysfunctional emotions and behaviours through a goal-oriented, systematic procedure. There is empirical evidence that CBT is effective for the treatment of substance use disorders and is widely used and recommended. For instance, 'Relapse prevention' (RP: a cognitive behavioural therapy based on the theory that learning processes play a critical role in the development and maintenance of maladaptive patterns of behaviours) can be used as a standalone programme or as a component of a more comprehensive treatment programme. Relapse prevention has been found to reduce the intensity and duration of relapse episodes and to be more likely to have sustained effects.[23]
- The **Matrix Model** is an evidence-based substance abuse out-patient treatment programme. It is an eclectic model that combines elements of several evidence-based treatment approaches (ie motivational interviewing, cognitive-behavioural therapy and twelve-step facilitation) into a single framework. It was initially developed for the

---

21 Miller, WR 'Motivational Interviewing: Research, practice and puzzles' (1996) 61 *Addictive Behaviours* 835-842.

22 Myers, B et al *A Review of Evidence-based Interventions for the Prevention & Treatment of Substance Abuse Disorders* (2008) Technical Report of the Medical Research Council, South Africa.

23 Marlatt, G & Gordon, JR *Relapse Prevention* (GuildfordPress 1985) 4, 17, 35.

treatment of stimulant (cocaine and methamphetamine) dependence but has been adapted and is effective for the broad range of substances of abuse (including alcohol and opiates). It is a standalone treatment designed to be used in community-based out-patient settings. Several evaluations have been conducted on the Matrix Model, all demonstrating statistically significant reductions in alcohol and drug use.[24]

- The **twelve-step programme,** originally proposed by Alcoholics Anonymous (AA) as a method of recovery from alcoholism, is a set of guiding principles outlining a course of action for recovery from addiction, compulsion, or other behavioural problems.[25] There is sufficient evidence for the effectiveness of this approach.

- **Brief Motivational Interviewing (BMI)** is a directive, client-centred counselling technique for eliciting behaviour change by helping clients to explore and resolve ambivalence. Compared with patient-centred counselling, it is more focused and goal-directed. The assessment and resolution of ambivalence is its central purpose, and the counsellor is purposely directive in pursuing this goal.[26] Brief Motivational Interviewing has been shown to be effective in changing various health-related behaviours.[27]

- **Contingency Management (CM)** is a behavioural treatment that is used to encourage behaviour change. It is designed to make continued alcohol or drug use less attractive and abstinence from alcohol or drugs more attractive and involves the delivery of rewards or consequences contingent on clients' responses. In other words clients receive tangible positive reinforcers for evidence of desired behaviour change.[28] Contingency Management has been shown to sustain substantial periods of abstinence.[29]

2.3.4(b)(ii) Group counselling

With this form of treatment, patients work with their therapist and other dependent individuals. This allows them to understand how different types of people can have the same problem and to support one another as they go through the recovery process together. They are also able to identify similar experiences. This helps instil confidence and hope through the realisation that they are not alone and unique. Group counselling can involve peer-group confrontation and role play and is often utilised when the patient is more stable.

This is the framework of the AA approach to treatment. It is founded on the belief that group support, confrontation and encouragement to abstain from drinking are far more effective than individuals' resolutions to do so on their own. When individuals join an AA group, their misconceptions of their drinking problem are identified by a group of individuals who have been through the same experiences. The strength of this type of

---

24 Myers (n 20).

25 Vandenbos, GR *APA dictionary of psychology* 1 ed (2007).

26 Rollnick S, & Miller, WR 'What is motivational interviewing?' (1995) 23 *Behavioural and Cognitive Psychotherapy* 325-334.

27 Miller, WR 'Motivational interviewing: research, practice & puzzles' in (1996) 61 *Addictive Behaviours* 835–842 .

28 Miller (n 27).

29 National Institute on Drug Abuse *Principles of drug addiction treatment: a research based guide* (1999) National Institutes of Health, Bethesda, Washington.

encounter lies in the sharing of mutual experiences and support; peer-group influences reinforce and monitor the patient's acceptance of treatment.

Manualised and structured group counselling sessions can also be found in treatment models such as the Matrix Model, specifically early recovery groups, during which strategies to achieve early recovery are discussed as well as relapse prevention. The programme also includes family education and conjoint (family) counselling sessions for family members affected by the substance use disorders.[30]

2.3.4(b)(iii) Self-help groups

Substance abusers are also likely to seek or gain help from organisations such as Alcoholics Anonymous (AA) or Narcotics Anonymous (NA). Though well established, these and similar organisations still attract criticism. Detractors claim that these groups are rigid, obsessive and dogmatic. It therefore has the potential to dissuade a percentage of possible clients.

Ironically, the alleged weaknesses of the AA are, for members and supporters of the organisation, its greatest strengths. Alcohol-addicted or -dependent individuals often lack structure and purpose in their lives; they also tend to have poor self-control. Under these circumstances the highly structured approach of the AA would, understandably, appeal to a great many problem drinkers. The fact that an individual can rely upon the support of a cohesive peer group further explains the organisation's popularity. Each new member is eligible for a sponsor; someone who is a long-standing member and who can provide one to one support as required.

These two organisations (AA and NA), and others that adhere to similar principles are characterised by spirituality and being single minded.

Each AA and NA group is autonomous and develops its own character. Groups may consist of individuals from the same social background, or who follow a similar lifestyle, or who belong to the same age group, for example. Other groups may be more catholic in nature, gaining strength from a diverse mix of social classes, lifestyles, and so on. Other groups may oppose the use of drug therapy such as Antabuse and antidepressants. (Note that a patient in receipt of prescription drugs who is considering joining such a group should consult his or her psychiatrist before doing so. The psychiatrist will be able to advise the patient on whether stopping drug use is likely to interfere with his or her recovery process.)

2.3.4(b)(iv) Family counselling

It is important to bring the family into the counselling process. Often the family (and usually the wife) has borne the brunt of the problem for many years, having attempted all along to hide its social impact. Typically, relatives feel isolated and do not know where to seek help; they may also feel a sense of loyalty towards the alcohol- or drug-dependent person and do not wish to jeopardise his or her status or job. In the later stages of dependency, alienation will enter into the relationships. However, attempts to maintain family cohesiveness will remain, particularly if there are children involved.

---

30 Rawson, RA, Marinelli-Casey, PJ & Huber, A 'A multi-site evaluation of treatment of methamphetamine dependence in adults' in Harrell, J & Straw, RB (eds) *Conducting Multiple Site Evaluations in Real-World Settings* (2002) 73-87.

Family members are often classified as co-dependents and enablers in the treatment process.

The treatment of alcohol and drug abuse patients is more successful when the family is involved, because family members provide both physical and emotional support. In some cases the partner, usually the wife, will have joined the partner as a substance abuser due to years of frustration, in which case both partners will need treatment.

Interviews with family members (or other individuals with whom the patient has a close relationship) should be conducted in the presence of the patient, but often the interviewee feels intimidated by the presence of the user. This joint consultation is useful in verifying the drinking or drug use history. Before this, however, the counsellor should reassure family members of the confidentiality of the interview process and that the purpose of counselling is to restore stability to the life of the patient and his or her family. The counsellor needs to stress the fact that substance users/abusers need their families' support and encouragement if they are to make a recovery and that anger and recrimination will only undermine the recovery process. The family should be encouraged to report to the counsellor any changes in the patient's behaviour that are not consistent with the treatment.

Alcoholics Anonymous is affiliated with organisations such as AL-ANON, a support group established particularly for the benefit of the families, friends and colleagues of problem drinkers.

2.3.4(b)(v) Continuation or reinforcement counselling (aftercare)

The majority of substance-abuse patients, particularly those who are alcohol- or drug-dependent, will experience relapses—this should be expected as part of the process of rehabilitation. But each relapse could be used as a positive resource to further strengthen the recovery. For the treatment to be successful the patient must feel able to come forward after each relapse event and discuss in depth the events leading up to the relapse. This enables the counsellor to identify the trigger mechanisms that initiated the relapse, to discuss these with the patient, and to think of ways in which these triggers can be avoided or their impact on the recovery process diminished or eliminated.

The importance of post treatment aftercare is widely recognised and should always be recommended, irrespective of the type of treatment (in-patient or out-patient) administered. Aftercare is an essential component of substance abuse treatment. The continuing support and care it provides reduces the risk of a relapse occurring. Participation in aftercare activities typically involves enrolment in a self-help group such as AA or NA, or even taking up residence in a half-way house or sober living establishment following completion of treatment.

2.3.4(c) Qualities and skills of counsellors

The qualities required of counsellors include self-awareness and sensitivity to how they themselves impact on the patient. They require empathy—the ability to understand and relate to the patient's position. They need to be trustworthy and to be perceived as trustworthy, otherwise poor communication will result. They need to be realistic in their expectations and non-judgemental.

Counselling skills include the ability to develop a rapport with clients, and to do so quickly. Rapport is established during the counsellor's meetings with the patient, which demand effective interviewing skills if these meetings are to be productive. Other skills include the ability to unravel complex issues so as to get to the root of the problem and the ability to identify problems and to set priorities with particular issues. The competent counsellor will also be able to identify options and to see alternative routes of treatment. Counsellors must be capable of formulating a plan of action and deciding who (the counsellor or the patient) should take responsibility for certain actions. By assigning responsibility to a patient, the counsellor facilitates the patient's capacity to cope on their own.

The skilled counsellor knows how to cope with a crisis, that is, he or she can determine what intervention is needed (this will depend upon the nature of the crisis) and how to utilise the crisis to enhance the treatment process. More and more addiction counsellors are being trained in Cognitive Behavioural Therapy (CBT) and Brief Motivational Interviewing (BMI), which are valued as fast and effective forms of treatment for patients with drink and/or drug problems. Cognitive Behavioural Therapy helps the individual to challenge the negative thoughts or triggers that can prompt a relapse, whilst BMI is advocated for use in early intervention and referrals.

The inability to manage stress is always a significant problem with substance-abuse patients and therefore stress management is an essential skill. Counselling for grief, particularly in women, is a further skill. Patients may also experience suicidal tendencies and the counsellor must be constantly aware of this.

Counsellors should, furthermore, have a sound knowledge of mental health, its diagnosis and treatment. They should also be knowledgeable in the fields of alcohol and drug dependency, particularly where the two are associated. Ethical and legal issues and their impact on confidentiality should be part of the training of the counsellor; he or she should also be aware of corporate policies regarding alcohol abuse.

3. MONITORING AND MAINTENANCE

Monitoring the treatment is important, because two-thirds of relapses occur within the first 90 days.[31] Monitoring can take place in many ways. Objective tests are a useful method of assessing the patient's commitment to the treatment; these can take the form of blood tests (alcohol, GGT, MCV, CDT) or breathalyser, urine or saliva tests (see chapter 10 above). They can also involve inquiry into recent relapses and reinforcement of the commitments that were agreed upon during previous treatment sessions. The indirect objective blood tests (GGT, MCV, CDT) are useful tools as the patient can observe their progressive improvement as treatment continues; likewise, the patient knows that if relapses occur these will be identified.

SUMMARY

In this chapter we looked at the issues surrounding the treatment of individual employee-patients who are experiencing drink and/or drug problems. However, it is important to remember that treatment of the organisation may also be needed. In other words, if alcohol or drug abuse is encouraged or condoned within the organisation it will first be necessary to investigate why and how this has developed, *before* considering how the problem manifests at the level of the individual employee. Institutionalised drink and/or drug abuse exerts a powerful influence on the behaviour of employees and on the outcome of any rehabilitation programmes that are introduced.

---

31 Marlatt, GA & Gordon, JR *Relapse Prevention* (Guildford Press 1985) 4,17,35.

The Employee Assistance Programme (EAP) is intended to combat substance abuse within the workplace. Research has shown that only a small proportion of alcohol abusers are identified in the EAP and that these individuals are usually in the later stages of dependency. This is because objective performance deterioration is often absent in the early stages of alcohol dependency. The linking of medical screening to the EAP can help to improve the efficacy of the programme.

The most powerful tool in the workplace treatment programme is constructive persuasion, which links the disciplinary inquiry into alcohol abuse to medical treatment. Constructive persuasion is intended to support the rehabilitation treatment of an alcohol-dependent employee; *not* to punish him or her.

We also discussed the advantages and disadvantages associated with in-patient treatment and out-patient treatment. The in-patient treatment centre is perhaps the most effective, but the high costs involved place this option beyond the reach of most companies (unless medical aid/insurance is available). The out-patient centre is more cost-effective; it also allows the patient to live normally, that is, without severe disruption to his or her daily activities. However, out-patient care is not suitable in cases of severe alcohol dependency, where in-patient care will be necessary.

Very large companies might consider corporate in-house facilities. The availability of a half-way house has the advantage of gradually weaning the patient from the protection of institutionalised life and would alleviate the problem of dependence on an external agency.

Detoxification treatment for problem drinkers usually necessitates the use of drugs. However, there is a higher risk of drug dependence occurring in individuals who have previously been alcohol-dependent. The drugs used during the detoxification process should therefore be used judiciously; otherwise alcohol dependency could be traded for drug dependency. Nevertheless, in dealing with acute alcohol withdrawal, drug treatment is often essential and must in any event be considered. Relapse prevention remains a significant challenge but is helped by certain pharmaceutical treatments.

Antabuse, or Disulfiram, is a useful drug for relatively short-term treatment, but is ill-advised for long-term treatment or when administered unsupervised. Opiate antagonists such as Naltrexone and glutamate inhibitors like Acamprosate play a role in relapse prevention

Counselling lies at the core of any rehabilitation treatment programme. Individual, group and family counselling can be used; each form offers distinct advantages. Family counselling provides support to family members affected by the problem drinking; the most severely affected member is often the wife of the employee-patient. The encouragement and support of a patient's family is an essential part of the recovery programme and the counsellor should try and elicit this support at every opportunity. Relapses are common in patients recovering from alcohol dependence or addiction and should therefore be expected. The counsellor should find out what triggered the relapse, discuss the specific trigger mechanisms with the patient, suggest how the patient could, in future, avoid these triggers, and consider what action is needed to negate or lessen the impact of these mechanisms on the recovery process.

The effective counsellor is someone who possesses certain skills (interviewing, problem-solving and crisis-management, for example) and qualities (empathy, sensitivity and self-awareness, among others). A percentage of alcohol-abuse patients who are not dependent will change their behaviour even if counselled by untrained personnel. The path of abstinence is not the only way and controlled drinking may be the advised route for some less dependent patients.

Note: we are greatful for the work done by Margaret Ann McCann for this chapter.

Chapter 17

*The Role of the Occupational Health Professional**

Mike McCann & Nadine Harker Burnhams

The information presented in this chapter provides a broad description of the nature, scope and challenges of the work of an occupational health professional (OHP). For a closer understanding of the OHP's interactions with individual employees suffering from drink and/or drug problems, please refer to chapters 1, 3, 5, 7, 8, 10 and 16.

We examine the complexities of the OHP's relationship with substance-abusing employees. This includes a consideration of the treatment options available and the problems associated with diagnostic testing. The professional independence of the OHP is essential if he or she is to gain the trust and cooperation of employees. We address this issue here. However, we also look at the ways in which management may try to influence the work of the OHP and the threat this poses to his or her autonomy. Attention is also given to the OHP's relationship with doctors and other health professionals in the local community.[1]

As mentioned in previous chapters, alcohol abuse accounts for the majority of workplace accidents or incidents where substance abuse is involved. Thus in this chapter we will discuss the role of the OHP in terms of his or her interactions with *alcohol*-dependent or -addicted employees, while noting that the OHP's relationship with *drug*-dependent or -addicted employees is structured along similar lines.

1. INTRODUCTION

Occupational health professionals should be able to identify the signs of alcohol abuse, both from the developing history in the clinical file and also when the employee presents him- or herself for treatment or counselling. They should be capable of assessing the degree of abuse and should be able to counsel the employee accordingly. They should be able to organise a direct referral system to external agencies, to facilitate either in-patient or out-patient treatment for the dependent abuser. It is particularly in the areas of rehabilitation and monitoring that the OHP has a very important role to play.

A company can invest a considerable amount of money in treatment programmes for its alcohol-misusing employees only to find that these programmes fail to deliver the expected results. This failure is largely due to inadequate monitoring of these employees once they return to their work environment. The success of a treatment programme mainly depends on how well the 'treated' employees readapt to life in the workplace,

---

* This chapter was written with Dr Margaret McCann, the Medical Director of Castle Craig Hospital, an addiction treatment hospital in Scotland.

---

1   Information for the occupational health professional is also considered in chapter 16 Treatment: The Employee Patient.

where they must confront their problems on their own, that is, without the guidance and support of the counsellor or OHP who has taken them through the treatment process. Too often, expensive and well-meaning treatment is rendered useless by poor follow-up of the rehabilitation process in the workplace. If the culture of the company continues (explicitly or implicitly) to encourage alcohol misuse, then treatment is often undermined.

Monitoring of the rehabilitated employee should therefore be an important part of the rehabilitation process. It should continue for at least two years and possibly longer in severe cases. Objective blood tests are the ideal monitoring tools. If these tests are conducted on a regular basis, they can be linked to counselling sessions. At the beginning, that is, the period following the employee's initial return to work, tests should be on a monthly basis; after six months, they should occur two-monthly; and after one year, three-monthly. (This is a suggested testing regime; alternative time intervals are of course possible.)

2. THE ROLE OF THE OHP: PRELIMINARY ASSESSMENT

Preliminary assessment is the first step in the treatment programme and arises when an employee is referred to the occupational health unit for help with his or her drink problem. He or she may have been referred because of actual or suspected intoxication or because he or she has exhibited other signs of impairment due to alcohol consumption; the OHP may also have detected a problem during screening of employees for alcohol use.

Diagnosis is facilitated by the use of one or more screening instruments, such as the CAGE, MAST and AUDIT tests. The CAGE is easy to administer and one of the most effective and efficient screening devices. In some countries, the CAGE and the MAST tests are 75% accurate. The AUDIT is more effective for younger people and is particularly useful for early intervention with problem drinking. However, caution is needed when using these assessment tools in the work environment (for more on this issue, see chapter 16 section 2.1.2 and chapter 10 section 3.2.12 and the questionnaires contained in Appendix 3).

During preliminary assessment, the OHP tries to find out as much information as he or she can about the employee's history of alcohol consumption, including the quantity and frequency of consumption. Objective evidence of alcohol-related problems can be obtained by reviewing the employee-patient's medical history. See Appendix 11 for Table of History, Signs and Diseases of Alcohol and Drugs

Problems may be physical, psychological, social, forensic or related to employment. A chronological history of problems should be gathered. By reviewing reports submitted by management or colleagues of the employee the OHP can glean useful collateral information; this information can then be compared to the employee's testimony and any anomalies or inconsistencies noted. The OHP should be aware of common presentations and risk factors for employees suspected of alcohol misuse or abuse. Common presentations include stress, anxiety, insomnia, depression, hypertension, accidents, GIT complaints, and sickness absence. Remember that the majority of alcohol patients are difficult to detect in general practice. People who are addicted generally do seek help on a voluntary basis but for different reasons. A family history of alcohol abuse occurs in 55% of problem drinkers compared with 17% of controls.

During the physical examination of the employee, the OHP should look for signs of longstanding misuse of alcohol or drugs (see chapters 7 and 8 and Appendix 11).

The OHP must explain to the employee that he or she will need to perform some blood tests, including three for liver function (GGT [gamma glutamyl transferase], AST [aspartate amino transaminase] and CDT [carbohydrate deficient transferrin]). Getting laboratories to do CDT tests can be difficult but we suggest you persevere – the test can be quite valuable.) A full blood count for MCV (mean corpuscular volume) should also be provided.

3. MATRIX OF CATEGORIES OF DRINKERS AND RELATED INTERVENTIONS

Assessing alcohol abuse in a workplace setting is not something that the general practitioner (GP) can accomplish, and yet he or she is usually the person to whom an alcohol-abusing employee is referred for treatment. The OHP can help here: he or she can suggest to the GP one or more interventions that the doctor could use in his or her treatment of an alcohol-dependent or -addicted employee. The interventions the OHP proposes will depend on the type of drinker involved, which in turn is based upon the severity of his or her drink problem. In the matrix below (Table 17.1 on page 264), the types of drinker are listed under the heading 'Categories of drinker'. Of the 9 categories shown, numbers 1 to 5 are also described in terms of the level of consumption involved (units per week; grams per week). The bottom half of the matrix lists the interventions ('Education', 'Well person check', and so on) and, horizontally, the categories of drinker (1, 2 ... 9); a small 'x' denotes the intervention that is best-suited to a specific category of drinker.

You can use the matrix to decide on the relevant intervention. For example, with misuse, shown as 'Moderate hazardous' under Categories of Drinker, a well person check and/or education is all that may be needed (see chapter 16 for more on treatment and counselling of the individual employee).

4. CHECKING FOR DEPENDENCY

It is important to consider if the employee-patient could be *alcohol dependent* and to assess for severity. Indicators of dependency include three or four positive responses to the CAGE questionnaire, which have occurred in the past year (see Appendix 3), or evidence of the following:

4.1 Compulsion to drink

The employee-patient is preoccupied with alcohol; he or she spends a considerable amount of time taking alcohol, thinking about it, planning how to get it, and recovering from its effects. There is a need to consume alcohol and this becomes more pressing and more urgent. Alcohol may be used by the employee for medicinal purposes, for example to induce sleep or to relieve anxiety. Solitary drinking, secretive drinking, and feeling uncomfortable if alcohol is not available are highly suggestive symptoms.

4.2 Impaired control

Here there is difficulty predicting how much one is going to drink and when one is going to stop. Repeatedly the person will drink more than planned. They are no longer really in charge of when they start or when they stop drinking.

As dependency becomes established, use becomes more involuntary and the person increasingly makes fewer conscious choices about drinking.

Table 17.1 Matrix of categories of drinkers and related interventions

Categories of drinker	Units/week F – M	Grams/week (1 unit = 8 g) F – M
1. Low risk drinker	<14 – <21	112 – 168
2. Moderate hazardous	21 – 25	168 – 200
3. Heavy hazardous	35 – 50	280 – 400
4. Problem harmful	35 – 63	280 – 504
5. Dependent harmful	70	560
6. Known chronic history		
7. Previous failure of treatment		
8. Dual psychiatric diagnosis		
9. Complicating medical Problems		

Staging of interventions	1	2	3	4	5	6	7	8	9
Education	X	X							
Well person check		X	X						
General counselling – controlled drinking			X						
OHP/GP – blood tests			X	X	X	X	X	X	X
OHP/GP – outpatient counselling (addiction Tx)				X					
Psychiatric addiction specialist assessment					X	X	X	X	X
Day treatment					X				
In-patient treatment					X	X	X	X	X
AA					X	X	X	X	X
Abstinence					X	X	X	X	X
Controlled drinking after 6 months				X	X				

4.3 Attempts to control

There is also a persistent desire or unsuccessful efforts to cut back or to control use.

4.4 Relief drinking

As an employee becomes increasingly dependent on alcohol, he or she may engage in relief drinking to overcome the withdrawal symptoms that he or she experiences. Because dependency raises a person's tolerance to alcohol, he or she is likely to consume progressively larger amounts of alcohol during relief drinking. An employee who continues to drink in this manner despite current health problems is particularly at risk. Relief drinking is a reliable diagnostic indicator of alcohol dependency.

Dependency and addiction develop insidiously. The affected individual often devises strategies for coping with or masking his or her problem, which means that his or her condition gradually worsens even though there may be few or no clear signs of impairment. Because of this it is not advisable to base the need for a diagnosis on the presence of withdrawal symptoms; an over-reliance on outward signs of alcohol abuse may mean that many patients end up not being diagnosed or under-diagnosed.

Obvious indications of alcohol misuse are of course important to the OHP. Absenteeism, sickness absence, accidents, and falling productivity are some of the ways in which alcohol abuse among employees may manifest. The more alcohol-related problems there are, the more likely there is to be serious dependence.

Remember that by the time alcohol causes problems in the workplace, it may already have been 'at work' for some time in other areas of the employee's life.

5. MANAGEMENT OF ALCOHOL-DEPENDENT EMPLOYEES

The management of an alcohol-dependent employee entails the following:
- The line manager's report documenting all incidents in chronological order, as well as witness reports of suspected intoxication should be made available.
- The personnel record of the employee should be studied to see if he or she has experienced drink problems at other times and/or with other employers. For example, if the employee has ever been disciplined for the misuse of alcohol, details of the action taken will most likely be on file.
- The GP's report and all other medical reports regarding the employee's health should be examined, provided that the employee gives his or her written consent beforehand.
- The OHP must inform the employee of the company's alcohol policy and of what treatment is available.
- A 'fitness to work' assessment must be performed. This could involve a *risk assessment* on the grounds of health and safety. The question that the OHP must consider here is 'Is it safe for the employee to return to work?' If the OHP determines that the employee cannot return to work until he or she has completed a detoxification or rehabilitation programme, the employee must be informed of this.
- The OHP will review all the information she or he has obtained and then make a tentative diagnosis. The type of intervention needed will be evaluated. The OHP may recommend interventions that involve the family since, as noted above, alcohol-induced problems usually surface in the home long before they do in the workplace.
- Referral to an addiction specialist may be advisable. The specialist will then define the extent of the dependency and the preferred treatment programme. It is, of course, essential to advise the employee-patient that all information will be treated confidentially and will not be disclosed to management. Except where it relates to fitness to work.

6. DIFFICULTIES WITH DIAGNOSTIC EVALUATION

Diagnostic evaluation is problematic for a number of reasons. The fact that the stereotypical view of alcoholism is seriously flawed is perhaps the most important reason. People who are addicted to or heavily dependent upon alcohol or drugs are not the physically and mentally diminished individuals that exist in our imagination or onscreen. The orthodox view of the alcoholic as a human wreck; someone devoid of judgement and incapable of lucid thought; is almost wholly inaccurate. Severe mental and physical debilitation can occur, of course, but it is wrong to assume that *all* problem drinkers will be affected in this way. Alcoholics (and drug addicts) are expert at hiding their abuse and can continue to lead lives of apparent normality for many years. They have relationships, careers and experiences like the rest of us and can be highly intelligent.

Alcoholics and problem drinkers achieve this through the process of denial. If we are going to successfully treat substance-abusing individuals we therefore have to understand their denial, which forms part of their illness. It is important to note that denial is not deliberate lying; it serves to cover up much of the shame and guilt the sufferer feels. Denial serves to protect both the addiction/dependency and the person's self-esteem. If denial becomes entrenched in a person's psyche it can be very difficult to dislodge and usually reinforces the (mis)perception of others that the individual is leading a healthy, stable life. Diagnosis should therefore take place as early as possible.

We also wish to emphasise the fact that *addictive drinking is not a symptom*. Problem drinkers and their families usually think the drinking is due to stress, depression or other situational factors. The reality is that addictive drinking is an illness that causes depression, stress, marriage breakdown, difficulties in the workplace, etc. Accepting this reality is critical if we are to provide alcohol-dependent and -addicted drinkers with meaningful solutions to their problems.

We can conclude this section by commenting on the ambiguity of diagnosis in the early stages of dependency. This is to be expected given that the problem drinker is unlikely to have revealed the full extent of his or her problems in this initial period. The OHP is thus required to make his or her diagnosis without knowing all the facts. In such circumstances a degree of uncertainty is unavoidable; however, this should not stop the OHP from considering the possibility that alcoholism or alcohol dependency exists.

7. TREATMENT: GOALS AND OPTIONS

Treatment goals will depend upon the nature of the presenting problem. All clinical treatment programmes are geared towards the eradication or minimisation of the drink problem. Unfortunately these goals are not achievable in each and every case of alcohol abuse. The more involuntary the drinking or misuse becomes; the more difficult it is to moderate consumption. Patients who succeed with controlled drinking are generally people with low levels of dependence and few related problems; they also tend to have a relatively short period of abuse and a high degree of social stability. These conclusions have been recorded by Valliant from meticulous long-term follow-up studies.[2] Prospective follow-up studies by Valliant and Helzer[3] show clearly that less than 6% of alcoholics can sustain problem-free drinking. Valliant's follow-up studies are

---

2   Vaillant, GE 'A 60 year follow up of alcoholic men' (2003) 98 (8) *Addiction* 1043-1051.

3   Helzer, JE, Robins, LN, Taylor, JR et al, 'The Extent of Long-Term Moderate Drinking among Alcoholics Discharged from Medical and Psychiatric Treatment Facilities'(1985) 312 (26) *N Engl J Med* 1678-1682 in Peele, S 'Why Do Controlled-Drinking Outcomes Vary by Investigator, by Country and by Era? Cultural Conceptions of Relapse and Remission in Alcoholism'(1987) 20 *Drug and Alcohol Dependence* 173-201.

particularly notable because they contain a large sample of alcoholics who were tracked over a period of 60 years.[4]

Treatment options include:

- brief interventions
- community detoxification
- outpatient treatment
- inpatient treatment.

7.1 Brief interventions

These are effective with non-dependent drinkers, misuse drinkers and early problem drinkers, all of whom may be able to adjust their use. Brief interventions can also reduce consumption by 20% and reduce drinking to below dangerous amounts for these categories of drinkers.

Brief interventions involve *feedback* based on the assessment, the blood test results and the other information collected. The OHP will meet with the employee-patient to discuss sensible drinking levels, triggers to drinking and the ways in which he or she can change his or her behaviour. For example, the OHP may advise a moderate hazardous drinker (level 2 in Table 17.1) to cut back on his or her consumption provided that there is no evidence of dependence. Where there is evidence of established dependence or repeated failed attempts to reduce consumption, however, the OHP may advise the employee-patient to abstain from drinking alcohol.

An action plan will be agreed upon and appropriate goals will be set. The OHP must of course demonstrate confidence in the employee's ability to achieve these goals and to adhere to the action plan. The employee should also be provided with relevant educational material and encouraged to undertake self-monitoring.

Brief interventions are less effective when used to treat dependent drinkers. Outcomes may be successful in the short term but are likely to be unstable in the long term, which suggests the need for other forms of treatment, that is, interventions.

7.2 Community detoxification

Community detoxification refers to the use of a local community's health resources to facilitate the planned withdrawal from alcohol or drugs of an employee-patient. This form of intervention may be successful with individuals who have mild to moderate withdrawal symptoms, which would thus exclude dependent drinkers and alcoholics. For low risk and non-dependent drinkers, treatment administered via community health professionals can be beneficial, although relapse is highly probable and compliance with counselling or therapy is often a problem.

---

4   Abstinence versus controlled drinking has been hotly debated over the years but as Stanton Peele states there does seem to be difference in cultural and treatment environments depicted by ethnic and national attitudes which lean towards one or the other types of treatment. These authors believe there is a place for both types of treatment but as stated in the text it is the severity of the condition which should decide on the type of treatment. Peele, S 'Why Do Controlled-Drinking Outcomes Vary by Investigator, by Country and by Era? Cultural Conceptions of Relapse and Remission in Alcoholism'(1987) 20 *Drug and Alcohol Dependence* 173-201.

7.3 Outpatient treatment

Outpatient treatment has been shown to be an effective, less costly form of intervention for a broad range of patients, including certain categories of employee-patients suffering from substance abuse. Table 17.1 suggests that outpatient care may be a viable option for level 1 to 4 drinkers but not for level 5 to 9 drinkers. The lower-risk drinkers (levels 1 to 4) are likely to require less direct supervision and to be more capable of functioning as independent individuals within the community, which suggests that hospitalisation may be unnecessary. By contrast, higher-risk drinkers (levels 5 to 9) often require a more intense form of intervention if they are to make progress, which presupposes the need for hospital care.

7.4 Inpatient treatment

There are groups of patients who require residential or inpatient treatment.[5] Authorities suggest that inpatient treatment may be appropriate if one or more of the following factors exist:
- patients lack social resources/family support
- serious medical and psychiatric conditions present (This would include patients with more complex alcohol problems, severe depression or liver disease.)
- environmental conditions seriously impede recovery—a strong drinking network, a stressful occupation and chaotic living conditions, for example
- patients with more complex problems—typically, chronicity and severity of dependence or serious psychological problems
- high levels of resistance to treatment (This would be reflected in a high degree of denial and/or a failure to keep outpatient appointments or follow treatment.)[6]
  Inpatient treatment should also be considered under the following circumstances:
- in cases where a complicated withdrawal syndrome exists or may develop. Most patients can be detoxified at home but those with a history of DTs, recent very heavy use, or significant use of other drugs of abuse should be considered for inpatient detoxification.
- where intoxication of the employee-patient could result in the death of other people (An alcohol-abusing airline pilot would thus qualify for inpatient treatment, as would a surgeon, shipmaster, oil rig worker, and so on.)
- if the employee-patient is seriously at risk of losing his or her job and livelihood due to alcohol and drug use
- in cases of failed outpatient treatment. (Rather than seeing patients as unmotivated, we have to see their denial as greater than the intensity of the current treatment effort.)

It is important to respond at an early stage with inpatient treatment for many alcohol-dependent patients. In fact the more severely dependent the patient, the more likely it is

---

5   Waterhouse, W *'Prevention and relapse in alcohol dependence'* from the 2003 Scotland Health Technology Board Report, SHAAP Conference (2008).
6   Finney, JW 'The effectiveness of inpatient and outpatient treatment for alcohol abuse' (1996) 91 (12) *Addiction* 1773-1796.

that they need inpatient treatment: 'The more severely dependent, and the less socially stable, alcoholics seem to fair better with inpatient and more intensive treatments'.[7]

As we mentioned earlier in this chapter, the OHP does not usually provide the clinical treatment the employee-patient requires. Medical evaluation, detoxification, treatment planning and medical care are instead undertaken by other health professionals in the community. However, a working knowledge of what is involved in these stages will be useful to the OHP since it may help him or her to motivate the patient and to influence the type of treatment chosen.

8. MEDICAL EVALUATION AND DETOXIFICATION

Dual diagnosis must be considered, the second condition may be psychiatric or organic.

Approximately 80% of patients referred to an inpatient unit have a co-existing medical problem of, for example, peripheral neuritis, pancreatitis or liver disease. Up to 50% of patients have significant cognitive impairment due to cortical atrophy. Some 50% suffer from psychiatric disorders such as depression, anxiety, phobic states or personality problems. This psychological disturbance is often secondary to the drinking and resolves within 4–6 weeks after detoxification and abstinence. The possibility of a co-existing primary psychiatric disorder must always be considered; for example, bi-polar patients have a high incidence of alcohol or drug dependence.

Likewise Attention Deficit Hyperactive Disorder (ADHD), Post Traumatic Stress Disorder (PTSD) and schizophrenia commonly occur with substance-abuse disorders.[8]

9. BIOCHEMICAL TESTS

Following the initial medical examination, a number of tests should be carried out. These tests include an LFT (liver function test), FBC (full blood count), U&E (Urea & Electrolysis) and other tests for blood borne viruses. Abnormal results should always be discussed with the patient. This is an important brief intervention. For example, making patients aware that the LFT results are abnormal and by exactly how much, can have a profound impact on how they perceive their condition. In other words, the news is likely to act as a short, sharp shock to the system that can penetrate denial and act as a strong motivator for change. An MRI scan that shows cortical brain damage or a neurobehavioural study that reveals evidence of cognitive and behavioural impairment may also prompt a change in behaviour and thought in the individual patient who receives the news.

10. DETOXIFICATION

Detoxification generally involves the prescription of a long-acting benzodiazepine such as Chlordiazepoxide, which is recommended by the Scottish Intercollegiate Guidelines Network (SIGN) healthcare organisation. Chlordiazepoxide provides a smooth withdrawal reflecting its long half-life. It also permits a rapid reduction over the first 24–48 hours.

---

7   Miller, WR & Hester, RK 'Inpatient alcoholism treatment: Who benefits?' (1986) 41 *American Psychologist* 794-805.

8   Brady, K & Sinha, R 'Co-Occuring Mental and Substance Use Disorders: The Neuorbiological Effects of Chronic Stress' (2005) 162 *American Journal of Psychiatry* 1483-1493.

Minor tranquillisers, which render alcoholic patients vulnerable to relapse or cross-addiction should not be prescribed after detoxification. Inpatient treatment usually requires higher amounts of Chlordiazepoxide.

Due to the poor nutritional state and health status of patients, parenteral administration of thiamine is usually required. Oral thiamine is very poorly absorbed in alcoholics and will be insufficient to replenish depleted brain supplies.

Evidence indicates that parenteral thiamine should be given to any patient who shows signs presumptive of Wernicke's encephalopathy, for example, ataxia, nystagmus, confusion, memory disturbance, delirium tremens, or opthalmoplegia. So there should be a low threshold for administering this drug to any patient with liver disease, peripheral neuritis or a confusional state.

Detoxification from opiates is with methadone or lofexidine. Both have proven effectiveness.[9]

11. REHABILITATION TREATMENT

Treatment could include psychotherapy, education, family therapy, relapse prevention and aftercare planning as well as an introduction to AA or AlAnon. The aim is not to focus on causes but to treat the primary dependence. It is important to address the factors which could perpetuate the alcohol or drug abuse and the factors which could precipitate a relapse. Further detailed reading on this subject can be found in chapter 16.

12. POST-TREATMENT—RETURN TO WORK

After the employee-patient has completed the treatment programme he or she is likely to want to return to work. This is usually possible provided that the following precautionary measures are taken:

- The rehabilitation centre's report should be consulted. This will include the proposed aftercare plan and recommendations to help the patient consolidate recovery. Note that the employee-patient's consent to the release of this confidential information must be obtained.
- If residential treatment has been necessary, an Employee Assistance Programme (EAP) counsellor, human resources manager or senior supervisor should have been in regular contact with staff at the rehabilitation centre or clinic. The counsellor/ manager/ supervisor can liaise with the therapists and treatment team regarding the employee-patient's medical history, current level of impairment and how well (or poorly) he or she is responding to treatment. The information gained during these discussions will prove useful when planning for the reintegration of the patient into the workplace.
- Baseline blood tests or urine screening should be available.
- A risk assessment should be made on the basis of the above findings.
- Re-entry to the workplace may be facilitated by adjusting the employee's workload for a period of time or modifying his or her work environment. For example, employee-patients in high-risk positions (airline pilots, active duty soldiers, mine workers, for example) may be relieved of some or all of their more onerous duties when they return to work, especially if work-related stress was a factor in the development of

---

9   SA Society for Occupational Medicine A *Guideline on Alcohol and Drug Problems at Work* (1991).

their addiction or dependency. Thus the airline pilot may remain on the ground and the soldier away from the front line for several months, and both would have to prove continuing abstinence and attendance at counselling/therapy sessions before being allowed to resume their regular duties.

- The OHP should continue monitoring for as long as necessary.
- Liaison with the employee's GP is advisable.
- The OHP will need to advise the line manager/supervisor of the need to support the employee on his or her return to work. At the same time, the OHP can reassure the line manager/supervisor that if a relapse occurs, it can be dealt with therapeutically provided the employee adheres to the two 'golden rules' (see immediately below).

In addition to the measures just outlined, there are two further golden rules that govern all aspects of employee-patients returning to work, namely if the drinking starts again, the individual

- must not attend work, and
- must report the incident to the OHP.

If the person attends work while under the influence of alcohol there is a probability that he or she will be dismissed. The reporting of the relapse to the OHP ensures that there is no return of denial and that the relapse becomes a therapeutic learning opportunity. The OHP and the employee can explore the reasons for the relapse and a strengthening of the negative reinforcement against alcohol can be further encouraged.

13. CONCLUSIONS

The OHP assessment is important for two main reasons: (1) it provides support to the employee referred for treatment and (2) it can help to ensure that the most appropriate treatment is administered. The OHP is in a good position to monitor the progress of the employee-patient on the latter's return to work, and to support the recommendations made by the rehabilitation team. The OHP should review the individual on a regular basis and facilitate the involvement of the employee's family and/or community if he or she decides that their support is needed.

14. ETHICAL CONSIDERATIONS

The medical profession's ethical rules of conduct maintain that an OHP, when he or she tests an employee-patient for alcohol or drugs, has a duty of confidentiality towards his or client. This means that the OHP cannot release details of the test results to a third party without the written informed consent of the employee-patient. In certain circumstances, however, some form of disclosure may be warranted. For example, where the OHP has a genuine reason to believe that the tested employee-patient represents a threat to him- or herself, to fellow employees, or to other persons (such as members of the public, for example), he or she should inform management that the employee is unfit to work

The duty of confidentiality is inevitably compromised in situations where management identifies actual or suspected intoxication or alcohol abuse in an employee and so refers him or her for assessment. Logic dictates that in these circumstances the OHP would inform management of the outcome of the assessment process and of whether the employee required counselling and/or treatment, or was fit or unfit to work.

Another form of acceptable disclosure is the release of statistical or group results since here the misuse of alcohol is identified in organisational terms and not in terms of individual employees.

While protecting the anonymity of individual employees who misuse alcohol, this method of disclosure also benefits management in that it is likely to shed light on the extent of alcohol abuse in the company *as a whole*. For example, if the OHP collates the results of all post-accident breathalyser tests and puts this data in his or her report, management can scrutinise the results to see what action is needed to improve company policy and practice in this area. In most circumstances, the relevant trade union(s) representatives would also be privy to this information.

However, there are also situations where it is permissible to reveal information regarding an individual alcohol-abusing employee. In any industry where dangers and high-risk safety factors exist, the medical personnel should consider the alcohol problem in a broader context. Because one is dealing with situations that are potentially lethal, not only for the individual employee but also for his or her co-workers, others present in the workplace and the general public, confidential information should be shared with the employee's direct manager, who should treat the information confidentially. Ethical standards and confidentiality are designed to protect the patient, but in a workplace setting medical staff also have a responsibility to protect the whole working community and the general public from potential dangers.

Despite these various exceptions to the principle of confidentiality, disclosure should still be regarded as a last resort. In most circumstances, the intoxicated or alcohol-abusing employee must be given every opportunity to correct his or her behaviour, including the chance to voluntarily disclose his or her problem. But if the employee refuses to take these opportunities and continues to attend work—and does so having disregarded the OHP's advice to stay away from the workplace since his/her continued presence at work constitutes a genuine threat to the health and safety of him- or herself and others—the OHP can inform management of the problem, having first informed the employee of this fact.

Occupational health services exist to monitor health and prevent work illness, not to police workers, and therefore OHPs should not involve themselves in any drug-testing programme carried out specifically for security or disciplinary purposes. A health service that does involve itself in drug testing for protective or punitive reasons may, understandably, be seen by workers as a managerial means of control and not as an objective service to which they would be willing to confide personal health information. Such conduct would, furthermore, breach the ethical obligations of the medical staff to their patients, the employees. They would be acting— and be seen to be doing so—as agents of management for non-health purposes, which would undermine their position.

Periodic testing for drug or alcohol abuse can be implemented as part of a regular health screening programme. In this context such testing becomes simply another health test, and if an abuse problem is identified during such screening, the next step should be confidential counselling and monitoring by the medical personnel. This could be written into the Alcohol and Drug or Substance Abuse Policy.

15. DEALINGS WITH MANAGEMENT

The OHP's relationship with management has several aspects; here we focus on the two most important: (i) the question of being given the freedom by management to perform their functions unhindered, and (ii) subjecting management to testing and treatment for alcohol or drug abuse.

The OHP must be able to assert the principles regarding the practice of occupational health care within a company. Management should not dictate to the OHP what tests or treatment should be done. Often an OHP feels isolated from management and vulnerable to management's authority. If an OHP feels that this authority is being exercised unfairly or improperly (such as when a senior manager instructs the OHP to release employee information to which the manager is not entitled, for example), he or she should immediately seek professional advice from the appropriate health council, association or other body.

The most difficult employee to treat for an alcohol problem is the senior manager. The work and social pressures on the senior manager, who may be required to do considerable entertaining for the company, are all highly stressful and will most likely be part of the cause of an alcohol problem. They may feel trapped by their responsibilities or their work; they may also have few opportunities to release their emotional or even rebellious feelings. Often they have been protected for many years by their secretaries or by other colleagues, which makes the task of confronting them about their problem particularly daunting. As denial is one of the first hurdles to overcome, the confrontation could become very difficult, particularly as confidentiality must be respected. The task is an onerous one. However, the OHP must acknowledge the fact that if he or she does not take action the manager's condition is likely to worsen, which will have serious consequences for the company and its employees in the long term.

One possible solution is for the OHP to persuade the senior manager to agree to being examined by an external specialist. The manager's acceptance of this alternative course of action is likely to be based on his or her perception that the external specialist will offer a more objective, less prejudicial assessment of his or her condition. The likelihood of a manager refusing to undergo 'in-house' treatment depends upon his or her level of seniority; the general rule being that the more senior the manager the more likely it is that he or she will reject the services of the company's OHP or other medical specialist. However, even if the manager should elect to use an outside specialist, the OHP will not disappear entirely from the picture. He or she will need to meet with the specialist to discuss the particulars of the case and to hand over any relevant information. The OHP can in return ask to see a copy of the specialist's report. This report will be added to the other documents the OHP will need in order to complete a medical profile of the manager, which in turn could be used to persuade the manager to accept that they have an abuse problem.

The role of the external specialist is dealt with further in the next chapter (chapter 16).

16. THE ROLE OF THE OCCUPATIONAL HEALTH PROFESSIONAL AS COUNSELLOR

Although it is widely accepted that substance-abusing patients require some form of counselling as part of their treatment, the question of who fulfils the role of counsellor remains a contentious issue. There are two broad schools of thought on the issue: those who insist that any genuinely empathetic, supportive individual can do the job and those who maintain that counselling should be done only by professionally trained counsellors.

Corney[10] evaluated twelve controlled studies comparing different counselling techniques and concluded that the type of counselling used was far less important than the relationship which developed between counsellor and client or patient. Durlak[11] found that there was no demonstrable difference, as regards outcome, between the help provided by paraprofessionals and professionals; in his study, the lay counsellors achieved results equal to or even better than those of the professionals. Durlak's findings are supported by the work of Berman and Norton.[12] Corney observes that these results led some researchers to hypothesise that it was the non-specific effects of the therapy which were important and that basic counselling skills should be developed in all health care workers. There may sometimes be an underlying psychiatric problem that needs the attention of a trained professional. The health care worker must be aware of his own fallibility and be prepared to refer a patient when the need arises.

Lazarus[13] states that psychosocially impaired persons such as employees with an alcohol problem are best treated in an occupational environment as such problems are usually poorly detected and inadequately treated in the community. An OHP is thus ideally placed to counsel the employee with a developing problem that has been identified by indirect medical tests; on the other hand, the employee with a severe dependency problem should be referred to a professionally trained counsellor.

17. RELATIONSHIPS WITH LOCAL COMMUNITY DOCTORS AND OTHER HEALTH CARE WORKERS

Doctors in general practice (private or public) are not faced with the realities that affect the OHP in the workplace. It has been estimated that only 10% of patients with a serious alcohol problem are likely to be routinely recognised by a general practitioner. Research on this subject suggests that the GP often finds it difficult to ask patients about their drinking habits and that such information is not acquired routinely in consultations.[14]

The OHP, by contrast, often has in-depth knowledge of the drinking habits of the individuals the GP sees for a variety of other reasons. By passing on this information to the GPs and other health care workers, the OHP can help raise awareness of the presence and extent of alcohol abuse in the community. The OHP can furnish community health professionals with statistics on the use and abuse of alcohol in one or a number of companies; outline the various Alcohol and Drug Policies that are in place, and indicate what company-led initiatives for the care and treatment of employee-patients exist. By taking this action the OHP directly supports the local health service's efforts to encourage at-risk individuals to come forward for treatment.

The GP can in turn support the work of the OHP. For example, suppose that the OHP of a particular company notices that short-term sick notes are being submitted on a regular basis by an individual employee. The OHP suspects that alcohol may be

10 Corney, RH 'Counselling in general practice –- does it work?'(1990) 83 *J Royal Soc Medicine* 253-257.

11 Durlak, JA 'Comparative effectiveness of para-professional and professional helpers'(1979) 86 *Psychol Bull* 80-92.

12 Berman, JS & Norton, NC 'Does professional training make a therapist more effective?'(1985) 98 *Psychol Bull* 401-407.

13 Lazarus, RS 'A cognitively orientated psychologist looks at bio-feedback'(1975) 30 *Am Psychol* 553.

14 Robertson, C 'Alcohol a public health problem. Is there a role for the GP?'(1990) 83 *J Royal Soc Medicine* 232-236.

a factor but feels that further investigation is needed. The OHP could telephone the employee's doctor and explain his or her concerns, and request that the doctor assess the underlying causes in more detail the next time the employee asks for a sick note. Details of the doctors commonly used by employees can be extracted from sick-note records.

SUMMARY

The role of the OHP in relation to alcohol or drug abuse is twofold: (i) to provide help to substance-abusing employees, and (ii) to protect the employee, other employees and the company from the hazards of substance abuse in the workplace. As we have discovered in this chapter, the duality of the OHP's position within a company creates a number of challenges; the fact that the needs of the first group (the employee-patients) very often conflict with those of the second being the greatest. The ethical implications associated with testing for drink or drug abuse represent another challenge.

If we recall that the OHP is sometimes pressured by management to use testing for disciplinary or security purposes, the precarious nature of his or her position becomes even more apparent.

Despite these challenges, the OHP must strive to maintain his or her independence within the organisational framework. If employees believe that the OHP is acting under the instructions of senior management it is highly unlikely that they will cooperate with or confide in him or her. The autonomy of the OHP is something that should be stated in any collective agreements between management and trade unions and in all corporate Alcohol and Drug Policies.

As well as the issues mentioned above, the chapter also discussed the various types of treatment that are available for employees suffering from alcohol addiction or dependency. Detoxification and post-treatment interventions were considered.

We also looked at the role of the OHP as counsellor and at his or her relationship with management, including senior management. The chapter ended with a brief consideration of the nature of the relationship between an OHP and the health care professionals of his or her local community. A company is part of the surrounding community and the success of an alcohol-abuse or drug-abuse programme can be increased by communicating with the local doctors and health care workers and seeking their support.

Chapter 18

The Workplace as a Setting for Substance Abuse Prevention Initiatives: A Brief Overview

Mike McCann & Nadine Harker Burnhams

1. INTRODUCTION

The increasing incidence of alcohol and drug problems in organisations and industrial settings has been widely discussed in recent years.[1] Substance abuse in the workforce has a negative impact on the workplace, which translates into enormous financial loss to industry, usually in the form of accidents, lost productivity, high turnover and extra training costs.[2,3] This suggests that there is a link between substance abuse and dangerous, dysfunctional behaviours such as workplace accidents and injuries.[4] The negative effects of substance abuse extend beyond the periphery of the workplace, however. The families of substance-abusing employees often have to deal with the consequences of a family member's alcohol or drug problem, and the tension this creates can lead to acrimonious relationships within the home. Since substance abuse has also been associated with financial, legal and other problems it has become clear that substance abuse is a societal problem and a legitimate workplace concern.

2. REASONS FOR INTRODUCING SUBSTANCE ABUSE PREVENTION PROGRAMMES TO THE WORKPLACE

The workplace represents an ideal environment for providing substance abuse prevention messages to working adults.[5,6] Two decades ago the Exxon Valdez oil spill disaster drew attention and aroused major concern about alcohol use and safety in the workplace and the need for policies and programmes to prevent substance abuse at work.

---

1   Elliott, K & Shelly, K 'Effects of drugs and alcohol on behaviour, job performance and workplace safety' (2006) 43 *Journal of Employment Counselling* 43, 130–134.

2   Ibid.

3   Spell, CS & Blum, TC 'Adoption of workplace substance abuse prevention programs: strategic choice and institutional perspectives' (2005) 48 (6) *Academy of Management Journal* 1125-1142.

4   Hersch, RK, Cook, RF, Deitz, DK & Trudeau, JV 'Workplace Substance Abuse Prevention Research' (2000) 27 (2) *Journal of Behavioural Health Services and Research* 144–151.

5   Ibid.

6   Zungu, LI, & Setswe, KG 'An integrated approach to the prevention and promotion of health in the workplace: a review from international experience' (2007)49 (6) *South African Family Practice* 6-9.

Many facets of the workplace require constant alertness as well as accuracy, and perhaps quick reflexes if machinery or other technical equipment is present.[7] Any impairment to these qualities can cause serious accidents and interfere with the precision and effectiveness of work. The Occupational Health and Safety Act 85 of 1993 prohibits the use of illicit substances in the workplace to ensure a safe working environment for all employees. In addition, the Act clearly states at s 8(1) that 'every employer shall provide and maintain, as far as is reasonably practicable, a working environment that is safe and without risk to the health of his employees.' The existence of this stringent legislation against substance abuse allows for organisations to have considerable influence over their employees' work-related behaviour, which makes the workplace the ideal locus for interventions.

Traditionally the focus of workplace interventions was on identifying the troubled employee and referring him or her for rehabilitation. This often happened when an employee was already in the late chronic stages of the disease or already dependent on alcohol or drugs. Organisations spend large sums of money on the rehabilitation of a worker with a chronic substance abuse problem. Costs often include, but are not limited to, hiring, training and paying a temporary replacement worker in the absence of the troubled employee. By introducing a prevention programme that targets the whole workforce or segments thereof, the organisation puts measures in place that delay or prevent workers from using alcohol or drugs at risky levels; the prevention programme can also act as a safeguard against future spending on employee rehabilitation.

Although specific data on substance abuse in the workplace is scarce, the few data sources that do exist highlight the substance abuse scourge. (We considered the extent of alcohol and drug abuse in chapters 2 and 4.) Additional sources of information such as a survey by Health24[8] mention that employees working fulltime in South Africa are more likely than their drug-free counterparts to have had more than two jobs, are five times more likely to have filed for a worker's compensation claim and have been absent without leave more often. They are also more likely to have undergone a disciplinary hearing or been fired in the past year.[9,10] On the international front, studies in Australia found that nearly half of the Australian workforce drank at levels associated with risk of harm.[11] The International Labour Organisation further highlights that the population at highest risk for developing substance abuse disorders is the 20- to 30- year-old age group, which forms part of the adult working population.[12] It is therefore clear that there is ample opportunity to target efforts at universal or other prevention levels in the workplace.

---

7   Canadian Centre of Occupational Health and Safety *Substance abuse in the workplace* (2010) http:// www.ccohs.ca/oshanswers/psychosocial/substance.html (accessed March 2010).

8   Rose-Inness. 2008. Health 24: Drugging on the job (accessed July 2008). http://www.health24. com/mind/sexual dysfunction.

9   Hersch et al (n 4).

10   Spell, CS & Blum, TC 'Adoption of workplace substance abuse prevention programs: strategic choice and institutional perspectives' (2005) 48 (6) *Academy of Management Journal* 1125-1142.

11   Pidd, K & Roche, A 'Prevention of alcohol-related harm in the workplace' (2009) 8 (1) *Prevention Research Quarterly*. National Centre for Education and Training on Addiction (NCETA), Flinders University, South Australia. www.druginfo.adf.org.au (accessed July 2010).

12   International Labour OrganisationCommunication and Public Information Unit (2010) http:// www.ilo.org/global/About_the_ILO/Media_and_public_information/Press_releases/lang–en/ WCMS_007992/index.htm (accessed March 2010).

Lastly, the workplace provides access to large groups of people who otherwise may not seek assistance[13] or who may not have been accessible. In addition, fulltime employees spend at least 8 hours of their day at work, which maximizes opportunities for exposure to intervention programmes.[14]

3. TYPES OF PREVENTION AND APPROPRIATE INTERVENTION STRATEGIES

Prevention at its broadest can be defined as a proactive process that creates and reinforces conditions that promote healthy behaviours and lifestyles,[15] but specific to substance abuse it can be defined as any activity designed to prevent or delay the onset of substance use disorders.[16] There are many different types of prevention, which can be categorised as follows: universal, selective or indicated.

Universal prevention measures target the general public or a whole population with the aim to promote healthy behaviour and reduce the use of alcohol and drugs in the workplace but also in the social and domestic environments.[17] Selective prevention interventions, on the other hand, are aimed at subgroups of the population whose risk of developing the disorder is significantly higher than that of the general population. Such interventions would mainly be focused on employees who may be more at risk for developing a substance-related disorder because their job exposes them to a higher degree of risk. Jobs involving the use of heavy machinery, mine work, and work with hazardous chemicals is associated with an increased probability of using illicit substances.[18] Indicated interventions aim to identify individuals who are exhibiting early signs of problematic use or substance abuse and/or other problem behaviours, and to target these behaviours with focused interventions.[19] This could possibly take the form of brief interventions aimed at mobilising an employee into treatment.

As indicated in previous chapters, substance use disorders occur along a continuum of severity ranging from no use to dependence, with various stages in between.[20] The World Health Organisation[21] recommends the use of different intervention strategies for each level of severity, with interventions increasing in intensity as problem severity

---

13   Cook, R & Schlenger, W 'Prevention of Substance Abuse in the Workplace: Review of Research on the Delivery of Services' (2002) 23 (1) *Journal of Primary Prevention* 115-142.

14   Pidd & Roche (n 12).

15   Atkinson, AJ, Tolbert, IK *Our common language: a quick guide to prevention terminology in Virginia* (2004).

16   World Health Organisation 'Prevention of psychoactive substance use: a selected review of what works in the area of prevention' Switzerland (2002).

17   Sloboda, Z & Bukoski, WJ *Handbook of drug abuse prevention: Theory, Science, and Practice* (2003) Kluwer Academic/Plenum publishers: New York.

18   Bennett, JB, Lehman, WEK & Reynolds, GS 'Team Awareness for Workplace Substance Abuse Prevention: The Empirical and Conceptual Development of a Training Program' (2000) 1 (2) *Prevention Science* 157–172.

19   Medina-Mora, ME 'Prevention of substance abuse: a brief overview' (2005) 4 (1) *World Psychiatry* 25-30.

20   National Institute on Drug Abuse *Principles of Drug Addiction Treatment. A Research Based Guide* (1999) National Institute of Health Bethesda, Washington.

21   World Health Organisation *National Drug and Alcohol Treatment Responses in 23 countries. Results of a key informant survey* (1993)Geneva WHO, Department of Mental Health and Substance Abuse.

increases.[22] Table 18.1 below depicts the appropriate intervention strategies for each level of substance use. For instance, universal prevention programmes are suitable for employees with no-use or occasional substance use as these activities attempt to prevent or delay substance abuse. Selective or indicated prevention programmes may be more suited to those misusing alcohol or drugs.

Table 18.1 Appropriate intervention strategies for each level of substance use (Myers, Harker et al, 2008).

Different stages of substance use and the appropriate intervention	
No use **Use**	Prevention Prevention—no treatment required
Misuse	Prevention and brief /early intervention
Abuse	Brief intervention and out- or in-patient treatment services
Dependence	Detoxification and in- or out-patient treatment, and sometimes mental health services, as well as aftercare (continuing support) services. Harm reduction services for individuals with chronic dependence.

This is also covered in chapter 17 (The Role of the Occupational Health Professional).

4. GUIDELINES FOR INTRODUCING PREVENTION PROGRAMMES TO THE WORKPLACE

Workplace prevention uses existing organisational structures in the workplace to deliver alcohol and drug abuse prevention messages. However, it is important to ensure that certain actions have been taken before introducing such programmes.

4.1 Understanding organisational context—the culture of the organisation

Before the introduction of any prevention or other programme into the workplace, it is crucial to gain an understanding of workers' pattern of substance use and the relationship between workers' consumption and the actual workplace. This can be done by conducting a needs analysis or risk assessment (see chapter 7). Rossi and colleagues highlight the importance of asking key questions about the nature and magnitude of the problem as well as the characteristics of the population in need,[23] which thus allows for the development of evidence-based strategies.

4.2 Policy development

If a company plans to introduce prevention programmes either as part of an existing health promotion programme or as an independently conceived EAP, it should be clearly stipulated in the company's substance abuse policy. If there is no policy in place, introducing one is advisable. Policy formation will require the input of management,

---

22 Myers, B, Harker, N, Fakier, N, Kader, R & Mazok, C *A review of evidence-based interventions for the prevention and treatment of substance use disorders* (2008) Technical Report Medical Research Council, South Africa.

23 Rossi., PH, Lipsey, MW, & Freeman, HE *Evaluation: A Systematic Approach* 7 ed (2004).

staff and the trade union(s) (see chapter 20, Proposed Substance Abuse Policy and Procedural Agreement). The policy should be a comprehensive document that provides a clear statement outlining the organisation's position on substance abuse and a set of guidelines and strategies for dealing with substance abuse in the workplace.[24] Effective policies are broad brush in nature, and are therefore implemented throughout the industry and designed to fit the operating requirements of the particular organisation.

5. PROGRAMME DEVELOPMENT

The development of any workplace programme should be a collaborative process that engages all key role players. Ideally, representatives from management and supervisors, the Human Resources department, trade unions, and the occupational health and medical departments should participate in the choice of a prevention intervention. The use of evidence-based prevention programmes is always encouraged and advised. Evidence-based practices are practices, interventions or programmes for which there is a large body of research evidence in support of its effectiveness.[25,26] In other words, evidence-based interventions are based on solid theories or theoretical perspectives that have been validated by research suggesting that the study has been subjected to at least one randomised clinical trial which shows the practice/intervention to be effective. In addition to the above, the chosen intervention/practice should have demonstrated effectiveness in several replicated research studies using different population groups. It is advisable to seek the assistance of workplace prevention programme specialists when selecting a programme for implementation.

6. WORKPLACE PREVENTION STRATEGIES

Workplace prevention strategies aim to effectively change the organisational culture and can be divided into five main categories: health promotion, peer interventions, psychosocial skills training, drug testing and employee assistance programmes. The latter two have received attention in chapters 10 (testing) and 19 (EAPs), and will therefore not be discussed in detail. Although they have been placed under the banner of workplace programmes, it should be understood that current prevention programmes have their roots in the EAP and drug testing.

6.1 Health promotion

The use of health promotion programmes is a relatively recent strategy for responding to alcohol and other drug issues in the workplace.[27] In general, health promotion programmes do not specifically focus on alcohol or other drugs, rather, they focus on improving the overall health of employees. The basic premise of health promotion programmes is that a healthy lifestyle is incompatible with heavy alcohol consumption and/or risky drug use. This being so, incorporating alcohol and other drug issues

---

24 Pidd & Roche (n 12).

25 Myers (n 18).

26 Ruiz, M & Auerbach, J 'What is the "evidence" in evidence-based HIV prevention?' www.hiv-prevention.org/docs/topics/Evidence_fact_sheet.pdf (accessed 29 September 2008).

27 Cook & Schlenger (n 14).

within the context of health concerns in general, can be seen as an effective method of motivating behaviour change regarding alcohol and other drug use.[28]

6.2 Drug testing

Workplace drug testing became popular in the 1970s[29] when the identification and removal of substance-abusing employees was considered to be the best way to manage problems of alcohol or drug misuse in the work environment. There is however very little research concerning the effectiveness of alcohol and drug testing as a standalone preventative measure for reducing alcohol- and drug-related harm.[30,31]

6.3 Peer interventions

Peer education first gained prominence in the 1960s and is now a well-established form of intervention, particularly within schools and the youth service.[32] Peer intervention has also been effectively used with adults in a workplace context. Strongly associated with drug use, peer education's appeal rests on the assertion that fellow workers are in the best position to respond to workers with alcohol or drug problems.[33] Peer interventions make use of workers that are trained as facilitators who are able to recognise alcohol and drug problems and to intervene appropriately.

6.4 Psychosocial skills training

Psychosocial skills training programmes aim to develop psychological skills among employees by using strategies such as motivational interviewing, cognitive behavior therapy, goals setting, problem solving and even coping skills.[34,35] There is a strong evidence base for the effectiveness of alcohol-related psychosocial intervention in primary prevention settings.[36]

7. PROGRAMME AWARENESS

Employees should be made aware of the existence of prevention programmes and the associated policy on substance abuse in the workplace. A series of short awareness programmes would achieve this objective. In this type of programme the focus is on delivering useful information in a concise, easily understandable manner. The programme co-ordinator typically presents a summary of the most important aspects of the substance abuse policy and programme, such as the consequences of alcohol or drug abuse in the workplace and the factors that can increase the risk of developing a substance-related disorder.

---

28 Elliott, K & Shelley, K 'Effects of drugs and alcohol on behavior, job performance and workplace safety' (2006) *Journal of Employment Counselling* 43, 130–134.
29 Albertyn & McCann (n 8) at 93–94.
30 Pidd & Roche (n 12).
31 Cook & Schlenger (n 14) at 115–141.
32 Shriner, M 'Defining peer education' (1999) 22 *Journal of Adolescence* 555–566.
33 Pidd & Roche (n 12).
34 Pidd and Roche (n 12).
35 Foxcroft, DR, Ireland, D, Lister-Sharp, G & Breen, R 'Longer-term primary prevention for alcohol misuse in young people: a systematic review' (2003) 1 (93) *Addiction* 397-411.
36 Ibid.

Such programmes also provide the opportunity to tell employees about the help that is available for individuals with drink and/or drug problems. According to Pidd and Roche,[37] the success of any workplace response to alcohol- and drug-related harm is dependent on changing existing attitudes and behaviours relating to alcohol and drug use.

8. PROGRAMME DELIVERY

Ideally, prevention programmes should be flexible, interactive and should make use of various methods for delivering and conducting the prevention programme.[38] Programmes can be delivered to small groups of employees or even to individual employees. Delivery can be done through the use of assorted communication methods, such as email, the intranet/internet, quarterly newsletters, pamphlets and bulletins. Some studies have also reported on the effectiveness of e-learning methods as a preventative tool.[39] Most of these methods (the exceptions are email and the intranet) allow the employee to access information anonymously, which may reassure those employees who believe they will be stigmatised should their problems be revealed to others. Some organisations even have an onsite wellness library where workers will find a wealth of material on a range of psychosocial issues.

9. PROGRAMME EVALUATION

Research and other academic literature emphasises the importance of monitoring and evaluating substance abuse prevention and treatment programs, not only because this helps identify areas in which services can be improved, but also because evidence of programme effectiveness can inform decision-making around the distribution of prevention programmes. However, despite the widespread use of prevention programmes worldwide in both the corporate and education sectors, external evaluations of programmes seldom, if ever, take place.[40] Organisations making use of prevention programmes should build evaluation into the programme budget and outline.

SUMMARY

This chapter's review of the literature reveals the importance of structured prevention programmes as a means of eradicating or minimising substance abuse in the workplace. The workplace is the ideal setting in which to introduce intervention programmes since it affords access to a large group of people who may otherwise have been out of reach. Programmes on substance abuse in the workplace can be introduced under the broad umbrella of health and safety or health promotion, thereby removing the stigma attached to substance abuse. The introduction of any prevention programme should follow the principles laid down in the organisation's policy document on substance abuse in the workplace; this document should also provide guidance on how incidents of substance

---

37 Pidd & Roche (n 12).

38 Foxcroft (n 36) 397–411.

39 Matano, RA, Koopman, C, Wanat, SF, Winzelberg, AJ, Whitsell, SD, Westrup, D. Futa,K, Clayton, JB, Mussman, L & Barr Taylor, C 'A pilot study of an interactive web site in the workplace for reducing alcohol consumption' (2007) 32 *Journal of Substance Abuse Treatment* 71 – 80.

40 Myers (n 18) at 557–565.

abuse are to be processed. The development of both the policy document and the prevention programme is a collaborative effort that requires the input of management and employees. The prevention programme should also take into account the views of personnel in the occupational health and/or medical departments.

Chapter 19

Treatment: Employee Assistance Programmes

Mike McCann & Nadine Harker Burnhams

1. INTRODUCTION

The Employee Assistance Programme (EAP) is one of the fundamental ways in which a company can attempt to treat the alcohol or drug problem in its constituency. The purpose of any EAP is to help employees who have or may develop social, behavioural or health problems that could affect work productivity or the safety of the employee or other employees.[1] Many EAPs also offer support to the families of troubled employees.

EAPs are generic in their service delivery; they do not focus solely on alcohol- and drug-related problems but are equipped to intervene when such cases arise within the workplace. Additionally, EAPs are restorative and preventative and not punitive in nature.[2]

Although the chapter focuses on the EAP, it is important to briefly discuss Employee Wellness Programmes (EWPs) in relation to EAPs. Over the last decade, organisations have adopted a more holistic method for maintaining and improving employees' health. EWPs are informed by the concept of wellness, which can be defined as 'an active process of becoming aware of and making choices toward a more successful existence'.[3] Wellness involves taking care of one's physical and mental self, expressing emotions effectively, fostering positive relations and being concerned for one's physical, psychological and spiritual environments. EWPs embrace the concept of prevention in addition to the therapeutic intervention, which is the sole focus of the EAP.

2. TYPES OF EMPLOYEE ASSISTANCE PROGRAMMES

An EAP can function as an internal corporate resource or together with the assistance of an external agency. It is however imperative that an EAP, whether run internally or externally, provides a service that is voluntary, ensures confidentiality and neutrality and is available and accessible to all employees.

Traditionally EAPs were focused on treating employees exhibiting alcohol- and drug-related problems. The unfortunate effect is that alcohol and drug abuse can make up

---

1 Csiernik, R 'Ideas on Best Practices for Employee Assistance Program Policies' (2003) 18 (3) *Employee Assistance Quarterly* 15-32.

2 Ibid.

3 Harker, Nadine 'Occupational Stressors experienced by persons working shifts at a local motor manufacturing plant.' (Nelson Mandela Metropolitan University unpublished Masters Dissertation, 2006).

only a relatively small percentage of the total number of such referrals.[4] Today EAPs apply the 'broad-brush' approach, whereby all problems that can impact on the individual employee—matrimonial, financial and psychological, as well as substance abuse—are included in the programme. Although there have been calls for the modification of the broad-brush approach to give greater emphasis to those employees with specific alcohol or drug problems, it should be stressed that EAP practitioners are skilled in the early identification of substance-abuse problems and speedily initiate referrals in instances where employees require immediate treatment.

A weakness of the first approach (a focus on only alcohol and drug problems) is that the supervisor's attempt to identify substance abuse factors that are relevant to the job performance can lead to unnecessary confrontation between the supervisor and the employee concerned. Moreover, confrontation in unskilled hands can be manipulated by the employee being confronted. Plausible explanations, generalisations such as 'there is always someone else who drinks more' and endless arguments can develop to such an extent that the supervisor could be reluctant to confront an employee again. The supervisor should therefore not confront the employee concerned with any accusation of alcohol or drug abuse; should he or she require the employee to attend an inquiry, he or she should at least be capable of identifying the performance indicators of substance abuse. The employee can then be informed of his performance or behavioural problem and be referred for assessment.

It is also important to consider the issue of stigma in relation to substance abuse. The broad-brush approach minimises stigmatisation, as an employee may seek EAP services for a multitude of problems and not necessarily for substance related problems only. Although substantial strides have been made toward the general acceptance of addiction as a treatable disease there is still much stigma attached to substance abuse. Employees may not be willing to take any action, such as approaching the EAP for services, that might, in the slightest way, indicate that they could have a substance abuse problem.[5]

3. ACCESS TO THE EMPLOYEE ASSISTANCE PROGRAMME

Self-referrals are the aim of a successful EAP.[6] They have been found to increase substantially with the implementation of the broad-brush EAP, but these self-referrals were often for problems besides alcohol. However, it has been recognised that those who seek assistance for a problem voluntarily are more successful in resolving their problems.[7] The extent of self-referrals seems to depend upon whether the programme is operated internally or by an external agency: in the latter case, there is a much higher rate of self-referral. The internal programmes, on the other hand, tend to generate a higher proportion of alcohol-problem referrals as compared to the external service, because the internal programmes tend to be supervisor- rather than employee-driven.

4   Levinson, H *Current trends in Employee Assistance Programs: will the pendulum swing?* paper presented at the International Institute on Prevention and Treatment of Alcoholism (Berlin, June 1990) 150.

5   Cook, R & Schlenger, W 'Prevention of Substance Abuse in the Workplace:
     Review of Research on the Delivery of Services' (2002) 23 (1) *The Journal of Primary Prevention* 115-142.

6   Galanter, M (ed) (1988) 6 *Recent Developments in Alcoholism* 333–349.

7   Csiernik (n 1) at 15–32.

From his experiences at a Copenhagen municipal out-patient clinic for alcoholics, Jensen[8] discovered that patients seldom came for treatment voluntarily. They did so because there was internal or external pressure on them as a result of the alcohol problem, and they felt that treatment was the lesser of the pressures to which they could be subjected.

Supervisor-driven referrals can be done formally or informally depending on the severity of the problem and previous attempts at referral. In the case of an informal referral the suggestion to use the EAP is made by a colleague, union member, medical staff member or supervisor, and has often been described as a 'gentle nudge' towards treatment. A formal referral, on the other hand, is made once an employee's work performance suffers and there is a clear pattern of decline. Formal referrals are not a disciplinary measure but a means to assist the employee. However, should the employee decide not to make use of the EAP and there is no visible improvement in work performance, this may lead to disciplinary measures. It is also important for employees to have access to follow-up services; this will ensure that they continue to receive the type of counselling or treatment needed to avoid, or at least to effectively manage, relapses.

> The majority of alcohol- and drug-abusing individuals go undetected.

4. THE SUPERVISOR'S ROLE IN AN EMPLOYEE ASSISTANCE PROGRAMME

According to the literature, the success of EAPs is largely determined by the supervisor— the key person in the entire process.[9] It is the supervisor who has to put up with the absenteeism, errors, personal problems and deteriorating job performance of the alcohol or drug abuser. It is the supervisor who may ultimately have to make the painful decision to discharge a once valuable employee because his drinking or drug taking has destroyed his ability to function at work. And it is the supervisor, second only to the drug-addicted or -dependent employee himself, who has the most to gain from a programme that couples early identification of the problem with prompt referral to a competent source of assistance.

Literature suggests that supervisors refrain from diagnosing an employee's alcohol or drug problem or acting as a counsellor to the employee. Supervisors should limit their intervention to only discussing employee performance issues.[10] This ensures that the supervisor does not fall into what is often described as the 'quicksand trap'.[11]

The quicksand trap describes the damage caused to workplace relations when a supervisor and a substance-abusing employee become caught in an unproductive role-playing cycle that tends to worsen an already difficult situation. The roles assumed are that of victim, rescuer or persecutor.

Consider the example of an employee who abuses alcohol, which has a negative impact on his performance. The supervisor decides to cover for the employee in the hope that his behaviour will improve and that the issue will in due course resolve itself. However, by allowing the inappropriate behaviour to continue the supervisor initiates the

---

8   Jensen, K 'Why does an alcohol abuser seek treatment?' in *A Danish Approach to the Treatment of Alcoholism* (1983) section 4.

9   SANCA Employee Assistance Programmes—Training Manual (2004).

10   SANCA 2004; Csiernik (n 1).

11   SANCA (n 9).

enabling process and assumes the role of rescuer; the employee being the victim. But the employee's behaviour does not improve; in fact the situation deteriorates. In spending time 'rescuing' the employee, the supervisor's own work begins to suffer. Senior management becomes aware of this and subjects the supervisor to closer scrutiny. The supervisor, who up to this point has been trying to help, starts to feel victimised. Resenting the fact that he or she has been placed in this position, the supervisor abandons the role of victim and assumes the role of persecutor. The supervisor-as-persecutor looks for opportunities to find fault with the employee with the aim of removing the problem or the employee. There will usually be a confrontation between the supervisor and the employee during this stage. During the argument the supervisor is likely to threaten the employee with disciplinary action unless his (the employee's) behaviour improves; the employee, in turn, will invariably promise to mend his ways. The cycle therefore completes itself when the supervisor accepts the promise and moves back into the rescuer or enabler role.

The supervisor should use objective criteria for assessing job performance to identify the alcohol or drug abuser and refer him or her on the grounds of poor or deteriorating work performance. The supervisor is advised not to delve into the reasons for the inadequate performance, but merely to refer the worker to the programme for assessment and treatment. As the poor job performance criteria build up, documentation is the important monitoring tool for developing a profile of the job performance. The supervisor's role is to observe poor work performance, document it and inform the employee of the observations before referring him or her for assessment to the EAP. It is essential to document all unacceptable behaviour, attendance, and job performance that fail to meet established standards.

The skill of the supervisor lies not only in the detection of often small changes in employee behaviour or work performance but also in the caring yet confrontational manner in which he or she deals with substance-abusing employees. In other words, the supervisor has to both support (care for) and challenge (confront) employees. This would seem to be an almost impossible task since the two duties (caring and confronting) appear to cancel each other out. The supervisor who *can* reconcile the need to be simultaneously empathetic and impartial towards employees is of great value to his employer. The truth, however, is that only a few companies engage supervisors of the required, that is, high, standard. Poor supervision is the norm in many organisations, which is one of the main reasons why many EAPs fail or are only partly successful. The expectations of management are that all the alcohol and drug abusers will be identified and the problem put to rest, but the reality is often very different. The EAP cannot be expected to yield positive results under conditions of poor supervisory control, particularly if inadequate supervision was wholly or partly responsible for the onset of substance abuse in the first place.

The success of an EAP depends upon proper performance appraisals by supervisors of the employees in their charge and upon correct confrontation with alcohol- and drug-abusing employees. This places a great onus upon them, and poses a particular difficulty for the lower-level supervisor, who may come from the same subculture of drinking as the workers he or she supervises. Generally, though, the greater the social distance between supervisor and employee, the more likely it is that the confrontation or management of the problem will succeed.

Meanwhile, the modern-day supervisor undertakes several tasks that his predecessor would not have been expected to perform. The role of supervisor has expanded to include a range of white-collar functions that have very little to do with the direct control and regulation of workplace activities. These functions include the compilation of reports for production, budgets and accident statistics, and participation in or management of maintenance projects, development strategies and human resource policies. On top of this he or she now has to observe and document progressive, often subtle, changes in the work performance of employees which he or she may find tedious and time consuming.

A supervisor may also find the task of confronting poor performance a challenge in instances where the supervisor has perhaps been promoted because he or she is the longest-serving employee in the section or the best at working with a particular machine. With a promotion his or her role has changed: he or she must acquire the skills to lead, motivate, instruct and give orders; often when under stress, and to administer ever-increasing paperwork. On the other hand the greater assertiveness of unionised workers is making the supervisor's task even more complex and difficult. The combination of these factors tends to make the supervisor more reluctant to confront intoxication, and as a result his or her pivotal role in the EAP may be undermined or compromised. In addition, numerous jobs are not closely supervised and quite often job performance is difficult to monitor, which results in there being no proper records by which to monitor performance. In such circumstances, the very foundation of the supervisor's role in the EAP is wanting.

5. LIMITATIONS OF AN EMPLOYEE ASSISTANCE PROGRAMME

Kurtz et al[12] showed that there is usually a collective awareness by co-workers of the employees who are developing a problem with alcohol or drugs. They interviewed supervisors who had referred employees to the EAP, and found that the first indication of a performance problem was usually a dramatic episode such as the employee passing out in the workplace. Forty per cent of the supervisors sampled stated that no performance problems were noted prior to the dramatic incident. A supervisor under pressure to complete a job, shared how he preferred to have an intoxicated employee working at 30–50% of his productivity than to send him home.

Unfortunately the majority of alcohol-abusing individuals go undetected. Reichman et al[13] estimated that the identification rate in EAPs ranged from 0,1–1,6% with a mean of 0,64% of the workforce per year.[14] Shain[15] also shows the discrepancy between the cases identified and the prevalence of alcohol abuse. He studied 10 broad-based EAPs and discovered that the number of alcohol abusers identified ranged from 0,18–1,4% with a mean of 0,18% of the workforce per year. These figures must be compared to the prevalence rates of alcohol abuse associated with the employed population: usually between 7% and 20% of the workforce experience alcohol problems. These percentages therefore represent employees in the later, more dependent and

---

12 Kurtz, B, Googins, B & Williams, C 'Supervisors' views of an occupational alcoholism programme' (1980) *Alcohol, Health* 44-49.

13 Reichman, W, Young, DW & Gracin, L 'Identification of alcoholics in the workplace' (1988) 6 *Recent Developments in Alcoholism* 171-179.

14 Ibid.

15 Shain, M 'Alcohol, drugs and safety: an updated perspective on problems and their management in the workplace' (1982) 14 *Accidents & Prevention* 239-246.

physically destructive stages of the problem. O'Reilly and Weitz[16] suggest that, if early identification of alcohol abuse amongst employees is considered, then the overall prevalence figure of the problem may more accurately be assumed to reach 20%. Thus, considering these references and using the 0,64% identification rate as an average, EAPs effectively identify only between 3,2% and 8,4% of all alcohol abusers in the workplace.

The South African Chamber of Mines estimates that its rate for identifying alcohol or drug abuse is 1% and that such identification occurs mainly at hospitals to which employees have been referred, often for reasons other than the identified alcohol- or drug-abuse problem.[17] Walker and Shain[18] have suggested that the low rate of identification of alcohol abusers in the EAPs reflects the programmes' inherent inability to identify most employees with a drinking problem. They suggest that organisations do not incur losses from most of their alcohol-dependent employees because these employees do not manifest objective job performance problems. What they mean here is that the employee's reduced performance is not easy to measure objectively—the decline in work performance will be subtle, eg the employee will select less taxing work, his or her decision-making will be less acute though not necessarily blatantly erroneous, the time he or she spends handling a task will be extended but not to such an extent as necessarily to invoke censure.

This subtle shift in the quality of an employee's work performance highlights the problems facing the supervisor and an EAP. Our aim is not to discourage the use of the EAP but to place such a programme in perspective. It has value, but it should be combined with the other techniques of identification and treatment which we propose.

More generalised screening than mere performance appraisal may indicate alcohol problems in the workplace. In addition, it is important to reemphasize that only between 6–10% of employees engaging in drinking in a workforce will be dependent drinkers. The remaining employees fall within the 'no-use' or 'light-to- moderate' drinker categories. Detecting alcohol-related problems amongst moderate drinkers, who account for more than half of the workforce, is extremely difficult in comparison to those exhibiting dependency because signs and symptoms are less visible. More recent literature suggests that low-to-moderate drinkers present a higher absolute number of absences and accidents in the workplace and therefore pose a bigger risk. According to the International Labour Organisation, moderate or occasional alcohol and drug users cause 60–70% of workplace problems, therefore efforts to address alcohol and drug abuse in the workplace should reach the entire workforce and not only those exhibiting signs of dependency.[19]

---

16 O'Reilly, CA & Weitz, BA 'Managing marginal employees: the use of warnings and dismissals' (1980) 25 *Admin Science Q* 467-484.

17 Du Toit & Duncan Pers comm from J Starker Centre, Transvaal, 1990.

18 Walker, K & Shain, M 'Employee assistance programming: in search of effective interventions for the problem drinking employee' 1983 (78) *Br J Addiction* 291-303.

19 United Nations Office on Drugs and Crime (2005) Program for drug abuse prevention in the workplace and the family. UNODC. Geneva; Loxley, W, Toumbourou, J & Stockwell, T 'The prevention of substance use, risk and harm in Australia: a review of the evidence' (2003). The National Drug Research Institute and the Centre for Adolescent Health, Australia.

6. DEVELOPING A SUCCESSFUL EMPLOYEE ASSISTANCE PROGRAMME

How can more effective EAPs be developed? Although EAPs are unique to each workplace and industry, there are common characteristics that ensure the success of any EAP. Considering that most EAPs in South Africa employ the broad-brush approach, the question will be addressed from this perspective.

The first step is for the company to prepare a formal written policy outlining the principles and intent of the EAP it wishes to introduce. Preparing an alcohol and drug policy at the same time would also make sense since the two policies need to be closely aligned. Each policy should contain a preface in which the purpose of the policy, the responsibilities of the employer and the employees, and the procedural issues involved are briefly described. It is also helpful to draw on the relevant legislation applying to each of the policies.[20] The policies should be endorsed and signed by senior management (on behalf of the employer) and by a designated member of the labour force or an authorised trade union official (on behalf of the employees); this ensures the status of the policies. The policies themselves would show clear procedures for access to EAP services.

Education and promotion of the EAP service and alcohol and drug policy should be communicated to management, trade unions, health professionals and other counselling staff who might be involved in the actual implementation and operation of the EAP. Employees with alcohol or drug problems should also be informed about the EAP and the alcohol and drug policy and should be kept abreast of new initiatives. Regular evaluation of the EAP is recommended to ensure the service continues to be of benefit to employees and management. This can be done on an annual basis.

Ideally the EAP should target the entire workplace, offering generic counselling services and a professional alcohol and drug referral source. Reichman et al[21] and Parker and Farmer[22] have indicated that all employees with alcohol problems should be targeted by the programme and not just those whose condition has led to an observable deterioration in work performance. The learned authors have clarified what we regard as a fundamental insight: indications of deterioration in an employee's performance will in all likelihood mean that the employee's retrogression to dependent drinking is almost complete. The focus of an alcohol and drug programme must be to assist employees with a drinking or drug problem who have not reached such a state of dependence, and who have therefore not yet shown any significant deterioration in job performance.

Thus it is important to monitor and identify developing alcohol and drug problems. More generalised screening than mere performance appraisal may reveal the cause(s) of alcohol and drug problems in the workplace. Perhaps a group may be identified in a certain department or area of work as having a particular difficulty, which is causing the development of alcohol or drug problems among its members. What is needed is a link between the EAP and periodic medical screening tests conducted confidentially on all employees by the medical department. This approach would enable the medical department to address the problem confidentially with counselling until such time as the supervisor refers the employee for assessment or to the EAP. Likewise, if a disciplinary

---

20 CsiernikR, 'Ideas on best practice for employee assistance programme policies'(2003) 18(3) *Employee Assistance Quarterly 15–32.*

21 Reichman (n 13).

22 Parker, DA & Farmer, GC (1988) 6 *Recent Developments in Alcoholism* 113.

route has been adopted for the assessment, the employee has already been made aware that alcohol or drug abuse is the cause of his poor work performance.

Paul Roman[23] has suggested that the training programme for EAPs is often forgotten and that individual coaching of supervisors should be implemented. What is needed is a system by which the programme co-ordinator or a health expert is available on a hotline to give advice to supervisors concerning the correct implementation of the programme, thus providing reinforcement of the initial training. The EAP should be utilised at management-union meetings to reinforce the need for continual awareness regarding substance abuse in the workplace, just as the company's health and safety programme would be invoked to reaffirm employer and employee commitment to safe working practices and procedures.

7. EVALUATION OF THE EMPLOYEE ASSISTANCE PROGRAMME

As we mentioned above, an annual review of the EAP is needed to ensure its continued credibility. This review will encompass an appraisal of the company's approach to the treatment of substance abuse and whether changes are needed. Evaluation can take several forms. For instance, the value of the EAP can be considered in terms of its impact on a number of objective criteria, such as sickness absence, accidents, lateness and disciplinary hearings. The medical department should be able to provide input on the number of cases of physical illness due to alcohol or drug abuse. The EAP co-ordinator or the external agency should provide statistics regarding the number of cases assessed, the number treated, and the success rate among those treated. Those treated should be categorised as 'successful', 'partially successful', 'ongoing', and 'failed'. The audit should also include an indication of the percentages of self-referrals and of management referrals. The personnel department should provide information on the number of disciplinary inquiries for alcohol or drug abuse.

A cost-benefit analysis should, if possible, form the final input of the evaluation, despite the fact that hidden or indirect costs may have to be excluded from the analysis. The evaluation should be in the form of an annual report to management and union officials who will then address any shortcomings identified and decide upon what changes are needed in the year ahead.

SUMMARY

Employee Assistance Programmes have a role to play in the treatment of substance abuse in the workplace. Any initiative that offers help and support to employees suffering from alcohol and drug problems is to be welcomed and EAPs represent one such initiative. However, we wish to reiterate a point we made earlier: EAPs should not be regarded as the solution to problems of substance abuse at work. As we have seen in this chapter, and as we discuss elsewhere in this book, the use and misuse of alcohol and drugs is a controversial, complex issue. A great many social, cultural and psychological factors determine the prevalence of substance abuse in the workplace, which would suggest that no single response, such as the introduction of an EAP, is likely to solve the problem. Furthermore, because the identification rate associated with EAPs is generally poor—often less than 1%—it would in our opinion be unwise to regard them as the sole means of combating substance abuse at work.

---

23 Roman, P 'From employee alcoholism to employee assistance' (1981) 42 (3) *Jnl of Studies on Alcohol* 244–272.

Chapter 20

Proposed Substance Abuse Policy and Procedural Agreement

Christopher Albertyn & Urmila Bhoola

INTRODUCTION

In this chapter we present two proposed substance abuse policy and procedural agreements for use in the workplace. The two documents are broadly similar and cover much the same ground. The only significant difference is that Policy No 1 includes comments on most, though not all, of the document's provisions, while Policy No 2 does not. The notes are attached to the sections of the (first) policy where we felt explanation or elaboration would be helpful. Further policies can be created by combining different elements of the two documents shown.

POLICY NO 1

This is a draft collective agreement between an employer and a trade union for the regulation of substance abuse in the workplace. We believe it offers a fair exchange of rights and obligations between the employer and the union. It would be suitable as a first draft from which both parties might negotiate.

PARTIES

ABC (PTY) LTD   (the Company)

and

XYZ UNION   (the Union)

PREAMBLE

1. The parties recognise that there is a problem of alcohol and drug abuse, with or without dependence, among the Company's employees.
2. The Union warrants that it is authorised by all of the employees within the bargaining unit to represent them and to enter into this agreement on their behalf.
3. The Company recognises that this agreement is concluded by the Union on behalf of all of the employees falling within the bargaining unit, whether or not they are members of the Union, and that the terms hereof will apply to all of them.

   The purpose of this clause is to record a commitment by the parties that the employees of the company are bound by the agreement concluded by the union. The union acts as collective bargaining representative for all of the employees in the bargaining unit. If all of the representative unions are represented in the discussions, then this scope clause should cover all employees.

4. The parties believe that drug or alcohol abuse and/or dependence is detrimental to the Company and to the employees who suffer its effects, and that drug and alcohol abuse and/or dependence among employees may have, inter alia, one or more of the following effects: low performance, low morale, absenteeism, impaired judgement, deteriorating interpersonal behaviour, poor health, and industrial accidents.

5. The parties believe that drug or alcohol abuse is either a behavioural problem or an addiction-dependence problem. The purpose of this clause is to anticipate that drug- or alcohol-abusing employees will fall into two principal categories: problem drinkers or drug-takers (including heavy drinkers/ heavy drug users) and casual drug or alcohol users; and dependent drinkers and drug addicts. Individuals in the former category tend to have a behavioural problem; those in the latter are likely to have a dependence problem.

6. The parties recognise that the remedy for drug or alcohol dependence is often beyond the control of the individual drug or alcohol abuser and that assistance may be required and should be available to such an employee to enable them to try themself to overcome the problem.

7. The parties accept that they have a responsibility towards employees who are drug or alcohol abusers/dependants to endeavour to assist them to manage their abuse/dependency.

8. The parties recognise that the prevention of drug and alcohol abuse by changed attitudes and a changed culture within the Company's establishment and the early detection of such abuse are the most effective means of combating the problem.

9. The parties accept that peer pressure is among the most effective methods of preventing drug or alcohol abuse.

10. The parties accept that if drug- or alcohol-abusing/dependent employees unreasonably refuse assistance, or fail to make reasonable efforts to co-operate with the assistance available to them, they may be disciplined for continued abuse which impacts on their work performance or attendance or on the safety of other employees or the public.

    This clause takes account of the principle that employees should be given the opportunity to seek to overcome their drug or alcohol problems, but if they fail to co-operate in their treatment/counselling, then they will face the consequences that they may be disciplined in the ordinary course if there is repeated evidence of abuse. Employees should be helped to overcome their problematic drinking or drug consumption, but if they fail to do so, then they may face a penalty for further abuse. If they are not able to comply with the reasonable standards of employment, they may be reasonably regarded to be behaviourally incapacitated (ie guilty of misconduct) or they may be found to be physically incapable.

11. The parties believe it to be important that employees who suffer from drug or alcohol abuse/dependence must be able to admit and face their problem with the support and assistance of the Company and of the Union, on the understanding that such admission will not jeopardise their job security.

12. The parties wish to identify the circumstances in which drug or alcohol abuse/dependence will be treated as a medical-social-psychological problem (ie as

incapacity) which requires treatment and attention, and the circumstances in which the Company may reasonably treat drug or alcohol abuse as a disciplinary problem (ie as misconduct).

13. In summary, the parties accept that they must make a reasonable attempt to recognise dependence among drug- or alcohol-abusing employees, and that such employees should be treated as being temporarily incapacitated, but that the Company may, in appropriate circumstances defined in this agreement, discipline employees who are guilty of drug- and alcohol-related offences occasioned by abuse.

14. The parties recognise that each case of drug or alcohol abuse is different. In applying this agreement, the Company shall take into account the individual situation of each employee concerned, and the agreement shall not be applied rigidly.

This provision is intended to address the requirement that discipline be applied consistently. In normal circumstances discipline should be applied consistently in the sense that:
- *like cases should be treated alike, and*
- *the same standard should be applied as was applied previously in earlier cases of the same sort.*

This clause acknowledges that the origin of a particular employee's drug or alcohol abuse or dependence is inherently particular and personal. In other words, the cause of drug or alcohol abuse is specific to each affected individual and the method of managing the dependency or the problem behaviour is likely to be specific to the individual concerned. Discipline or treatment should be applied in a manner which is fair to that individual. In the absence of a clause such as this, an adjudicator may subsequently be persuaded by the argument that, because one drug- or alcohol-abusing employee was not treated like another, there has been unfairness. The clause therefore protects the employer against a possible charge of unfairness by making explicit the need to regard the issue of substance abuse on a case-by-case basis.

AGREEMENT
1. DEFINITIONS

'alcohol or drug abuse' means the consumption of intoxicating drugs or alcohol by an employee which impairs the performance of the work, or which detrimentally affects his or her performance or ability to do the work and/or the relationships at work, and it includes intoxication or impairment at work;

'alcohol or drug dependence' means the habitual reliance upon or addiction to the consumption of excessive quantities of alcohol or intoxicating drugs, or an inability to limit alcohol or drug consumption to within reasonable limits;

'bargaining unit' means all the employees [here define the bargaining unit in terms of the recognition agreement between the Union and the Company];

The purpose of defining the bargaining unit is to ensure that all employees falling within the bargaining unit are covered by the same terms and conditions of employment as regards the regulation and prevention of alcohol or drug abuse. It may be (and this is certainly to be preferred) that the parties define the bargaining unit as encompassing all of the company's employees, including all of its management staff.

'breathalyser' means an SABS-approved breathalyser [here describe the type of breathalyser to be used—the different types are described above; our recommendation is to use an electronically calibrated, portable breathalyser]. A positive breathalyser test result shall be a reading which is consistent with a blood-alcohol level of 0,05 g/dl or 50 mg/100 ml of blood or 0,38 g of alcohol in a litre of breath, or above;

We have taken the norm as 0,05 g/dl. We have included the breath equivalent measurement to avoid the problems of the conversion factor. This need not be the standard for all employees. The parties may agree upon different standards for different categories of employees. Those who perform particularly dangerous, hazardous or responsible tasks may have more stringent standards regarding what constitutes a positive reading applied to them. That is a matter for determination by the parties.

The use of the crystal tube test was rejected as being unreliable in the arbitration award Castle Lead Works (Tvl) (Pty) Ltd v National Union of Metalworkers of SA (1989) 10 ILJ 776 (Arb) *at 778. The arbitrator stated the following:*

> *... the test using the system called 'Alcolyser' is quite unsatisfactory for the purposes of determining either the extent of the alcoholic consumption or whether or not the employee was under the influence of alcohol and no possible finding can be made on this test.*

This rather overstates the position, in our view. The crystalline test has an inherent unreliability factor of 25 per cent, which is substantial, but that does not render it entirely useless. On its own it is insufficient, but it is indicative and should suggest a further test.

'the counsellor' means the person appointed by the parties, charged with the responsibility of endeavouring to counsel employees suffering from drug or alcohol abuse and/or dependence;

'work group' means a group established in terms of this agreement.

Provision is made for work groups so as to encourage co-worker responsibility for the prevention of drug or alcohol abuse. We provide in the draft agreement for benefits to be received by work groups for assisting their members to address their problem drinking or drug taking. The establishment of work groups should be a joint undertaking by management and the union. If the groups are created by management only, there is likely to be a perception among the workers that the groups are intended to be informers on the drinking or smoking habits of their fellows. We do not intend this. The work group is a forum in which employees with drink and/or drug problems can receive support and encouragement. Discrimination and victimisation of such employees is not permissible in these groups or indeed anywhere else in the workplace. It is therefore vital to the success of the work groups that they be established as a joint venture, with the support and understanding of the workers.

2. COMPANY RESPONSIBILITIES

2.1 The Company will not in any manner promote the use of alcohol or intoxicating drugs by employees.

This clause obliges management to investigate the ways in which the consumption of alcohol or drugs is promoted via the formal or informal culture of the company. The inappropriate or harmful practices or customs, once identified, need to be eradicated or minimised. In certain circumstances, however, the promotion of alcohol may form an integral part of the company's core business—breweries, restaurants and bars are the obvious examples here. There may have to be a redefinition of what constitutes legitimate or acceptable promotion in these types of environment, which common sense and good judgement should be able to determine.

2.2 To this end, but subject to clause 2.3, no alcohol will be kept or served on the Company's premises by the Company, the Company will not permit its representatives to consume alcohol in the course and scope of their employment, and nor will the Company make alcoholic drinks available at business lunches or social events on its premises.

This provision, sensible as it is, may be too severe a restriction in certain circumstances. A company that regularly entertains clients on-site, for example, might disappoint its guests if no alcohol at all were available (see also clause 2.3 below). In this situation the clause could be modified to permit the serving of alcohol at company-client functions only, provided that food is also obtainable. Where alcohol consumption is deemed acceptable, as in the example just given, the alternative of soft drinks and low-alcohol beverages should also be available and visibly promoted.

2.3 In cases where an employee of the Company may offend or embarrass guests of the Company, the employee may be permitted to drink alcoholic beverages off the Company's premises, provided they stay within legal drink-driving guidelines.

2.4 The Company will provide opportunities for all of its employees to be educated in and informed of the hazards of alcohol abuse, and of the content of this agreement.

The union may want to take part in the process of educating and informing employees (clause 2.4). Such a request for involvement should be encouraged and accepted, because union participation is likely to add credibility to the process.

3. WORK GROUPS

3.1 The Company and the Union will jointly establish work groups for all employees within the Company's establishment. The work groups will meet periodically to consider the problem of alcohol and drug abuse, and to give consideration to methods of assisting any employee within the work group referred for treatment or counselling or who is undergoing such treatment or counselling in terms of this agreement.

3.2 The Company will confer with the work groups at the earliest opportunity and, in any event, before making changes to their work practices or to their work environment which may have a bearing upon the matters dealt with in this agreement.

3.3 Each work group will be encouraged by the parties to identify and consider alcohol and drug abuse problems in the workplace; and to urge any of their members to make use of the assessment and treatment facilities provided in terms of this agreement if any such member is an alcohol or drug abuser.

4. COUNSELLOR

4.1 The Company and the Union will meet each year to appoint a trained alcohol counsellor on such terms and conditions as may be agreed upon between the parties.

4.2 The counsellor will be employed in terms of an annual contract by the Company and be paid by the Company.

The union is an equal party with management in determining who should be employed as counsellor. Union involvement should reassure employees that the person hired is likely to be an unbiased, independent individual. Conversely, should the union be excluded from the selection process and management made solely responsible for this, employees may believe, rightly or wrongly, that the counsellor has been hired to protect and/or promote their employer's interests only. The duration of the counsellor's contract may be extended if it is not possible to secure the services of a suitable candidate on an annual basis. The post of counsellor may be a full-time or part-time one. In smaller enterprises a part-time position may be most suitable.

4.3   A counsellor will be eligible for reappointment by the parties.

4.4   The counsellor will be responsible for the assessment of potential alcohol or drug abusers and for endeavouring to counsel employees suffering from alcohol or drug abuse/dependence and to do such other things as are reasonably required expressly or impliedly by this agreement with a view to preventing or combating alcohol or drug abuse/dependence among the Company's employees.

4.5   The counsellor will not be subjected by either party to intimidation, nor to any coercion or unreasonable pressure, nor to any requirement to participate in discipline other than in terms of this agreement.

4.6   The counsellor will treat the information received from any employee as confidential, except as otherwise provided for under this agreement.

4.7   Every employee is deemed to give consent to the counsellor to read and retain any medical information pertaining to that employee.

5. IDENTIFICATION

5.1   The Company will endeavour to identify the emergence of alcohol or drug abuse/dependence in an employee by monitoring factors such as: decline in work performance, absenteeism (especially over weekends (for weekend workers) and on Fridays and Mondays), sick leave (especially on Fridays and Mondays), accidents at work, and behavioural changes towards other employees.

5.2   If, as a result of such monitoring, the Company concludes that an employee's conduct reveals the one or more of the factors referred to in clause 5.1 hereof, the Company may convene a meeting of the employee concerned, his/her shop steward, and his/her manager and supervisor to address and consider the reasons for the decline in the employee's performance.

5.3   If, as a result of such monitoring, and after the meeting referred to in clause 5.2 hereof, the Company is satisfied that an employee's conduct reveals one or more of the factors referred to in clause 5.1 hereof, the Company may require the employee concerned to meet with the counsellor to consider the results of the Company's monitoring. The employee concerned may have his/her shop steward present in such meeting.

5.4   If the Company has reasonable cause to take a test of an employee (reasonable cause being occasioned by one or more of the following: apparent impairment; an accident or near miss; part of a rehabilitation or accommodation agreement with the employee), it shall make use of only a SABS-approved equipment which has established accuracy. In the case of a breathalyser, it will use a portable, electronically calibrated breathalyser to determine employee intoxication, if any, to which end:

   5.4.1   the breathalyser will be calibrated weekly if used frequently, or otherwise as directed by the manufacturers;

5.4.2   the calibration will favour the employee in the sense that the margin of error adjustment will be in the employee's favour;

5.4.3   the Union shall be entitled to appoint a shop steward or any other employee to be present when the breathalyser is calibrated;

5.4.4   the employee will be advised, at the time the test is to be administered, that they are entitled to the presence of a shop steward, and if requested, a shop steward will be summoned to witness the test, unless the delay occasioned in summoning the steward is likely to vitiate the test result;

5.4.5   the person conducting the test will have been trained in its use and in the proper custody and retention if a sample has been taken from the employee.

An intention of this clause is to identify the person who should conduct the breathalyser tests, and the agreement should stipulate the person(s) who are entitled to conduct the test. As far as possible, the test should be done by someone other than the employee's immediate superior so as to avoid additional scope for tension between them. The choice of who should conduct the test is a matter for agreement between management and the union. The advantage of agreement between them is that the process is given credibility and there can be no doubt as to when the test is being applied correctly or incorrectly.

5.5   If the test proves positive:

5.5.1   the name, clock number and department of the employee will be noted by the person administering the test;

5.5.2   the person administering the test will inform a departmental superior of the employee of the above, and, in the presence of the departmental superior and the employee's shop steward, the employee:

5.5.2.1   will be advised, if so requested, to return home and to report sober for work at a stipulated time to attend a disciplinary meeting;

5.5.2.2   will be sent home, if necessary (if the employee is not sufficiently sober to arrange his or her own transportation home) by taxi;

5.5.2.3   the employee will not be paid for the portion of the shift not worked by him or her in the above circumstances;

This provision (clause 5.5.2.3) applies unless the employee can subsequently establish that he or she was not intoxicated.

5.5.3   at the stipulated time, the employee will be required to attend a meeting of the shop steward, the safety or work group representative and the counsellor at which the counsellor will inquire of the employee whether he or she is an excessive consumer of alcohol or drugs and whether he or she wishes to undergo assessment to determine whether or not he or she is alcohol- or drug-dependent or has an alcohol- or drug-use problem;

The safety officer need not necessarily be present at the inquiry—this depends upon the parties. The advantage of having the safety officer present is that this ensures that any safety considerations are taken into account. The attendance of the work group representative is to ensure that the work group is aware of the consumption issues of the particular employee.

5.5.4   if the employee admits to the excessive consumption of alcohol or drugs, he or she will be requested to undergo assessment in terms of this agreement and if the employee agrees to undergo assessment in terms of this agreement, he or she will be referred by the meeting to the counsellor for assessment in terms of this agreement. By agreeing to undergo assessment the employee will be deemed to have consented to the disclosure by the counsellor of the assessment report to the medical officer/occupational health unit of the employer;

This provision authorises the counsellor to inform the company's medical department or occupational health unit of the outcome of the assessment. The medical department/health unit can then decide if further counselling is required or if treatment is necessary.

5.5.5   if the counsellor's assessment is that the employee is alcohol- or drug-dependent or has an alcohol- or drug-use problem, the counsellor will endeavour to persuade the employee to undergo treatment and/or counselling.

5.5.6   if the employee agrees to undergo treatment and/or counselling, the employee will be deemed to have consented to the counsellor's submitting a report of the success or failure of the treatment to the employee's departmental manager, and the counsellor will submit such a report in due course.

We have provided for the report to be made to the employee's departmental manager (clause 5.6.7). The union and management may agree that someone else should receive the report. The purpose of the report is to inform line management that the employee will be undergoing treatment and that he or she may be absent from work for periods of time on account of such treatment. Line management needs to be informed of the accommodation arrangements reached between the employer and the particular employee and his or her union. However, details of these arrangements will be confined to a description of the impact the treatment will have on the employee's attendance and work performance; line management is not entitled to receive information regarding the exact nature of the employee's treatment or his/her medical condition.

5.5.7   if the employee does not admit to the excessive consumption of alcohol or drugs, or if, having made this admission, the employee refuses to undergo assessment by the counsellor, or if, having agreed to undergo assessment and the counsellor thereafter requests the employee to undergo treatment for alcohol or drug dependence, the employee refuses, then a report will be submitted by the counsellor to the employee's departmental manager advising that the employee is unwilling to cooperate with treatment recommended by the counsellor;

5.5.8   in the event of the employee's departmental manager receiving such a report from the counsellor, subject to a sunset period[1] with regard to disciplinary penalties in the Company's establishment; the employer may initiate disciplinary proceedings against the employee.

This section describes the procedure to be followed in the event of an employee refusing to cooperate with management on the issue of his or her substance abuse. The employee may refuse to admit to his or her problem; may admit to the problem but refuse to be assessed; or may agree to be assessed but refuse

---

1   A sunset period refers to the automatic expunging of a particular law, rule or regulation after a specified period of time.

to undergo the treatment the counsellor recommends. The employer, having given the employee these opportunities to address his or her problem, has fulfilled its responsibility to act fairly towards employees identified as problem drinkers or drug users. If the employee rejects these offers of assistance, he or she may then be subject to discipline in the ordinary course. We propose a system of graduated disciplinary sanctions, with each recurrence of misconduct resulting in a more severe penalty being imposed.

Assessment of the progress of a substance-abusing or -dependent employee is best performed over a fairly long period of time (one or two years, for example) since relapses and uneven progress are to be expected. Furthermore, if the employee's treatment programme requires him or her to undergo periodic medical tests as a means of assessing his or her progress, more rather than less time will clearly be needed to conduct such tests.

If discipline is enacted, it may be advisable to have this linked to some form of negative reinforcement of the penalty. Perhaps the discipline itself could be suspended for an extended period (eg 6 or 12 months), depending upon progress made by the employee. This approach would be consistent with the policy of using constructive coercion to help substance-abusing employees manage their problem. Thus an arrangement could be reached with an alcohol-abusing employee, for example, to exempt this employee from disciplinary action should his or her breathalyser test results be consistently below the agreed upper limit, and his/her MCV and GGT test results return to normal. This incentive bolsters any potential discipline issued to the employee. The employee's reward for co-operating is that no disciplinary steps will be taken (or recorded) against him or her.

5.6 A work group may request any employee of that work group to meet with the counsellor to consider whether or not that employee should undergo assessment, counselling and/or treatment in terms of this agreement. The employee shall be entitled to have the shop steward present in that meeting.

No disciplinary steps should be implemented against an employee who is referred for assessment by his or her own work group. The purpose of this clause is to assist employees in identifying their alcohol or drug problem and to help them to overcome it. One purpose of the agreement—to encourage voluntary and frank confrontation of alcohol and drug abuse—would be defeated if employees stood the risk of being disciplined if they were referred for assessment.

5.7 At least once per annum the Company will arrange for its employees to undergo glutamyl transferase (GGT) and mean corpuscular volume (MCV) medical tests, or other specific clinical tests, on the Company's premises and at the expense of the Company, to assist in the identification of alcohol or drug abuse or dependence, subject to the following:

5.7.1 no employee will be forced to undergo the defined periodic clinical tests;

5.7.2 an employee who declines to undergo the periodic clinical tests will not be prejudiced in any manner as a consequence;

5.7.3 the results of the tests will be provided to the medical officer responsible for the tests and to the employee, and to no-one else, unless the employee is subject to an accommodation agreement, in which event the employer and the union will be entitled to know only whether the employee is cooperating with their rehabilitation or not.

The tests need not occur every year, but they ought to be done on a regular, periodic basis. The advantage to the employees of this provision is that the company provides them with a free, regular medical check-up. The opening clause (5.9) could provide for other tests to be undertaken, eg heart functioning, cholesterol, blood pressure, cancer, lungs, etc. The tests will assist in the early identification of medical problems; in the present case, those occasioned by alcohol or drug abuse. No employee can be forced to undergo an invasive examination. The purpose of clinical examination is to enable the counsellor and the worker concerned to be informed as early as possible of whether the worker is drinking or consuming drugs to excess. Early identification offers the best prospect of reversing problem drinking or drug-taking and the chances of returning to moderate social behaviour are significantly improved. Note that a worker who chooses not to be clinically examined should not to be prejudiced as a result of this decision.

5.8 If, upon consideration of the said annual examination, the medical officer concerned concludes that in his/her opinion the employee may be an alcohol or drug abuser/dependant:

5.8.1 the medical officer concerned will endeavour to persuade the employee to undergo assessment by the counsellor. If the employee agrees to undergo assessment, they will be deemed to have consented to the disclosure by the counsellor to the medical officer of the counsellor's report of the assessment;

It is noteworthy that the report of the assessment goes to the medical department and not to management. This is deliberate. The annual or periodic medical check-up is intended to help employees to identify any health problems before they become serious or difficult to cure or correct. The information contained in the report is confidential to the employee concerned and the company's medical officer: management has no right to it;

5.8.2 if the counsellor's assessment is that the employee is alcohol- or drug-dependent, the counsellor will endeavour to persuade the employee to undergo treatment;

5.8.3 if the employee agrees to undergo treatment, the employee will be deemed to have consented to the counsellor's submitting a report that the employee in undergoing treatment on the recommendation of the counsellor and advising what impact the treatment will have on the employee's attendance at work;

This clause provides for management to be informed of whether the treatment will impact on the employee's attendance at work, nothing more. None of the details of treatment may be disclosed. No report is necessary if the treatment will not have an impact on the employee's performance or attendance at work;

5.8.4 if the employee refuses to undergo assessment or treatment as recommended, or if the assessment of the counsellor is that the employee is not alcohol or drug dependent and no counselling is necessary, nothing further will be done at that point.

5.9 If, in the case of an employee who is a driver of a vehicle or who works on a dangerous machine or in a dangerous environment, the employee's departmental manager receives a report that the employee has failed a sobriety test, reasonably undertaken, the departmental manager may thereafter:

5.9.1 require that employee to undergo a breathalyser or other non-invasive test at reasonable intervals for a reasonable period until the employee's medical report suggests they are no longer an alcohol or drug abuser, provided that the employee may, at intervals of not less than 2 months from the previous examination, require the medical test(s) to be repeated, and the Company will arrange such further examination to be done at its cost. Should such test(s) establish that the employee is no longer suffering from alcohol or drug abuse, the employee will immediately be excused from the requirement to undergo further breathalyser or other tests in terms of this clause.

5.10 Provided that the Company is able to arrange for a venous blood test to be taken within two hours of the employee being requested to undergo a breathalyser or other non-invasive test, any employee required to undergo such a test may require that a blood test be taken in addition to or instead of the other test, in which event:

5.10.1 the Company will enable this to occur;

5.10.2 the venous blood test will be regarded as definitive provided it has been taken at least half an hour after the breathalyser test was administered;

5.10.3 the employee shall be deemed to be under the influence of alcohol if the test reveals blood-alcohol level of 50 mg per 100 ml (0,05 mg/dl) of blood, or above.

There is no need for a venous blood test if a reliable breathalyser test has been taken. A reliable breathalyser is one which can be, and is regularly, calibrated and therefore gives an accurate reading. The only reason why a blood test is offered at all is because of the popular misconception that a blood test is more reliable than a breathalyser test. There is no empirical reason why a blood test should be administered in addition to a reliable breathalyser test for alcohol consumption.

A venous blood test does not produce reliable results if it is conducted within half an hour of alcohol being consumed, which is why clause 5.10.2 is necessary. A breathalyser test, on the other hand, would produce accurate results if administered during this half-hour time period.2 For more on the different tests available for alcohol use and their advantages and disadvantages, refer to chapter 11—Testing for abuse in individual employees.

The blood-alcohol level stated in clause 5.10.3 is that of the legal driving limit in South Africa. The parties may agree that different limits should apply for different categories of workers.

5.11 If the Company refuses to admit an employee to its premises because of suspected or confirmed alcohol or drug abuse, the Company should recommend to the employee that he or she not drive a vehicle because of their intoxication, provided that if the employee is so intoxicated as to be unable to make a reasoned decision, the Company should ensure that the employee is not permitted to drive a vehicle

---

2 Note: If alcohol has been consumed immediately before the breathalyser test is to be administered, the worker should be required to swill his mouth with water to clear it of superficial traces of alcohol, or the test should be taken after 15 minutes, by which time any surface trace of alcohol will have dissipated.

away from the Company's premises until sufficiently sober to do so safely, or the Company should arrange transport for the employee concerned.

This clause can hardly be contested: if an employee is too intoxicated to work; he or she must also be too intoxicated to drive. If the employer arranges for the employee to be transported home by some other means (usually by taxi), provision could be made for the costs of such transport to be borne by the employee.

5.12 An employee may at any time voluntarily request to be breathalysed or otherwise tested and the Company will make that opportunity available to the employee.

6. COUNSELLING TREATMENT AND INCAPACITY

6.1 The counsellor will, with the co-operation of the Company and of the Union, establish an employee assistance programme (EAP) to enable those who agree to treatment to undergo a process of counselling and treatment arranged by the counsellor. The programme may be conducted with the assistance of SANCA or an equivalent consultant.

6.2 Any employee who agrees to undergo counselling and treatment in terms of this agreement will be permitted time off work as required by the counsellor, during working hours, without loss of pay, for such period as the counsellor considers necessary.

We propose that the company pay the costs of the employee's time off to be treated (clause 6.2), but this is clearly a matter for negotiation. Our reason for making this recommendation is that the company will benefit from the employee's treatment and cure. It may be used as a coercive incentive to encourage the employee to co-operate with his treatment: if the treatment is successful, the company will pay for it; if not, he or she will refund the company the cost of the treatment. Alternatively, the employee may be required to pay for the treatment, as a show of commitment; thereafter, if treatment is successful, the employer can refund the employee.

6.3 At the conclusion of the period of counselling and treatment required by the counsellor, the counsellor should make a report on the success or failure of the counselling and treatment to the Company and to the Union and to a meeting of the employee concerned, his or her shop steward and a Company representative.

The report issued must respect the confidentiality of the employee–counsellor relationship. The counsellor should only inform the employer and the union of the success or failure of the counselling and treatment; no further details should be included. What the employer and the union are entitled to know is whether the employee cooperated and acted in accordance with the purpose of the treatment, or not. This enables the parties to fashion a suitable accommodation arrangement for the employee.

6.4 If the counsellor's said report is that the employee has co-operated in the treatment and the employee has either ceased consuming alcohol or drugs or reduced consumption to a level where alcohol or drug intake does not interfere with job performance and/or relationships in the workplace, then the parties may review the discipline issued to the employee that gave rise to the counselling and treatment.

6.5 If the counsellor's said report is that the employee has not co-operated in the treatment and the employee has not ceased consuming alcohol or drugs to excess, then the counsellor will advise whether, in the counsellor's opinion, a further period of treatment will achieve the desired result.

6.5.1 If so, the employee will be referred for a further period of counselling and treatment, and at the conclusion thereof the provisions of this clause will apply, *mutatis mutandis*.

6.5.2 If the counsellor is satisfied that the employee will not benefit from the opportunity of a further period of counselling and treatment, the employee will be dealt with on the following basis:

6.5.2.1 if the employee is no longer capable of performing the job on account of alcohol or drug dependence, they will be regarded as being permanently disabled, and employment may be terminated by the Company on grounds of incapacity;

6.5.2.2 if the employee is capable of performing the job notwithstanding the lack of co-operation or lack of success in the counselling and treatment, the employee will be subject to discipline for any alcohol- or drug-related offence, and any punishment short of dismissal imposed for such offence may include a requirement to undergo at reasonable frequency, or randomly a breathalyser or other suitable test as contemplated in this agreement for a period of 1 year thereafter and, with the employee's consent, defined periodic medical tests.

6.6 Any employee may voluntarily elect to undergo a counselling and treatment programme under the supervision of the counsellor and the provisions of this clause will apply, *mutatis mutandis*.

6.7 If the counsellor believes that the redeployment of an employee will benefit the treatment, the counsellor may recommend redeployment of an employee during the course of the treatment, in which event the parties may agree that the employee will be so redeployed for the duration of the treatment, without loss of pay, provided there is a suitable vacant position available for the employee to fill.

6.8 All discussions between the employee concerned and the Company's medical officer, the counsellor and the Company's management will be in confidence, and details of any treatment will be retained only in medical records.

6.9 Notwithstanding anything to the contrary in this agreement, the counsellor shall be entitled to disclose any information to the Company's medical officer concerning any matters pertaining to the assessment or treatment of any employee in terms of this agreement, and the counsellor shall be at liberty to seek the advice or assistance of the medical officer in respect thereof.

This is an important provision. It enables the medical practitioner responsible for the health of the company's employees to be informed of the state of treatment or counselling of any employee. Often it will have been the medical officer who first detected an employee's alcohol or drug problem, and the doctor is well placed to supervise and guide the counsellor as regards the employee's treatment and counselling. A useful method of checking upon the employee's progress during treatment is to carry out periodic blood tests (eg MCV and GGT). The medical officer would in all likelihood perform these tests.

7. DISCIPLINE

7.1 Besides the discipline provided for elsewhere in this agreement, an employee who does not avail themself of or co-operate with the counselling and treatment opportunities provided in this agreement may be disciplined by the Company in the following manner:

The tenor of this agreement is that employees are first given a reasonable opportunity to identify and to overcome the problem. If they do not avail themself of this opportunity and continue to abuse alcohol or drugs, they run the risk of being intoxicated at work or being unable to perform their duties at work on account of their alcohol or drug problem. Employees may not be physically incapacitated, but their drug or alcohol problem may be such as to render them behaviourally incapacitated. In other words, the blameworthy behaviour may be such that they can no longer adhere to the rules and requirements of employment. That constitutes misconduct.

7.1.1   if the employee works other than on a dangerous machine or in a dangerous area, for being under the influence of alcohol or drugs at work, a final written warning, subject to the obligation of the employee to undergo random tests at the reasonable request of management;

7.1.2   if the employee works on a dangerous machine or in a dangerous area, or drives a vehicle, for being under the influence of alcohol or drugs at work, dismissal following an inquiry in terms of the Company's disciplinary procedure.

7.2   If an employee is reasonably required to undergo a drug or alcohol test, the test will be administered in the presence of the employee's shop steward. Should:

7.2.1   an employee refuse to take the test, they will be assumed to be under the influence of alcohol or drugs. They will be required to leave the Company's premises and they will not be paid for the shift concerned;

7.2.2   the test prove positive, the employee may be required, in the presence of a shop steward, to leave the Company's premises, in which event the employee will not be paid for the shift concerned;

7.2.3   the test prove negative, the employee will be entitled to resume work normally, save that if the employee's superior is anxious that the employee may be a danger to themself or to other employees, the superior may require the employee to leave the Company's premises, in which event the employee will be paid for the full shift as if it had been worked;

7.2.4   the employee refuse to leave the Company's premises in any of the above circumstances, the employee may be disciplined for insubordination.

An intoxicated employee may resent being asked to leave the work premises and might even become hostile. Aggressive, threatening behaviour constitutes misconduct in its own right and can thus be addressed as a separate matter, even if the employee's aggression arose while he or she was intoxicated.

7.3   As the outcome of a disciplinary hearing, the Company may suspend the imposition of a penalty upon an employee who is guilty of an alcohol- or drug-related disciplinary offence conditional upon the employee's:

7.3.1   undergoing counselling and treatment;

7.3.2   being required to take a breathalyser or other suitable test at reasonable frequency, or randomly; and/or

7.3.3   being required to undergo defined periodic medical tests not more than once every three months, with the employee's consent;

7.4   Any suspension of a disciplinary penalty shall be for a period of 12 months, and such penalty may come into operation only if:

7.4.1   the employee concerned has committed an alcohol- or drug-related offence during the period of suspension; or

7.4.2   a medical report from the Company's medical officer or from the counsellor reveals that the employee has not co-operated with the counselling and treatment.

The period of 12 months will likely establish whether the employee has overcome the substance-abuse problem. A longer period may be stipulated, perhaps 2 years. A shorter period may not be as reliable because the risk of relapse is strongest in the early stages of rehabilitation.

7.5   Any employee who has been offered the opportunity of counselling and treatment and who has either refused that opportunity or failed to overcome the addiction following such counselling and treatment may be disciplined for alcohol- or drug-related offences in the ordinary course.

7.6   Discipline should be tempered with the assurance to the employee that as long as the employee makes genuine efforts to overcome the substance dependence, the Company will assist the employee in that process.

7.7   The parties recognise a clear distinction between the counselling and supportive facilities provided by this agreement for alcohol or drug dependence or acknowledged problem drinking or drug use and the disciplinary stage of handling the problem of alcohol or drug abuse. The former should be flexible and informal, whereas the latter has the characteristics of a formal disciplinary inquiry.

7.8   Subject to the terms of this agreement, all other terms and provisions of the disciplinary procedure agreed between the parties will apply to the exercise of discipline in terms of this agreement.

8. DEEMED CONSENT

Any report made by a medical officer or by the counsellor to the Company and/or to the Union in respect of any employee in terms of this agreement shall be deemed to have been made with the informed consent of the employee concerned, and the Union hereby vouches that such consent has been obtained; provided that the disclosure to the Company shall be of the result of an assessment or treatment, and not its content, which shall remain confidential as between the employee and the medical officer and/or the counsellor.

9. BONUSES

The agreement might make provision for the payment of a bonus to work groups should the groups achieve certain attendance targets. Employees with drink or drug problems often miss work or report late for work, most notably on Mondays and Fridays and on the day (or days) following pay day. On these occasions, the recovering employee usually submits a sick leave request. The incidence of sick leave and absenteeism among alcohol- and drug-dependent employees is generally higher than that of the rest of the employee population. Thus a collective bonus scheme based on good attendance—or, to express it otherwise, on the absence of sick leave—may be useful in terms of motivating non-substance-abusing employees to help their drink- or drug-troubled co-workers, by urging them to seek assessment, counselling and assistance.

A possible objection to the scheme is that it discriminates on grounds of disability. If substance-abusing employees can be compensated for their disability, so the argument goes, why should employees who are otherwise disabled (physically or mentally), and through no fault of their own, be deprived of this bonus? To exclude these employees is therefore inherently discriminatory.

10 ORIENTATION

10.1 The parties agree that this agreement will become effective only four weeks after the signature hereof by both parties in order that the Company's management and supervisory staff and the employees of the Company may be informed fully of the terms hereof.

10.2 During the said period of four weeks the Company and the Union shall jointly conduct an intensive educational programme to inform employees of the implications for health and work of alcohol and drug abuse and dependence, and of the terms of this agreement. To this end they will conduct such seminars and training sessions as they consider necessary, either jointly or severally, and they will utilise such other methods as they are able, including the issue of notices to each employee, and the use of posters, videos and team briefings.

One aspect which ought particularly to be brought to the employees' notice during the orientation process is the fact that the effects of intoxication can last for some time, often for many hours, and irrespective of whether the individual has slept or not. Management, taking note of this, may want to introduce a rule to deal with this specific problem. Following proper negotiation with the relevant trade union(s), the rule might read something like this

> *Because of the nature of the company's business and the need, for safety reasons, for you to start your shift fully competent and in an alert and fully sober state, you will be required to conduct yourself sensibly before the start of your shift. This may mean that you will have to abstain from any alcoholic beverage or prescribed drugs several hours before your normal starting time, since taking them during this time may affect your ability to perform your duties or may potentially endanger your health and safety or the health and safety of others.*[3]

11. DISPUTES

11.1 In the event of any dispute arising as to the interpretation of this agreement or its application, such dispute shall be referred for determination on an expedited basis by mediation-arbitration.

The parties may consider an expedited mediation-arbitration process so that the substance of the issue can be addressed promptly and in a manner that enables the parties to fashion an appropriate outcome.

---

3   This provision takes account of the fact that during the metabolisation process (the 'hangover' period) the employee is likely still to be under the influence of alcohol.

POLICY NO 2[4]

SUBSTANCE MANAGEMENT POLICY
This document sets out the substance abuse policy of _____[name of organisation].

1. PREAMBLE, GLOSSARY, PURPOSE AND APPLICATION
1.1 Preamble
The misuse of alcohol or drugs is a national problem of immense proportions. The social, psychological, emotional and physical consequences affect the lives of men and women regardless of age or status, ethnic origins, sexuality or disability. Most people with a drink or drug problem are employed. Alcohol and drug misuse is therefore also an industrial problem. The negative effects of alcohol and drug misuse in the workplace include the following: higher rate of absenteeism, rising medical costs due to increased use of benefits, more worker's compensation claims due to alcohol- or drug-related accidents, poor productivity, interpersonal conflict, injuries and damage to property.

A workplace alcohol and drug policy may be defined as a formal set of principles, guidelines and rules governing the job-related behaviour of employers, employees and volunteers with regard to the use, misuse and abuse of alcohol and drugs.

Workplace alcohol and drug policies generally serve four goals:
• to increase productivity
• to reduce safety risks
• to improve employee health
• to reduce employer liability.

The policy recognises the need for effective and consistent action, while striking a proper balance between work, privacy and concern for the individual.

_____[name of organisation] is committed to maintaining the highest possible standards of occupational health and safety and considers alcohol and drug abuse to be disruptive of and detrimental to a safe and productive working environment.

_____[name of organisation] views substance abuse and dependency as treatable health problems and accepts that employees who experience such problems should be provided with assistance, subject to certain conditions outlined in this policy.

_____[name of organisation] does not support the intrusion into the private lives of employees; however it does expect all employees to report to work in a condition to safely and effectively perform their duties.

_____[name of organisation] will ensure that the contents of this policy and procedure will be communicated to all employees, unions and management.

---

4   This policy was prepared by Grant Wilkinson, labour attorney and reproduced here with his kind permission.

1.2 Glossary

The terminology of this policy contains several key words and phrases, which are listed and described below. The descriptions should be read in the context of the nature and purpose of this policy.

Acceptable work performance—to conform to all reasonable requirements and expectations regarding work-related matters

Alcoholism—a chronic illness and behaviour disorder, characterised by the repeated drinking of alcoholic beverages to an extent that exceeds customary dietary use and/or ordinary compliance with the social drinking customs of the community and/or which interferes with the drinker's physical or emotional health, interpersonal relations or economic functioning (ie job performance).

Alcohol-related problem—any employee whose use of alcohol interferes with the efficient and safe performance of assigned job duties is considered to have an alcohol-related problem. They may or may not yet be acutely or chronically alcohol dependent.

Client—an individual/group/family member utilising the Employee Assistance Programme due to personal and/or alcohol- or drug-related problems.

Chemical dependency—psychological and/or physical dependency from alcohol and/or other drugs

Co-dependent—a relative, close friend, or colleague of an alcohol or drug-dependent person, whose actions perpetuate or may perpetuate that person's dependence and thereby retard the recovery process

Dependence—a person is dependent on a drug or alcohol when it becomes very difficult or even impossible for them to stop taking the drug/alcohol without help after having taken it regularly for some time. Dependence may be physical or psychological or both.

Drug—any chemical substance that produces physical, mental, emotional or behavioral change in the user

Denial—a psychological defence mechanism or range of mechanisms that alcohol- or drug-dependent persons unconsciously or subconsciously establish to protect themselves from the reality of their situation

Fitness for duty—to report for work in a sufficiently acceptable physical, psychological and emotional condition to be able to work in an effective, safe manner; such fitness to be determined by approved alcohol- and drug-testing methods where appropriate

In-patient treatment—patients remain in an institution for the duration of the treatment

Intervention—therapeutic and professional guidance given to an employee with alcohol or drug problems in order to help them overcome such problems

Intoxication—the acute effects of excessive amounts of alcohol or other drugs in the body

Organisation—_____[details of organisation]

Out-patient treatment—patients attend treatment sessions at a clinic/centre at scheduled times but do not remain in the clinic/centre overnight

Prevention—appropriate action to counteract the emergency and/or development of unfavourable conditions in a given population/community

Reasonable cause/reasonable suspicion—supported by evidence strong enough to establish that a policy violation has occurred

Prohibited alcohol- or drug-related activities—including the manufacture, transportation, transfer, distribution, sale, purchase, possession, or unauthorised consumption or use of alcohol or other habit-forming drugs

Registered treatment centres – a licensed health centre or clinic for the treatment of alcohol- or drug-dependent individuals, which may be either a private or a public (state) facility

Substance abuse—the harmful use of alcohol or drugs by an employee, which has or may have a damaging effect on that employee's work performance and productivity and his or her relationships with others in the workplace

Substance dependence—a clinical diagnosis characterised by specific physiological and behavioural symptoms caused by a pattern of pathological substance use that leads to personal distress or significant impairment in social or occupational functioning

Treatment – the help given to an alcohol- or drug-dependent individual by a range of health professionals for the purpose of restoring or improving the quality of life of that individual and his or her spouse or partner, family members, friends and other individuals with whom he or she has a close relationship

Under the influence—the condition whereby an employee, having consumed an amount of alcohol or drugs that exceeds accepted legal and medical limits, is impaired to the extent that he or she (i) is unable to perform in a safe, productive manner and (ii) poses a risk to the health and safety of himself and/or others and to the safety and security of the employer's property

Well-being—a positive state of physical, psychological and emotional wellness

1.3 Purpose
This policy has two main purposes:
— to balance respect for the privacy and dignity of individuals with the need to maintain a safe, productive, alcohol-free and drug-free work environment.
— to offer a helping hand to those who need it while sending a clear message that the abuse of alcohol or drugs is incompatible with employment at _____ [name of organisation]

The objectives of this policy are:
— to identify and remove the adverse effects of alcohol or drugs on job performance, and to protect the health and safety of employees by providing education and treatment
— to define corporate responses to violations of the policy, including progressive disciplinary procedures and a treatment option in appropriate instances
— to define employer and employee responsibilities with respect to the prevention of substance-abuse problems.
— to create an awareness of alcohol- and drug-related problems through the provision of training and educational programmes

The aims of this substance abuse policy and programme are:
— to promote the sensible and appropriate use of alcohol and drugs among employees
— to encourage and assist employees who suspect or know that they have a problem with alcohol or drugs to seek help, in confidence, at an early stage

— to encourage senior staff and supervisors to offer referral to an appropriate agency for specialist help to those members of staff who request support, or whose work performance may be affected by the inappropriate use of alcohol or drugs;

— to protect employees of_____[name of organisation] and members of the public from the potential adverse effects of inappropriate use of alcohol or drugs by employees of _____[name of organisation]

— to provide mechanisms for the early detection and treatment of persons who may have an alcohol- or drug-abuse problem

— to provide procedures for defining the role and responsibilities of management when dealing with alcohol- or drug-use problems at work.

1.4 Application
The provisions of this policy apply to all employees of_____ [name of organisation] and not to any other persons other than the employees of _____[name of organisation].

1.5 Statutory authorisation
SOUTH AFRICAN LAW ON SUBSTANCE ABUSE IN THE WORKPLACE

1.5.1 Labour Relations Act 66 of 1995, the Code of Good Practice: dismissal

• the employer has an obligation to make available counselling for employees suffering alcohol or drug (and other) problems prior to dismissal

• dismissal on grounds of incapacity: an employee incapacitated through ill health or injury depends upon the degree of incapacity suffered; the employer must first try to find an alternative position for the employee should he or she be unable to perform his or her normal job

• an employee may be dismissed on grounds of misconduct, or poor work performance Labour Relations Act 66 of 1995, section 89(2): disclosure of information
An employer is not required to disclose information:

• that is legally privileged;

• that the employer cannot disclose without contravening a prohibition imposed on the employer by any law or order of any court;

• that is confidential and, if disclosed, may cause substantial harm to an employee or the employer;
or

• that is private personal information relating to an employee, unless that employee consents to the disclosure of that information.

1.5.2 Employment Equity Act 55 of 1998
The Act promotes equal opportunity and fair treatment through the elimination of unfair discrimination. This Act also addresses the issue of disclosure of information and enhancement of confidentiality.

1.5.3 Basic Conditions of Employment Act 75 of 1997
The Act ensures that the working conditions of unorganised and vulnerable workers meet minimum standards.

1.5.4 Compensation for Occupational Injuries and Diseases Act 130 of 1993
The Act provides for compensation for disablement or death caused by occupational injuries or diseases sustained or contracted in the course of employment. Advice must be given to traumatised clients regarding claims.

1.5.5 Occupational Health and Safety Act No 85 of 1993
This Act places a duty on employers to ensure the health, safety and welfare of their employees. Specifically,
- Every employer shall provide and maintain a working environment that is safe and without risk to the health of its employees (section 8(1))
- An employer is not permitted to allow any person who is or who appears to be under the influence of intoxicating liquor or drugs, to enter or to remain at the workplace (section 10(1))
- An employer must ensure that employees do not injure themselves or endanger co-workers or members of the public. This has particular relevance to alcohol and the use of machinery or vehicles.
- Employees should also take reasonable care of themselves and others who could be affected by their actions whilst at work.

1.5.6 Constitution of the Republic of South Africa, Act 108 of 1996
The use of 'breathalyser tests' in the workplace is a justifiable limitation of the right to privacy. Section 36 of the Constitution entitled 'Limitation of Rights' states that the rights entrenched in the constitution may be limited by a law of general application, provided that such limitation:
(a) shall be permissible only to the extent that it is–
    (i) reasonable; and
    (ii) justifiable in an open and democratic society based on freedom and equality.
The law of general application is the Occupational Health and Safety Act.

1.5.7 National Road Traffic Act 93 of 1996
Any person driving, or attempting to drive, a motor vehicle whilst under the influence of alcohol or a drug that has a narcotic effect, can be prosecuted under this Act. This includes driving as part of work duties.

1.5.8 Prevention and Treatment of Drug Dependency Amendment Act 14 of 1999
The Act outlines the services to be rendered to persons who are dependant or addicted to drugs and/or alcohol. (This act was not yet in force at date of publication of this book.)

1.5.9 Prevention and Treatment of Drug Dependency Act 20 of 1992[5]
The Act considers ways in which the state can help drug-dependent or drug-addicted individuals. Section 6 lists the types of programmes available to such individuals; it also (s 6(e)) refers to the help available to the families of drug users. Section 6 reads:
> *The Minister may establish or cause to be established programmes which are aimed at–*
> *(a) the prevention of drug dependency;*

---

5   The whole of this Act has been repealed by Act 70 of 2008 not yet in operation.

(b) information to the community on the abuse of drugs;
(c) the education of the youth in regard to the abuse of drugs;
(d) the observation, treatment and supervision of persons who-
　　(i)   are in a treatment centre or a registered treatment centre;
　　(ii) have been released from a treatment centre or registered treatment centre or who have been placed under supervision by a court;

　　...

(e) the rendering of assistance to the families of persons detained in a treatment centre or registered treatment centre.

The type of person who may be eligible for treatment for drug abuse or misuse is described in section 21(1) of the Act as someone
　　...who is dependent on drugs and in consequence thereof squanders his means or injures his health or endangers the peace or in any other manner does harm to his own welfare or the welfare of his family or fails to provide for his own support or for that of any dependant whom he is legally liable to maintain...

1.5.10 Criminal Procedure Act 51 of 1977
Under section 296 of this Act, a person may also be referred to a treatment centre if the court concludes from evidence or any other information placed before it that such a person is as defined in terms of section 21(1) of the Prevention and Treatment of Drug Dependency Act 20 of 1992 (see above).

2. POLICY STATEMENT:

_____[name of organisation] is committed to providing a safe work environment and to fostering the well-being and health of its employees. That commitment is jeopardised when any _____[name of organisation] employee comes to work under the influence of alcohol or drugs or abuses alcohol or drugs while at work.

3. POLICY PRINCIPLES

_____[name of organisation] will implement a comprehensive drug and alcohol abuse education programme. As part of that programme, information will be provided on the availability of Employee Assistance Programme ('EAP') services for employees of _____[name of organisation].
　　Alcoholism and other drug addictions are recognised as diseases responsive to proper treatment, and this will be an option as long as the employee cooperates. The employer will treat an issue of alcohol or drug dependency as a health problem and not as an immediate cause for discipline or dismissal.
　　Being under the influence of alcohol on company or client property is prohibited.
　　Managers should receive appropriate training to implement the policy.
　　Where a staff member, having been encouraged to seek assistance for an alcohol or drug problem, fails to do so, that staff member should understand that normal disciplinary procedures will be applied to redress the problem of impaired work performance.

Employees who may seek assessment or treatment for an alcohol or drug problem should be encouraged to follow through with treatment. In so doing:
— they will not jeopardise job security, promotion opportunities or the conditions of service contained in their contract of employment
— their medical records will be treated in confidence.

4. EMPLOYEE ASSISTANCE PROGRAMME:

4.1 _____[name of organisation] maintains an Employee Assistance Programme ('EAP') to assist employees with personal problems, including those related to substance abuse/dependency, which have an impact on workplace performance.

4.2 Hence the EAP policy provision and procedure is applicable in the identification, referral and treatment of employees with substance abuse/dependency problems.

4.3 The EAP will provide employees and their families with confidential, professional assessment and referral services for assistance in resolving or accessing treatment for addiction to, dependence on, or problems with alcohol, drugs, or other personal problems adversely affecting their job performance.

4.4 Confidential assessment and referral services will be provided without cost to the employee or any member of his or her family.

4.5 The cost of treatment, counselling or rehabilitation resulting from EAP referral will be the responsibility of the employee.

4.6 When documented job impairment has been observed and identified, a supervisor may recommend participation in the EAP.

4.7 Any action taken by the supervisor, however, will be based on job performance. Supervisor referrals to the EAP must include the employee's release of information consent form.

4.8 Refusal to participate in, or failure to complete the EAP-directed programme will be documented.

4.9 Should job performance not improve after a reasonable amount of time, the employee will be subject to progressive corrective action up to and including termination of employment.

4.10 Self-referral by employees or family members is strongly encouraged. The earlier a problem is addressed, the easier it is to deal with and the higher the success rate. While self-referral in itself does not preclude use of corrective actions, participation in an EAP-directed programme may enable the supervisor to allow time for completion of such programme before initiating or determining additional corrective actions.

4.11 EAP-related activities, such as referral appointments, will be treated on the same basis as other personal business or health matters with regard to use of sick leave. Confidentiality is assured. NO information regarding the nature of an employee's personal problem will be made available to supervisors, nor will it be included in the permanent personnel file of that employee.

4.12 Participation in the EAP will not affect an employee's career advancement or employment, nor will it protect an employee from disciplinary action if substandard job performance continues.

4.13 The EAP is a process used in conjunction with discipline; it is not a substitute for discipline.

4.14 An employee can access the EAP through self-referral or through referral by a supervisor.

4.15 Information about the EAP will be distributed to employees for their confidential use.

5. REFERRAL PROCEDURES:

_____[name of organisation] will provide an environment in which those with alcohol- or drug-related problems are encouraged to obtain guidance and advice as soon as possible.

Names and contact details of specialist agencies can be obtained, in confidence, from the EAP Office.

Referral to specialist agencies must always include the agreement of the person with the alcohol- or drug-related problem and self-referral may be the most effective way of addressing the problem.

5.1 Self-referral

5.1.1 An employee who believes that they are experiencing alcohol- or drug-related problems is encouraged to obtain specialist advice.

5.1.2 When an employee decides to seek specialist advice directly, that is, by making personal contact with the specialist or the specialist's organisation or facility, this is known as self-referral

5.1.3 An employee may contact the person or organisation offering specialist advice without the knowledge or participation of his or her supervisor.

5.1.4 Any employee who, as a result of self-referral, is required to undertake a course of treatment that requires absence from work will be deemed to be absent from work on grounds of ill-health.

5.1.5 Any such absences from work should be arranged and agreed upon in advance and should be under the direction of the employer's occupational health unit liaising with the employee's departmental management.

5.2 Supervisory referral

5.2.1 A supervisor who has reasonable evidence to support the view that an employee for whom they have responsibility may have an alcohol- or drug-related problem that is affecting work performance should arrange to discuss this with the person concerned.

5.2.2 The purpose of the discussion is not for the supervisor to diagnose an alcohol or drug problem, but to bring to the attention of the employee the perceived problems regarding his or her work performance.

5.2.3 A supervisor may refer an employee to the EAP under the following circumstances:

- if the employee is not meeting the minimum requirements of a job that he or she should be able to perform,
- if the employee's work performance has dropped noticeably,
- if the employee's work performance is very unpredictable
- if the employee acts or behaves in an unusual, inappropriate or unpredictable manner and such behaviour is affecting his or her work performance.

5.2.4 If normal supervisory procedures do not help to rectify the situation, a supervisor may refer the employee to the departmental programme coordinator.

5.2.5 While it is appropriate for the supervisor to raise questions about performance in the context of the employee's use of alcohol or drugs, the employee has the right to refuse to discuss that matter.

5.2.6 If the employee does not wish the matter to be considered under _____[your organisation's name] alcohol and drug policy, it will be dealt with under the normal disciplinary procedures.

5.2.7 If the employee accepts that the use of alcohol/drugs have adversely affected aspects of his or her work performance, the supervisor will offer assistance. Normally the matter will be passed to the EAP for further action.

5.2.8 Any employee who, as a result of supervisory referral, is required to undertake a course of treatment that requires absence from work will be deemed to be absent from work on grounds of ill-health.

5.2.9 Training should be provided for managers giving them the confidence and skills to make early identification and to intervene should problems arise in the workplace.

5.2.10 Staff, especially managers, should be encouraged to examine their own attitudes to alcohol and drug problems as this affects their responses to situations.

5.3 Indicators of alcohol or drug misuse or abuse in employees

Absenteeism: multiple instances of unauthorised leave, excessive sick leave, frequent Monday and/or Friday absences, excessive tardiness, especially on Monday mornings or when returning from lunch, leaving work early, peculiar and increasingly improbable excuses for absences, higher absenteeism rate than other employees for colds, flu, gastritis, etc.

'On-the-job' absenteeism: recurrent absences from work station for non-work reasons (trips to the restroom, staff canteen, recreation area, etc)

High accident rate: accidents on the job, accidents off the job (but affecting job performance)

Difficulty in concentration: completion of work requires greater effort, jobs take more time

Confusion: difficulty in recalling or following instructions; inability to recall or process detailed information or complete complex assignments; difficulty in recalling own mistakes

Spasmodic work patterns: alternate periods of high and low productivity

Lowered job efficiency: missed deadlines, mistakes due to non-attention or poor judgement, complaints from users of services, improbable excuses for poor job performance

Poor workplace relationships: over-reaction to real or imagined criticism; mood swings; abrupt changes in morale; uncooperative, resentful or obstructive attitude and/or behaviour; complaints from co-workers

The supervisor should be prepared to discuss the performance problem with the employee. The supervisor may set guidelines for improving work performance. If the performance problems continue, the supervisor should suggest referral to the EAP for professional counselling. The supervisor should be aware that some instances of poor employee work performance may lie beyond his or her area of expertise, in which case he or she should refer the matter to a suitably skilled senior manager.

5.4 Referral outcomes

5.4.1 Employees referred under these procedures accept and are accepted by _____ [name of organisation] as having had performance problems because of the misuse of alcohol or drugs. Any disciplinary action that might have been pending as a result of alcohol or drug problems will be held in abeyance pending the outcome of the referral programme.

5.4.2 If, as a result of the referral programme, the employee is able to sustain a return to working at an acceptable level of performance, references to pending disciplinary action will be deleted. The period of sustained evidence of a successful outcome of the referral programme will normally be two years.

5.4.3 Employees who embark on, but refuse to follow, the referral programme will be dealt with under the normal disciplinary procedure.

5.4.4 Employees who return to working at an acceptable standard but whose performance again deteriorates as a result of alcohol- or drug-related problems may, if appropriate, be given further opportunities under the referral procedures. It should be noted, however, that the opportunities to deal with problems created by alcohol or drug misuse under the referral procedures would not be unlimited.

5.4.5 If an employee appears incapable of dealing with the problem, _____[name of organisation] may take steps to terminate the employment on the grounds of incapacity and/or misconduct.

5.5 Treatment services

5.5.1 Seeking private counselling or treatment outside _____ [organisation's name] is always an individual option.

5.5.2 The counsellor or health worker will provide the employee with a certificate of attendance, if requested to by the employee or supervisor.

5.5.3 Employees may attend treatment or counselling in their own time or work time in accordance with normal _____ [organisation's name] procedures (flexi-time, sick leave or by special arrangement with supervisor).

5.5.4 Should the employee decline the offer of assistance following substance abuse related misconduct or poor work performance, or fail to co-operate with the assistance offered, this will be documented and the employee will be informed that any further incidents of substance abuse related misconduct or poor work performance occurring within a six-month period from the date of such a documented offer may be dealt with as a matter of discipline without repeating the offer of assistance.

5.5.5 If a professional counsellor's report indicates that the employee has been uncooperative and/or that excessive alcohol or drug intake persists, _____[name of organisation] will assess whether the employee is still capable of performing the job satisfactorily.

5.5.6   If the employee is no longer capable of performing the job satisfactorily as a result of alcohol or drug dependence, employment may be terminated on grounds of incapacity.

5.5.7   If the employee is capable of performing the job satisfactorily despite non-compliance and/or continued alcohol or drug intake, he or she shall be subject to standard disciplinary measures for any further substance abuse related offences.

5.6   Dealing with relapses

Where an employee, having received treatment, suffers a relapse, _____ [name of organisation] will consider the case on its individual merits. Medical advice will be sought in an attempt to ascertain how much more treatment/rehabilitation time is likely to be required for the employee to make a full recovery. At _____ [name of organisation]'s

discretion, more treatment or rehabilitation time may be given in order to help the employee to recover fully.

5.7   Recovery unlikely

5.7.1   If, after the employee has received treatment and recovery seems unlikely, _____[name of organisation] may be unable to wait for the employee any longer, in which case dismissal may result. However, in most cases a clear warning will be given to the employee beforehand and a full medical investigation will have to be undertaken.

5.7.2   If the employee declines to allow _____[name of organisation] access to his or her medical records, a decision about future employment would be made using the information that is available to _____[name of organisation].

6. DISCIPLINE

6.1   Whilst recognising the need to investigate the possibility of alcoholism or drug dependency, _____[name of organisation] places a high premium on its statutory and common-law obligations to ensure the safety of its employees and members of the public. It therefore takes a serious view of employees using drugs or alcohol on the premises or whilst on duty (except during social functions and promotions as described hereunder) or being under the influence of drugs or alcohol on the premises or whilst on duty.

6.2   In determining whether an employee may be under the influence, clinical observations (as listed in the Observation check sheet) will be considered along with on-site alcohol and/or drug screening tests, which will be offered to suspected intoxicated employees.

6.3   _____[name of organisation] will consider all relevant facts in determining an appropriate sanction, including whether the employee's conduct caused a safety risk to themself, co-workers or members of the public and/or harm to _____ [name of organisation]'s good name and standing.

6.4   The following transgressions and sanctions are as set out in _____ [name of organisation]'s disciplinary code will serve as guidelines. These may vary on a case-by-case basis, subject to the principles of consistency:

6.4.1 Being under the influence or using alcohol or illegal drugs whilst on the premises or on duty—
First offence: final written warning effective for six months plus offer of assessment/counselling and/or welfare support
Second offence: (within the operative six-month period following a previously issued final written warning): dismissal

6.4.2 Being in possession of alcohol or illegal drugs (excluding controlled medicines for which the employee has a legal prescription) whilst on the premises or on duty—
First offence: Written warning effective for six months plus the offer of assessment /counselling and/or welfare support
Second offence: (within the operative six-month period): final written warning effective for six months plus the offer of assessment/counselling and/or welfare support
Subsequent offence: dismissal

6.5 Notwithstanding these guidelines, _____[name of organisation] reserves the right to vary the sanction depending on the circumstances of each case.

6.6 The following constitute particularly serious acts of misconduct, which may be grounds for dismissal for a first offence, depending on the facts of each case:

6.6.1 Consuming intoxicating substances whilst on duty and/or providing other employees with such substances whilst on duty.

6.6.2 Driving a _____[name of organisation] vehicle or operating safety sensitive equipment whilst under the influence of intoxicating substances.

6.7 An employee who is suspected of being under the influence of an intoxicating substance as described herein will be subject to a disciplinary enquiry to investigate the matter and to ascertain whether the employee had indeed been under the influence.

6.8 If an employee's abuse of intoxicating substances whilst performing regular work duties is reasonably likely to endanger his or her own safety, or the safety of co-workers or members of the public, _____[name of organisation] reserves the right to:

6.8.1 suspend the employee from such work or assign alternative duties to the employee until such time as a counsellor's report and/or appropriate tests confirm that the employee no longer abuses intoxicating substances, and/or;

6.8.2 require the employee to submit to routine breath testing before commencing duties for a period which may be deemed reasonable by the Chairperson of the enquiry.

7. STAND-BY /CALL-OUT EMPLOYEES

7.1 An employee instructed to perform stand-by duties will be considered to be on duty and will be subject to the same provisos as those that pertain to employees during normal working hours.

7.2 An employee summoned to perform call-out duties outside of normal working hours and where no prior arrangement had been made for the employee to report at a specified time, shall inform the duty foreman or manager whether he or she (that is, the employee) has used any alcohol since the last shift. Should the employee fail the Observation Check sheet, he or she will be sent home and no disciplinary action will be taken. Should the employee fail to inform the duty foreman or manager and test positive after having commenced his or her duties, normal disciplinary action shall be taken.

8. MANAGEMENT OF SUSPECTED INTOXICATION

8.1 If a duty foreman or a manager is of the opinion that an employee is or appears to be under the influence of drugs or alcohol, the employee's manager and/or a fellow employee or shop steward shall be called to act as a witness. If the employee's manager and/or fellow employee or shop steward is not available, any other manager or fellow employee or shop steward may be called.

8.2 The responsible manager will, in the presence of the witness and/or shop steward, document signs of suspected intoxication. An Observation Check Sheet form may be used for this purpose.

8.3 Should the employee refuse to submit to the Observation Check Sheet, the employee should be informed that he or she will be giving up an opportunity to contest the allegation of being under the influence. The employee's refusal will then be recorded on the verification form.

8.4 Should the breathalyser test and Observation Check Sheet result be positive, or where testing is refused and/or where clinical or behavioural signs of intoxication are apparent, the employee will, in the interests of workplace safety, be deemed to be under the influence and instructed to leave the work premises.
Regardless of any test result, where clinical or behavioural signs of intoxication are apparent and the supervisor, observing such signs, concludes that the employee's continued presence constitutes a safety risk and may tarnish the name and status of _____[organisation's name], the supervisor will instruct the employee to leave the workplace.

8.5 The manager should take all reasonable steps to ensure that the employee has a safe means of returning home by contacting a relative or friend to accompany the employee. Whilst waiting for assistance the employee will be accompanied to a safe area where they are least likely to cause harm to themself or others. Employees who choose to leave the premises without assistance, that is, unaccompanied, do so at their own risk.

8.6 An employee who is required to return home for reason of actual or suspected intoxication, and an employee who is refused entry to the workplace for the same reason, will not be paid for the hours he or she is unable to work due to his or her actual or suspected intoxication, unless a subsequent enquiry finds the employee not to have been intoxicated at the time he or she was asked to leave or refused entry to the workplace, in which case the employee will be paid for the hours he or she would otherwise have worked.

9. INFORMATION, EDUCATION AND TRAINING:

9.1 _____[name of organisation] is committed to providing employees with information, education and training on all aspects of alcohol or drug use in the workplace during their induction into the company and through the provision of health and safety updates.

9.2 Supervisors and managers will be trained in how to identify problems of substance abuse in employees and equipped with the skills and knowledge needed to assist substance-abusing employees and co-workers affected by their behaviour, which will involve the acquisition of effective interviewing techniques and basic counselling skills.

9.3 _____[name of organisation] will provide drug and alcohol awareness information to all employees. This information includes _____ [name of organisation] policy on drug and alcohol abuse, and information on the following issues:
- the magnitude and dangers of drug and alcohol abuse
- the health and safety implications of drinking at work
- where to go for further information and support
- the services available to employees through the Employee Assistance Programme.

9.4 _____[name of organisation] will provide drug and alcohol awareness training to all employees. This will include:
- exploring and understanding the effects of alcohol and drugs in the workplace
- exploring and understanding attitudes to alcohol and drugs
- exploring and challenging myths surrounding alcohols and drugs
- identifying alcohol and drug problems in the workplace (signs and symptoms)
- implementing the alcohol and drug policy
- interviewing skills
- putting procedures into practice
- confidentiality issues
- identifying and accessing support services
- referrals.

10. ROLES AND RESPONSIBILITIES

Every employee must take on some responsibility in making this policy work.
   The roles defined below are intended as guidelines.

10.1 Role of staff in a managerial or supervisory capacity
- to set a good example to their subordinates and others
- to be familiar with policies and procedures
- to ensure that their subordinates and students understand the policy and their own responsibilities
- to be alert to, and monitor changes in, work or study performance, attendance, sickness and accident patterns
- to take an objective and non-judgemental approach when counselling or interviewing employees
- to review the progress of employees on a treatment programme
- to refer employees for assistance as appropriate
- to be aware of or seek to identify aspects of the work environment that aggravate or may aggravate problems of substance abuse among employees
- to intervene at the earliest opportunity in cases of actual or suspected substance abuse.

10.2 Role of employees

- to find out about the damage caused by alcohol or drug abuse and how such abuse affects workplace relations
- to avoid covering up for or colluding with colleagues who abuse alcohol or drugs
- to encourage colleagues who abuse drugs or alcohol to seek help, especially if they are experiencing problems as a result of this abuse, or advise a senior member of staff of the matter
- to seek help if they themselves have problems with substance misuse
- to be familiar with the policy and procedures.

10.3 Role of the Employment Assistance Programme:
- to provide advice and guidance to employees experiencing problems due to substance misuse
- to provide an impartial and confidential service to employees experiencing problems due to substance misuse, which may include counselling, assessment and referral to other agencies
- to assist in the education and training of employees on all aspects of substance abuse
- to inform the supervisor(s) of employees undergoing counselling and/or treatment of the progress being made by such employees

10.4 Role of the Human Resources Department
- to assist employees experiencing problems due to substance abuse by referring such employees to the EAP, advising on the employer's disciplinary procedure as it relates to issues of substance abuse, and providing further information where necessary.
- to increase the awareness and understanding of all employees regarding matters of substance use, misuse and abuse and to promote the advantages of healthy living;
- to facilitate the provision of induction and refresher training on all health-related issues, including the issue of substance abuse in the workplace.
- to plan and provide training for those in a managerial or supervisory capacity, such training to be in accordance with the provisions of section 9 of this policy (Information, Training and Education)

10.5 Role of employee representatives
- to take part in discussions about the policy
- to help inform employees about the policy
- to encourage employees experiencing substance abuse problems to seek help voluntarily
- to advise employees of their rights and responsibilities under the policy
- to encourage employees to take part in appropriate educational and training programmes
- to represent employees, if requested, in any problem or dispute regarding the application of the policy.

11. TESTING FOR ALCOHOL AND DRUGS/INTOXICATION AND SEARCHES

11.1 Only management or senior officials who have been duly authorised/delegated by their Heads of Department shall carry out testing.

11.2 Where there is a reasonable suspicion that an employee is under the influence of an intoxicating substance a test shall be carried out. Should an employee be found to be intoxicated such employee *shall* be instructed to leave the workplace/premises and the disciplinary process shall be invoked.

11.3 Where an employee unreasonably refuses to consent to any form of testing, the employee should be advised that the refusal will lead to the conclusion that the employee is under the influence of an intoxicating substance and suspension and disciplinary action will follow.

11.4 The test to be conducted will be the test that is appropriate in the circumstances.

11.5 Before an employee can be tested, he or she must be given an explanation of why the test is needed and informed of the possible consequences of a positive test result.

11.6 Testing can only take place if two employees, one of whom must be a supervisor, agree that the observed employee is or appears to be under the influence of an intoxicating substance.

11.7 Supervisors will be provided with a check sheet of behavioural and physical characteristics commonly displayed by individuals under the influence of an intoxicating substance, which they can consult should they reasonably suspect that an employee at work or on the work premises is under the influence of alcohol or drugs.

11.8 Testing for substance abuse may be done immediately following a workplace incident, eg an accident, subject to the requirements of the abovementioned check sheet.

11.9 Failure to comply with, or respond to, rehabilitation shall result in either dismissal on grounds of incapacity due to ill-health or disciplinary action.

11.10 An employee identified as intoxicated shall be immediately suspended for the remainder of the shift on full pay with the instruction to report for duty the following day and that the disciplinary procedure shall apply accordingly.

11.11 Searches

11.11.1 Searches may be conducted when there is a suspicion and/or a situation of disputed possession of a substance of abuse. No consent is necessary for a specific search. Any substance of abuse found on the employee shall be confiscated and be submitted as proof of possession.

(A Senior Official shall conduct searches).

12. SOCIAL FUNCTIONS AND PROMOTIONS

12.1 In the event of functions and promotions where liquor may be served, all employees are expected to at all times behave in a becoming and respectful manner

12.2 No alcohol will be served by _____[name of organisation] during training courses or seminars, except in the event of evening functions and then only with food and with the alternative available of non-alcoholic or low-alcohol beverages.

12.3 No employee may consume alcohol during normal working hours, including lunchtimes, tea breaks and other designated rest and relaxation periods.

12.4 At social functions which have been arranged by _____[name of organisation] and where alcohol consumption is permitted, the alternative of soft drinks and low-alcohol beverages should be available and food should be provided.

12.5 Employees attending such functions who intend driving home afterwards must ensure that they drink responsibly in order to avoid possible prosecution under section 65 of the National Road Traffic Act 93 of 1996 ('Driving while under the influence of intoxicating liquor or drug having narcotic effect …')

12.6 Employees whose behaviour during such events becomes offensive, causing embarrassment to _____[name of organisation], fellow employees or guests, or whose conduct jeopardises the safety of those attending and/or of members of the public as a result of excessive alcohol intake, will be charged with having been under the influence of alcohol whilst on the premises or on duty (see clause 6.4.1) and disciplined accordingly.

13. DISPUTES

In the event of any dispute arising regarding the interpretation of this policy or its application, such dispute shall be resolved through the existing dispute procedure.

14. EVALUATION

14.1 This policy will be evaluated on an annually to ensure that it remains up to date with current developments in the field of substance abuse in the workplace.

15. POLICY DISCLAIMERS

15.1 The treatment of an alcohol- or drug-related problem does not negate the employee or the supervisor's responsibility for adhering to policies and procedures.

15.2 _____[name of organisation] reserves the right to interpret, change, suspend, cancel or dispute, with notice, all or any part of this policy, or procedures or benefits discussed herein.

15.3 Employees will be notified before implementation of any change. Should this policy or any provision thereof be amended, the amended policy or provision thereof will supersede the previous one.

Appendix 1

Standard Procedures for Breathalyser Testing

OBJECTIVES

1. to identify and control alcohol intoxication in the workplace
2. to provide an objective assessment of alcohol intoxication

DEFINITIONS

intoxication: level of tissue alcohol measured via the breath that is equivalent to 0,38 mg of alcohol per one litre of blood (0,38 mg/l).

Note: If testing for alcohol via urine or via the venous blood, a level of tissue alcohol that is equivalent to 0,08 g% or 80 mg/100 ml blood denotes intoxication.

adequate breath required for the reading:

minimum breath pressure	7,5 cm H_2O
minimum breath flow period	2,3 secs
minimum breath flow rate	28 l/min
minimum breath discard volume	1,25 l/min

breathalyser: a digital alcoholmeter breath-alcohol screening device with digital readout in alcohol percentage volume—equivalent to a particular blood alcohol concentration (in milligrams of alcohol per 100 ml blood)
   operator: a security officer or supervisor, trained in administering breathalyser tests and authorised to perform such tests

STANDARD OPERATING PROCEDURE FOR BREATHALYSING

1. An employee who has been requested to take a breathalyser test must first be told:
   (i)   that if he or she refuses to take the breathalyser test, he or she will be deemed to be intoxicated
   (ii) that being intoxicated at work is a serious offence
   (iii) that he or she will be sent home and will be subject to disciplinary action on his/her return to work

(iv) that if he or she voluntarily undergoes a blood or urine test he or she will be sent home but that he or she will only be subject to disciplinary action on his or her return to work if the results of the blood or urine test confirm that he or she was intoxicated at the time the test was taken

(v) that if he or she so requests, he or she will be entitled to have a blood or urine test done *as well as* the breathalyser test

(vi) that he or she may request the presence of a witness during breathalyser testing and/or during blood or urine testing.

2. Before testing, the operator must also ask the employee if he or she has consumed alcohol within the previous 20 minutes. If the employee replies 'yes', the operator must take the employee to an office or other safe area and request him or her to wait there for a further 20 minutes before he or she can be breathalysed.

3. The breathalyser will only record a reading if the employee being breathalysed blows sufficiently hard enough. The employee can be asked to repeat the test if

(i) no reading is recorded after the initial test *and*

(ii) the reason for this is that, in the opinion of the operator, the employee did not blow sufficiently hard enough.

If the employee refuses to repeat the test, the supervisor must be called (see clause 4 below).

4. If in the opinion of the operator the employee is intoxicated irrespective of the breathalyser reading, the line supervisor on duty must be called and, if the supervisor confirms the opinion of the operator, the employee will be deemed intoxicated and sent home and the decision recorded.

5. The employee is informed of the reading recorded upon successful completion of the breathalyser test and told that a reading of 0,38 mg/l[1] or above will indicate intoxication.

OPERATOR FUNCTION

1. The operator must breathalyse the employee in the presence of

(i) another security officer or supervisor and

(ii) the employee's witness, should the employee request a witness.

2. If the first breathalyser test records a reading and the operator is satisfied that the test has been properly conducted, then this reading will be used *unless* the operator is of the opinion that the employee has a rising level.

3. If the reading indicates a breath-alcohol level of 0,35 mg/l[2] the employee concerned must be held for a further 20 minutes, when the test will be repeated. The employee's supervisor must be informed of the delay.

4. If the second test records a reading below a breath-alcohol level of 0,38 mg/l[3] then the employee may resume work.

5. If the second test records a reading for breath-alcohol of 0,38 mg/l[4] or above, the employee will be deemed intoxicated and sent home.

---

1   Equivalent to a blood-alcohol level of 0,08 g% or 80 mg/100 ml blood.
2   Equivalent to a blood-alcohol level of 0,06–0,075 g%.
3   See n 1.
4   See n 1.

6. A health professional should be contacted only if the employee asks for a blood-alcohol test to be taken—the health professional is not to act as a witness.
7. If a blood-alcohol test does take place the operator will remain present as a witness. The employee may also request a further witness to be present.
8. The operator cannot request a blood-alcohol test to be taken; only the employee.

ALCOHOL POLICY FOR CALL-OUT, STANDBY AND PRIOR ARRANGEMENT SITUATIONS

DEFINITIONS

call-out: without prior notice or arrangement an employee is required to report for duty outside his/her normal working hours
standby: an employee is paid to make available his/her services outside his/her normal hours of work for a pre-agreed period
prior arrangement: an employee and his/her supervisor or manager agree in advance that the employee will report for duty at a specified time outside his/her normal working hours

CALL-OUT EMPLOYEES

Alcohol policy

Employees on call-out, on reporting for duty, must inform the security officer at the entrance to the work premises whether they have drunk alcohol since the last time they were at work.

Procedure

1. The employee on call-out, on reporting for duty, informs the security officer whether he/she has drunk alcohol since the last time he or she was at work.
2. If the employee declares that he or she has drunk alcohol during this period the security officer may request the employee to take a breathalyser test if he or she reasonably suspects that the employee may be intoxicated.
3. If the employee consents to being tested and the breathalyser records a reading that shows the employee to be intoxicated, the employee will be sent home and no disciplinary action will be taken.
4. If the employee fails to advise the security officer of any prior alcohol intake and on subsequent breathalysing upon entering the work premises is found to be at or over the prescribed limit, formal disciplinary action will be taken against him or her.

STANDBY EMPLOYEES

Alcohol policy

Employees on standby duty must ensure that their alcohol intake is such that at no time during that period of standby can they legally be declared intoxicated, ie that upon being breathalysed their breath-alcohol level will not exceed 0,38 mg/l.[5]

---

5   See n 1.

Procedure

The procedure follows that described for call-out employees.

PRIOR-ARRANGEMENT EMPLOYEES

Alcohol policy

Employees who have made a prior arrangement to report for duty at a specified time outside their normal working hours must regulate their alcohol intake as if they were reporting for duty *during their normal working hours*, that is, they must ensure that they are not in a state of intoxication.

Procedure

The procedure follows that described for call-out employees.

Notwithstanding anything contained in the above, the Company reserves the right to request any employee to undergo a random breathalyser test (i) when reporting for duty, or (ii) while on Company premises, and to initiate normal disciplinary action should the test reveal the employee to be intoxicated.

Appendix 2

Protocol for Blood Testing

This protocol is for the confirmatory blood testing of an employee suspected of alcohol and/or drug abuse where disciplinary action is likely to be taken against that employee.

1	Donor identification should be obtained.	*donor identification*
2	A signed and witnessed statement stipulating that the employee-donor agrees to provide a blood sample should be obtained.	*written consent of employee*
3	The test should only be conducted by a suitably qualified medical professional.	*use of medical professional*
4	A chain of custody needs to be established. This is to ensure the safe handling and storage of the specimen, from the time the employee-donor provides his/her blood sample to the release of the test results. The chain of custody also links the employee-donor to the sample.	*chain of custody*
5	The area of skin for drawing venous blood should be dry and used without the application of any solvent or alcohol cleanser, ethyl or otherwise.	*drawing venous blood sample*
6	The sample must be split between two containers. Only one container is used for testing purposes; the other is stored. (If the test result is positive the donor can ask for the sample contained in the second container to be tested.)	*use of two containers*
7	The specimens should be sealed in the presence of the employee-donor. A witness should be present when the specimens are sealed.	*sealing of specimen*
8	The documentation should be signed by the screen testing officer, the employee-donor and the witness.	*specimen details*
9	The time and date of providing the specimen should be written on the labels of the containers.	*specimen details*
10	The employee-donor's name should be written on the labels of the containers.	*specimen details*
11	The labelled specimens should be sealed and refrigerated in a secure area. The date and time of storage should be recorded.	*specimen storage*

12	The time, date and method of transportation should be recorded.	*transportation of specimen*
13	The time and date of arrival at the laboratory should be recorded. Laboratory personnel must acknowledge in writing that the specimen has not been tampered with.	*laboratory (arrival of specimen)*
14	The specimen should be tested at least twice by arecognised laboratory with established levels of standardisation and accreditation. The screen test can be performed in front of the employee-donor and the initial screen test results should be given to him or her. The employee-donor then has the option of requesting a GC/MS validity test.	*laboratory (testing of specimen)*
15	The name of every individual handling the specimen should appear in the documentation of the chain of custody.	*chain of custody documentation*
16	The report must be in writing and handled with the strictest confidence. The test results are issued to the employee-donor and/or to any other person he or she has authorised, in writing, to receive the results.	*written report of test results*

Blood testing for alcohol/drug abuse is a highly complex and intricate process. For this reason, we strongly advise all organisations to engage the services of an accredited and competent external testing and collecting agency. Professional guidance is particularly important in the following areas:
- Donor identification verification
- Site preparation
- Screen test procedure
- Specimen collection procedure
- Specimen validity testing
- Screen test result interpretation.

Appendix 3

Questionnaires used to Screen for Alcohol or Drug Misuse

1. ALCOHOL USE DISORDERS IDENTIFICATION TEST (AUDIT)

Circle the number that comes closest to the patient's answer

1. How often do you have a drink containing alcohol (use standard drink of 10 g of alcohol)?
   (0) Never
   (1) Less than monthly
   (2) Two to four times a month
   (3) Two to three times a week
   (4) Four or more times a week
2. How many drinks containing alcohol do you have on a typical day when you are drinking?
   (0) 1 or 2
   (1) 3 or 4
   (2) 5 or 6
   (3) 7 or 8
   (4) 10 or more
3. How often do you have six or more drinks on one occasion?
   (0) Never
   (1) Less than monthly
   (2) Monthly
   (3) Weekly
   (4) Daily or almost daily
4. How often during the last year have you found that you were not able to stop drinking once you had started?
   (0) Never
   (1) Less than monthly
   (2) Monthly
   (3) Weekly
   (4) Daily or almost daily
5. How often during the last year have you failed to do what was normally expected from you because of drinking?
   (0) Never
   (1) Less than monthly
   (2) Monthly

(3) Weekly
(4) Daily or almost daily
6. How often during the last year have you needed a drink first thing in the morning to get yourself going after a heavy drinking session?
(0)Never
(1) Less than monthly
(2) Monthly
(3) Weekly
(4) Daily or almost daily
7. How often during the last year have you had a feeling of guilt or remorse after drinking?
(0) Never
(1) Less than monthly
(2) Monthly
(3) Weekly
(4) Daily or almost daily
8. How often during the last year have you been unable to remember what happened the night before because you had been drinking?
(0) Never
(1) Less than monthly
(2) Monthly
(3) Weekly
(4) Daily or almost daily
9. Have you or someone else been injured as a result of your drinking?
(0) No
(1) Yes, but not in the last year
(2) Yes, during the last year
10. Has a relative or friend or a doctor or health worker been concerned about your drinking or suggested you cut down?
(0) No
(1) Yes, but not in the last year
(2) Yes, during the last year

SCORING
A score of around 8 gives the highest sensitivity and a score of 10 or more results in higher specificity
High scores on questions 1–3 only suggest hazardous alcohol use
Highs scores on questions 4–6 suggest emerging or present dependence
High scores on questions 7–10 suggest harmful alcohol use
Hazardous alcohol consumption
1. Frequency of drinking
2. Typical quantity
3. Frequency of heavy drinking

DEPENDENCE SYMPTOMS
4. Impaired control over drinking
5. Increased salience of drinking
6. Morning drinking

HARMFUL ALCOHOL CONSUMPTION
7. Guilt after drinking
8. Blackouts
9. Alcohol-related injuries
10. Others concerned about drinking

2. THE MICHIGAN ALCOHOL SCREENING TEST (MAST)

Please answer YES or NO to the following questions:
1. Do you feel you are a normal drinker? (Drink as much or less than most other people)
2. Have you ever awakened the morning after some drinking the night before and found that you could not remember a part of the evening?
3. Does any near relative or close friend ever worry or complain about your drinking?
4. Can you stop drinking without difficulty after one or two drinks?
5. Do you ever feel guilty about your drinking?
6. Have you ever attended a meeting of Alcoholics Anonymous or other self help groups?
7. Have you ever gotten into physical fights when drinking?
8. Has drinking ever created problems between you and a near relative or close friend?
9. Has any family member or close friend gone to anyone for help about your drinking?
10. Have you ever lost friends because of drinking?
11. Have you ever gotten into trouble at work because of drinking?
12. Have you ever lost a job because of drinking?
13. Have you ever neglected your obligations, your family, or your work for two or more days in a row because you were drinking?
14. Do you drink before noon fairly often?
15. Have you ever been told you have liver trouble such as cirrhosis?
16. After heavy drinking have you ever had delirium tremens (DTs), severe shaking, visual or auditory (hearing) hallucinations?
17. Have you ever gone to anyone for help about your drinking?
18. Have you ever been hospitalised because of drinking?
19. Has your drinking ever resulted in your being hospitalised in a psychiatric ward?
20. Have you ever gone to any doctor, social worker, clergyman, or mental health clinic for help with any emotional problem in which drinking was part of the problem?
21. Have you been arrested more than once for driving under the influence of alcohol?
22. Have you ever been arrested, even for a few hours, because of other behaviour while drinking?

SCORING

Score 1 point for each 'yes' answer—except for questions 1 and 4, where 1 point is allocated for each 'no' answer—and then total the responses.
0–2   No apparent problem
3–5   Early or middle problem drinker
6 Or more   Problem drinker

3. BRIEF MAST (BMAST)[6]

		Points	
		yes	no
1.	Do you feel you are a normal drinker?	–	2
2.	Do friends or relatives think you are a normal drinker?	–	2
3.	Have you ever attended a meeting of Alcoholics Anonymous AA?	5	–
4.	Have you ever lost friends or girlfriends/boyfriends because of your drinking?	2	–
5.	Have you ever gotten into trouble at work because of drinking?	2	–
6.	Have you ever neglected your obligations, your family, or your work for 2 or more days in a row because you were drinking?	2	–
7.	Have you ever had delirium tremens DTs, severe shaking, after heavy drinking?	2	–
8.	Have you ever gone to anyone for help about your drinking?	5	–
9.	Have you ever been in a hospital because of your drinking?	5	–
10.	Have you ever been arrested for drunk driving or driving after drinking?	2	–

SCORING

< 3 points	nonalcoholic
4 points	suggestive of alcoholism
5 > points	indicates alcoholism

4. FAST ALCOHOL SCREENING TEST (FAST)

For the following questions please circle the answer which best applies

1. Men: How often do you have EIGHT or more drinks on one occasion?
   Women: How often do you have SIX or more drinks on one occasion?
   Never
   Less than monthly
   Monthly
   Weekly
   Daily or Almost daily

2. How often during the last year have you been unable to remember what happened the night before because you had been drinking?
   Never
   Less than monthly
   Monthly
   Weekly
   Daily or Almost daily

3. How often during the last year have you failed to do what was normally expected of you because of drinking?
   Never
   Less than monthly

---

6   Selzer ML. 'The Michigan Alcoholism Screening Test: The quest for a new diagnostic instrument (1971) 27(12) *American Journal of Psychiatry*: 1653-1658.

Monthly
Weekly
Daily or Almost daily
4. In the last year has a relative or friend or a doctor or other mental health worker been concerned about your drinking or suggested you cut down?
NO
Yes, on ONE occasion
Yes, on MORE THAN ONE occasion

SCORING

Score questions 1–3:   0, 1, 2, 3, 4
Score question 4:   0, 2, 4
A score of 3 or more suggests probable hazardous drinking.

5. CAGE

C—Have you ever felt you should cut down on your drinking?
A—Have people annoyed you by criticising your drinking?
G—Have you ever felt bad or guilty about your drinking?
E—Eye opener. Have you ever had a drink first thing in the morning to steady your nerves or to get rid of a hangover?

Two 'yes' answers indicate harmful drinking and the need for further assessment.

6. DRUG ABUSE SCREENING TEST (DAST)[7]

1.	Have you used drugs other than those required for medical reasons?	Yes	No
2.	Have you abused prescription drugs?	Yes	No
3.	Do you abuse more than one drug at a time?	Yes	No
4.	Can you get through the week without using drugs (other than those required for medical reasons)?	Yes	No
5.	Are you always able to stop using drugs when you want to?	Yes	No
6.	Do you abuse drugs on a continuous basis?	Yes	No
7.	Do you try to limit your drug use to certain situations?	Yes	No
8.	Have you had 'blackouts' or 'flashbacks' as a result of drug use?	Yes	No
9.	Do you ever feel bad about your drug abuse?	Yes	No
10.	Does your spouse (or parents) ever complain about your involvement with drugs?	Yes	No
11.	Do your friends or relatives know or suspect you abuse drugs?	Yes	No

---

7   Gavin DR, Ross HE, Skinner HA. 'Diagnostic validity of the Drug Abuse Screening test in the assessment of DSM-III drug disorders'. (1989) 84(3) *British Journal of Addiction* 84(3): 301–307. (23 refs.)

12.	Has drug abuse ever created problems between you and your spouse?	Yes	No
13.	Has any family member ever sought help for problems related to your drug use?	Yes	No
14.	Have you ever lost friends because of your use of drugs?	Yes	No
15.	Have you ever neglected your family or missed work because of your use of drugs?	Yes	No
16.	Have you ever been in trouble at work because of drug abuse?	Yes	No
17.	Have you ever lost a job because of drug abuse?	Yes	No
18.	Have you gotten into fights when under the influence of drugs?	Yes	No
19.	Have you ever been arrested because of unusual behaviour while under the influence of drugs?	Yes	No
20.	Have you ever been arrested for driving while under the influence of drugs?	Yes	No
21.	Have you engaged in illegal activities to obtain drugs?	Yes	No
22.	Have you ever been arrested for possession of illegal drugs?	Yes	No
23.	Have you ever experienced withdrawal symptoms as a result of heavy drug intake?	Yes	No
24.	Have you had medical problems as a result of your drug use (eg memory loss, hepatitis, convulsions, or bleeding)?	Yes	No
25.	Have you ever gone to anyone for help for a drug problem?	Yes	No
26.	Have you ever been in hospital for medical problems related to your drug use?	Yes	No
27.	Have you ever been involved in a treatment programme specifically related to drug use?	Yes	No
28.	Have you been treated as an outpatient for problems related to drug abuse?	Yes	No

SCORING

Each item in bold = 1 point
6 or more = substance use problem (abuse or dependence)

7. DRUG USE DISORDERS IDENTIFICATION TEST (DUDIT)

Male   Female   Age

1. How often do you use drugs other than alcohol? (See list of drugs on next page.)
   Never
   Once a month or less often
   2–4 times a month

2–3 times a week
4 times a week or more often
2. Do you use more than one type of drug on the same occasion?
Never
Once a month or less often
2–4 times a month
2–3 times a week
4 times a week or more often
3. How many times do you take drugs on a typical day when you use drugs?
0
1–2
3–4
5–6
7 or more
4. How often are you influenced heavily by drugs?
Never
Less often than once a month
Every month
Every week
Daily or almost every day
5. Over the past year, have you felt that your longing for drugs was so strong that you could not resist it?
Never
Less often than once a month
Every month
Every week
Daily or almost every day
6. Over the past year, has it happened that you have not been able to stop taking drugs once you started?
Never
Less often than once a month
Every month
Every week
Daily or almost every day
7. How often over the past year have you taken drugs and then neglected to do something you should have done?
Never
Less often than once a month
Every month
Every week
Daily or almost every day
8. How often over the past year have you needed to take a drug the morning after heavy drug use the day before?
Never
Less often than once a month
Every month
Every week

Daily or almost every day

9. How often over the past year have you had guilt feelings or a bad conscience because you used drugs?

Never

Less often than once a month

Every month

Every week

Daily or almost every day

10. Have you or anyone else been hurt (mentally or physically) because you used drugs?

No

Yes, but not over the past year

Yes, over the past year

11. Has a relative or a friend, a doctor or a nurse, or anyone else, been worried about your drug use or said to you that you should stop using drugs?

No

Yes, but not over the past year

Yes, over the past year

Appendix 4

Protocol for Urine Testing

FOR ALCOHOL/DRUG ABUSE WHEN DISCIPLINARY ACTION IS LIKELY TO BE TAKEN

This protocol is for the urine testing of an employee suspected of alcohol and/or drug abuse where disciplinary action is likely to be taken against that employee.

1	Donor identification should be obtained.	*donor identification*
2	A signed and witnessed statement stipulating that the employee-donor agrees to provide a urine sample should be obtained.	*written consent of employee*
3	A chain of custody needs to be established. This is to ensure the safe handling and storage of the specimen, from the time the employee-donor provides his/her urine sample to the release of the test result. The chain of custody also links the employee-donor to the sample.	*chain of custody*
4	Anti-tampering precautions are needed to protect the specimen against contamination. These precautions include: • the use of a tamper-proof toilet cubicle • the use of coloured water in the toilet • turning off the water supply • the screen testing officer asking the employee-donor to remove all personal belongings (take off coat, empty pockets, etc) • the screen testing officer (same gender as donor) escorting the employee-donor to and from the toilet • the screen testing officer taking charge of the specimen as soon as possible after it has been voided • checking the temperature of the sample (this should be between 35–37° C; a lower temperature indicates that the sample is probably not the one just voided by donor) • reducing the risk of sample contamination (eg clean the thermometer between tests or rather use a stick on thermometer; do not use a test device before the sample has been split) • strictly observing the procedures covering the documenting and handling of the sample after voiding.	*protection of specimen*
5	The sample must be split between two containers. Only one container is used for testing purposes; the other is stored. (If the test result is positive the donor can ask for the sample contained in the second container to be tested.)	*use of two containers*

6	The specimen must be sealed in the presence of employee-donor. The employee-donor and the screen testing officer add their signatures to the seal.	*sealing of specimen*
7	The time and date of voiding the specimen should be written on the labels of the containers.	*specimen details*
8	The employee-donor's name should be written on the labels of the containers.	*specimen details*
9	The labelled specimens should be sealed and refrigerated in a secure area. The time and date of storage should be recorded.	*specimen storage*
10	The time, date and method of transportation should be recorded.	*transportation of specimen*
11	The time and date of arrival at the laboratory should be recorded. Laboratory personnel must acknowledge in writing that the specimen has not been tampered with.	*laboratory (arrival of specimen)*
12	The specimen should be tested at least twice by a recognised laboratory with established levels of standardisation and accreditation. The screen test can be performed in front of the employee-donor and the initial screen test results should be given to him or her. The employee-donor then has the option of requesting a GC/MS validity test.	*laboratory (testing of specimen)*
13	The name of every individual handling the specimen should appear in the documentation of the chain of custody.	*chain of custody documentation*
14	The report must be in writing and handled with the strictest confidence. The test results are issued to the employee-donor and/or to any other person he or she has authorised, in writing, to receive the results.	*written report of test results*

Urine testing for alcohol/drug abuse is a highly complex and intricate process. For this reason, we strongly advise all organisations to engage the services of an accredited and competent external testing and collecting agency. Professional guidance is particularly important in the following areas:

- Donor identification verification
- Site preparation
- Screen test procedure
- Specimen collection procedure
- Specimen validity testing
- Screen test result interpretation.

Appendix 5

Units and Formulae

Ethanol: units of measurement and conversions
1 millilitre of ethanol equals 798 milligrams ethanol
or,
1 ml ethanol = 798 mg ethanol

1 gram of ethanol equals 21,7 millimoles* ethanol
or,
1 g ethanol = 21,7 mmol ethanol

To convert mg/100 ml to mmol/l multiply by 0,217
thus, 60 mg/100 ml = 13,02 mmol/l (60 × 0.217 = 13,02)

To convert mmol/l to mg/100 ml divide by 0,217
thus, 13,02 mmol/l = 60 mg/100 ml (13,02 ÷ 0,217 = 60)

*A millimole is one thousandth (10^{-3}) of a mole.
A mole is the base SI unit of amount of substance.
   Millimolar describes the amount-of-substance concentration of a chemical compound in a water-based (aqueous) solution. Millimolar can thus be used to describe the concentration level of alcohol (a chemical compound) in blood (an aqueous solution).
   Standard units of measurement used in calculating blood alcohol content (BAC)

Unit of measurement	symbol	description
decilitre	dl	metric unit of volume equal to one tenth (10^{-1}) of a litre
millilitre	ml	metric unit of volume equal to one thousandth (10^{-3}) of a litre
milligram	mg	a metric unit of mass equal to one thousandth (10^{-3}) of a gram
microgram	µg or mcg	a metric unit of mass equal to one millionth (10^{-6}) of a gram
nanogram	ng	a metric unit of mass equal to one billionth (10^{-9}) of a gram

Alcohol content measurements: blood, breath and urine

blood alcohol content	0,08 g/100 ml	0,08 g%	80 mg/100 ml	80 mg/dl	80 mg%	17,4 mmol/ℓ
breath alcohol content (absorption phase) * breathalyser testing is best-suited to the absorption phase of alcohol	38 mcg/dl	0,38 mg/ ℓ	38 µg/dl	0,08 g/ 210 ℓ		
urine alcohol content	107 mg/ dl or 107 mg/100ml					

FORMULAE

1. Calculating alcohol content (in grams) in a given volume of alcoholic drink

$$\text{alcohol in grams} = \text{volume in millilitres} \times \frac{\%\ \text{alcohol volume}}{100} \times 0,789$$

2. Widmark formula
   Calculates blood alcohol content (BAC) based on a person's gender, weight, the amount of alcohol consumed, and the time that has elapsed since the first drink was consumed. The exact formula is
   $A = P \times C \times r \times 10 \times 0,947$
   where
   A = amount of alcohol absorbed in grams
   P = body mass in kilograms
   C = blood alcohol concentration (BAC) in grams per 100 ml of blood
   R = diffusion rate
   Note: the diffusion rate varies according to the percentage of body fat, thus:
   obese person   r = 0,5
   muscular male   r = 0,75
   average male   r = 0,67
   average female   r = 0,6

Example of a Letter to Non-unionised Employees regarding the Introduction of an Updated Alcohol and Drugs Policy

ABC PRODUCTS LIMITED

PO Box 222
SWEETWATER
9098
TEL: (6678) 4444
TEL: (6678) 4457

Dear _____

The Company's updated Alcohol and Drug Policy will be introduced in a few weeks time. The new Policy aims to improve upon the existing Policy in a number of ways. The most significant change is the new rule that *no alcohol is to be allowed on Company premises*. A total ban on alcohol is the best way of ensuring the safety of employees in a busy factory like ours, where accidents can cause loss of life or limb. Alcohol increases the chances of slip-ups or mistakes occurring, which is why we believe a complete ban is needed.

We are not asking people to give up alcohol completely. We are only asking that you refrain from drinking at work and that you make sure that when you arrive at work you are not suffering from the effects of too much alcohol.

A minority of employees may have a drink problem and to them we offer a simple message: We have a caring policy and would like to give all the help and support we can.

But there may be isolated cases where someone with difficulties doesn't ask for help, or the support given doesn't achieve results. In these cases we plan to get tough and disciplinary action will be taken.

The employees of ABC Products Limited are the Company's most valuable asset and their health is of paramount importance. The new Policy aims to safeguard what all of us would agree is life's number one priority—good health.

The new Policy also has a section on drugs, which was not in the original document. Drug abuse is, sadly, a reality of modern life. The Company acknowledges this and accepts that some members of its workforce may be affected. Employees with drug problems are therefore also encouraged to come forward—we will care for them as best we can. But please note that if such an employee refuses to seek help or fails to control his or her drug problem, he or she will be disciplined.

If you have any queries, comments or suggestions to make regarding the improved Policy, please contact the Human Resources Manager.

Subject to the above, the new Policy on Alcohol and Drugs will become effective from 1 January 20–, from which time the new Policy will be deemed to be part of your terms and conditions of employment.

Yours sincerely

COMPANY REPRESENTATIVE

Appendix 7

Glossary of Medical Terms relating to Alcohol and Drug Misuse

acetaldehyde	the breakdown product of ethanol in the liver and is toxic
acne rosacea	permanent redness of the face with associated pustules like acne, made worse by, among many other causes, sunlight, stress, heat and alcohol
addiction	a chronic, relapsing disease characterised by compulsive drug seeking and use
adenomatous polyps	a fleshy growth occuring on the lining of the colon or rectum; untreated they can develop into cancer
adulterant	a substance, either biologically active or inert, which is added to a drug when processed
adulteration	to make something impure
alcoholic fugue	a fugue or state of amnesia for personal identity, memory. Dissociative fugue involves wandering and on recovery an amnesia of the event.
amblyopia	progressive dimness of vision
amnesia	when associated with substance abuse it results in lapses of short term memory
aplastic anaemia	a condition where bone marrow does not produce sufficient new cells to replenish blood cells
arrythmias	abnormal or irregular heart rate
ascites	fluid on the abdomen
asterixis	flapping tremor of the hands associated with high levels of blood ammonia
ataxia	a balance problem
atrial fibrillation	rapid non-functioning contractions of the atria of the heart
atrophy	shrinking of an organ or muscle
beri beri heart	heart failure associated with thiamine deficiency

bradycardia	a slow heart rate
bronchiectasis	a form of obstructive lung disease where there is permanent dilation of part of the bronchial tubes and often associated with chronic infection
bronchospasm	narrowing of the bronchioles usually associated with asthma
caput medusae	swollen veins in the abdominal wall
cardiomyopathy	damage to the heart muscle
cardiovascular system	the heart and blood vessels
centrilobular necrosis	death of liver cells in the centre of the liver lobules
cerebrovascular accidents (CVA)	stroke
cholecystitis	inflammation of the gall bladder
cirrhosis	chronic liver disease where the liver tissue is replaced by fibrosis, regenerating liver nodules and scarring
co-carcinogen	a chemical which promotes the effects of a carcinogen in the production of cancer
cognition	the process of thinking and understanding
confabulation	inventing stories to cover up for memory deficiency
coproporphyrin	either of two porphyrin compounds normally found in faeces as a decomposition product of bilirubin
cortisol	hormone released by the adrenal gland usually in response to stress or anxiety. Its primary function is to increase blood sugar and liver glycogen levels.
craniofacial	pertaining to the skull and face
Cushing's disease	caused by excessive cortisol in the blood. Noticeable symptoms are rapid weight gain in the trunk and face (moon face) with thin skin yet dilated capillaries.
delerium tremens (DTs)	the reaction associated with withdrawal of alcohol involving tremor of the hands or even shaking of the body, anxiety, panic attacks, confusion, disorientation and paranoia and even visual hallucinations.
dopamine	brain neurotransmitter which gives activity and alertness found in parts of the brain that regulate movement, emotion, motivation and feelings of pleasure
Ecstasy	common street name of MDMA or methamphetamine
emphysema	chronic obstructive lung disease (COLD), also known as chronic obstructive pulmonary disease (COPD), where the lung parenchyma or structure of the lung has been destroyed
encephalopathy	disease of the brain

erythropoiesis	manufacture of red blood cells
euphoria	refers to a feeling of elation. A reaction associated with substance abuse, which with drugs invariably uses up the body's dopamine supplies ending with a crash
executive functioning	the lead functioning of the brain from the the frontal cortex involved in abstract thinking, planning, deciding on actions, control of inappropriate actions
FAS	Foetal Alcohol Syndrome associated with growth deficiencies in the foetus
fibrosis	scarring associated with non-functioning fibrous tissue
gastrointestinal system or tract	the stomach and intestine as a functional unit
gluconeogenesis	formation of blood glucose by the liver
'Half-life'	The half-life of a drug is the time it takes for the drug to lose one-half of its activity
Hallucinations	Auditory or visual hallucinations are when the patient hears voices or sees things. With substance abuse the condition is usually associated with brain damage or severe withdrawal of alcohol. Also associated with the use of hallucinogens, for example LSD.
Hallucinosis	hallucinating without other symptoms
hepatitis	inflammation of the liver
hippocampus	situated in the medial temporal lobe of the brain and is associated with long term memory and spatial navigation
hyperacussis	increased sensitivity to noise
hyperlipidaemia	excess fats in the blood
hyperthermia	a potentially dangerous rise in body temperature
hypopharyngeal	bottom part of the pharynx or throat which connects to the oesophagous
hypospermia	low sperm count
jaundice	yellow discolouration of the skin and sclera (white of the eyes) associated with hepatitis or liver failure
larynx	voice box
macrocytosis	enlarged red blood cells
Mallory-Weiss syndrome	lacerations of the internal lining of the oesophagous
MDMA	common chemical name for 3,4-methylenedioxymethamphetamine
mesenteric adenitis	inflammation of the mesenteric lymph nodes in the abdomen
meta-analysis	a powerful combination of numerous databases to assess the overall result

MRI	Magnetic Resonance Imaging
myopathy	damage to muscles associated with muscle disease
myositis	inflammation of muscle
narcosis	the unconsciousness induced by a narcotic drug
neurobehavioural	relationship between the nervous system and behaviour
neurocognitive loss	memory loss associated with brain cell damage
neurogenesis	regeneration of nerve cells
neuron	nerve cell
neuronal death	death of nerve cells
neurophysiology	physiology of the nervous system
neuropsychiatry	psychiatry associated with understanding nerve damage. Associated with assessing an individual with potential brain damage.
neurotoxic	toxic to the nerves
neurotransmitter	a chemical that acts as a messenger to carry signals or information from one nerve cell to another
norepinephrine	a neurotransmitter present in regions of the brain that affect heart rate and blood pressure
ocular palsy	eye muscle paralysis
oedema of the brain	fluid on the brain which can increase pressure, sometimes dangerously
oesophagitis	inflammation of the oesphagous
oropharyngeal	situated on the posterior wall and above the hypopharynx
osteoporosis	thinning of and weakening of the bone structure
pancreatitis	inflammation of the pancreas
pellagra	nicotinic acid deficiency causing a rough thick brown skin with associated 'rickety rosary' or necklace effect around the neck
perinephric abscess	abscess adjacent to the kidney
peripheral neuropathy	neuropathic pain, pins and needles, loss of sensation, numbness and/or weakness of the arms or legs
petechiae	very small haemorrhages in the skin
phlebotomist	a person trained to take blood. Usually a nurse practitioner or medical laboratory technician
portal hypertension	high blood pressure in the portal venous system associated with cirrhosis of the liver due to the blood vessels being blocked
portal venous blood	blood from the intestine carrying nutrients to the liver for metabolism or detoxification
potentiation by alcohol abuse	accelerating or enhancing the effect by alcohol abuse

pre-senile	associated with the early signs of dementia
promoter	in genetics, a part of DNA which helps the transcription of a particular gene
prothrombin	a blood clotting enzyme
psychosis	a loss of contact with reality
pulmonary aspiration	the entry of secretions or foreign substances into the trachea or lungs
pupillography	the measurement of the reaction of the pupil of the eye
REM sleep	Rapid Eye Movement sleep. Part of the natural sleep process associated with deep sleep.
respiratory acidosis	abnormal body chemistry which becomes acidic due to breathing problems
rhinophyma	a form of rosacea with a swollen red nobbly nose more prominent with chronic excess alcohol abuse
scotoma	central blind spot in the retina of the eye affecting central vision
serotonin	powerful neurotransmitter used in widespread parts of the brain, which is involved in sleep, movement and emotions
spastic colon	Irritable bowel syndrome
spermatogenesis	formation of sperm cells
spider naevi	enlarged branching end arterioles in the skin
splenomegaly	enlarged spleen
steatorrhea	fatty stool
synergistic	two or more factors which when working together give more than double the effect
telangiectasia	spider-like swollen arterioles in the skin usually on the face
thiamine	one of the B vitamins which is depleted in alcoholics
tinnitus	ringing in the ears
tik	street name for crystal methamphetamine
tolerance	a decrease in the effect of a drug that occurs with repeated administration
triglycerides	a glyceride associated with the fats in the blood
varices	engorged swollen veins and usually not functioning efficiently
ventricular extra systoles	additional contractions of the ventricles of the heart

Appendix 8

Strategy for Managing Alcohol and Drug problems in the Workplace: A Summary

The management of alcohol and drug problems at work covers five areas of concern, namely
1. the development and implementation of an alcohol and drug policy
2. the education of employees
3. the training of supervisors and managers
4. the provision of effective treatment programmes for identified dependent employees
5. the provision of effective, structured rehabilitation programmes for recovering employees.

1. **Alcohol and drug policy**
   The policy is the lead document governing all aspects of alcohol and drug use, misuse and abuse in a company. As such, the policy will outline the company's attitude towards substance abuse at work and the measures it plans to introduce to combat the problem. These measures are likely to be proscriptive—the banning of all alcohol and illegal drugs on the work premises, for example—and supportive—the provision of free in-house counselling for employees with substance-abuse problems, for example. Details of the employee assistance programme (EAP) will be included, as well as those of the disciplinary code.
   The policy should be developed in conjunction with employee representatives and, very importantly, trade unions.

2. **Education of employees**
   Education on the dangers associated with substance abuse is essential. Some employees may simply be unaware of these dangers; others may downplay the risks involved because they themselves are alcohol- or drug-dependent. While it is of course important to enumerate the health risks associated with substance abuse, attention must also be given to the debilitating effect such abuse can have on workplace and social relationships, and on organisational safety, morale and productivity.
   This part of the programme also provides the opportunity to inform employees of the warning signs of drug or alcohol abuse, outline the counselling and treatment

services available for troubled employees, and explain what constitutes unacceptable behaviour in terms of corporate policy.

3. **Training of managers and supervisors**
Line managers and supervisors ('supervisor(s)' hereafter) are pivotal to the successful implementation and maintenance of an alcohol and drug policy.

They are responsible for the day-to-day running of the organisation, which inevitably involves a great deal of interaction between themselves and the workers under their control. The supervisor is therefore ideally positioned to assess the work performance of employees and is usually the first to notice if an employee is struggling to maintain performance targets. If a failing employee's behaviour indicates that substance abuse may be a factor—the employee takes too many long lunch breaks and often smells of alcohol on his or her return, for example—the supervisor must know how to handle the situation. He or she must be careful not to antagonise the employee concerned, for example by strongly reprimanding him or her in front of others, since this may only antagonise and alienate him or her; it may also alienate other employees who feel that the supervisor is acting unfairly or vindictively. The supervisor may in any event be unwilling to act in this way, or possibly unwilling to act *at all*, given that he or she may instinctively wish to protect someone coming from the same or a very similar background to him- or herself.

But the supervisor needs to take action of *some* sort. He or she cannot ignore a problem of (actual or suspected) substance abuse, especially if the problem has the potential to disrupt productivity, jeopardise worker safety, damage the company's reputation, and so on.

There are ways in which the supervisor can remain fair both to employees and to the company. For example, the employees must know—and the supervisor must make this abundantly clear—that any concerns they may have about their own alcohol or drug consumption or that of any of their co-workers will be treated with the utmost confidence. The supervisor should also remind the troubled employee that the company's policy on substance abuse is primarily concerned with *helping* employees with drink or drug problems, and that disciplinary action will only be used as a last resort.

As well as reassuring the employee in this way, the supervisor must also remind him or her of the need to comply with the prescribed treatment programme. He or she must be gently but firmly advised that the company will not tolerate uncooperative or obstructive behaviour on the part of the employee and that should such behaviour persist, disciplinary action may be the only course of action left open.

4. **Effective treatment programmes**
The alcohol and drug policy should recognise that alcohol or drug dependency is an illness and that the individual employee will receive treatment for this illness as if it were any other. Treatment of alcohol- or drug-dependent employees can be very rewarding for the employer. Research shows that dependent persons in work are more likely to recover than those out of work. An unemployed person's social life has often disintegrated to such an extent that it is only when they are at work that they feel more or less in control, safe and normal. An effective recovery inevitably

produces a highly motivated employee – grateful for having been given a second chance.

Initially the case should be managed by the Occupational Health Professional (OHP) or an EAP professional, who can provide a preliminary assessment.

For this assessment the OHP or EAP professional (hereafter 'the OHP') should be provided with the following:

- *the supervisor or line manager's report.* This will document all incidences of actual or suspected intoxication, behavioural inconsistencies, absenteeism from work, and so on, identified in chronological order. Employees who claim to have seen a co-worker in an intoxicated condition should be asked to submit a report testifying to this, and this report should be included along with the supervisor's.
- *details of previously identified substance-abuse issues.* The personnel records of the employee should note other alcohol- or drug-related incidents and the action taken at the time (warnings, referral for treatment, etc). This information will relate to the employee's period of service with his or her present employer but *may* also refer to similar incidents that have arisen elsewhere, that is, when working for another company.
- *previous medical history.* This may indicate a long-term problem vis a vis substance abuse.
- *general practitioner's (GP's) report.* The employee must give his or her written consent to the release of this report. It is important that the company advises the GP that it has an alcohol and drug policy in place and that it views alcohol or drug dependency as an illness. The GP should also be told about the company's detoxification and rehabilitation programme.

Preliminary assessment

The preliminary assessment takes place after the OHP has read the GP's report but before he or she refers the employee to an addiction specialist. The aim of the preliminary assessment is to familiarise the employee with the counselling/treatment/rehabilitation process and to obtain commitment to this process. Briefly, the assessment will involve:

i. advising the employee that he or she is suspected of having a drink or drug problem and discussing the supervisor/line manager's report with him or her

ii. advising the employee that a medical history and medical examination is required to establish, among other things, the employee's fitness to work. The types of tests that can be conducted (blood, urine or saliva) should be explained to the employee and an explanation given as to the purpose of these tests, namely that they will be used to establish the severity or otherwise of the physical aspects of the employee's condition.

iii. establishing the employee's level of dependency. He or she may be highly dependent, moderately dependent or only mildly dependent. An employee who is highly dependent (that is, he or she is in the late stages of dependency) will require radically different treatment to an employee who is only mildly dependent/in the early stages of dependency.

iv. establishing the possibility of a dual diagnosis (psychiatric or organic). A substance-abusing employee with a co-existing mental health illness will require specialised help, which is why the possibility of dual diagnosis needs to be taken into account.

v.   advising the employee of the confidential nature of the relationship. This means that the OHP will not disclose any information to a third party (in effect, management), but that non-compliance (on the part of the employee) may compel the OHP to inform management that the individual employee is unfit for work.

vi. undertaking a risk assessment on the grounds of health and safety to ensure that the safety of the employee, his or her colleagues and/or the general public is not jeopardised. Consideration should also be given to organisational risks, that is, the negative impact the employee's behaviour and actions may have on the company's performance, productivity and public image.

vii. reassuring the employee on the issue of confidentiality. The previous exercise (the risk assessment) is likely to have unsettled the employee since it will have necessitated an examination and exploration of his or her character and conduct.

viii. advising the employee that they must complete the treatment programme if they wish to remain with the company. While the company will do what it can to help a substance-abusing employee, the success of the treatment largely depends upon the degree of commitment the employee invests in the process. In other words, the employee has to 'do the work'; no one else can do it for him or her.

ix. assessment by an addiction specialist. The specialist will define the extent of the dependency and the preferred treatment programme for that individual employee.

x.   treatment options. These include:
  • home detoxification
  • in-patient detoxification
  • day hospital rehabilitation
  • in-patient rehabilitation
  • halfway house.

5. Post-rehabilitation return to work
On returning to work the following steps need to be taken:
1. The individual needs to be re-assessed by the OHP. Re-assessment should include
  • the alcohol/drug rehabilitation centre's report on the success of the treatment
  • base line blood tests
  • a risk assessment in relation to findings
  • work modifications or alternative work, if required.
2. The OHP needs to counsel the individual on the effect that return to work may have on other employees. If the individual's pre-treatment behaviour was particularly unpleasant (verbally or physically abusive, for example) it is very likely that he or she will be treated with suspicion, at least at the beginning. Alternatively, some colleagues may derive pleasure from making fun of a recovering employee-patient, perhaps in the hope that this will provoke a further relapse or an inappropriate outburst of some sort. The OHP should forewarn the individual or these possibilities and advise him or her that reintegration is a gradual process that requires patience and self-discipline.
3. The individual should be told that they will continue to be monitored for as long as the OHP considers necessary.
4. There should be some ongoing support of therapy. This could be via support groups such as Alcoholics Anonymous or Narcotics Anonymous, a halfway house, or further counselling from an addiction counsellor.

5. Return to work is subject to two golden rules, namely
    i.   If drinking or drug taking starts again the individual must not attend work.
    ii.   If drinking or drug taking starts again the individual must report the incident to the OHP.

    These two rules are of paramount importance. A recovering employee-patient who attends work while under the influence of alcohol or drugs is likely to be dismissed. Conversely, the employee-patient who reports the relapse to the OHP acknowledges that denial is not a problem. Thus the incident becomes part of the therapeutic process and can be used to strengthen existing coping mechanisms or techniques or to develop new ones.

6. The OHP should liaise with the local GP regarding the employee's progress.

7. The OHP needs to inform the manager of his or her responsibilities in respect of the returning employee. The manager will be responsible for supporting and encouraging the employee on his or her return to the workplace, as well as monitoring his or her performance. The manager should also remind the employee of the disciplinary procedures relating to his or her situation and that he or she should seek the help of the OHP when or if problems arise. The OHP needs to explain to the manager that relapses are to be expected, especially in the early stages of recovery, and that the incident can be put to good (therapeutic) use *provided that* the employee does not try to conceal his renewed drinking or drug taking (see the two 'golden rules' above).

Appendix 9

Verification Form for Use by Security, Health and Safety Officers or Line Managers in Suspected Alcohol/Drug Use

VERIFICATION OF SUSPECTED ALCOHOL/DRUG INTOXICATION FORM

Name of Employee_____

Employee / ID number _____

Business Area_____

Name of observer: _____

Business Area_____

The following results were obtained during a visual test in the presence of _____

a representative of _____

1.	Speech	Talkative		Slurred		Incoherent		Slow/ deliberate	
2.	Speech	Red, puffy		Fixed stare		Droopy lids		Enlarged pupils	
3.	Walking & balance			Impaired		Unsteady		Stumbling	
4.	Co-ordination			Poor judgement		Impaired		Shaky hands	

5.	Behaviour	Loss of inhibition		Passive		Normal
		Argumentative		Uncontrolled laughing		Hyperactive
		Restless		Nervous/edgy		Aggressive
				Sleepy appearance		Nausea

Should any one or more of the above be positive, an alcohol/drug screen test must be done by a test operator

Result of alcohol/drug screen test   Positive   ·   Negative   ·

A copy of the screen test chain of custody form indicating the result to be attached to this form.
If positive, inform the employee of his/her rights to a laboratory confirmation test.

Signature of Employee _____ Date _____ Time _____
Signature of Observer _____ Date _____ Time _____
Noted by Representative_____ Date _____ Time _____
Signature of Test Operator _____ Date _____ Time _____

Appendix 10

A Short Policy on the Management of Alcohol and Drug Abuse

The Company is aware that alcohol and drug abuse (hereafter referred to as 'substance abuse') can damage the health and safety of employees, disrupt workplace relationships, and reduce productivity.

The Company is also aware that substance-abusing employees may require specialist treatment in order to overcome or to successfully manage their problem and that such treatment is more likely to be required for employees who are dependent upon or addicted to alcohol or drugs.

It is the policy of the Company to make every effort to eradicate or minimise substance abuse among its employees and to assist in the rehabilitation of those employees who are dependent upon or addicted to alcohol or drugs.

In pursuing this policy, the following steps will be necessary:

1. EDUCATION

The Company will provide education to employees on the risks associated with substance abuse, how to identify signs of substance abuse in others, and the types of treatment available to individuals experiencing substance-abuse problems.

Education will commence on induction of employees to the Company and continue during the period of their employment through the provision of written material (reports, memoranda, posters, etc), videos, lectures and one-to-one counselling on all aspects of substance abuse.

The Company resolves to maintain a high-profile education policy on the issue of substance abuse in the workplace.

2. IDENTIFICATION

The Company has employed an independent testing agency to provide random testing of any person entering the Company's premises, including employees, contractors, suppliers and visitors.

A computer generated random number system will be used to select individuals for testing. This system represents the most impartial selection method currently available.

In addition to the random testing referred to above a person may be requested to submit to testing in the following circumstances:

- if requested by security when entering the Company's premises on suspicion of abuse
- as part of an accident investigation
- in the event of a supervisor being concerned about the behaviour of an employee under his or her control
- on exiting the premises (computer generated random number system).

Any person refusing to be tested will not be allowed to enter or to remain on the Company's premises. An employee refusing to be tested will not be allowed to begin work or to continue working and his or her refusal will be recorded.

All managers and supervisors are responsible for informing the Company's Occupational Health Department as soon as reasonably impossible if they have good cause to believe that an employee's job performance, time-keeping or behaviour has been affected as a result of substance abuse.

3. DISCIPLINARY ACTION

Any employee who attempts to enter or to remain on the Company's premises while under the influence of alcohol or drugs or in possession of alcohol or drugs will be subject to disciplinary action. Nothing in any clause in this policy will alter or detract from the above statement.

Any employee under the influence of alcohol or drugs or reasonably suspected of being under the influence of alcohol or drugs must clearly understand that his or her continued employment is in jeopardy unless he or she accepts and follows treatment. Failure to do so could result in disciplinary action and eventual termination of his or her services.

4. REHABILITATION

Those employees who are identified as having abused alcohol or drugs will be referred to the Company's Occupational Health Department for assessment and possible inclusion in the Company's Employee Assistance Programme. This programme offers one-to-one counselling, group therapy, and out-patient and/or in-patient therapy for employees experiencing substance- abuse problems.

Employees undergoing rehabilitation treatment will not be subject to any disciplinary action and their security of employment is assured until treatment has been fully explored and the results assessed provided that they adhere to and cooperate with the treatment prescribed for their particular alcohol- or drug-related problem.

Employees undergoing rehabilitation treatment may suffer relapses, especially in the early stages of treatment. The Company accepts that such relapses are possible and will take no disciplinary action where the Occupational Health Department advises that the employee concerned is genuinely attempting to overcome his or her problem. Should the Occupational Health Department advise that the employee is not making such an attempt and/or is refusing or not fully cooperating with treatment, then the rehabilitation treatment will be terminated.

All information regarding an employee undergoing treatment remains strictly confidential between the Occupational Health Department and the employee concerned. This provision applies

(i) where the employee voluntarily seeks treatment

(ii) where the Occupational Health Department advises that the employee should seek treatment

(iii) where management refers the employee for assessment and/or treatment.

However, if in the opinion of the Occupational Health Department an employee's substance abuse could endanger himself or herself and/or co-workers, the Company must be advised.

Where, as a result of disciplinary action, an employee has been referred to the Occupational Health Department for treatment, the Occupational Health Department shall submit progress reports to management regarding such treatment.

Employees who are members of the Company's medical aid scheme will be eligible for treatment for alcohol/drug abuse in terms of the rules of the scheme.

5. MANAGEMENT OF NON-COMPLIANCE OR UNSUCCESSFUL TREATMENT

Failure to comply with or respond to rehabilitation will result in either retirement due to ill-health or discipline up to and including dismissal, depending on the individual circumstances.

In certain circumstances and at the discretion of the trustees of the Company pension fund, a long-serving employee who can no longer work due to the progressive impairment of his or her health through alcohol or drug abuse may be eligible to receive a medical disability pension, provided that he or she is not subject to disciplinary action in respect of alcohol or drug abuse.

6. MAINTENANCE OF POLICY

This policy and the Employee Assistance Programme will be evaluated according to the maintenance procedure devised, implemented and maintained by the Occupational Health Department, the Security Department and the Human Resources Department in consultation with all departmental managers and the designated trade union representative or representatives or other person or persons authorised to act on behalf of employees.

7. RESPONSIBILITY

The responsibility for ensuring the policy is implemented has been allocated to the Human Resources Manager who will liaise with the relevant department heads and personnel department and the employees.

Table of History, Signs and Diseases of Alcohol and Drugs

GENERAL APPEARANCE

Flushed or blotchy red face
Staggering gait
Red, bleary eyes
Hand tremors with nicotine stains
Periodically smelling of alcohol
Untidy or dishevelled appearance

WORK HISTORY

Absenteeism
Absence due to sickness — frequency of short periods
Absence without leave — Monday, Friday or day after payday.

On-the-job absenteeism

Sickness presence
Sleeps on the job
Difficulty concentrating, tired, confused
Less prioritised work done first
Procrastination.
Deteriorating work performance
Faulty decision-making
Frequent temporary absence from workstation
Frequent use of rest room
Unreliability
Details overlooked
Complaints from customers
Extended lunch hours
Poor afternoon performance

Behaviour

Loud talking, slurred speech
Aggressive
Argumentative
Oversensitive to criticism

Paranoid tendencies
Mood swings particularly after lunch
Unpredictable behaviour
Unusual excuses for absence from work
Poor ability to communicate
Grandiose behaviour

TRAUMA HISTORY

Injuries on duty
Falls
Tripping over or stepping on objects
Handling faults
Assaults
Other injuries
Motor-vehicle accidents, particularly at night and 'one-person accidents'

SOCIAL HISTORY

Financial problems
Wife or child abuse
Married or divorced
Lives in digs or hostel
Nature of the alcohol or drug problem, including severity
Other co-occurring health and medical problems
Co-occuring psychiatric disorders
Co-existing social and interpersonal problems (among family members, friends or within the workplace)
Co-existing legal problems
Previous substance abuse treatment history

MEDICAL HISTORY[8]

Recurring medical complaint	Related sign	Possible related condition or diagnosis
Gastrointestinal Indigestion/heartburn/ dyspepsia		Oesophagitis
Sternal chest pain		
Vomiting blood	Epigastric tenderness	Mallory-Weiss syndrome
Nausea and vomiting		Gastritis
Upper abdominal pain		Pancreatitis
Diarrhoea		Enteritis
Liver		

---

8   Paton, A, Potter, JF and Saunders, JB (1988) 'Detection in hospital' in *ABC of Alcohol*, Paton, A (ed) *British Medical Journal*, London. Also adapted from Levine J 'The relative value of Consultation, Questionnaires and Laboratory investigation in the Identification of excessive alcohol consumption' in *Alcohol and Alcoholism* 1990, Vol 25 No 5, 539–553.

Recurring medical complaint	Related sign	Possible related condition or diagnosis
Abdominal distension	Enlarged palpable spleen	Cirrhosis
	Enlarged palpable liver/spleen	Fatty liver
Fluid in abdomen	Ascites	Cirrhosis
Jaundice	Yellow mucosa and sclera	Portal hypertension
Pruritus	Yellow skin	and/or liver failure
Abdominal varices	Caput medusae	Portal hypertension
Vomiting blood	Oesophageal varices	Portal hypertension
Bleeding per rectum	Haemorrhoids	Portal hypertension
Fever	Acute inflammation of the liver	Alcoholic hepatitis
Jaundice		
Loss of appetite		
Nausea		
Abdominal pain		
Bruising	Reduced prothrombin	Cirrhosis
Bleeding per rectum		
Melaena		
Confusion	Raised blood ammonia	Toxic hepatic
Irritability	and portal hypertension	encephalopathy
Foul breath		
Flapping tremor		
Coma		
Weakness	Hypoglycaemia	Suppression of
Confusion		gluco-neogenesis
Dizziness		of the liver by
Blackouts		alcohol
Fits		
Hormonal imbalance	Gynaecomastia/low andro-	
Enlarged breasts in males	gens	Alcoholic liver disease
	Testicular atrophy	and
Shrunken testicles	Testicular atrophy	
Infertility		low androgen levels
Impotence		
Swollen moonshaped face		Low androgen levels
Obesity		Pseudo-Cushing's disease
Lethargic, polydipsia and		
polyuria	Sugar in urine	Diabetes mellitus
Frequency, dysuria		
Pruritus vulvae	Urinary tract infections	Diabetes mellitus
Vaginal discharge		Candidiasis
Balanitis		
Cardiac	Tachycardia	Coronary heart disease
Palpitations	High blood pressure	Alcoholic
Chest pain	Arrhythmias	cardiomyopathy
Shortness of breath		Congestive cardiac failure

Recurring medical complaint	Related sign	Possible related condition or diagnosis
Respiratory Cough Purulent sputum Shortness of breath Night sweats	Lowered resistance to-infection	Bronchitis Upper lobe pneumonia Tuberculosis
Musculoskeletal Gouty tender swellings Muscular weakness Back pain Generalized pains Recurring injuries Contractions in the palms	Gouty tophi, gouty joints Raised uric acid Wasted muscles Fixed flexion, deformity of digits	Gout Alcoholic myopathy Osteoarthritis Osteoporosis Dupuytrens contractures
Skin Red blotchy facial rash with papules and carbuncles Red, swollen nose Groin and feet rashes Pruritus Scaly round lesions White nails Dark pigmented skin Loss of body hair Red palms Spider-like arterioles Raw, red gums Striae on a pot belly Cutaneous ulcers	Acne rosacea Rhinophyma Fungus infections Sweat rashes Psoriasis Hypoproteinaemia Palmar erythema Spider naevi greater than 5 below root of neck Poor oral hygiene	Excessive sweating Excessive sweating Alcoholic liver disease Alcoholic liver disease Alcoholic liver disease Alcoholic liver disease Alcoholic liver disease
Nervous System **Acute** Tiredness Depressed mood Headaches Nausea Oversensitivity	 Dehydration Electrolyte imbalance	 Mild alcohol withdrawal

Recurring medical complaint	Related sign	Possible related condition or diagnosis
Tremor of hands, face, body		
Nausea		
Sweating		
Mood changes		
Depression		Severe alcohol
Anxiety		withdrawal
Agitation		
Ringing in the ears	Tinnitus	
Muscle cramps		
Sleep disturbances		
Sensitivity to noise	Hyperacusis	
Hallucinations: auditory and visual		Delirium tremens
Grand mal seizures		
Fits	Hypoglycaemia	
Amnesia		
Blackouts		
Confusion		
Loss of equilibrium		
Staggering gait	Ataxia	Wernicke's
Abnormal eye movements	Ocular palsy	encephalopathy
Chronic		Pre-senile dementia
Personality changes		
Memory deterioration		
Depression		
Morbid jealousy		
Anxiety		
Paranoia		Wernicke's
Hallucinosis		encephalopathy
Confusion		followed by Korsakoff's
Loss of equilibrium	Ataxia	psychosis
Staggering gait		
Abnormal eye movements	Ocular palsy	
Short-term memory loss		
Confabulation		
Numbness in the legs	Peripheral neuropathy	Thiamine deficiency
Diminished reflexes		
Walking on cotton wool		
Dimness of vision		
Loss of colour vision	Peripheral neuropathy	Thiamine deficiency
	Peripheral neuropathy	Thiamine deficiency
	Alcohol toxicity to optic nerve	Amblyopia

SYMPTOMS AND SIGNS SPECIFIC TO DRUGS

Recurring symptoms	Related sign	Possible related condition or diagnosis
Hallucinogens Flashbacks Psychotic like symptoms Acute Toxicity	Changed behaviour Changed behaviour Pupil dilatation Tachycardia Raised Blood Pressure Tremor Nausea Increased body temperature Dizziness Emotional reactions Drowsiness Weakness Numbness	Previous or current use of Chronic use Hallucinogens Overdose of Hallucinogenic Drugs: LSD Mescaline Phencyclidine (PCP) Ketamine
Stimulants Acute toxicity	Binge usage Sweating High temperature Tremors Excitability Restlessness Agitation Paranoia Hallucinations Delusions Hyperarousal Violent/bizarre behaviour Possible related condition or diagnosis	Cocaine/Crack Crystal Methamphetamine (Tik) MDMA Amphetamine and derivatives
Stimulants Chronic toxicity	Weight loss Poor concentration Memory impairment Sleep disturbance Hallucinations Flashbacks Depression Anxiety Agitation Panic attacks Psychotic disturbance Paranoid delusions Hallucinations Violent behaviour Dependence Stroke Seizures	Can lead to acute paranoid schizophrenia Delirium

Cannabis Acute Toxicity	Anxiety Panic Attacks Delusions Hallucinations Psychotic reactions Memory loss Slowing of reaction time Specific task skill loss Motor dysfunction Short term memory loss Likely impact on those with other mental health problems Psychiatric symptoms exacerbated	Dagga Marijuana Can lead to a substance induced psychosis Hallucinations
Opiates Acute Toxicity	Pin point pupils Meiosis Drowsiness Euphoria Pruritis Dry mouth Constipation Nausea Vomiting Headache Flushing Confusion Delirium Stupor Urine retention Urticaria Hypothermia Bradycardia Hypotension(orthostatic) Pulmonary oedema Coma Respiratory depression	Heroin Morphine Codeine Spontaneous abortion in pregnant females HIV/AIDS Hepatitis Pulmonary complications
Chronic toxicity	Dependence Social deprivation Hypoxic brain damage Withdrawl reactions Antisocial behaviour Drug impurities reaction Blood-borne diseases Immune dysfunction (Macrophages & Lymphocytes) Subnormal testosterone Osteoporosis Hallucinations	

www.ingramcontent.com/pod-product-compliance
Lightning Source LLC
Chambersburg PA
CBHW081734270326
41932CB00020B/3270